How to use this book

ORGANIZATION

Paris Is, Paris Was
Discusses aspects of life and culture in contemporary Paris and explores significant periods in its history.

A–Z
An alphabetical listing of places to visit, including suggested walks. Within this section fall the Focus On articles, which consider a variety of subjects in greater detail.

Excursions
Provides a selection of popular excursions from Paris.

Travel Facts
Contains the strictly practical information vital for a successful trip.

Accommodations and Restaurants
Lists recommended establishments throughout Paris, giving a brief summary of their attractions.

ADMISSION CHARGES
Standard admission charges are categorized in this book as follows:

Inexpensive	under 20 francs
Moderate	20–30 francs
Expensive	over 30 francs

ABOUT THE RATINGS
Most places described in this book have been given a separate rating. These are as follows:

▶▶▶	**Do not miss**
▶▶	**Highly recommended**
▶	**Worth seeing**

MAPS
To make each particular location easier to find, every main entry in this book is given a map reference to the right of its name. This comprises a number, followed by a letter, followed by another number, such as 176B3. The first number (176) refers to the page on which the map can be found, the letter (B) and the second number (3) pinpoint the square in which the main entry is located. The maps on the inside front cover and inside back cover are referred to as IFC and IBC respectively.

Contents

CHEZ EUGENE
CHEZ EUGENE

Fiona Dunlop lived in Paris for over 15 years. Her taste for tropical travel and interest in developing countries has led her to write *Explorer Singapore & Malaysia, Mexico, Costa Rica, Vietnam,* and *India.* She is now based in London.

My Paris

I am not the only foreigner who went to live in Paris for a short period and ended up spending a formative chunk of my life there. This is arguably Europe's most seductive capital, with architecture made to measure for aesthetes, restaurants for food lovers, boulevard cafés for people-watchers posing as intellectuals, the banks of the languid Seine for romantics, and art galleries and shops for those in search of the unique ... the list goes on.

All levels of society exist here, from the stereotypical artist or writer-in-a-garret to the *grand bourgeois* of Neuilly. Flung together in stylish unison, they mingle in a compact, cosmopolitan city that can disconcert by its aggressiveness or enchant by its sophistication. The boom years of the 1980s that produced new cultural landmarks and movements had their flip-side in the 1990s when recession led to a much-quoted *morosité*. Social upheaval and revelations of political corruption plunged the city into a period of self-doubt. A sudden drop in unemployment, heralded by an economic upturn, gave Paris back its old confidence. By the beginning of the 21st century, a new spirit emerged bringing innovation and a dynamism in its wake.

When in Paris, I search out the up-and-coming quarters emerging from the shadows of a less well-to-do past. Recent examples are the north-eastern areas of the Bastille and Ménilmontant, although the old classics of St.-Germain and St.-Honoré are also seeing traditions upturned, for both the good and the bad. My favorites remain the apparently characterless faubourgs, where local *boulangeries* and pre-war cafés flank an unusual museum or a specialist shop, and courtyards reveal an atmosphere straight out of a Cartier-Bresson photograph. Everyone should allow time to wander the backstreets and build up their own picture of this incomparable city.

Perhaps the only word to encapsulate these numerous strata is quality, for this is Paris' strength. Quality of culture, of material, of craftsmanship, of display, of dress, of service, of transport, and, not least, of the fiercely defended French language. Some may say it is all in the wrapping, but Paris remains an utterly beguiling and complex package that takes years to unfold.

Fiona Dunlop

Paris Is
Paris Was

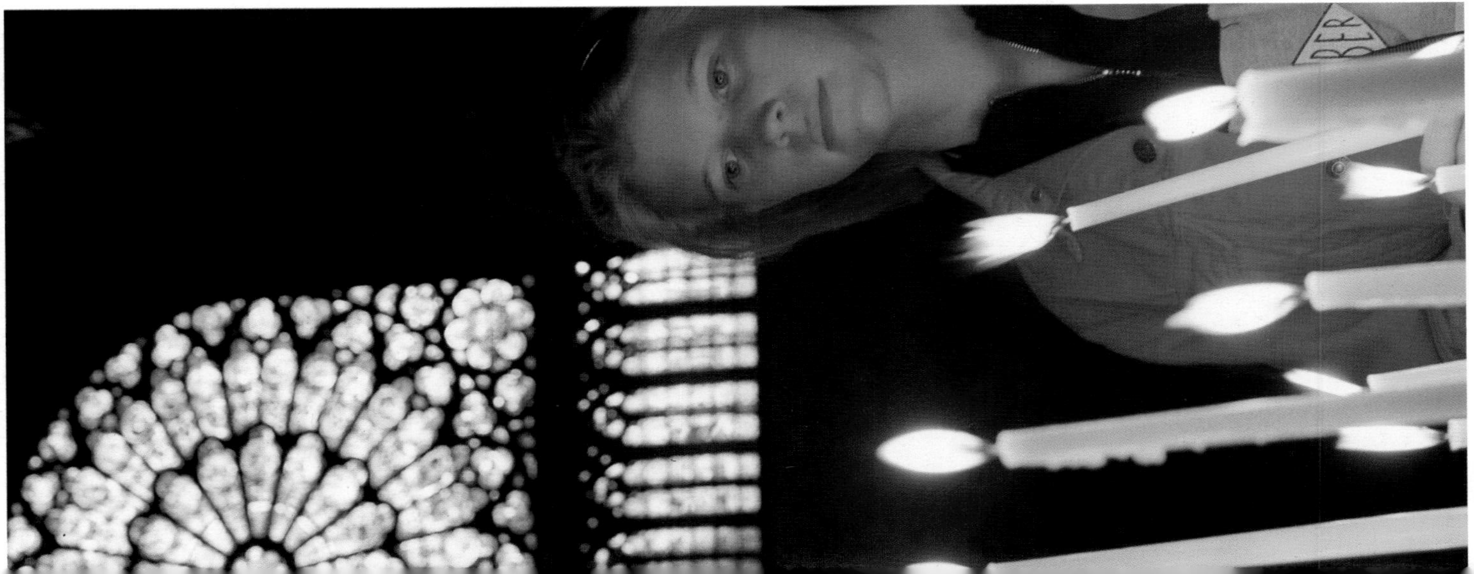

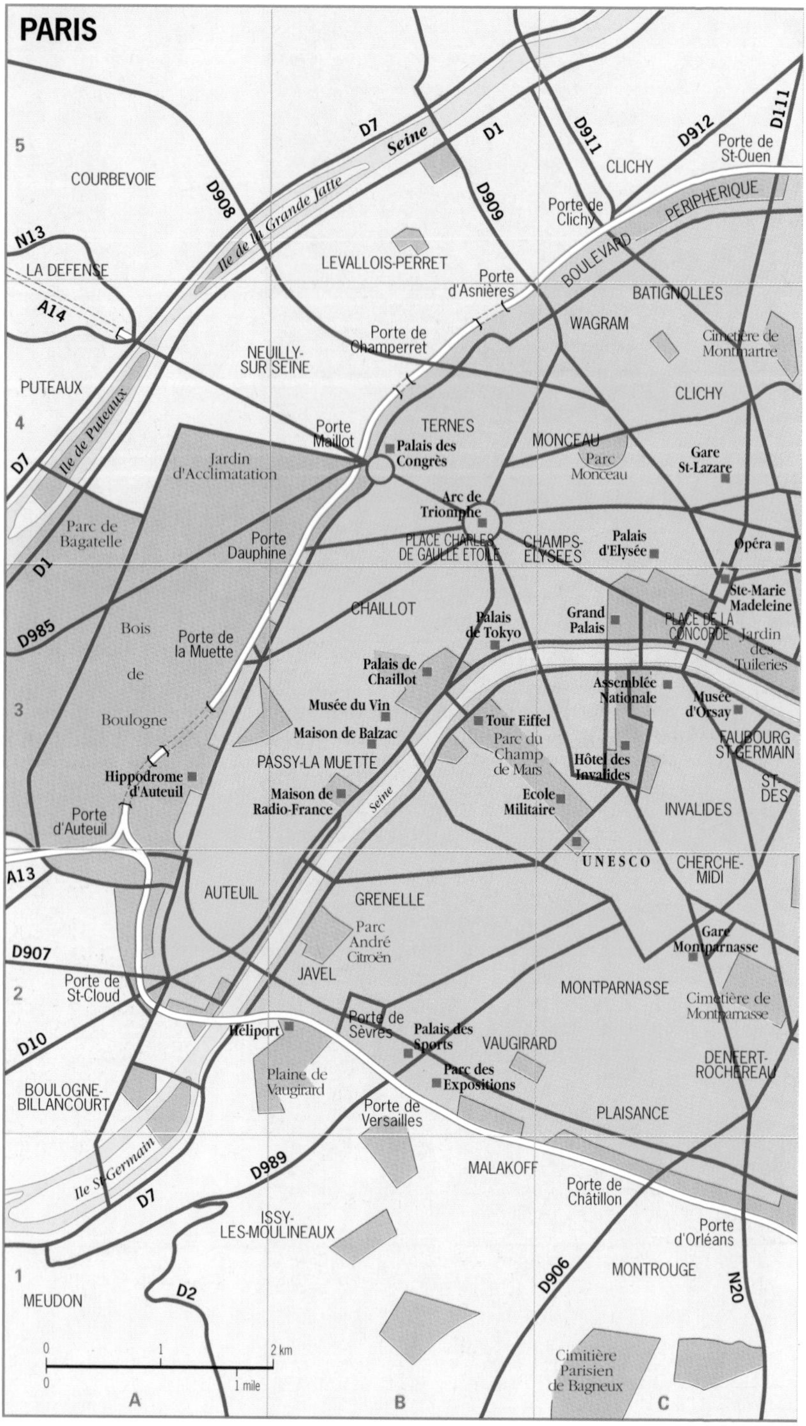
PARIS
COURBEVOIE
LA DEFENSE
PUTEAUX
Ile de Puteaux
Ile de la Grande Jatte
Seine
CLICHY
Porte de St-Ouen
Porte de Clichy
LEVALLOIS-PERRET
Porte d'Asnières
BOULEVARD PERIPHERIQUE
BATIGNOLLES
WAGRAM
Cimetière de Montmartre
Porte de Champerret
NEUILLY-SUR SEINE
CLICHY
Porte Maillot
TERNES
Palais des Congrès
MONCEAU
Parc Monceau
Gare St-Lazare
Jardin d'Acclimatation
Arc de Triomphe
Parc de Bagatelle
Porte Dauphine
PLACE CHARLES DE GAULLE ETOILE
CHAMPS-ELYSEES
Palais d'Elysée
Opéra
Ste-Marie Madeleine
CHAILLOT
Grand Palais
PLACE DE LA CONCORDE
Jardin des Tuileries
Bois de Boulogne
Porte de la Muette
Palais de Tokyo
Palais de Chaillot
Assemblée Nationale
Musée d'Orsay
Musée du Vin
Tour Eiffel
Maison de Balzac
Parc du Champ de Mars
FAUBOURG ST-GERMAIN
PASSY-LA MUETTE
Hôtel des Invalides
Hippodrome d'Auteuil
Maison de Radio-France
Ecole Militaire
INVALIDES
Porte d'Auteuil
UNESCO
CHERCHE-MIDI
AUTEUIL
GRENELLE
Parc André Citroën
Gare Montparnasse
JAVEL
Porte de St-Cloud
MONTPARNASSE
Cimetière de Montparnasse
Porte de Sèvres
Héliport
Palais des Sports
VAUGIRARD
DENFERT-ROCHEREAU
Plaine de Vaugirard
Parc des Expositions
BOULOGNE-BILLANCOURT
Porte de Versailles
PLAISANCE
Ile St-Germain
MALAKOFF
Porte de Châtillon
ISSY-LES-MOULINEAUX
Porte d'Orléans
MONTROUGE
MEUDON
Cimitière Parisien de Bagneux
D7
D1
D908
D909
D911
D912
D111
N13
A14
D985
A13
D907
D10
D989
D2
D906
N20
5
4
3
2
1
A
B
C
0
1
2 km
1 mile

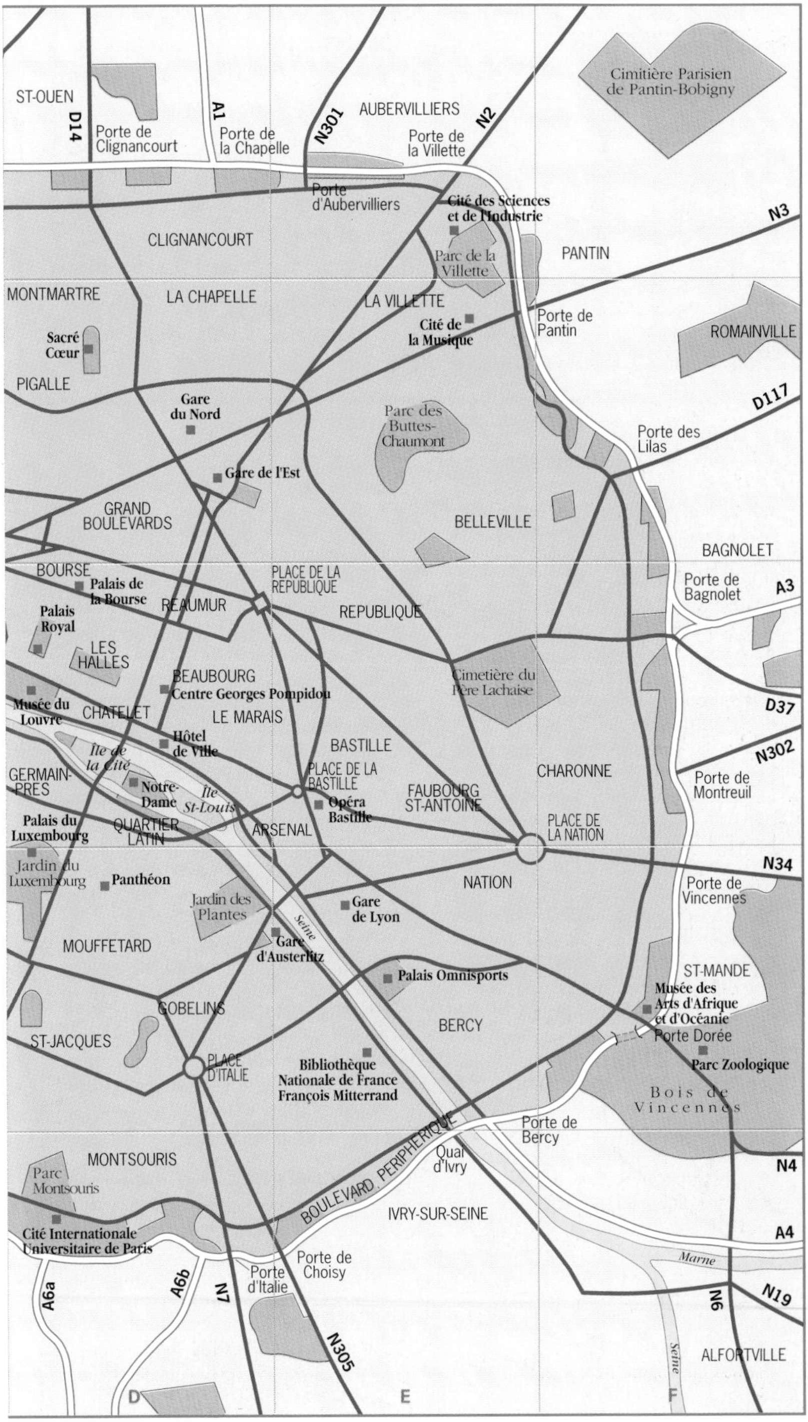

Cimitière Parisien de Pantin-Bobigny
ST-OUEN
D14
Porte de Clignancourt
A1
Porte de la Chapelle
N301
AUBERVILLIERS
Porte de la Villette
N2
Porte d'Aubervilliers
Cité des Sciences et de l'Industrie
N3
CLIGNANCOURT
Parc de la Villette
PANTIN
MONTMARTRE
LA CHAPELLE
LA VILLETTE
Porte de Pantin
ROMAINVILLE
Cité de la Musique
Sacré Cœur
PIGALLE
D117
Gare du Nord
Parc des Buttes-Chaumont
Porte des Lilas
Gare de l'Est
GRAND BOULEVARDS
BELLEVILLE
BAGNOLET
BOURSE
Palais de la Bourse
PLACE DE LA REPUBLIQUE
Porte de Bagnolet
A3
Palais Royal
REAUMUR
REPUBLIQUE
LES HALLES
BEAUBOURG
Centre Georges Pompidou
Cimetière du Père Lachaise
D37
Musée du Louvre
CHATELET
LE MARAIS
Hôtel de Ville
BASTILLE
N302
Île de la Cité
GERMAIN-PRES
Notre-Dame
Île St-Louis
PLACE DE LA BASTILLE
CHARONNE
Porte de Montreuil
Opéra Bastille
FAUBOURG ST-ANTOINE
Palais du Luxembourg
QUARTIER LATIN
ARSENAL
PLACE DE LA NATION
N34
Jardin du Luxembourg
Panthéon
NATION
Porte de Vincennes
Jardin des Plantes
Gare de Lyon
Seine
MOUFFETARD
Gare d'Austerlitz
Palais Omnisports
ST-MANDE
Musée des Arts d'Afrique et d'Océanie
GOBELINS
BERCY
Porte Dorée
ST-JACQUES
PLACE D'ITALIE
Bibliothèque Nationale de France François Mitterrand
Parc Zoologique
Bois de Vincennes
Porte de Bercy
BOULEVARD PERIPHERIQUE
Quai d'Ivry
MONTSOURIS
N4
Parc Montsouris
IVRY-SUR-SEINE
Cité Internationale Universitaire de Paris
A4
Marne
Porte de Choisy
Porte d'Italie
A6a
A6b
N7
N6
N19
N305
Seine
ALFORTVILLE
D
E
F

Paris is one of the most densely populated cities in the world. Not only that: it is perhaps the capital most talked about, most written about, most hyped, most dreamed about. A vacation spent there leaves indelible memories—whether of the clear spring light on the Seine, a gastronomic fantasy, an exhausting string of masterpieces at the Louvre, or an irascible waiter serving a tray of delectable oysters. Full of contrasts, thick with history, it is also a city on the move, looking to the future.

Parisians themselves remain a mystery. Their general love of the good things in life—food, sex, and fashion (not necessarily in that order) is accompanied by a strong intellectual streak. T.V. programs regularly feature groups of writers chatting about their books, ideas, and projects, while newspapers contain long columns written by philosophers. This interest in abstraction spins off into conversations in which heated arguments are commonplace and a necessary part of any friendship. For some, such a strong emphasis on abstract thought stops action, or at least postpones it, and the business world suffers directly.

Defining a typical Parisian means taking into account not only the many provincials who flock to the city but also a traditional foreign influx, whether from Central Africa, North Africa, Vietnam, or Europe. Communities form rapidly, from the African, Arab and Asian quarters in Belleville to the Chinese and Vietnamese in the 13th *arrondissement*. Racism is disturbingly well entrenched, particularly in certain soulless suburbs bereft of social life and structure. In contrast, the prosperous and sacrosanct 16th *arrondissement* remains intact with its breed of bourgeoisie sprinkled with the odd princess, sheikh, or retired Hollywood diva. In between the extremes lies the heart of French business and social trends.

PARIS STYLE Ever since the heady days of the 1920s, Paris has harbored a hotbed of foreign artists, thinkers, and political refugees, all of whom have contributed to the clichés of bohemianism. Glamor is never far: Paris is a city where enjoyment can cost little, as it is always on display. Appearances are paramount, and the impeccably groomed businessman or woman, totally at ease drinking a glass of champagne in the latest hip restaurant, may well turn out to live in a minute studio-flat in a distant *arrondissement*. Money is worn on the back, or on the plate, and this can also be interpreted as a sheep-like trait. Fashion is not invented, it is followed; woe betide the pretender who misses the season's mark.

Yet this apparent conformism is peppered with strong anarchistic qualities, as traffic wardens and tourists well know. The notion of queueing (although originally from a French word) still seems to escape the Gallic consciousness; individualism wins hands down over any civic conscience or community sense.

CHANGING CITY Compared to the 1980s, the face of Paris in the first decade of the 21st century is radically different. Fourteen years of a socialist President Mitterrand who, to some, seemed to mould himself on predecessors such as Louis XIV or Napoleon III, left their distinctive mark. *Grands projets* hit the skyline, new *quartiers* are still being created and Paris is gradually undergoing total gentrification. An obsession with history and their role in the continuum is another characteristic of French rulers, and former President Mitterrand was no exception. Which other world capital has invested so much in cultural structures as a national trademark?

> ❑ The population of Paris (intramuros, or within the ring road) stabilized in 1990 at 2,154,600 after 30 years of dropping. Each residence/flat/house has 1.92 inhabitants, compared with 2.35 in 1954. Ten percent of lodgings are empty, rising to 18 percent in the center. ❑

MIND AND BODY If the Parisians love culture and abstract ideals, they have few inhibitions about sex, from the hot spots of Pigalle to advertisements whose blatancy makes Anglo-Saxon feminists blanch. Parisian women somehow manage to retain an ambivalence: supremely elegant, they are increasingly prominent in French business and politics.

Thus a renovated Paris, its sense of pride (and sometimes superiority) intact, faces a new Europe. Times have changed and a non-French-speaking visitor is no longer ostracized. A new generation eagerly bridges the language barrier; and remember that however reserved a Parisian exterior may be, humor will always permeate it. The Parisian character lies somewhere in between Latin demonstrativeness (they would kiss even their worst enemy on the cheek, left and right), and bourgeois restraint. Underneath is a *bon viveur* who, whatever his faults, helped coin the phrase *savoir vivre*.

All life is here: café society still flourishes in Paris, despite many other changes in the city

France has at last attained political stability and is now regarded as one of the most powerful Western democracies. In the last two centuries it has been ruled by no fewer than 16 constitutions, and only a few decades ago, in the immediate post-war period, government after government failed in their attempts to rule an ebullient nation undergoing profound socio-economic changes. Then came de Gaulle and the Fifth Republic. And then, after the dramatic events of 1968 and two intermediary Presidents, came "the quiet strength" of Mitterrand.

Modern France reached its lowest ebb with the national disgrace of Pétain's Vichy Régime. In 1945 the Fourth Republic was accepted by referendum and women were at last given the vote. But inherent constitutional weaknesses led to 30 successive governments, often rocky coalitions. The Algerian War of Independence finally brought down this Republic: under threat of a military *coup d'état*, the National Assembly admitted defeat in 1958 and called on de Gaulle to bail his country out.

Although a national referendum ratified the new constitution, many doubted that the Fifth Republic would survive the General's departure. Yet, although severely shaken by the events of 1968 (student

The National Assembly, where Presidents dare not tread

revolts and national strikes brought the country to a standstill), it still survives today.

POLITICAL STRUCTURE At the head of the government stands the President, elected every seven years by universal suffrage. Far from being a mere figurehead, as in many other European republics, he is head of the army, responsible for nuclear defence, nominates the Prime Minister, can call referendums or dissolve Parliament. Based in the Elysée Palace, the President is not allowed to set foot in the National Assembly at the Palais Bourbon. He is answerable to the *Conseil Constitutionnel*, an independent body.

Nominated by the President from the majority party in the National Assembly, the Prime Minister heads the government. Based at the Hôtel Matignon, he nominates ministers for the approval of the President, but owes his authority to the confidence of the National Assembly. The government can be censured by parliament with a vote of absolute majority. Government's inner core, the cabinet, meets every Wednesday at the Elysée for a working meeting chaired by the President.

Parliament is composed of two chambers: the National Assembly, with 577 deputies elected every five years, and its upper body, the Senate, with 318 senators, elected by local representatives every nine years.

The differences in duration of power between the President (still seven years, despite various proposals to shorten the term) and the Assembly (five years) has led to potentially divisive situations. In 1986, when Mitterrand was already five years into his first mandate, new legislative elections produced a right-wing parliamentary majority. This led to the paradoxical and thorny situation of a Socialist President ruling with a right-wing (Gaullist) Prime Minister—Chirac—and the phrase "cohabitation" was coined. A repeat situation was produced in 1993 when RPR Edouard Balladur was appointed Prime Minister under the then still-presiding Mitterrand. In 1997, the reverse situation occurred when right-wing President Chirac called on Socialist Lionel Jospin to form a government.

QUICK CHANGES Chameleon-like, French political parties are constantly changing initials, allegiances, and coalitions. Divided roughly equally between right- and left-wing, there are currently three main tendencies: the *gauche plurielle* including the PS (Socialist Party), PC (Communist), and les Verts (ecologists); the moderate right including the RPR (Gaullist) and UDF (center right); and the extreme right, namely the FN (National Front). The latter, after years of growth under Le Pen, has split in two and is on the wane.

TECHNOCRACY As a nation, the French are not strongly unionized and members are diminishing in number: only 13 percent of the workforce are now registered. But the area where the French maintain overwhelming numbers is in the army of civil servants. The traditionally heavyweight state administration dates back to the 17th century, was perfected by Napoleon, and assured a legal and technical continuity throughout the turmoil of French political history. Exemplary in many fields, it has some of the best training-grounds for top-ranking administrators. Yet it is also stifling, encumbering the nation with an excessive bureaucracy. It also ensures that governmental power is far-reaching and all-encompassing—not always a healthy situation.

Above all, France is a technocracy in which civil servants often play dominant roles in economic or technical development. One time-honored tradition has now changed: parking tickets handed out by that most despized of civil servants, the traffic warden, are no longer automatically amnestied by the new, thriftier breed of incoming Presidents.

❑ Over 4,900,000 men and women work in state and regional government. ❑

"Frenetic" is the only word to describe architectural activity in Paris over the last 20 years. Cranes groan on the horizon, while other machinery burrows away underground. Little remains untouched and, as a result, Paris has undergone a major facelift, with entire quartiers *like Le Marais restored to their former gleaming glory and countless sheets of glass lovingly installed into the facades of Paris' new landmarks.*

The key building is the **Centre Pompidou**, more commonly known as **Beaubourg**, completed in 1977 and already being renovated, which now attracts more visitors than the Eiffel Tower. Controversially high-tech, in marked contrast to the surrounding 18th- and 19th-century town houses, it set the tone for a new generation of architects and a new attitude towards public building. Although instigated by President Georges Pompidou, it was finished under Giscard d'Estaing —who had attempted to axe the plan— and was soon followed by more ambitious projects such as the **Parc de la Villette**, a kind of glorified urban playground, and the transformation of a former railway station and hotel into the **Musée d'Orsay**. Politics and architecture have always gone hand in hand (see pages 44–45) and the 1980s saw a particularly complex wrangle, with Gaullist prime minister Jacques Chirac stalling the grandiose, some say megalomaniac, projects of Socialist François Mitterrand. In the end all were built after Mitterrand defeated Chirac in the 1988 presidential election!

GRAND FINALE With Mitterrand's 14 years of presidency over, so his *grands projets* are virtually completed. The last one on the board was Dominique Perrault's national library, nicknamed the **TGB** (Très Grande Bibliothèque), whose four 328-foot-high glass towers imitate the form of open books.

The cement-mixers did not leave when the TGB was completed, as the Mairie de Paris has instigated an ambitious plan to overhaul this rather neglected quarter in the south-east of Paris. Immediately north across the river, in Bercy, there has already been a transformation, with Chemetov's one-legged **Ministry of Finance** limping into the Seine, while Frank Gehry's whimsically designed, but financially disastrous American Center, has been transformed into France's national Cinémathèque, and new office and apartment blocks overlook the landscaped **Parc de Bercy**.

❑ The new Bibliothèque François Mitterrand, built at a cost of over 5 billion francs, provides 248 miles of shelves. The old Bibliothèque Nationale is now an art-history library. ❑

NEW LOOK LOUVRE After initial resistance by traditionalists, Parisians have taken to their hearts I.M. Pei's glass and metal pyramid, personally chosen by Mitterrand as the centrepiece of the *Grand Louvre*. When completed in 2001, at a cost of over $1 billion, the Louvre will be the world's largest museum.

The pyramid's symbolic position on the east–west axis marks a straight line from the **Opéra Bastille** in the east to the **Grande Arche**, far to the west at La Défense, with the **Tuileries, Concorde, Champs-Elysées** and **Arc de Triomphe** in between. Apart from pleasing a Cartesian sense of logic and geometry and bowing to a tradition of French rulers from Catherine de Médicis onwards, it also makes life easier for landmark-seeking visitors.

The Louvre: I.M. Pei's pyramid

LA GRANDE ARCHE crowns the new business district of La Défense and has created a desperately needed focal point for what was previously a mass of tower blocks left over from the 1960s and 1970s. Von Spreckelsen's gateway design leaves the axis open for development, and the city without limits.

Completed just in time for the 1989 Bicentenary celebrations, the Grande Arche had a warmer reception than Mitterrand's other pet project, the "people's" opera-house at the Bastille, designed by relatively unknown Canadian architect Carlos Ott. Plans were radically modified, but it eventually opened in 1990.

Although completely overpowering the rest of the place, the **Opéra Bastille** improves inside and seems to have overcome its teething problems.

NOUVEL ARCHITECTURE Paris in the 1990s cannot be discussed without mentioning the *enfant terrible* of architecture, Jean Nouvel. His much praised **Institut du Monde Arabe**, completed in 1987, is a masterpiece of sculptural purity, and was followed in 1994 by the equally intriguing new Fondation Cartier.

The city's architectural renaissance has added to its unique style, not only in status-symbol monuments, but also in the far-flung *arrondissements* and the suburbs.

There are enough stars and "would-be's" in Paris to launch another galaxy. Below is a checklist of prominent characters who have been part of Paris life during recent years—though not all have been worthy of gracing the cover of the gossip mag Paris Match.

ISABELLE ADJANI Born in Paris of a German mother and Algerian father, Adjani started acting aged 14 and later joined the Comédie Française. She became famous with Truffaut's *Adèle H* in 1975. In 1981 she won the Cannes prize for best actress for her role in James Ivory's *Quartet*.

AZZADINE ALAIA Of Tunisian origin, Alaïa was adopted by the French fashion world when he worked from his living-room in the early 1980s, selling clinging dresses in black leather and slinky jerseys. He opened a boutique in the Marais and is now an international fashion name.

PIERRE BOULEZ The great classical composer was born in 1925 and studied music at the Paris Conservatoire under Messïaen. He worked as a conductor in London and New York before directing acoustic research at IRCAM.

DANIEL BUREN France's most controversial contemporary artist, Buren was born in 1938 near Paris. Since the 1960s he has specialized in scandals and in taking intellectual stands in the art world. Stripes are a constant theme as his columns in the Palais-Royal clearly show.

HENRI CARTIER-BRESSON This world-famous globe-trotting photographer was a founding member of the Magnum photo-reporters' agency. The underlying sensitivity of his images has made them into icons of the 20th century.

CESAR A diminutive, bearded figure from the south of France, César's "pop art" sculptures astonished the public in the early 1960s. He is particularly famous for his giant bronze thumbs. See his *Centaur* at the Carrefour de la Croix Rouge in St.-Germain.

PATRICE CHEREAU Theater and movie director Chéreau first achieved international fame in the 1970s, with a revolutionary production of Wagner's *Ring* cycle in Bayreuth and Berg's *Lulu* in Paris. After successfully directing the Théâtre des Amandiers in Nanterre, Chéreau resigned in 1990 to concentrate more on personal work.

CATHERINE DENEUVE A blonde beauty propelled to fame by director Roger Vadim in the 1960s. Jacques Démy's *Les Parapluies de Cherbourg* and Polanski's *Repulsion* sealed her destiny. Her face was a model for every town hall statue of *Marianne*.

Face of France: Catherine Deneuve

GERARD DEPARDIEU His bulky muscular frame is now world-famous, following major roles in films by Wajda, Truffaut, Ferreri, Pialat and Resnais. Dépardieu recently turned to directing, with *Tartuffe*. He divides his time between tending his Burgundy vines and his Parisian apartment.

MARGUERITE DURAS Author and movie director Duras' entire output expresses the incommunicability of love in a tense, lonely world. She became famous in the 1950s, confirming her status with her movie *India Song* and by writing the screenplay for Resnais' *Hiroshima mon amour*. Her bestseller *L'Amant* (1984) was based on her childhood in Indo-China.

PIERRE GAGNAIRE Perhaps the most famous chef in Paris and a legend in his own lifetime: his bold move from St.-Etienne in the provinces to the capital won him the unreserved admiration of the business world and his superbly inventive cuisine conquered the tastes of even the most conservative of gourmets.

SERGE GAINSBOURG Although he died aged 62 in 1990, Gainsbourg's influence on French rock music and youth culture continues. Iconoclastic, with a sardonic humor inspired by Surrealism, he revolutionized the French *chanson*, changing the writing and sonority of sung French. He was married to Jane Birkin and their daughter Charlotte Gainsbourg is now a talented young actress in her own right.

JEAN-PAUL GAULTIER The ultimate French fashion designer of the 1980s, this recognized *enfant terrible* introduced the androgynous look, baroque caricatures and extra-ordinary fabrics. He started designing at Cardin's and created his own label in 1976.

JEAN NOUVEL One of a new generation of architects who put French design on the map, Nouvel's first major Parisian project was the Institut du Monde Arabe (1987). His designs make sophisticated use of high-tech materials and are often technical feats. His *Tour sans fin* at La Défense is a 1,312-feet-high tower which stands as a testament to his skills. Nouvel is often spotted at Les Bains nightclub.

Internationally-known film actor and director Gérard Dépardieu

CHRISTINE OCKRENT Coming to fame in the 1980s as a TV newscaster, Belgian-born Ockrent soon had clones on every other channel. Her "superwoman" legend grew when she had her first child at the age of 40. She worked for C.B.S. in the U.S. and the BBC in the U.K., and now presents political programs on French television.

YVES SAINT-LAURENT Born in Algeria in 1936, Y.S.L. divides his time between Marrakesh and Paris. He designed for Christian Dior from 1957 to 1960 and founded his own fashion house in 1962. The first couturier to introduce *prêt-à-porter*, he developed licensing for accessories, thus revolutionizing the fashion business. He invented the pantsuit in the 1970s.

When all is said and done, what remains of a civilization is its culture and this the French understood long ago. The electricity of Parisian cultural life has always attracted foreign artists and today the capital is a stage for top international figures. Stimulated by a healthy rivalry between theaters and encouraged by generous state subsidies, the situation for the arts is enviable.

France's all-powerful Minister of Culture does not only cover traditional forms but is also Minister for rock music and comic strips, while guiding the destiny of the fashion industry. But this paternalistic umbrella has its negative effects, creating a climate of dependency. The hard edge—a will to succeed and survive—is sometimes lacking.

PICTURE PALACE Living up to its role as inventor-nation of the cinema, France's capital offers over 300 different movies weekly. Since the heyday of the *nouvelle vague*, new blood has appeared (**Jean-Jacques Beneix, Léo Carax, Bertrand Blier, Coline Serreau, Luc Besson, Chantal Akermann, Jean-Jacques Annaud, Alain Corneau**) while the older intimist generation of **Rivette, Chabrol, Rohmer, Resnais,** or **Tavernier** has not said its last word. The third largest producer of movies in the world, much of France's cinema is filmed in the studios of Billancourt in west Paris, while once a year all eyes are on the Cannes Film Festival. All this has helped to maintain movie theater audiences at a healthy level.

Théâtre des Champs-Elysées

❑ In 1990 admissions to movie theaters in France numbered 121 million. In 1998 they numbered 170 million. ❑

MUSIC Whether jazz, rock, or classical, sounds emerge from clubs, theaters, hotels, churches, or concert halls all over the capital. Maintaining its pivotal role as the European jazz center, Paris has attracted a stream of top American musicians since **Sidney Bechet's** days. Jazz clubs abound; traditionalists vie with experimentalists, **Miles Davis** would appear for a lightning set; and local musicians create their own syntheses. Rock music, on the other hand, remains the black sheep of French culture—despite desperate state support. Exceptions such as the **Gypsy Kings,** or **Les Négresses Vertes** bend the rule, but ultimately creative rock escapes the French character and language, which may be too analytical for such basic rhythms. The explosion of "world music" has given black Africans and North Africans (mainly Algerians

La Comédie Italienne is a striking feature of rue de la Gaîté

and notably **Khaled**) a chance to express new sounds, amalgamations of their native harmonies with westernized arrangements.

Opera and classical music are centralized fields in France: 75 percent of French composers over 40 studied at the Paris Conservatoire, and the sophisticated new Conservatoire at La Villette will no doubt maintain this *status quo*. **Pierre Boulez, Henri Dutilleux, Edgar Varèse,** and the Greek-born **Iannis Xenakis**, with **Olivier Messïaen** (who died in 1992) as a strong background influence, are France's contemporary masters who, although sometimes open to electro-acoustic innovation, avoid minimalist American models.

DANCE has been transformed throughout the 1980s and, unlike music, has found its place in the regions. However, the companies of young choreographers such as **Jean-Claude Gallotta** (Grenoble), the late **Dominique Bagouet** (Montpellier), **Karine Saporta** (Caen), and **Angelin Prelocaj** (Chambéry) still have to perform in Paris, usually at the Théâtre de la Ville, to confront the capital's sophisticated audiences and critics. The Opéra de Paris ballet company, now directed by the brilliant young dancer **Patrick Dupond** after years of Rudolf Nureyev's vagaries, wavers between the classics and occasional avant-garde choreography.

THEATER covers traditional boulevard farce, **Molière** or **Racine, Brecht, Beckett,** or **Koltès** and includes that uniquely Parisian institution, café-théâtre. As in other fields, injections of foreign talent are welcome and the theater scene would not be the same without **Ariane Mnouchkine's** theater complex in Vincennes, La Cartoucherie, or **Peter Brook's** company based at Les Bouffes du Nord. Director **Patrice Chéreau** remains the *enfant chéri* of both public and critics and mounts his innovative productions all over Europe. A vital motor is the Festival d'Automne which, every autumn, invites foreign directors from **Luc Bondy** to **Heiner Müller,** or **Robert Wilson**, thus providing Paris with an enviable and dynamic window on world theater.

ART Parallel to the performing arts is a lively visual art scene. Slowly recovering now from world recession, private and public galleries are still aided by government subsidies. But state aid does not create talent, and French artists still tend to look too closely at their American and German contemporaries, although exceptions such as **Boltanski** or **Buren** have international status. Paris still attracts creative talent and culture vultures alike; and with three weekly book programs on TV, France is unlikely to lose touch with its literary roots.

Despite repeated offensives from Milan, New York, London, and Tokyo, Paris remains the uncontested center of fashion. With an arrogant, relentless hold on women's wardrobes worldwide, its high fashion dictates are unashamedly copied in countless sweatshops from Hong Kong to Taiwan to Paris itself. Haute couture *may be having a hard time but the new generation of* prêt-à-porter *designers is flourishing and keeping the tricolor flag flying. Fashion and its accessories are France's best ambassadresses.*

Paris quite simply breathes fashion. No central street is complete without its chic boutique and no woman rightfully self-assured without her designer accessories. Non-French designers, models, and photographers flock to Paris for essential training and, more than anything else, sensitizing to a general spirit of fashion awareness. It may be a cut-throat, backbiting business but it is also glamorous and/or outrageous: no self-respecting fashion professional can ignore it.

BIG BUSINESS In the 1990s **Haute Couture** and **Fashion Creators** together represented a several billion franc industry, 67 percent of which was exported. It is hardly surprising that most of the 3,000 or so private *haute couture* clients are foreigners: prices range from 25,000 to 50,000 francs, a level more accessible to wives of sheikhs or Hollywood film moguls. Fashion Creators (Créateurs de Mode) is the name given to upscale *prêt-à-porter* designers (**Chloé, Kenzo, Sonia Rykiel, Thierry Mugler** etc) whose fame is often as great as their elders, and who officially joined forces with the couturiers' federation in 1975.

Strangely anachronistic, the *grands couturiers* have to follow a rigid set of rules to be allowed into this hallowed legally protected circle, currently numbering 18. These include

presenting twice-yearly collections of at least 75 models to the press and at least 45 times to clients inside the Couture house. January and July are the big months for, respectively, the Spring–Summer and the Autumn–Winter collections. The fashion creators show their new designs, carefully juxtaposed, in early October and March (when Parisian hotels are full to the brim). Some 100 shows take place in various venues from the custom-designed area of the Carrousel du Louvre to the Grande Halle at La Villette or the place de l'Alma by the river.

INVENTION AND TRADITION

Dreaming up innovative garments has been a Parisian tradition since the first couturiers started up in the 1880s and 1890s. In the first part of the 20th century, the master was **Paul Poiret**, the man who declared the corset undesirable and swathed his customers in Arabian Nights gear but later admitted, "I freed the bust but enslaved the legs." **Chanel** first recognized a new direction for women after World War I and created soft, loose boyish-looking cuts as well as the famous "little black dress." Much to her annoyance the exuberant personality of **Elsa Schiaparelli** soon stepped in with humor, a clever antidote during the 1930s depression. When **Dior** stunned the postwar world with his "New Look," women were ready to return to a more feminine line and be extravagant with yards of cloth: this carried on throughout the 1950s. Since then couturiers like **Courrèges** (1960s space age), **Saint-Laurent** (1970s retro-influences), and the latest to be admitted to the inner circle with a flamenco flounce, **Christian Lacroix**, have influenced and reflected the spirit of the time. Rule-breaking is part and parcel of Parisian fashion extremism. Waists are clinched or forgotten, skirt lengths short or long, trousers baggy or drainpipe, dresses clinging or billowing. Certain younger designers have led the way: **Thierry Mugler** (in luxury Hollywood kitsch), **Jean-Paul Gaultier** (for outrageous, humorous designs), and **Claude Montana** (for moody science fiction heroines), while **Alaïa** was the man to bring back the feminine figure with a vengeance. Foreign designers such as **Karl Lagerfeld**, the Japanese contingent (from the precursor **Kenzo** to **Miyake, Yamamoto** and **Rei Kawakubo** of Comme des Garçons), and the new British contingent of **Stella McCartney, John Galliard, Alexander McQueen**, and the American **Tom Ford** have all gravitated to Paris, naturally or forcibly, confirming the city's dual role as respected guardian and juvenile tearaway.

Fashion on show along the catwalks of Paris

Of all the countries in the world France is the most closely associated with food, with gourmets and gourmandize. Food is a subject taken seriously, and has at least 15 national magazines devoted to it. Fortunes are spent on ingredients, let alone on restaurants. But food combines both science and pleasure, and so corresponds perfectly to the dual French psyche.

Although this "science" has been the nation's prerogative since the days of Rabelais, most French choose to forget that the dreaded Catherine de Médicis was responsible for bringing chefs from Italy to introduce new dishes in the 16th century. But the advent and spread of public restaurants and cafés in Paris did not happen till the Revolutionary period. Before the Revolution Paris boasted fewer than 2,000 cafés; by the early 1800s they had more than doubled in number. *Ancien régime* cuisine was known for being elaborate, rich and heavy, with diners often struggling through twenty courses. In 1783 the first grandiose *dîner philosophique* was launched, creating the link between literature and gastronomy that is so much a part of France.

CHANGE OF DIET World War I ended the gourmet golden age of the 19th

Simple and stylish: poulet à l'estragon *(chicken with tarragon), originally a Lyonnais dish*

century, bringing a sense of measure and even in some cases frugality. With the spread of motoring, a new accent was put on regional cuisine, echoed by the famous Guide Michelin, and when in 1936 annual paid holidays became law, restaurants were at last opened up to all classes. The gastronomic variety of the provinces was soon discovered with a vengeance by crowds of foreign tourists armed, as always, with the little red book. Culinary dynasties in family inns scattered throughout France, from the Bocuse at Collonges to the Daguin at Auch, soon gained national and international status.

CULINARY REVOLUTION A new consciousness of ecology, macrobiotics, and dietary considerations influenced the cuisine of the 1960s and 1970s, culminating in **Michel Guérard's** famous *cuisine minceur*. Its emphasis on balanced nutrition and adventurous experiment created the subversive *nouvelle cuisine*. A new generation of chefs looked beyond France for inspiration. Partly through the influence of apprentice Japanese chefs in Paris kitchens, aesthetic presentation became paramount and classic table service disappeared.

However, by the late 1980s the tide was turning. Too many unworthy chefs jumped on the two-carrot *nouvelle cuisine* bandwagon, leaving customers unsatisfied and hungry. As a result, wholesome, old-fashioned bourgeois cooking is back in fashion. Yet Guérard's techniques, applied to traditional recipes, now inspire a lighter cuisine which satisfies both sophisticated and hungry appetites.

❑ The *crêpe suzette* was invented by mistake in Monte Carlo at the turn of the century. Chef Henri Charpentier was preparing some crêpes for the Prince of Wales and accidentally set fire to the alcohol in the sauce in which he was cooking them. Delighted with the result, the Prince suggested naming them after his young companion. ❑

GREAT CHEFS

Antoine Beauvilliers opened a famous restaurant in Palais-Royal in 1790. He wrote *L'Art du Cuisinier* in 1814, analyzing cooking with a clear, scientific approach.

Paul Bocuse Descendant of a line of chefs since 1765 and an apprentice at Lucas-Carton and Lapérouse, Bocuse returned to his family restaurant outside Lyon in 1959. Very soon he became known as France's unofficial gastronomic ambassador.

Alain Ducasse who took over Joël Robuchon's restaurant in magnificent art nouveau premises, offers a perfect example of the return to traditional yet lighter cuisine (such as crisp pork with caramelized potatoes).

Auguste Escoffier The creator of the peach melba started in the kitchens aged 13 in 1859 and lived to be 90. He worked mainly in London's Savoy and Carlton hotels.

Pierre Gagnaire left a renowned 3-star restaurant in St.-Etienne to try his hand in Paris, just off the Champs-Elysées. Here his meteoric rise to the top Michelin rating created quite a stir in gourmet circles.

Michel Guérard started as a pastry chef at the Crillon. In 1972 he opened his famous restaurant at Eugénie-les-Bains in southwest France, where he created imaginative, light, aromatic food with the accent on fish, fowl, and veal.

Guy Savoy As unpredictable in his repertoire as Robuchon, Savoy experiments with textures and flavors and has a restaurant in the *17th arrondissement*.

Taillevent Cook to 14th-century kings including Philippe VI, Taillevent wrote the oldest known treatise on cooking, *Le Viandier*.

Children's Paris is not all Punch and Judy shows. Specially designed facilities are installed all over the city and keep the whole range, from toddlers upward, out of mischief. Every arrondissement *has public squares equipped with sandpits and/or swings and slides. Although it may seem as if this diminutive section of the local population is rather thin on the ground, it emerges visibly on no-school days Wednesdays, Saturdays, and Sundays. Avoid most destinations mentioned below on these days.*

If museum-visiting is your priority, the Atelier des Enfants at the Centre Pompidou is a possible solution. Any child aged 6 to 12 can be booked in immediately prior to sessions on Wednesday mornings and left in capable hands. There are extra sessions in the school holidays. Nearby is another supervized playground, this one a labyrinth full of slides, swings, and tunnels. The Jardin d'Enfants accepts children aged 7 to 11, but check exact opening hours (105 rue Rambuteau, tel: 01 45 08 07 18).

PUPPETS The traditional puppets (*guignols*), whose squeaky language won't mean much to a non-French child, are still good value. All shows take place afternoons only on Wednesdays and at weekends. The following parks provide shows: Montsouris, Rond-point des Champs-Elysées, Champ-de-Mars, Luxembourg, Georges Brassens, and Jardins du Ranelagh. Best of all in the parks arena is the Jardin d'Acclimatation in the Bois de Boulogne (*Open* daily 10–5; summer 10–6. *Métro* Sablons), where Parisian children revel in pleasure trains, donkey rides, and boat trips. A children's zoo, a hall of mirrors, a *guignol* theater, and an educational Musée en Herbe complete the package. At the eastern end of Paris, the Bois de Vincennes has an equivalent area, the Parc Floral, which features a miniature train, a games area, and a mini-golf course.

MUSEUMS Top of the list of museums catering for children comes the Cité des Enfants at the Cité des Sciences et de l'Industrie (*métro* Porte de la Villette), where children are encouraged to crack the mysteries of science: the computer games are as instructive as the keyboard experiments (see pages 175 and 183). In the same scientific vein but less high-tech is the Palais de la

Découverte, part of the Grand Palais (see page 124). Ardent star-gazers shouldn't miss its fascinating planetarium.

Children with budding creative talents can participate in artistic activities at the Atelier des Enfants in the Centre Georges Pompidou, which has reopened after extensive renovations. The waxworks at the Musée Grévin (see page 124) never fail to provoke thrilled squeals.

CIRCUSES For chilly or rainy days the heated Cirque Diana Moreno in the Jardin d'Acclimatation is ideal and boasts breathtaking acrobats. Going strong since 1854, the Cirque Alexis Gruss is also in the Bois de Boulogne: Allée de la Reine Marguerite (tel: 01 45 01 71 26; *métro* Porte Maillot, then bus 244 to Route des Lacs, afternoon shows Wed, Sat, and Sun).

Outside Paris the field widens, from the Parc Astérix to Thoiry and Disneyland Paris (see pages 196–197). None of these attractions is more than 25 miles away, and Thoiry can be reached by train from Montparnasse (go to Montfort l'Amaury, then take the Shuttle). Astérix, of course, has more meaning if your children have spent time perusing the comic-strip hero's life. In any event, the park makes a lively outing.

Thoiry (*Open* daily 10–6) is however the star here, as between the 800 wild-ish animals, the Renaissance château and the Museum of Gastronomy, few tastes are neglected. The interesting château and its gardens, beautifully landscaped by Le Nôtre, are worth visiting in themselves, but may fade into insignificance in comparison with the safari park, the largest park of its kind in Europe.

To the southwest of Paris in Elancourt is France Miniature. Children can pretend they are giants in this "mini-France" where 200 French monuments have been scaled down to a 30th of their original size, and reproduced in exact detail.

Concentration: being entertained is a serious business

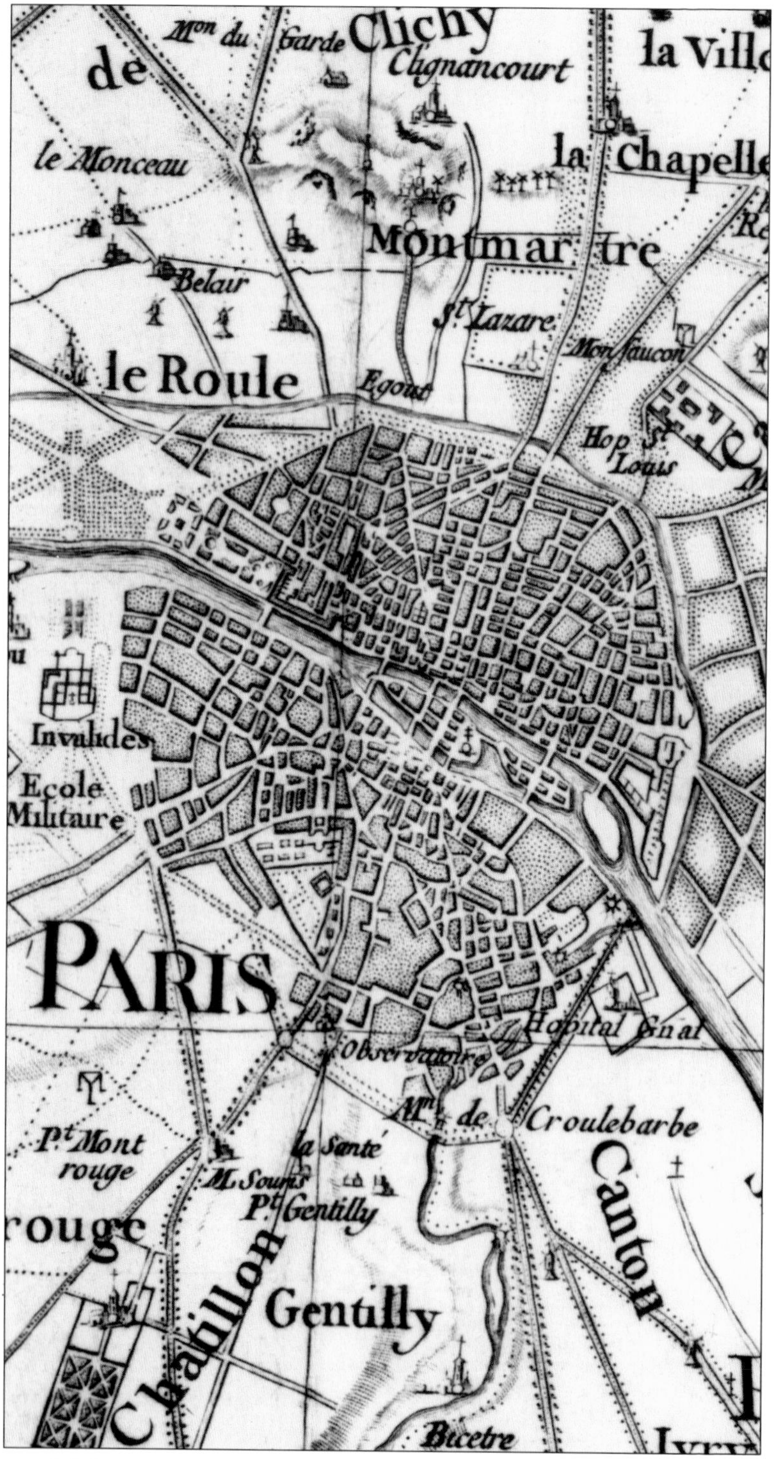
Mon du
Garde
Clichy
Clignancourt
la Villo
de
le Monceau
la Chapelle
Montmartre
Belair
St. Lazare
Mon faucon
le Roule
Egout
Hop. St. Louis
Invalides
Ecole Militaire
PARIS
Hopital Gnal
Observatoire
Mn. de Croulebarbe
Pt. Mont rouge
la Santé
M. Souris
Pt. Gentilly
rouge
Canton
Chatillon
Gentilly
Bicetre

Paris' first occupants were a Celtic tribe called the Parisii, who settled on the Ile de la Cité. Strategically located at the confluence of three rivers, the Seine, the Marne, and the Oise, they flourished on trade until Caesar's Gallic Wars engulfed them in 52 BC.

Renaming the settlement *Lutetia*, the Romans soon set about creating their own structures, which continued to thrive for almost 500 years. After rebuilding the Ile de la Cité the Romans moved across the Seine to the Left (south) Bank, where some monuments still stand today. The amphitheater (now called **les Arènes**) on the Montagne Ste.-Geneviève could hold up to 15,000 people and became the backdrop for gladiator fights as well as more sober and less bloody entertainment.

GROWING NEEDS The rapidly expanding population demanded baths, and of the three sites uncovered (**Collège de France, rue Gay-Lussac** and **Cluny**), the latter, built around AD 200, remains remarkably well-preserved. In true Roman style, no fewer than 28 miles of richly decorated aqueducts were built to supply water to these establishments. The central forum was located in the **rue Soufflot** (now below ground), while the adjacent **Montagne Ste.-Geneviève** became the main residential quarter.

ROMAN ROADS Although nothing remains of the Imperial palace (apparently on the site of the present Palais de Justice) or the theatre (on boulevard St.-Michel), the Romans left a network of firmly traced roads. Their north–south axes form the basis of Paris' main arteries, such as the **rue St.-Martin**, which cuts straight as a die across the Seine to the rue St.-Jacques, or the parallel **boulevard St.-Michel**, the east–west **rue des Ecoles** or the **rue de la Montagne Ste.-Geneviève**, which steadfastly climbs the slope to become the **rue Mouffetard**.

END OF AN ERA River and road trade assured a peaceful prosperity until around AD 275, when increasingly frequent Barbarian attacks eventually destroyed most of the Left Bank, forcing the inhabitants to withdraw on to the Ile de la Cité. This soon became a walled enclave, its ramparts built with the ruins of the Left Bank. Although a fragile peace was restored and the population spread to the Right Bank, the northerners eventually won the day in 486 when Clovis, chief of the Franks, conquered the Roman ruler Syagrius at the Battle of Soissons.

The frigidarium from the Roman baths, at the Musée de Cluny

Although the courageous Geneviève had saved Paris fronr Attila's Huns in the 5th century, later becoming the city's patron saint, the Ile-de-France soon fell under the rule of a series of Frankish kings. Power fell into the hands of rulers with the exotic names of Clovis, Childebert, and Dagobert, but when Charlemagne moved the capital of his powerful empire to Aix la Chapelle in the early 9th century, Paris went into a dramatic decline.

Concentrated on the Ile de la Cité, the only signs of the city's former prosperity and importance were now at the neighboring abbey of St.-Denis, the royal graveyard since Dagobert. Only in the 10th century, with the rise to power of the Capetians, Dukes of France, and Counts of Paris, did the city regain its luster. The development of agriculture and trade in the Middle Ages ensured new growth and wealth. For the first time, the Right Bank was settled and the swamp to the east, the Marais, was drained and cultivated. A port was established on **place de la Grève** (now l'Hôtel de Ville) opposite the Cité and a central market appeared at the end of the road from St.-Denis, named after its wooden pavilions: Les Halles.

FINANCIAL PULSE The Right Bank soon became the city's commercial heart. Its streets were still exceedingly narrow (the smallest 3 feet wide) and filthy. Muddy, badly lit, congested, and a haven for nocturnal thieves, they remained the terror of the visitor well into the 19th century. The houses were plain and narrow, made of wood beams and plastered rubble, with high-pitched gables. They took up every available space within the city walls and even piled up onto the town's four bridges, notable chiefly for the frequency with which they collapsed into the Seine.

A few buildings, like the royal palace (now the Palais de Justice), with its flamboyant Gothic chapel (**Sainte-Chapelle**), the splendid new cathedral of **Notre-Dame** or the fortress guarding the city's western gates, the **Louvre**, provided a note of distinction in this otherwise crowded, unplanned, and mostly very smelly city.

SCHOLARLY CITY In the late 12th century, under Philippe Auguste, the **University of Paris** was founded and trades and crafts came under the control of tightly organized, prosperous guilds. The university, which

France emerged from the Middle Ages under the reign of François I

Charles VII's reign saw the end of the Hundred Years' War: here he enters Paris in 1436

gave its name to the Latin Quarter on the Left Bank, soon became one of the most renowned in Europe, boasting scholars like Guillaume de Champeaux and Abelard.

ABELARD AND HELOISE Two of the most colorful and tragic figures of medieval Paris were the great scholar and theologian Abelard and his beloved Héloïse, niece of a Notre Dame canon, Fulbert. After a passionate love affair they had a child and secretly married. Fulbert wrought a terrible revenge: tied up by three hired thugs Abelard was castrated. Further pursued by the Church for alleged heresy in his writings, Abelard wandered from monastery to monastery until he found refuge at the abbey of Cluny. Eight poignant letters survive, exchanged by Abelard and Héloïse after their separation. They are buried together in the Père Lachaise cemetery, and at 9 quai aux Fleurs you can see their sculpted heads.

BIG CITY By the reign of Philippe Auguste's famous grandson, Saint Louis (1226–1270), Paris was already a major European capital and, with its 200,000 inhabitants, the most populous city on the Continent.

A memorable moment for the city came in 1263, when the Parisian merchants elected their first representative, the Prévôt des Marchands.

AT WAR The Hundred Years' war (from the mid-14th to mid-15th century) plunged the city back into turbulence, bringing medieval peace and prosperity to a violent end. Paris was at times ruled by the English, who defended the city successfully against Jeanne d'Arc. Violence also returned in the form of a rebellion in 1358 led by the Prévôt, Etienne Marcel, against the sovereign, the Dauphin Charles. Unable to bear numerous humiliations, the Dauphin was forced to escape to the south of France to rally the nobles to his cause. Marcel was eventually murdered, enabling the Dauphin to return to Paris. Yet this first act of rebellion gave birth to the distrust which existed between the rulers of France and their capital city well into modern times. Abandoning the central Cité palace in favor of mansions closer to the city wall, the kings increasingly favored provincial châteaux—a trend taken up to the full by the king who in many ways characterized late medieval France: François I.

Despotic and capricious, yet also a refined Renaissance gentleman, François I epitomized the contradictory aspects of French society in the 16th century. Still based on feudalism, this society nevertheless felt the increasing weight of royal authority as François I centralized power from his capital, Paris, seat of the Treasury, the Mint, and the law courts.

The court diligently followed François I from one splendid Loire château to the next. In Paris it settled in the Louvre, rebuilt by the king in the brand new Renaissance style imported from Italy. Elaborate costumed balls, ballets, and ceremonies kept the courtiers amused, and the title of "Majesty," previously reserved for the Holy Roman emperor, was now applied to the French king.

AGE OF REBIRTH The breath of the Renaissance swept France in the wake of Italian artists imported to decorate Fontainebleau. The new passion for antiquity, poetry, literature, and philosophy culminated in the founding of the Collège de France (1530), the kingdom's first secular educational institution. This was the age of Rabelais, Montaigne, the Humanist publisher Robert Estienne, and of noble patrons of the arts and humanities, notably François I's sister, Marguerite de Navarre, and Henri II's mistress, Diane de Poitiers.

MASSACRE AND WAR This enlightenment was brought to an abrupt end by the Wars of Religion that swept through France in the latter half of the century (1562–1598), a period dominated by the cunning Catherine de Médicis, wife of Henri II and domineering mother of the last three Valois kings (François II, Charles IX, Henri III). Its darkest episode occurred on Saint Bartholomew's day (24 August, 1572) when, pressed by his mother, the vacillating Charles IX ordered the massacre of Protestant nobles gathered at the Louvre to celebrate the wedding of Henri de Bourbon (the future Henri IV) to the king's sister. Three thousand strangled and knifed Protestant corpses were thrown into the Seine on that fateful day, and for over 20 years civil war raged throughout France.

"Paris is well worth a Mass" are the famous words uttered by Henri IV, the first Bourbon king, before abjuring his Protestant faith, last obstacle to his accession to the throne of France. His triumphal entry into a devastated and hungry Paris in 1594 spelt the temporary end to the Wars of Religion.

NEW ERA A pleasure-loving man, with as many mistresses as his predecessors, Henri IV was nevertheless the king who seriously set to reorganizing the kingdom and notably its capital, Paris. Completing the great gallery of the Louvre, the Hôtel de Ville started by François I and endowing the city with new squares (place des Vosges, place Dauphine), bridges (Pont Neuf) and a hospital for plague victims (St.-Louis), Henri began the process that would transform the still largely medieval city of the 16th century into the classical capital of the 17th and 18th centuries.

The first half of the 17th century (the Grand Siècle) was dominated by foreign and civil wars and the anxious personality of the chronically ill homosexual Louis XIII, sustained by the efforts of his brilliant but equally hypochondriac minister Cardinal Richelieu. This was the Paris of Alexandre Dumas' *Three Musketeers*, teeming with intrigue and the ongoing rivalry between the Cardinal and the Queen,

Henri IV pictured with the royal mistress, Gabrielle d'Estrées

❑ "People of quality know everything without ever having been taught."—Molière, *Les Précieuses Ridicules* ❑

the wilful and Catholic Anne of Austria, who was forever conspiring with the English and the Spanish against French interests.

MIDDLE CLASSES Amid court conspiracies and religious turmoil there emerged a Parisian class composed of the new civil servants, financiers and wealthy merchants, who provided the backbone of a great religious and cultural revival in the capital. Among the new churches and convents rose the sober, well-proportioned mansions of the Marais, in which cultivated women of taste, the hostesses, presided over the first Parisian salons. The most celebrated of all was the Marquise de Rambouillet, in her rue St.-Honoré house, who received all the great luminaries of her day from La Rochefoucauld to Corneille. Molière, whose theater troupe settled in Paris in 1658, satirized the new manners in his great play, *Les Précieuses Ridicules*.

The Fronde (1648–1652) was the last great civil disturbance experienced by Paris before the French Revolution. The victory of the regent, Anne of Austria and her wily prime minister, Cardinal Mazarin, over the rebellious Paris bourgeoisie and the nobility paved the way for the absolute power of Louis XIV.

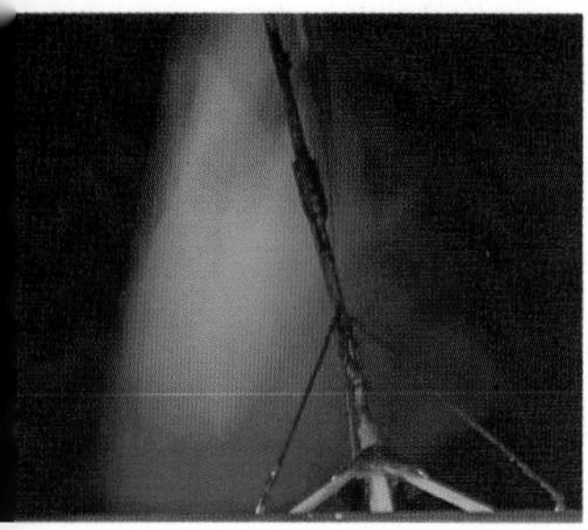

When at the death of his mother's old prime minister, the Cardinal Mazarin, in 1661, Louis XIV announced he would govern on his own, his ministers and the court were stupefied. Yet l'Etat c'est Moi *perfectly describes the spirit of the later 17th century, a time when all the energies and resources of the kingdom were harnessed into the service and glorification of one single being and symbol: the Sun King.*

Though refusing to name a new prime minister, Louis XIV would have been unable to carry through his ambitious projects without the help and administrative talent of his finance minister, the dour, workaholic Colbert. Colbert's dream, a great palace for the king in Paris—the Louvre—was abandoned (literally without finishing the roof) in favor of Versailles, yet other projects of his were carried through. Royal Academies were established to control every facet of French cultural and intellectual life, and a great Royal factory, the Gobelins, was set up to produce the furniture, silver, and tapestries needed to fill Versailles.

CULTURAL CAPITAL By the end of the century, the talents of architects,, painters, cabinetmakers, musicians, and playwrights trained to serve the king were already turning Paris and Versailles into the artistic and cultural center of Europe. Nor did the removal of the court into the glittering and tightly controlled environment of Versailles mean that Paris was neglected. New squares, hospitals, bridges, churches, and monumental avenues (Champs Elysées, the Grands Boulevards), better policing and lighting transformed the city more than ever before.

❑ "You are going to be a great king. Do not copy me in my love of building or in my love of warfare; on the contrary, try to live peacefully with your neighbours."—Louis XIV to the future Louis XV ❑

Much of the vitality of the Great King's reign was, however, extinguished long before his actual death (1715). The removal of the five-year-old Louis XV to the Tuileries palace by the regent signaled a renewal for the capital. Bored with the rigidity, etiquette, and dusty grandeur of the Sun King, the court and nobility returned to Paris to throw themselves enthusiastically into a life entirely devoted to pleasure and dalliance.

FRIVOLITY AND FLOWERS Thus sensual, frivolous rococo was born in the aristocratic mansions of the Faubourg St.-Germain and the bankers' houses of the quartier St.-Honoré. Watteau's flirting couples in romantic parks, Boucher's rosy mythological posteriors, shells, flowers, and tendrils interpreted in chair legs and sofas, all provided the decorative background to the first half of Louis XV's reign.

Yet this was also the period of the revival of the literary salon. As the century wore on, touches of intellectual curiosity, moralism, and pedantry invaded the witty, polished atmosphere of the salons of Mesdames du Deffand and Epinay. Beginning with Voltaire, this libertarian spirit, alternately flirting with and defying royal authority, was enshrined in the circle of the new philosophers and *encyclopédistes*, the compilers of the world's first dictionary—Diderot, Buffon, Condorcet, Rousseau, D'Alembert, and Helvétius.

❑ "In an aristocracy, honors, pleasures, power, and money are easily obtainable. Great discretion, however, is necessary. If abuse is flagrant, revolution will be the consequence."—Voltaire, *Philosophical Dictionary* ❑

SHIFT OF FOCUS Though the court returned to Versailles in 1724, it would never again be the focus of French life as it was under Louis XIV. It was to Paris that the aristocrats, even the King, now escaped for their fun, to the masked balls, the opera and, the latest rage, the first public art exhibitions the salons held every other year in the Louvre.

This spirit of reform found its first visual outlet in the city's architecture. Though still elegant, from 1750 a sobriety and studious historical allusion pervaded the neoclassical style, with its Corinthian columns, swags and triangular pediments spreading across Paris from the place Louis XV (Concorde) to the Eglise Ste.-Geneviève (Panthéon) and the new Royal Mint, La Monnaie.

By the middle of the reign of Louis XVI (1774–1793) and his beautiful, frivolous, unpopular Queen, Marie Antoinette, the still polite reformist mood of the earlier half of the century had turned into a flood of open sedition. Malicious printed jokes openly circulated at the Palais Royal and ended up beneath the Queen's plate at Versailles. The well-intentioned but indecisive Louis XVI, unable to control the situation any longer, called for the representatives of all classes, *Les Etats Généraux*, to meet in Versailles in May 1789. No-one could have dreamed it, but that fateful spring was to mark the end of the Ancien Régime.

The Water Gardens at Versailles: under Louis XIV's reign, Versailles became the focus of court life

The Revolution signaled the end of royal excesses and the rise of popular democracy in a momentum that continued throughout the uprisings of the 19th century. Long before the gathering in Versailles of the Etats Généraux, *which brought together the Clergy, Nobility and the Commons, trouble was afoot and the air rife with political agitation. Much of this was fermented at the Palais Royal, residence of the Dukes of Orléans, the rival branch of the royal family.*

The Palais Royal, though open to the public, was out of bounds to the police; so speechmaking and the distribution of anti-government pamphlets went on unhindered. It was here that in July 1789 a young journalist, Camille Desmoulins, gave the battle cry "*aux armes!*" to defend the city from a rumored attack by the King's army. A great mob invaded the city hall and raided the Invalides barracks for muskets. Next morning, on July 14, the same mob presented itself at a fortress on the eastern edge of the city, the Bastille. A four-hour battle, the first violent act of the Revolution, led to the fall of the fortress, the liberation of six prisoners (mostly counterfeiters), and the beheading of the governor. From here on events moved at a breathtaking pace until the Revolution finally ran out of steam in July 1794.

ROYAL PRISONERS A new mayor was nominated and the city organized its very own "National" guard, headed by the Marquis de Lafayette. In October, the Royal family was forcibly brought back from Versailles and installed in the Tuileries palace, virtual prisoners of the people and the new National Assembly. A period of relative calm, in which a Constitution and new laws were promulgated, came to an abrupt end with the King's failed attempt to escape on June 21, 1791. Now the anti-monarchist and left-wing forces in the city, radicalized by the outbreak of war, gained the upper hand. On August 10, 1792, the Paris mob attacked the Tuileries palace, massacring 600 of the King's Swiss guards and a few unlucky cooks and servants. A terrified royal family fled to the Assembly and the next day were locked up in the old medieval tower of the Temple.

Soon the new Assembly, the Convention, abolished the monarchy and proclaimed the First Republic, along with a new calendar: 1792 became Year 1 of the new era. The King was tried, found guilty of high treason and guillotined on 21 January, 1793. This was the year that opened the most violent period of the Revolution: the Reign of Terror. Nobles who had failed to emigrate, priests, the Queen, and ordinary citizens were whisked to the Conciergerie prison on the Ile de la Cité. Judged by a mock court, they were then sent by the cartload, their hands tied and napes shaved, rattling along the rue St.-Honoré to the guillotine on place de la Révolution (Concorde). As the stench of blood on the square led to complaints from the neighbors, the guillotine was transferred for a brief period to place

❏ Originally a revolutionary song, next a chant for the Republicans confronting the monarchists, the *Marseillaise* became the national anthem in 1880. It was written in 1792 by Rouget de Lisle and became known as the *Marseillaise* when Parisians heard troops from the south of France singing it as they entered the capital. ❏

de la Nation, but soon returned to the more central and convenient Concorde. Political power was now concentrated in the hands of the misnamed Committee of Public Safety, led by a former lawyer, the calculating Robespierre. By now, the Revolution was devouring her own children. Beginning with the Mayor of Paris, a stream of moderate deputies was led to the blade. In March 1794 Robespierre eliminated the left wing and hit the center, including the revolutionary leaders, Desmoulins and Danton. Robespierre now stood alone. But he had gone too far. The remaining deputies in the Convention, sensing their own short life expectancy, finally found the courage to gang up against him. In July, Robespierre was arrested. He escaped and called the Paris citizens to his defence, but for the first time since 1789 the Paris mob, tired and dispirited, did not respond. Robespierre was guillotined on July 28, 1794. The Terror, and the Revolution, were over.

A social system on trial: Louis XVI comes before the people's court in 1792 (above) and (below) the march to Versailles, 1789

Following the bloody days of the Terror and before France's first Emperor arrived on the scene with due pomp and ceremony, France was ruled by an intermediary government, known as the Directoire (1795–1799). This was a time of winding down of tensions and of gradual economic recovery, despite the continuing social and political instability.

With the old nobility and Church decimated by Revolutionary fervor, the bourgeoisie now controlled all political and financial power. The selling off of confiscated religious and noble properties during the Revolution further ensured that the new class of profiteers and property owners, no matter how conservative, would never accept a return to the old status quo.

DEFEAT AND CAUTION The Paris municipality, last stronghold of the left wing and the working classes, the *sans-culottes* (meaning "without breeches," that is not aristocratic), was suppressed in 1794. From Napoleon's era on, the city fell under the authority of the Prefect of the Seine, appointed by the government. So wary did the government become of the Parisians' seemingly endless potential for rebellion (borne out by the events of 1830, 1848, 1871, 1936, and 1968) that it took nearly two centuries for Paris to be allowed a freely elected Mayor, in 1977.

REACTION AND RELEASE Three years of revolutionary terror and patriotic fervor were succeeded by a mood of frivolity and unprecedented sexual liberation. Long-haired dandies and ladies, known as the *incroyables* and *merveilleuses*, danced the night away at the Café Frascati on the Grands Boulevards. Among the fashionable accessories of the day was a red ribbon worn around the neck, a discreet allusion to the past ravages and excitement of the guillotine.

One of the smartest Parisiennes of the period was the widow of a guillotined aristocrat, now mistress of the most powerful Directeur, **Joséphine de Beauharnais**. In 1796 she fell into the arms of an ardent, rising young general, **Napoleon**

Napoleon at the peak of his career: as the conquering general, portrayed by David ...

Bonaparte. Eight years later, already owner of the most ravishing country house near Paris, Malmaison, she was crowned in Notre Dame as Empress of the French.

THE NAPOLEONIC AGE Napoleon's meteoric rise to power resulted in a glorious epoch (1800–1814) that left an indelible imprint on France, its capital city and much of Europe, too. Named First Consul of the Republic after the 1799 *coup d'état*, the ambitious young general soon proclaimed himself "Emperor of the French." A new nobility, composed of princes and barons (as opposed to the old dukes and counts) was invented.

Most European territories conquered in the 1806–1810 campaigns were carved out into kingdoms and principalities for the rest of the family and in-laws such as Murat, named "King of Naples." Paris was now capital of the greatest European Empire since Charlemagne.

RECONSTRUCTION A far-reaching programme of renovation and building was drawn up by the two official architects of the reign, **Percier** and **Fontaine**, whose object was to turn the city into a monumental New Rome. The result was an unprecedented proliferation of columns and "temples" (the new **Assembly**, the **Bourse**, the **Madeleine**), Roman military monuments (**Colonne Vendôme, Arc du Carrousel, Arc de Triomphe**), and straight streets (**Castiglione, Rivoli**). Just as notable were the practical improvements in the city's infrastructure, the first signs in Paris of the dawning of an industrial age: the building of canals, the new stock exchange, an improved water supply and sewerage, modern cemeteries, a new meat market, even an iron bridge. The odd and even numbering system for the city's streets, with the low numbers beginning closest to the Seine, also dates from Napoleon I.

Napoleon's most permanent legacy to France and Paris were, however, the great national institutions in the fields of culture, education and law that he initiated or reformed. The **Louvre Museum**, inaugurated during the Revolution, was greatly enriched by the artistic booty hauled in from all corners of the new Empire. The prestigious Grandes Ecoles, still the training ground for France's ruling élite today, the **Polytechnique, Ecole des Mines, Ponts et Chaussées, Ecole Normale Supérieure,** and the **Natural History Museum** all date from Napoleon, as does the first national legal system in France, inspired by Roman Law, the Code Civil.

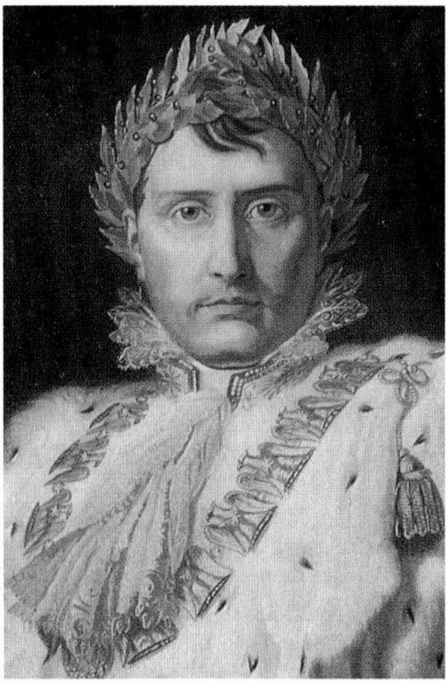

... and as self-styled Emperor Napoleon I of France, shown here wearing his Coronation robes in a tapestry by Gérard

CAPITAL CITY The concentration of the country's culture, government, education, financial, and political power in the capital, begun by the Bourbons and pursued by the Revolution, was brought to a climax by Napoleon. His ambitious plans for France brought added status to the city. The pre-eminence of Paris in France would now remain unchallenged by every succeeding régime until the election in 1981 of François Mitterrand.

Nineteenth-century Paris can largely be characterized by a tapestry of weak rulers, violent social conflicts, rising liberal intellectualism, and a new, monied bourgeoisie. Beyond the barricades and banks the arts flourished and foreign artists flocked to contribute to the capital's movements, but even greater designs were afoot. Symbolic of a will and need to change the fabric of society, Haussmann's mid-century urban transformations were a turning point for a newly industrialized society.

Before Napoleon III manoeuvred into place, France underwent the last convulsions of its luckless monarchy during the Restoration. Under Louis XVIII and Charles X, a new romantic spirit developed in the arts (Delacroix, Géricault, Victor Hugo, Balzac, Berlioz, followed by Baudelaire, and Rimbaud), partly inspired by the philosophy of Rousseau and a nostalgia for the "purity" of the Middle Ages—controversially practiced by the architect Viollet-le-Duc.

REBELS AND ROYALTY The 1830 uprising, which rapidly turned into a bloody insurrection, ended the Bourbons' lineage and brought to power the "citizen-king" Louis-Philippe of Orléans, more acceptable to the populace. Beneath a superficial self-satisfaction ("France is a nation which is bored" wrote Lamartine in 1839), however, the country was in ferment: strikes, spreading republicanism, assassinations, and a falling standard of living, accompanied by the rising power of a corrupt monied class, all combined to make an explosive situation.

The year 1848 signaled the end of the "July Monarchy." Blood and barricades soon heralded victory for the republicans, and elections brought to power Louis-Napoléon, nephew of Bonaparte, described by Toqueville as "an enigmatic, somber, insignificant numbskull." Yet inspired by the parks of his London exile and determined to end the overcrowded conditions of the capital (as well as its potential for revolution), Napoleon III immediately implemented an urban shake-up. And onto the stage now stepped the Protestant administrator Baron Haussmann, who in 18 years managed to transform the face of the capital and prepare it for the 20th century.

❏ "Paris is the heart of France. Let's put all our efforts into embellishing this big city. Let's open new roads, make the populous neighborhoods which lack air and daylight healthy, and may charitable light penetrate everywhere in our walls."—Napoleon III ❏

CITY FACE-LIFT Between 1800 and 1850, the population of Paris had doubled to over a million; in 1832, a cholera epidemic claimed 19,000 victims. Housing and proper sanitation were thus desperately needed. Conscious of the imbalance in activities between the east and west, north and south of the capital, as well as the imminent asphyxiation of its narrow, overcrowded streets, Haussmann traced an urban web of wide boulevards and avenues. Against a backdrop of sparkling social gatherings, operettas by Offenbach, and *haute couture* by Worth, he set about tearing down 20,000 houses, building 40,000, constructing 110 miles of roads, 348 miles of sewers and two reservoirs, and landscaping two woods, three parks, two gardens and 19 squares. The final jewel in Napoleon III's crown was Charles Garnier's ostentatious Opera House, the only real symbol of Second Empire architecture.

WHOLESALE CLEARANCE The Emperor's approach was romantic, that of Haussmann more inclined to straight lines. For 15 years Paris was one gigantic building site, as Haussmann, with little consideration for preservation, swept away entire *quartiers* such as the Ile de la Cité, where only Notre Dame, its immediate vicinity and the western tip were spared. Many of the Faubourg St.-Germain's finest mansions crumbled to make way for the rue de Rennes and the boulevard St.-Germain, and much of the picturesque medieval Latin Quarter succumbed to demolition.

NEW CONFLICT Modern sewerage, abattoirs (La Villette), a hygienic central market-place (Les Halles), a public bus company, squares, and parks completed this metamorphosis. However, the drums were rolling again with the Franco-Prussian War of 1870, the ensuing siege of Paris, when Parisians ate anything from rats to inmates of the zoo, and finally the last of the great revolutionary movements of the 19th century, the Paris Commune. Parisian radicals, disgusted with the peace treaty negotiated with Bismarck, had taken up arms and controlled the city, declaring it a free Commune. After a week of desperate fighting, when the Hôtel de Ville and the Tuileries Palace went up in smoke, Communards massacred priests, and government troops shot on sight, the last stand took place at the Père Lachaise cemetery. In that one week over 20,000 people died. It was the 19th century's last lesson in civil uprising.

Charles Garnier's Opera House, a Second Empire symbol

The shaky régime installed in France after the humiliating defeat inflicted by Bismarck's Prussia proved in the end to be the longest lasting since the Revolution. Paris hosted three Universal Exhibitions (1878, 1889, and 1900), which helped restore French morale and promote the prestige of the Third Republic.

The Eiffel Tower illuminated, 1889

As well as boosting morale, the Universal Exhibitions left several new landmarks on the horizon: the Palais de Chaillot (later rebuilt); the Eiffel Tower, built for the first centenary of the Revolution; and the Pont Alexandre III. The Grand and Petit Palais appeared in 1900, the year when Paris was consecrated as "World Capital" and France was recognized as one of the great industrial and colonial Empires.

NOSTALGIA The "Belle Epoque" refers to the period between 1885 and the outbreak of the Great War in 1914. Industrial squalor, labor strikes, and anarchist assassinations (like that in 1894 of the President Sadi Carnot) were forgotten in favor of the good life at the Opéra, new boulevard cafés, and music and dance halls (Folies-Bergère, Moulin Rouge).

Middle-class weekends spent boating and picnicking in the country or the suburbs (now accessible by train) became the subject-matter for a new generation of painters, the Impressionists: Monet, Renoir, Degas, Caillebotte, Sisley. The artists themselves lived in the new Batignolles district, north of St.-Lazare station, and met in the cafés of Pigalle and Clichy.

CHANGE OF MOOD By the 1880s the sunny insouciance of 1870s' Impressionism gave way to a more imaginative, but also pessimistic, mood. In poetry this was expounded by the Decadents, later the Symbolists, inspired by the writings of the explosive lovers, Verlaine and Rimbaud. The leading *fin de siècle* Symbolist was undoubtedly Mallarmé, whose enigmatic verses best convey the melancholy that overcame his generation.

The late 1880s were marked by modern art's first martyrs: Gauguin and Van Gogh, the latter's style having developed in the Bohemian atmosphere of the still half-rural Montmartre. By the 1890s a new intricate decorative style, art nouveau, blossomed on the apartment buildings of Guimard, the new Métro and department stores (Galeries Lafayette). This was also the city of Proust and Toulouse-Lautrec – a teeming, cosmopolitan Paris, where an over-indulged high society rubbed shoulders in a frisson of pleasure with alcoholics, morphine addicts,

A dance capturing the exuberance of the Belle Epoque: the can-can

prostitutes, can-can dancers, and singers at the Moulin Rouge and the new "artistic" cabarets of Montmartre. The Bohemian life, epitomized by low dives like Montmartre's *Lapin Agile*, gradually shifted into a more sophisticated gear as artists and poets moved to the new Montparnasse cafés, Le Dôme, and La Rotonde. This was when Derain, Matisse, Picasso, Braque, Delaunay, and Léger laid the foundations of 20th-century art.

THE BANQUET In 1908, Picasso threw a dinner party at his Montmartre studio that later became one of the legends of early Modernism. Guest of honor was Henri Rousseau, the great "naïve" painter. Other guests included the poets Max Jacob, André Salmon, and Apollinaire, the American collectors Leo and Gertrude Stein, and the painters Vlaminck, Braque, and Marie Laurencin. Marie Laurencin danced, while her lover Apollinaire, unperturbed, caught up with his correspondence in a corner of the room. Frédé, owner of the *Lapin Agile*, wandered in with his donkey Lolo, who consumed the last of the food. To crown the evening, two of the poets faked an attack of delirium, frothing at the mouth (they chewed soap), which sent the smartly dressed American guests scurrying home. This mix of exaltation and buffoonery perfectly conveys the atmosphere of Parisian Bohemia before the Great War—a certain innocence and *joie de vivre* later lost in the more worldly ambience of 1920s' Montparnasse. In the same years Eric Satie, Stravinsky, Alfred Jarry, Proust and Diaghilev revolutionized modern music, theater, literature, and ballet. Rarely had so much innovative talent gathered in the same place at the same time as in the Paris of 1900 to 1914.

❏ The Bateau Lavoir was a ramshackle wooden piano factory below the Moulin de la Galette, used as a studio by Picasso and his contemporaries—the city's poorest painters and poets. It was so named because of its resemblance to the laundry boats on the Seine, adorned with sheets and trousers hanging out to dry. ❏

Paris between the wars was described as "a magnificent and well-equipped showcase." Its frenetic cultural pleasures attracted a stream of foreign artists, firstly political refugees from Eastern Europe and then, as the 1920s gained momentum and became les années folles, *an influx of Americans living high on their dollars. Jazz was the rhythm, Chanel the fashion, Charleston the step, art deco the style, Surrealism the art, and Montparnasse the quartier that epitomized the cultural climate of this period.*

Profoundly marked by World War I, in which 1.4 million Frenchmen had died and over a million were disabled, the nation licked her wounds and embarked on an energetic and creative commitment. Victory celebrations were held in an attempt to wipe out memories of Big Bertha, the huge German cannon that had bombarded Paris, and national pride was restored by the return of Alsace Lorraine from German annexation. But could France after 1914 really hope to know another Belle Epoque?

SHOCK VALUE Although Apollinaire, the inventor of the term "Surrealism," died in 1918, it was only after the war that Tristan Tzara brought the Dada movement from Zürich to Paris. "Art is nonsense" cried its protagonists, the poets Breton, Eluard, and Aragon, rejecting traditional values and aiming to shock, as did Duchamp by exhibiting his "ready-made" urinal. However, they soon realized the limitations of negativity and by the time art students ceremonially drowned a Dada effigy in the Seine in 1921, the movement was dead.

Drawn to Freud's discoveries, Breton and his band, joined by the German Max Ernst, turned to free association, to the power of the subconscious, and to images generated by dreams. In 1924 their influential Surrealist Manifesto announced a Parisian movement that was to infiltrate much of European creativity (art, literature, film) right up to World War II and beyond.

Although their political affiliations were largely pro-communist, it was over this point that the group eventually broke up. Nevertheless, artists such as Dali, de Chirico, and the movie-maker Buñuel, despite disputes with the authoritarian leader Breton, spread its images throughout the world. Magazines were used to spread surrealist ideas, starting with *La Révolution Surréaliste* in 1924. Other magazines brought the gospel to Belgium, England and New York.

> ❑ "Pure automatism"—André Breton, describing the Surrealist movement ❑

KIKI AND CO Alongside these purveyors of fantasy, other creative individuals gathered around the tables of the famous Montparnasse cafés, Le Dôme, La Rotonde, and La Coupole. These included émigrés from Russia and eastern Europe (Chagall, Kisling), Léger, Soutine, the stylish Foujita, and the vivacious Kiki de Montparnasse, dancer and model,

> ❑ "Hand-painted dream photographs"—Salvador Dali, describing his own work ❑

who lived with photographer Man Ray. Montparnasse meant cheap accommodations and meals, freedom, and congenial company, but this foreign influx sometimes encountered French xenophobia from supporters of the fascist *Action Française*, then steadily gaining popularity.

THE US FACTOR Less integrated was a growing American community, steeped in dreams of Paris and busily penning some of the 20th century's most innovative literature. At the center of this web was Shakespeare and Company, Sylvia Beach's bookshop on the rue de l'Odéon, which attracted expatriate scribes such as Hemingway, Ezra Pound, Henry Miller, Scott Fitzgerald, and Gertrude Stein. Her devotion to James Joyce stretched to typing his illegible manuscripts and actually publishing *Ulysses*, a feat that nearly bankrupted her bookshop but gave the world a masterpiece. The Wall Street crash in 1929 announced the end of high living for many of the American expats, although the economy of France itself had a delayed reaction. With the advent of "talkies," American movies dominated Paris, but there was soon another, hotter import: that of jazz and black culture. The Bal Nègre, in the 5th *arrondissement*, was packed nightly with elegant women shaking to the new dance rhythms in the arms of West Indians or Africans. But the climax came in 1925, when the *Revue Nègre* hit town. Josephine Baker, attired in Poiret, Sonia Delaunay, or Schiaparelli, outshone home-grown star Mistinguette.

Meanwhile, three World Fairs proved to the world that native French culture was far from dead. In 1925 the Exposition des Arts Décoratifs marked, in Le Corbusier's words, "the decisive turning point in the quarrel between the old and the new." Art deco was acknowledged king, with the modernist designs of Ruhlmann, Dunand, Mallet-Stevens, and Chareau reinforcing Le Corbusier's *Esprit Nouveau*. The 1931 Exposition Coloniale, symbolizing France's strong colonial power, bequeathed the city the striking Musée des Arts Africains (now called the Musée des Arts d'Afrique et d'Océanie). But it was the 1937 Universal Exhibition that left the strongest architectural mark, in Trocadéro's Palais de Chaillot and the Palais de Tokyo. It also exhibited Picasso's *Guernica*—a sign of what was to come.

The Palais de Chaillot, built for the Exposition Universelle in 1937

When the bells of liberation finally rang out at Notre-Dame on August 26 1944, Paris emerged from 50 months of German occupation. Humiliated by the all-powerful German army which had taken over the capital, some Parisians had escaped, others turned a blind eye, some collaborated and some resisted. Hundreds of thousands died. Miraculously the city itself survived and General Von Choltitz disobeyed Hitler's final desperate orders to blow it up.

At the outbreak of war in September 1939, little changed for Paris but by May 1940, when the German army crossed the French borders, the capital woke up. Traumatized by memories of the Great War, the French army was by then in disarray: 100,000 escaped via Dunkirk but thousands more were taken prisoner, and others fled to the south of France. Refugees poured in, including herds of abandoned cattle, and a frenzied exodus southwards from the capital saw ministries, the press, the civil service, and the contents of the Louvre taking to the road. When the German tanks finally rolled in on June 14, they were greeted with an eerie, deserted city; only a quarter of its inhabitants remained.

FRANCE DIVIDED Soon Paris adopted a different rhythm. Four days after de Gaulle's impassioned though unheeded radio message from London, an armistice was signed between the aging French President, Marshal Pétain, and Hitler, allowing the Germans to occupy and use Paris "temporarily" as its military headquarters for the occupied zone. Some 40 percent of the country remained officially free, with its government based in Vichy.

For many, relieved to see the end of war and disorder, Pétain was seen as a savior, despite disastrously unfavorable peace terms, and the reality that France had become a colonized country.

OCCUPIED CITY In Paris clocks were changed to central European time, all luxury hotels and public buildings were requisitioned, swastikas fluttered from their roofs, road signs appeared in German, and the German soldiers goose-stepped down the Champs-Elysées daily at 12:30 PM at the changing of the guard. Commerce was stimulated by the big-spending habits of the occupiers, who could pay in Deutschmarks. For the average Parisian, shortages and rationing became part of daily life as the cost of living rose dramatically along with the mortality rate. Soon a flourishing black market was controlled by criminal gangs making vast fortunes. Petrol was unobtainable and Paris fell silent. Meanwhile Jews had to wear yellow stars, 30,000 Communists were arrested, trade unions were abolished, and the left wing banned.

German troops in Paris

In July 1942, 13,000 Jews were rounded up in abominable conditions at a sports stadium before being deported to concentration camps. This was the turning point, and the silent majority began to form an underground resistance movement. From all classes and ages, their only common purpose was a desire to rid France of its invaders.

❏ At the Mémorial de la Déportation, 200,000 quartz pebbles line the tunnel of a crypt which commemorates the same number of French who died during the Holocaust. Buried at the eastern tip of the Ile de la Cité, this monument was built in 1962 to a stark and effective design by G.H. Pingusson. ❏

Initially operating through individual acts of sabotage, the Resistance achieved a unity when Jean Moulin was parachuted in to co-ordinate all regional networks. Perturbed by Resistance activities, the Germans and the Vichy police reacted violently, arresting, assassinating, and deporting. Moulin himself was arrested and died under torture in June 1943, but by then the underground or *maquis* was riding high on de Gaulle's growing momentum from Algiers, where he set up a government in exile.

THE TIDE TURNS Strikes and demonstrations spread, clandestine newspapers boosted morale and by the time the Allies landed in June 1944, posters and tracts called for an insurrection. Between August 19 and 24 Paris resumed its street-fighting. Trees were felled, paving-stones dug up, barricades erected, ambushes laid, and sharp-shooters installed. When General Leclerc's tanks rolled in, it was to an accompaniment of ringing bells, ecstatic crowds, and the refrain of the Marseillaise. The next day Von Choltitz capitulated and on August 26 de Gaulle led the emotional liberation celebrations down the Champs-Elysées to Notre-Dame.

A city is characterized by its architecture and monuments, but a less definable spirit is created by its culture, a product of personalities from all epochs. Below are some of the Parisians who have left their mark.

APOLLINAIRE (1880–1918) Of Polish and Italian descent; one of the early 20th-century intelligentsia who led the schools of Cubism and Futurism, and France's first modern poet. *Alcools* and *Calligrammes* abandoned punctuation and experimented with typographical patterns.

BAUDELAIRE (1821–1867) Poet, critic, translator of Edgar Allan Poe. Introduced a modern sensibility and explored the musicality of the French language. With his mistress, he led a debauched life of opium and alcohol, haunted by a sense of his own damnation. Many poems in *Les Fleurs du Mal* were banned for offending against public morals. He died of syphilis.

SIMONE DE BEAUVOIR (1908–1986) Sartre's lifelong companion, and a novelist and essayist in her own right. *Le Deuxième Sexe* (1949) and *Les Mandarins* (1954) became handbooks for French feminists. Contributed to the existentialist review *Les Temps Modernes*.

BRASSAÏ (1899–1984) Of Hungarian origin but Parisian by adoption, Brassaï was a photographer who became "the eye of Paris," chronicling the nightlife and street-life of the city in the 1920s and 1930s.

ANDRE BRETON (1896–1966) Founder and theorist of Surrealism, an art collector and mentor for many painters. Breton was a poet and writer; *Nadja* was his semi-autobiographical novel.

COCO CHANEL (1883–1971) The first truly modern couturier introduced jerseys, short skirts, simple box jackets, and "the little black dress" in the 1920s. She started a vogue for costume jewelry and aimed to democratize fashion.

❑ "Each frill discarded makes one look younger."
—Coco Chanel ❑

COLETTE (1873–1954) The first woman to preside over the Académie Goncourt. Her writing was supple, sensuous and intuitive,

Colette poses for a 1909 magazine

often exploring more perverse sides of human nature.

LE CORBUSIER (1887–1965) Of Swiss origin, Le Corbusier settled in Paris in 1917 as a painter, and then became an architect who propagated the use of reinforced concrete. His rigid style revolutionized architecture.

CLAUDE DEBUSSY (1862–1918) Debussy entered the Paris Conservatoire aged 10. His music used mood and suggestion in works such as *Prélude à l'après-midi d'un faune* (1894) and *Pelléas et Mélisande* (1902).

ANATOLE FRANCE (1844–1924) Parisian novelist, critic, and essayist. France was elected to the Académie Française, and won the Nobel Prize for Literature in 1921. He confessed to finding Proust unreadable. His erudite work emulated 18th-century Classicism with an ironic style.

LEON GAMBETTA (1838–1882) Gambetta was a barrister before entering politics, a brilliant orator who opposed the Second Empire. He became a Deputy but left Paris by balloon during the 1870 Prussian siege to organize resistance from Tours. With Thiers, he was instrumental in forming the Third Republic in 1875.

ANDRE GIDE (1869–1951) Critic, essayist, novelist, and founder of the influential *Nouvelle Revue Française* in 1908. *La Porte Etroite* was his first major public success. Gide's questioning of moral dilemmas included his own homosexuality.

VICTOR HUGO (1802-1885) Champion of Romanticism in poetry, drama, and novels, famous for *Notre Dame de Paris*. Hugo was politically active as a Royalist and then a Republican, and exiled himself in Guernsey after Napoleon III's *coup d'état*. After his death, his body lay in state under the Arc de Triomphe before being transported to the Panthéon.

ANDRE MALRAUX (1901–1976) A charismatic idealist, aesthete, novelist, essayist, traveler, and Minister of Culture. He wrote *La Condition Humaine*, based on his days in Indo-China. During the Spanish Civil War Malraux organized Republican volunteers. Called upon by de Gaulle to "change the color of Paris," he renovated the center and took culture to the suburbs.

Debussy, master of mood music

JEAN-PAUL SARTRE (1905–1980) Paris-born philosopher, novelist, dramatist, and exponent of existentialism, starting with the novel *La Nausée*. He wrote prolifically during the war and in the 1950s, and was active in the Communist Party. Sartre refused to accept the Nobel Prize for Literature in 1964.

FRANÇOIS TRUFFAUT (1932–1984) Movie director of the post-war *Nouvelle Vague* movement, who started as a critic in the influential *Cahiers du Cinéma*. In a series of five movies, starting with *Les Quatre Cent Coups* (1959), Truffaut explored the dreamy personality of Antoine Doinel.

EMILE ZOLA (1840–1902) A novelist of the Realist school, conveying the tumultuous life of Paris and grim details of a growing industrial society. He defended Dreyfus with a celebrated open letter, *J'accuse*, accusing the government of a miscarriage of justice.

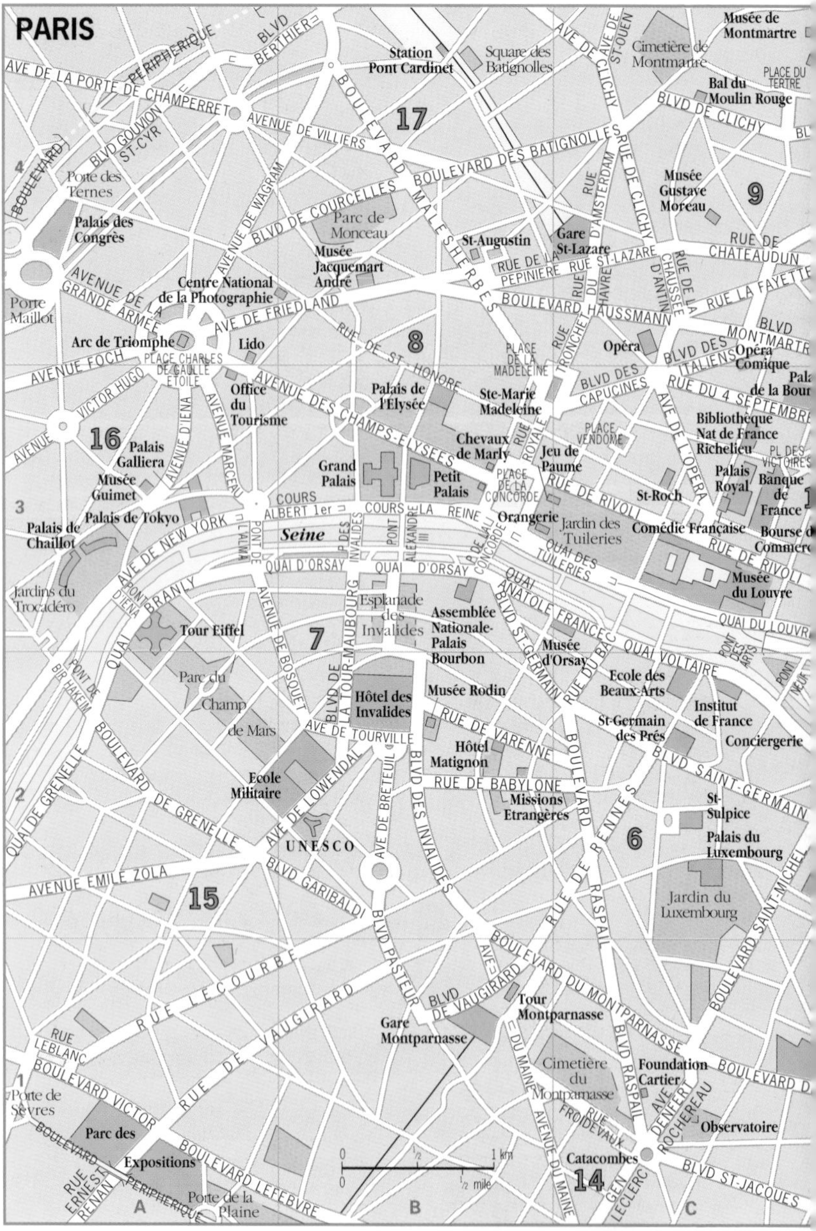
PARIS
Musée de Montmartre
Station Pont Cardinet
Square des Batignolles
Cimetière de Montmartre
PLACE DU TERTRE
Bal du Moulin Rouge
17
BLVD BERTHIER
PERIPHERIQUE
AVE DE LA PORTE DE CHAMPERRET
AVENUE DE VILLIERS
BOULEVARD MALESHERBES
BOULEVARD DES BATIGNOLLES
AVE DE CLICHY
AVE DE ST-OUEN
BLVD DE CLICHY
RUE DE CLICHY
RUE D'AMSTERDAM
BLVD GOUVION ST-CYR
BOULEVARD
Porte des Ternes
Palais des Congrès
AVENUE DE WAGRAM
BLVD DE COURCELLES
Parc de Monceau
Musée Gustave Moreau
9
St-Augustin
Gare St-Lazare
RUE DE CHATEAUDUN
Musée Jacquemart André
RUE DE LA PEPINIERE
RUE ST-LAZARE
RUE DU HAVRE
CHAUSSEE D'ANTIN
RUE DE LA
RUE LA FAYETTE
Centre National de la Photographie
AVENUE DE LA GRANDE ARMÉE
Porte Maillot
AVE DE FRIEDLAND
BOULEVARD HAUSSMANN
Arc de Triomphe
PLACE CHARLES DE GAULLE ETOILE
Lido
8
RUE DE ST-HONORE
PLACE DE LA MADELEINE
RUE TRONCHET
Opéra
BLVD DES ITALIENS
BLVD MONTMARTRE
Opéra Comique
AVENUE FOCH
VICTOR HUGO
Office du Tourisme
AVENUE DES CHAMPS-ELYSEES
Palais de l'Elysée
Ste-Marie Madeleine
BLVD DES CAPUCINES
RUE DU 4 SEPTEMBRE
Palais de la Bourse
AVENUE
16
Palais Galliera
AVENUE D'IENA
AVENUE MARCEAU
Grand Palais
Chevaux de Marly
RUE ROYALE
PLACE VENDOME
Jeu de Paume
AVE DE L'OPERA
Bibliothèque Nat de France Richelieu
PL DES VICTOIRES
Musée Guimet
Petit Palais
PLACE DE LA CONCORDE
Palais Royal
Banque de France
3
Palais de Tokyo
COURS ALBERT 1er
COURS LA REINE
RUE DE RIVOLI
St-Roch
Palais de Chaillot
AVE DE NEW YORK
PONT DE L'ALMA
Seine
P DES INVALIDES
PONT ALEXANDRE III
P DE LA CONCORDE
Orangerie
Jardin des Tuileries
Comédie Française
Bourse du Commerce
QUAI D'ORSAY
QUAI DES TUILERIES
Musée du Louvre
Jardins du Trocadéro
PONT D'IENA
QUAI BRANLY
AVENUE DE BOSQUET
BLVD DE LA TOUR-MAUBOURG
Esplanade des Invalides
Assemblée Nationale-Palais Bourbon
QUAI ANATOLE FRANCE
BLVD ST-GERMAIN
QUAI DU LOUVRE
Tour Eiffel
7
Musée d'Orsay
QUAI VOLTAIRE
PONT DES ARTS
PONT NEUF
PONT DE BIR HAKEIM
Parc du Champ de Mars
Hôtel des Invalides
Musée Rodin
RUE DU BAC
Ecole des Beaux-Arts
Institut de France
RUE DE VARENNE
St-Germain des Prés
Conciergerie
AVE DE TOURVILLE
Hôtel Matignon
BLVD SAINT-GERMAIN
BOULEVARD DE GRENELLE
Ecole Militaire
AVE DE LOWENDAL
AVE DE BRETEUIL
BLVD DES INVALIDES
RUE DE BABYLONE
Missions Etrangères
BOULEVARD RASPAIL
RUE DE RENNES
St-Sulpice
2
QUAI DE GRENELLE
UNESCO
6
Palais du Luxembourg
AVENUE EMILE ZOLA
BLVD GARIBALDI
15
Jardin du Luxembourg
BOULEVARD SAINT-MICHEL
RUE LECOURBE
BLVD PASTEUR
BLVD DE VAUGIRARD
Tour Montparnasse
BOULEVARD DU MONTPARNASSE
RUE DE VAUGIRARD
Gare Montparnasse
RUE LEBLANC
DU MAINE
Cimetière du Montparnasse
BLVD RASPAIL
Foundation Cartier
BOULEVARD
1
BOULEVARD VICTOR
Porte de Sèvres
RUE FROIDEVAUX
AVE DENFERT ROCHEREAU
Observatoire
Parc des Expositions
BOULEVARD LEFEBVRE
0 ½ 1 km
0 ½ mile
Catacombes
AVENUE DU MAINE
14
GEN LECLERC
BLVD ST-JACQUES
RUE ERNEST RENAN
Porte de la Plaine
A
B
C

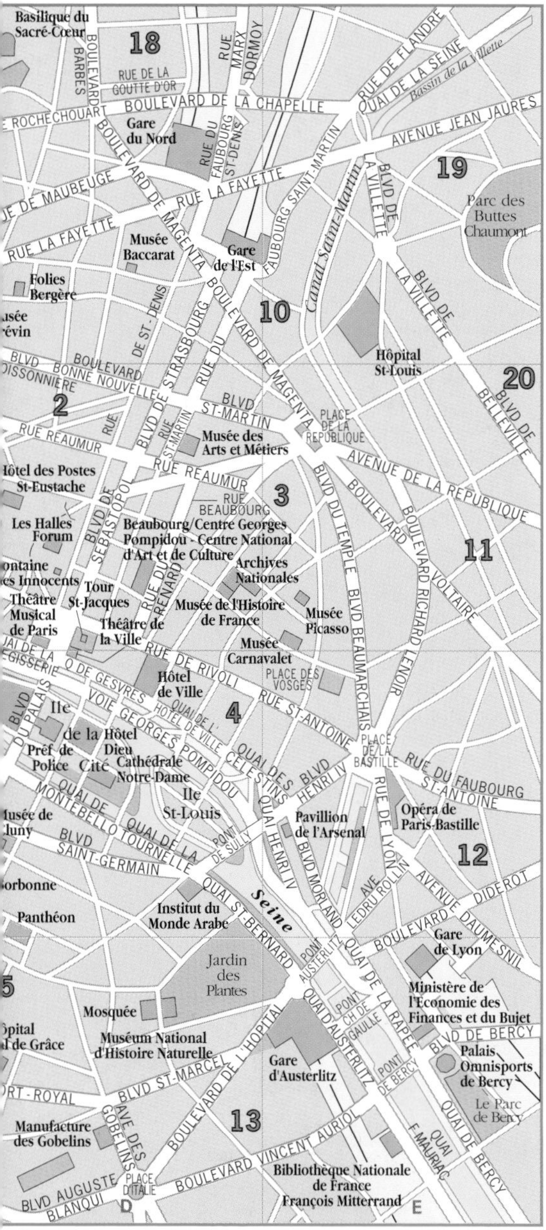

A–Z Paris

▶▶▶ CITY HIGHLIGHTS

Arc de Triomphe
pages 60–61

Arts Décoratifs, Union Centrale des
pages 64–65

Beaubourg *page 81*

Concorde, place de la
page 110

Eiffel, Tour
pages 114–115

Louvre *pages 133–137*

Le Marais *pages 142–145*

Montmartre and Sacré-Cœur *pages 148–150*

Notre-Dame
pages 154–157

Orsay, Musée d'
page 161

St.-Germain-des-Prés
pages 176–177

Tuileries, Jardins des
pages 179–180

It is impossible to tire of Paris' central Left Bank area (Rive Gauche). Its narrow streets, lined with shops and restaurants, combine with breathtaking monuments and Parisian chic to create a unique atmosphere. However the city may develop, nothing can change the historic streets and buildings of the **Quartier Latin**, the **Montagne Ste.-Geneviève** and **St.-Germain-des-Prés**.

TRANSFORMATIONS There have, however, been changes further afield. **Montparnasse**, the quarter famous for its literary and artistic connotations in pre-war Paris, is a flagrant example. Today the main boulevard presents a rather artificial, plastic face. The architectural *faux pas* of the 685-foot-high **Tour Montparnasse**, part of Pompidou's heritage, is so extraordinarily out of place that it almost assumes a perverted monumental glory. The urban developments behind the city's most confusing station (Montparnasse) are best ignored. Many Left Bank residents claim that they hardly ever cross the Seine. They have their Roman ruins, their movie theaters, galleries, literary cafés, and halls of learning. They also have France's government, concentrated in the **Faubourg St.-Germain**, once again the height of bourgeois fashion. Between the **rue du Bac** and **Les Invalides** is yet another world: hidden ministry gardens and embassies housed in superb 18th-century mansions. Immediately to the west are the stately residential avenues of the 7th *arrondissement* leading south to the heavily populated 15th. Apart from the **Eiffel Tower**, **Les Invalides,** and the Musée Rodin this area is devoid of "tourist attractions:" all the more reason to give it some attention. In the southern 13th *arrondissement*, southeast Asian immigrants have created a firmly identifiable **Chinatown**. Here you can celebrate Chinese New Year or sample ethnic cuisine. Towering over you are high-rise blocks, a far cry from the historic town houses and middle-class apartments near by, and impressive proof that even the Left Bank of Paris is still evolving.

A NEW PARIS SKYLINE
A huge redevelopment project in the 13th *arrondissement* has as its skyline symbol four glass towers—part of the new Bibliothèque National de France (National Library), a vast and ambitious operation which closed former President Mitterrand's 14-year reign of *grands projets*. Meanwhile the entire surrounding quartier of Tolbiac, which runs east along the Seine from the Gare d'Austerlitz, is being restructured at a projected cost of 25 billion francs: all part of a massive boost for the Left Bank image.

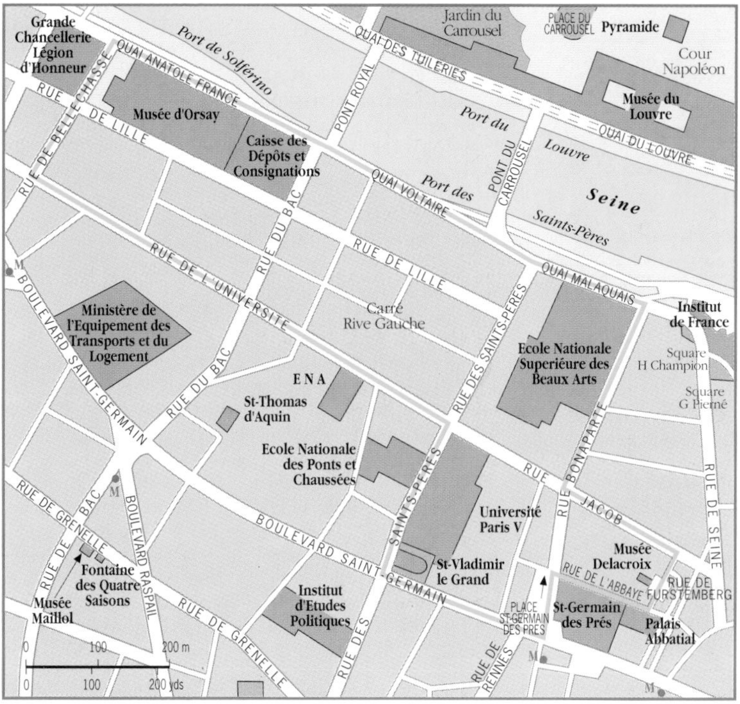

Walk

Exploring the Rive Gauche

Starting at the 12th-century church of St.-Germain-des-Prés, walk down the rue Bonaparte and turn immediately right after the corner garden into the rue de l'Abbaye. Turn left into the rue de Furstemberg.
Here you cross the square once inhabited by the painter Delacroix, before coming to the rue Jacob.

Follow rue Jacob to the left.
This street has numerous antique and interior decoration shops.

At the rue Bonaparte, follow this fascinating shopping street to the right.
On your left you will pass the grand entrance to the **Beaux Arts**.

Having reached the Seine, walk along the quai Malaquais, which leads directly into the quai Voltaire and the quai Anatole France.
From here there is a good view of the Louvre across the Seine. The *quais* themselves are lined with up-market antique shops and the odd restaurant. At **No. 19 quai Malaquais** stands a literary landmark; Anatole France was born here, and it was previously the home of George Sand, who was deeply involved with Alfred de Musset.

Cross the rue du Bac.
Pass the courtyard of the **Caisse des Dépôts et Consignations,** dominated by a sculpture by Dubuffet, before coming to the mighty Musée d'Orsay.

Circle round to the left, following the chic rue de Bellechasse to the rue de l'Université. Turn left.
The route continues past more antique shops and galleries.

At the rue des Saints-Pères, turn right to rejoin the boulevard St.-Germain, with the church along to the left.

Louis XIV looks out over the 17th-century place des Victoires, now a focus for 20th-century fashions

PLACE DES VICTOIRES
The imposing place des Victoires was developed in 1685 by the dauphin's tutor, Maréchal de la Feuillade. Laid out by architects Hardouin-Mansart and Prado, it continued a century-old Parisian tradition of majestic squares, started by Henri IV. Although many of the facades have since been altered, this circle of elegant mansions has lost none of its original grandeur, housing the chic boutiques of Kenzo, Cacharel and other leading fashion names.

Look at a map of Paris. Notice how the Seine gently curves around the Left Bank, almost enclosing it, leaving the Right Bank more open and more extensive. Covering a much greater area, it governs the north, east, and west of Paris, and over the centuries has suffered for it. Baron Haussmann created his wide arteries here; kings built their palaces here; and every ruler left at least one monument. Less intimate in scale, more disparate in style, its atmosphere can be stately or decidedly tacky, and is certainly less easy to define. This is also the banking and business center, and its rhythm is fast: those notorious long Paris lunches are here generally replaced by a quick sandwich.

CHANGING PACE This is contemporary Paris. It also boasts two opera houses, two museums of contemporary art, the Louvre, countless other monuments and museums, and a dense concentration of gastronomic halts and nocturnal haunts. Cushioning the grandeur are burgeoning new *quartiers*, rebuilt or redeveloped. The most obvious is the **Marais**, which over the last 20 years has undergone intensive renovation and is now a hive of avant-garde art galleries and trendy restaurants. Historic buildings have become museums, like the **Musée Picasso**, while at the eastern end the **Bastille** has developed along similar lines. Towering over the central square is a mammoth and prestigious new opera-house, while in the back streets flourish a mass of tiny boutiques, shady bars, and experimental galleries.

LES HALLES The central area of the Right Bank is monopolized by another renovated area, **Les Halles**, the hub of Paris which kicks off the *arrondissement* system (this curls outwards snail-like from here). The **Centre Pompidou** remains a controversial landmark, offering hot culture and panoramic views, while just a few streets away is the infamous **rue St.-Denis**, thick with sex shops and prostitutes. Unfortunate in the spectacular and protracted bulldozing of its past, Les Halles has taken on a peculiar identity, closely linked with a vast underground shopping center and the RER station which speeds in surburban teenagers for their nights on the town.

Once again, things change radically only a few streets away. Here you enter the realm of fashion victims and ultra-chic designer clothes shops which revolve around the superb 17th-century **place des Victoires**. Continuing the paradox, this area skates round the **Banque de France** and the **Bourse** before, deep in the 2nd *arrondissement*, becoming a maze of wholesale rag-traders and basement sweatshops. Punctuating all the above are the main press offices and agencies of the capital.

NIGHTLIFE For the visitor the Right Bank also means glamor and glitter. While the **avenue Montaigne** and the **Faubourg St.-Honoré** maintain their monopoly on haute couture and related boutiques, the **Champs-Elysées** has had a welcome facelift. Many of Paris' luxury hotels and exclusive nightclubs cluster around this major axis, and the temples of its top chefs are generously sprinkled between the 8th and adjoining 17th *arrondissements.*

Meanwhile the 16th *arrondissement* maintains its discreetly chic residential atmosphere, at the same time displaying some of France's most innovative turn-of-the-century architecture as well as monumental relics from various Expositions Universelles.

MONTMARTRE Few come to Paris without the obligatory pilgrimage to Montmartre, which, although still attracting residents from the world of film and media, has turned over many of its charms to the tourist masses. At the bottom of the hill in **Pigalle** tourist buses line the boulevard, while sex shops and clubs ply their trade, but in the streets running downhill through the 9th *arrondissement* you will find some of the city's more genuine nightlife. This village-like area runs down to the *grands boulevards,* and is being renovated to become once more one of the social hubs of central Paris.

NEW DEVELOPMENTS are legion on this side of the Seine, from the mega-development of **La Défense**, ongoing since 1958, to (marginally) more modest projects such as **La Villette** and **Bercy**, the latter due to complement the new Bibliothèque Nationale de France. This policy of injecting life and facilities into neglected outlying areas attempts to combine the latest architectural styles harmoniously with historical features and structures. But traditionally working-class districts such as **Belleville** and the **Bastille** are both suffering at the hands of property developers. Nothing is built without controversy: all the more fuel for Parisian polemics; all the more coffees to accompany the endless debate and discussion. At least those essential Parisian characteristics are saved.

A view across the Seine of the 8th arrondissement *on the Right Bank—a bustling district dominated by the Champs-Elysées and the rue St.-Honoré*

Happily floating mid-stream in the Seine, the **Ile de la Cité** and the **Ile St.-Louis** are as different in character as the two banks they separate. One is the site of the first (pre-Roman) settlement of the Parisii tribe; the other is the symbol of a successful 17th-century property development. Linked by a fragile footbridge, both are surrounded by extensive water-level *quais*, favorites with anglers, sunbathers, young couples, bookreaders and a cross-section of the Parisian gay community.

ILE ST.-LOUIS Densely inhabited by successful literati and a cosmopolitan breed of wealthy business people, the Ile St-Louis has become an exclusive residential area inevitably frequented by tourists. One long street which runs from end to end is a mass of restaurants and shops more geared to foreigners than to locals, although many residents swear by the quality of the food shops. The locally produced, world-famous ice cream is a strong attraction, but the architectural unity and beauty of Le Vau's 17th-century town houses and the elegant comfort they exude make neck-craning the favorite pastime here. One of Paris' best views is from the western tip of the island along the Seine.

FAMOUS FOOD STORES
One of Paris' most famous food institutions is on the Ile St-Louis. Big queues gather outside Berthillon in the rue St.-Louis-en-l'Ile, reputedly one of the best ice cream shops in Europe. Here they sell over thirty delicious flavors of creamy ices and sorbets, including best-sellers marron glacé and wild strawberry.

ILE DE LA CITÉ Historically the heart of Paris, the Ile de la Cité boasts three major monuments: **Notre-Dame**, **Sainte-Chapelle,** and the **Conciergerie**. Also strong on government buildings such as the **Palais de Justice**, the **Hôtel Dieu** (a hospital), and the **Préfecture**, the result is a bizarre mixture of the sublime and the banal. Some residents manage to squeeze in between the medieval monuments, living along the *quais* or on the delightful **place Dauphine**, while the flower market occupies a square behind the Préfecture, constantly passed by police cars and ambulances which, sirens wailing, tear past the Gothic towers of Notre-Dame. This relaxed eclecticism is perhaps symbolic of the entire city: nothing is sacred, but every area eventually has its monument.

Sainte-Chapelle and the gates to the Palais de Justice, Ile de la Cité

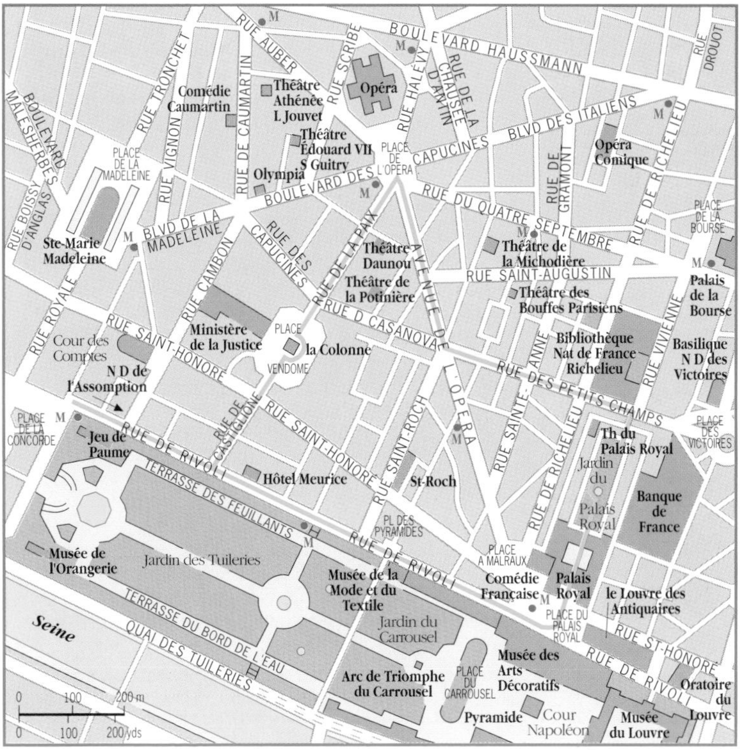

Walk

Exploring the Rive Droite

From place de la Concorde cross to the Tuileries gardens beside the Jeu de Paume.

From here you can either walk along the **Terrasse des Feuillants**, set up by Le Nôtre in the 1660s, and enjoy the view of the gardens or follow the **rue de Rivoli** and its tourist shops.

After an underpass, walk beside the Musée de la Mode et du Textile, soon followed by the Musée des Arts Décoratifs, before reaching the Louvre itself. At the place du Palais Royal turn sharp left, cross the rue St.-Honoré to the Comédie Française and enter the Jardin du Palais Royal through a discreet arch on the left.

Here you confront the controversial art installation by Daniel Buren, before entering the gardens proper. Walk to the end, leaving on the left side past the historic restaurant **Le Grand Véfour**.

Go up to the rue des Petits Champs. Turn left here, passing the old Bibliothèque Nationale on your right, and go on to the avenue de l'Opéra.

Japanese restaurants down the side-streets indicate the proximity of Paris' "Little Tokyo."

Turn right towards the opera-house, cross the avenue, then turn left and walk down the rue de la Paix,

This is Paris' high-class jewelry street, which leads to the no less classy **place Vendôme**. The legendary **Ritz Hotel** occupies the right half of the square.

Go straight on down the rue de Castiglione, until you reach the rue de Rivoli and place de la Concorde.

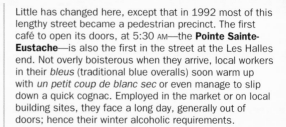

As dawn breaks over Les Halles, clusters of bleary-eyed, home-bound night-hawks cross paths with the first wave of workers. The rue Montorgueil, one of the main market streets when Les Halles was really Les Halles, still has many classic suppliers and services intact.

PAVING PARIS
Three and a half miles of paved streets around the rue Montorgueil make up one of Europe's largest pedestrian areas.

ROYAL PASTRIES
Pâtisserie Stohrer, one of the oldest and finest in Paris, was opened in 1730 by a Polish pastry cook who had moved to Versailles, following the marriage of Marie Leszczynska to Louis XV. The interior of the shop is decorated with 19th-century wall paintings: one shows La Renommée carrying a tray of "*Puits d'Amour*" (Wells of Love), an 18th-century specialty still sold today.

Little has changed here, except that in 1992 most of this lengthy street became a pedestrian precinct. The first café to open its doors, at 5:30 AM—the **Pointe Sainte-Eustache**—is also the first in the street at the Les Halles end. Not overly boisterous when they arrive, local workers in their *bleus* (traditional blue overalls) soon warm up with *un petit coup de blanc sec* or even manage to slip down a quick cognac. Employed in the market or on local building sites, they face a long day, generally out of doors; hence their winter alcoholic requirements.

Early risers Also starting the day early are the municipal workers, emptying dustbins into their poison-green dust-carts. When Paris regained its first mayor since the Revolution, in 1977, it also gained an army of street-cleaning machinery, including motorized "pooper-scoopers," Streets are cleaned in the morning by streams of water gushing through the gutters, channeled by strategically positioned lumpy rags. In the wake of the dustcart, *concierges* soon emerge to pull in their bins and restore order to the building in their care. Their net-curtained *loges* still exist and *concierges* continue to fulfil an important social role in Parisian residential life. By 8 AM a few white-collar workers start appearing, some hurrying straight to the *métro*, others taking time to stop for a coffee and croissant as they peruse the morning paper. By now the market is getting into its swing, although officially most stalls and shops open at 9 AM. *Boulangeries* are an exception, opening at around 7:30, when the baguette is often at its optimum. Queen of the pâtissiers in the rue Montorgueil is **Stohrer**, at No. 51, founded by Louis XV's *chef pâtissier* in 1730.

Cosmopolitan tastes Montorgueil literally means "proud mount," a poetic way of describing the road's gentle slope upward toward the *grands boulevards*. The southern end was once the central oyster and seafood market where produce from the northern ports ended up. This explains the proximity of the all-night seafood counters on the adjoining **rue Coquillière**. Today, cosmopolitan tastes have moved in and the choice is more eclectic: an Oriental grocer sells manioc, lychees, and sweet potatoes; a North African wholesaler displays buckets and barrels piled high with olives, grains, dates, and nuts; further up, a pungent Greek grocery offers humus or stuffed vine leaves, while the windows of two Italian delicatessens are full of fresh pasta of all shapes and sizes and strings of salamis. As you wander through the market crowds you will hear Spanish, Arabic, or even English and German. The fresh, colorful fruit and

vegetable stalls attract every nationality, generation, and status, as do the prices, which are a fraction of neighborhood grocery stores.

Lunch break By midday it is lunchtime for numerous office and street workers. Bistros abound in this street. **La Grille-Montorgueil** at No. 50 boasts a monumental zinc bar (1904) and fine entrecôte steaks, and **L'Escargot-Montorgueil** at No. 38 was the first restaurant in Paris to serve snails. They're still a specialty. Shoppers disappear as 1 PM approaches: this is closing time for the fish, meat, fruit, and vegetable shops which shut till 4 PM. With its pedestrian status, rue Montorgueil is a lunchtime haunt for fashion victims from nearby boutiques. The afternoon session closes again at around 7:30 PM, though some late-opening stores benefit from the last few dedicated office workers hurrying home to catch the 8 PM T.V. news.

Twilight zone If rue Montorgueil quietens down in the evening, the neighborhood remains lively. At 6 rue Coquillière, the famous **Au Pied de Cochon** stays open all night long. The side-streets are where it is all happening: the **rue Tiquetonne** boasts Thai transvestite bars or an all-night African restaurant, and the **rue Marie-Stuart** an equally eccentric selection, covering ethnic flavours from Spain to the Cameroons, all of which keeps the locals going until the 24-hour cycle starts again.

TOUR DE JEAN SANS PEUR

Near the junction of rue Montorgueil and rue Etienne-Marcel lies a rare example of a domestic Gothic tower, the Tour de Jean "Sans Peur" (without fear). Despite his name, Jean, Duc de Bourgogne, feared retaliation following the assassination on his orders of the Duc d'Orleans in 1408. So he added a massive square 88-foot stone tower to his home and slept at the very top, as far as possible from his would-be attackers.

Business as usual in the rue Montorgueil, retaining the spirit of the original Les Halles market, once the center of Paris' food trade

PARIS' ARCHES
The Arc de Triomphe stands in line with two other famous arches: the Arc de Triomphe du Carrousel to the east and the Grande Arche de la Défense to the west. To emphasize the progression along this *Voie royale* from the Louvre to the Défense, the Grande Arche is twice as tall as the Arc de Triomphe de l'Etoile, which in turn is twice as tall as the Arc de Triomphe du Carrousel! Two older and less well known arches are the Porte St.-Denis and Porte St.-Martin, situated along the *grands boulevards*. They were both erected in the late 17th century to celebrate Louis XIV's victories, and some of the carvings are by famous artists who worked at Versailles.

The Institut de France, home of the Académie Française

▶ Académie Française *176C3*
Institut de France, 23 quai de Conti, 75006
tel: 01 44 41 44 41. Métro: Pont-Neuf
This venerable institution remains a heeded voice in certain French circles, its 40 members occasionally emitting dictums that just have to be obeyed. Founded by Richelieu in 1635, the Académie's rule over the standards of the French language, which includes a high level of protectionism, is embodied in the *Dictionnaire de la Langue Française*, a 10-tome affair that is periodically revised and published, volume by hefty volume. The Académie's weekly meetings, which once a year become solemn occasions in the famous domed hall, are held at the Institut de France, an edifice that you cannot fail to spot in its prime Left-Bank position overlooking the Pont des Arts. The building itself was designed in 1663 by Le Vau, one of the architects of the Louvre, and was financed by a generous donation from Cardinal Mazarin to found a college for selected provincial students. The College of Four Nations was closed in 1790 and five years later the Convention founded the Institut de France, transferred here by Napoleon in 1805. Elected only when a seat is liberated by a member's death, the average age of the *académicien* is consequently advanced. Today the Académie Française is a concerted voice of historians, writers, doctors, and representatives of the church, army and diplomatic circles. Although the Institut is not open to individual visitors, which means nobody can pay homage to Mazarin's tomb, you can enter the courtyard to have a closer look.

▶ Angleterre, Hôtel d' *176B3*
44 rue Jacob, 75006; tel: 01 42 60 34 72
This elegant 18th-century town house in the heart of the antique district once housed the British Embassy, whence its name. This generated a diplomatic incident when Benjamin Franklin refused to set foot on "British soil" to sign the U.S. Declaration of Independence. More recently Hemingway lived here (modestly), and it is now a charming and discreet hotel preserving many of its historic features, including a flowery courtyard.

▶ Aquariums *11F2*
Apart from the small aquariums squeezed between cages of rabbits in the shops along the quai de la Mégisserie, underwater enthusiasts can also see no fewer than eight aquariums at the **Centre de la Mer et des Eaux**, 195 rue St.-Jacques, 75005 (tel: 01 44 32 10 90). Set up by Jacques Cousteau, it explains his ambitious underwater projects undertaken since the 1960s. However, Paris' largest liquid universe and the second in Europe is housed at the **Musée des Arts d'Afrique et d'Océanie** (see page 63).

▶▶▶ Arc de Triomphe *50A4*
tel: 01 43 80 31 31
Open: daily 10 AM–10:30 PM; 9:30 AM–11 PM in summer
Admission: moderate
Along with the Eiffel Tower, the Arc de Triomphe remains the great Paris landmark, dominating the axis leading east down the Champs-Elysées and west down

the avenue de la Grande Armée toward Porte Maillot and La Défense. The central point of a web of 12 avenues, constantly swirling with traffic, this major crossroads is known as the Etoile (star). The Arc's conception goes back to Napoleon, who in 1806 commissioned an awesome memorial to be built for the French army, but it was not until 1836, under Louis-Philippe, that the monument was completed. By the time Haussmann had finished with redesigning Paris, the Etoile had assumed the form it has today, and its symbolic role was confirmed after World War I with parades of victorious troops marching through and the burial of the unknown soldier beneath. Over 70 years later, a ceremony takes place every November 11 (Armistice Day). The flame is lit daily at 6:30 PM. The sculpted facade is the work of three different sculptors, and the 30 shields studding the crown of the arch each bear the name of a Revolutionary or Imperial victory (Waterloo does not figure ...). The Arc stands 165 feet high, and it is worth braving the queues to take the lift or laboring up the steps—the view is superb and gives a clear vision of Haussmann's urban layout. Access is via the underpasses beneath the chaos of the traffic.

Symbol of military victory and power, and a long-lasting landmark: the Arc de Triomphe

▶ Archives Nationales *51D3*

60 rue des Francs-Bourgeois, 75003; tel: 01 40 27 60 00
Open: Wed–Mon 2–5. Admission: inexpensive

The bureaucratic personality of France is well symbolised by its Archives Nationales, which fill 217 miles of shelves in the Marais. Napoleon was responsible for housing them in the remarkable Hôtel de Soubise (see page 126), but they have since spilled over into adjacent mansions and in 1988 a new center was built in the rue des Quatre Fils.

Walk

From the Etoile and along the avenues

Start at the Etoile métro and walk down the Champs-Elysées.
Stop at the famous **Fouquet's** at No. 99, an exclusive restaurant recently declared a historic monument.

Continue to the Rond Point and turn right into the avenue Montaigne.
This is the mecca of French *haute couture*. You will pass Louis Vuitton, Chanel, Cartier, Givenchy *et al*, as well as the luxurious Plaza-Athénée hotel, and, at No. 15, the **Théâtre des Champs-Elysées**. Designed in 1911–1913 by Auguste Perret, it saw the first scandalous performance of Stravinsky's *Le Sacré du Printemps*, danced by Nijinsky. The marble facade and the interior were recently restored and crowned by a controversial restaurant.

Cross the place de l'Alma and take the avenue du Président Wilson.
Pass the mammoth colonnaded 1937 buildings of the **Palais de Tokyo**, housing the **Musée d'Art Moderne de la Ville de Paris**. On the other side of the avenue rises the imposing **Palais Galliera**.

Turn right on to the avenue Pierre 1er de Serbie, from the place d'Iéna.
The entrance to the Palais Galliera is on this avenue.

Walk straight on, crossing the avenue Marceau with the church of St.-Pierre-de-Chaillot on your left, until you come to the avenue George V.
A short detour to the right takes you to the neo-Gothic **American Cathedral**.

Turn left and pass the prestigious hotels George V and Prince de Galles before returning to the Champs-Elysées.

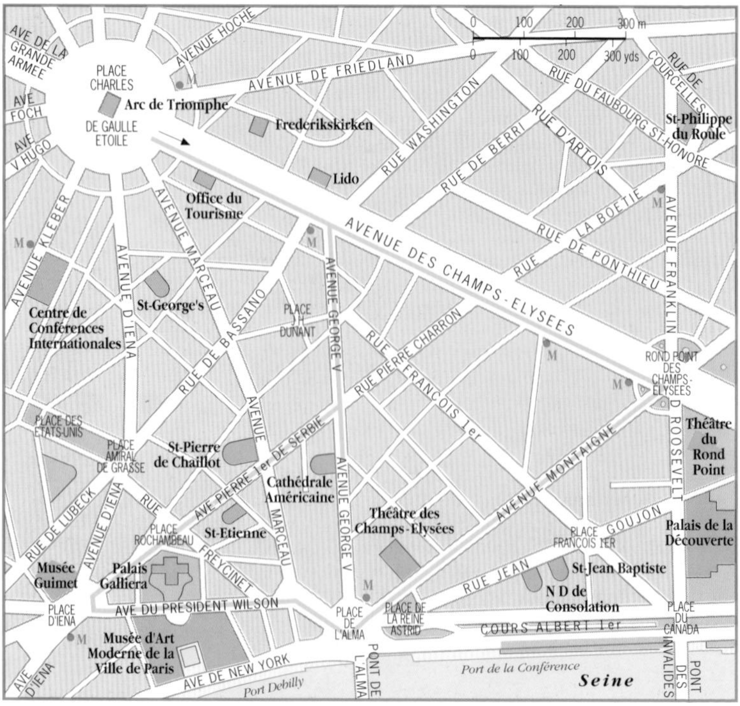

►► Arts d'Afrique et d'Océanie, Musée des 11F2

293 avenue Dausmesnil, 75012; tel: 01 44 74 84 80
Métro: Porte Dorée. Open: Wed–Mon 10–noon, 1:30–5:30; weekends 12:30–6. Aquarium 10–6. Admission: moderate

This museum is a perennial favorite with children. The basement aquarium is a constant draw: leopard sharks swim in the company of a fish named Grace Kelly, yellow-tailed Picasso ballistas, bewhiskered

catfish, or a mound of slow-motion turtles all circulate eternally. Apart from this aspect, the museum is yet another Parisian monument to the aesthetics of art deco. Built for the 1931 Exposition Coloniale in reinforced concrete, its colonnaded facade is backed by an extraordinary stone bas-relief by Alfred Janniot depicting the glories of the French colonies. Inside, two floors of galleries open on to an enormous ballroom with a superb "pagoda" ceiling, mosaic floors, and murals by Ducos de la Haille. More astonishing examples of art deco are found in two circular rooms leading off the main entrance hall: both boast murals, this time by Lemaître and Louis Bouquet, and are respectively decorated by Printz and by Ruhlmann.

The actual collections cover parts of the Pacific (Melanesia, New Hebrides, Australia), Central and West Africa and finally, on the top floor, the arts of the Maghreb (Algeria, Tunisia, and Morocco). The latter displays silver jewelry, ceramics, Koranic tablets, arms, and textiles as well as architectural features. However, the main riches of the museum lie in the African department on the second floor: here the tone is set by Dogon masks, rings and statues, reflecting a fascination with the coexistence of life and death. Other tribes such as the Bambaras, Lobi, Akan, Benin, and Kongo are represented by items ranging from basic to sacred.

The Pacific islands are represented on the first floor by masks, carved wooden statues, and a large collection of Australian aboriginal art. Bark paintings represent the aborigines' approach to their natural world.

The popular Musée des Arts d'Afrique et d'Océanie, set in splendid isolation on the edge of the Bois de Vincennes

A MEMORABLE AVENUE
Originally an unpaved track across swampy ground, the avenue des Champs-Elysées, just over 2 miles long and 232 feet wide, is today one of the world's most famous thoroughfares, full of movie theaters, clubs, shops, and sidewalk cafés. From the top of the Arc de Triomphe, with its breathtaking views toward La Défense and Place de la Concorde, it is easy to imagine the numerous grand processions through the arch over the centuries.

PAPAL PORCELAIN
In the 1990s, the museum acquired a Venetian glass cup decorated with enamel and gilt motifs representing the arms of the Medici popes of the early 16th century. However, this priceless object retains some of its mystery, for experts have not been able to decide whether it was made for Leon X or Clement VII! The gift/bookstore sells a choice of beautiful copies (porcelain, glass, and crystal objects, jewelry, wallpaper, textiles, and toys), a good range of contemporary design (objects of daily life as well as fashion accessories and decorative objects), books, catalogs, posters, and postcards published for special exhibitions.

▶▶▶ Arts Décoratifs, Union Centrale des *50C3*
107 rue de Rivoli, 75001; tel: 01 44 55 57 50
Métro: Palais-Royal
Open: weekdays 11–6 (Wed 9 PM); weekends 10–6; closed Mon
Admission: moderate

The **Union Centrale des Arts Décoratifs** was founded at the end of the 19th century by a group of industrialists and collectors whose aim was to display "beauty in function." Its didactic role reached its zenith in the 1920s and 1930s, with designers such as Le Corbusier, Charlotte Perriand, and Mallet-Stevens greatly contributing to its reputation. Today, the Union Centrale des Arts Décoratifs includes four museums, a library, and three art schools. Three of the museums, the **Musée des Arts Décoratifs, Musée de la Mode et du Textile,** and **Musée de la Publicité**, are housed in a wing of the Louvre which is being entirely renovated as part of the *Grand Louvre* project. The fourth museum is a private mansion modeled on the Petit Trianon in Versailles, donated to the state by Count Moïse de Camondo and named after his son Nissim, killed during World War I. It is almost exclusively devoted to the decorative arts of the second half of the 18th century (see page 188).

The gradual reopening of the **Musée des Arts Décoratifs**, housed since 1905 in the Marsan wing of the Louvre, should be completed by the year 2002.

Medieval and Renaissance Department The nine rooms of this department, the first to be reopened (1998), contain a rich collection which reflects religious art and domestic

life from the 13th to the 16th century. Paintings, sculptures, and furniture from churches and monasteries alternate with exquisite objects of daily life exhibited in period rooms. Whereas the Louvre contains a high proportion of exhibits of Royal origin, owing to its historical background, the period rooms of the Musée des Arts Décoratifs display a fine selection of works and objects reflecting the life and aspirations of the middle class. Some of the rooms are remarkable. The **Galerie des Retables** suggests a church interior—it contains a fine collection of Belgian, Italian, German, French and Spanish altarpieces in carved wood or stone. Among them, the *St. John the Baptist* retable by the Spanish painter Luis Borrassà, a particularly rare example, is exhibited to best advantage over a modern altar. Isolated statues from various altarpieces line the "nave." In the **Salle des Tapisseries**, themed selections of the museum's tapestries are exhibited in rotation owing to their sheer number (more than 300 items) and fragility; the extensive collection offers an insight into the themes that dominated 15th and 16th-century art. The **Salle du Maître de la Madeleine** contains medieval sculptures, and paintings from the primitive to the late-Gothic style, including a number of masterpieces: *The Virgin and Child between St. Andrew and St. James* by the 13th-century Italian painter known as the Maître de la Madeleine is the oldest work of its kind within French State collections. The Cabinet de Travail is a delightful period room decorated with refined marquetry paneling, and suggests the interior of a private study (usually located next to the bedroom in Renaissance homes). The **Salle des Vitraux**, which re-creates a great hall at the time of Henri II, contains French and Italian furniture, Flemish tapestries, paintings, 16th-century stained glass, and *objets d'art*. The remainder of the collections spanning the 17th, 18th, and 19th centuries, including a choice of fine wallpaper and porcelain, will be exhibited in chronological order, on three levels following the medieval and Renaissance collections. Special exhibitions continue to be organized while renovation work is in progress. The **Pavillon de Marsan** will house the modern and contemporary collections with an interesting selection of art nouveau furniture by Hector Guimard and a reconstruction of fashion-designer Jeanne Lanvin's apartment in the 7th *arrondissement*.

Musée de la Mode et du Textile▶▶▶ (*tel: 01 44 55 57 50. Open* weekdays 11–6, Wed 11–9; weekends 10–6; closed Mon. *Admission: moderate*.) Part of the same umbrella structure as the above, the Musée de la Mode et du Textile was reopened in 1997 after being entirely modernized and reorganized. The museum presents themed annual exhibitions such as *Touches d'Exotisme* showing stunning items designed by Poiret in the 1920s and Yves Saint-Laurent in the late 1960s as well as the latest designs by John Galliano; these will be drawn from the museum's stock of costumes from the 17th to the 20th century.

Musée de la Publicité▶ This museum, the third housed in the Marsan wing, has a research department. Museum information is available on the Internet: http://www.ucad.fr/pub

HECTOR GUIMARD

Hector Guimard (1867–1934), one of the leading lights in the French Art Nouveau Movement, initially made his mark on Paris with his Castel Béranger, a spectacular block of stained glass, mosaics, and elegant wrought-ironwork at 14 rue La Fontaine in the Auteuil district. He then went on to design the entrances for the Paris *métro*. Today only a few remain, including the striking Porte Dauphine and the Abbesses *métro* with its unusual amber lights and green iron arches.

Revelling in its historic reputation, the Paris art scene is, at the start of the 21st century, slowly recovering from the shock of recession. After experiencing a low ebb with international attention firmly focused on New York throughout the 1960s and 1970s, Paris has nevertheless re-emerged as a contemporary art crossroads.

PURCHASING ART AND ANTIQUES
There seems to be a limitless choice of art and antiques, ranging from the famous galleries around the rue du Faubourg St.-Honoré to the avant-garde galleries of the Marais and Bastille, or even one of the many flea markets. To export designated *objets d'art* worth more than 1 million francs you need a certificate of authenticity available from the Centre Français du Commerce Extérieur (tel: 01 40 73 30 00).

The late 1980s saw an unprecedented boom in the art market worldwide, and Paris reaped the rewards with galleries monopolizing areas such as the Marais, their scale often directly proportional to the conceptual nature of the work shown. The Bastille too had its renaissance, and many younger gallery-owners turned to this booming quarter as an alternative to the high-flying rents now common in the Marais. But since then economic reality has hit hard and many have closed their doors.

Left Bank But what about the traditional hotbed of art in St.-Germain-des-Prés? The rue de Seine, rue Mazarine and adjoining characteristic streets have put their avant-garde days behind them. Today this area has its own distinct flavor, nothing to do with what is going on across the Seine. Antiques, art deco furniture, prints, ethnographical wonders, and 1950s abstract paintings are the mainstay of hundreds of small galleries lining a well-defined territory between the rue Bonaparte, rue Guénégaud, and the rue de Seine. High-quality antiques

stores are concentrated farther west in what is known as the Carré Rive Gauche, a grid of streets running between the quai Voltaire, the rue du Bac, the rue de l'Université and the rue des Saints Pères, including the famous rue de Beaune.

Back in the epicenter of the Left Bank galleries, head for the eclectic atmosphere of the rue des Beaux Arts. Beautiful objects are all around while galleries like **Albert Loeb** and **Claude Bernard** still promote the figurative style that made their reputations a few decades ago. The rue de Seine offers anything from floral prints to Jean Cocteau originals. The **Galerie Montenay** at 31 rue Mazarine concentrates on young European and American artists and is worth checking out. For contemporary sculpture go to **JGM** in the short but sweet rue Jacques-Callot.

Meanwhile there is no shortage of prospective painters in the area: the **Ecole des Beaux Arts** on the rue Bonaparte regorges flocks of portfolio-lugging students and the eternal café meeting-point, **La Palette**, remains a favorite for gallery-owners and artists alike. The **Galerie du Chevalieret des Collectionneurs** is out of the chic gallery territory in Montmartre, but displays contemporary and classical works at more accessible prices.

Right Bank chic For strictly high price-brackets, head for another traditional gallery agglomeration over on the Right Bank. Here, between the avenue Matignon, the Faubourg St.-Honoré and (further north) the boulevard Haussmann, you can track down works by artists, dead or alive, who have hit the heights. The **Galerie Lelong**▶

BARGAIN HUNTING

For anyone unconcerned with the latest volatile trends of the art world, Paris has an unbeatable selection of back-street galleries showing classical paintings and drawings, both old and new. If you like the object, you can buy it; but unless you have real flair, don't think you're making an investment—only dealers govern that domain and the last few years have proved how wrong even they can be.

A spacious converted workshop is the setting for European and American art in the Galerie Yvon Lambert's collection (see page 68)

AUCTION HOUSES
The leading Paris auction centre is Drouot-Richelieu at 9 rue Drouot, 9e, named after the Comte de Drouot, Napoleon's aide-de-camp, and founded in 1858. Viewing is from 11 AM to 6 PM the day before the sale. The auction takes place in French and a 10–15 percent buyers' premium is added to the purchase price. Sale details are available in *La Gazette de l'Hôtel Drouot*.

The Galerie Maeght, run by Yoyo, grand-daughter of artistic talent-scout Aimé Maeght

at 13/14 rue de Téhéran, founded by the former director of the Maeght Gallery, still shows artists such as Magnelli, Alechinsky, Francis Bacon, and Tapiès, as well as younger names such as James Brown or García-Sevilla. Near by, the prestigious **Galerie Louis Carré** could be exhibiting anything from Delaunay to Hartung or a French contemporary such as Jean-Pierre Raynaud. For more accessible purchases go to **Artcurial**, the art department store at 9 avenue Matignon, which specializes in multiples (prints, jewelry, carpets) and boasts one of the best art bookstores in town.

On a very different note, clustered around Beaubourg and spreading east through the Marais are hundreds of contemporary galleries promoting today's avant-garde. From the narrow rue Quincampoix parallel to the boulevard Sébastopol to the labyrinth circling around the Musée Picasso and over toward the place des Vosges, galleries exhibit installations, large-format paintings or photographs and occasionally words. To find your way in this circuit, pick up one of the specialized listing maps, *Rive Gauche Rive Droite*, which are distributed free throughout the galleries. This itinerary is strictly for the initiated, the state of art today often being generally inaccessible.

Architecturally speaking, it is an opportunity to look at some remarkable renovations of mansions or factories—ceilings are high and often skylit, courtyards are commonplace and floors are bleached wood or painted concrete. The **Galerie Yvon Lambert** in the rue Vieille du Temple (showing top European and American names from Kiefer to Barcelo and Richard Serra) glows in the natural light of a converted workshop while underneath, around and above it a Greek dealer, Renos Xippas, has designed a labyrinthine gallery space. This is ideal for exhibiting contemporary talents including Richard Nonas, Robert Irwin, Franz Graf, Takis, and Per Barclay.

The youthful Bastille For unknown talent, the Bastille is perhaps the best bet. Although the area between the rue de Charonne, rue de Lappe and rue Keller has experienced a gallery invasion in the 1990s, quality is not always the common denominator, so don't be fooled. An exception is the impressive **Galerie Durand-Dessert** at 28 rue de Lappe, which occupies four floors of former factory space and exhibits highly regarded international work by the likes of Mario Merz, Kounellis, William Wegman, Barry Flanagan, as well as Gérard Garouste and Bertrand Lavier. However, you're unlikely to find a bargain here.

The attention of the arts world recently shifted to the 13th *arrondissement* where a group of galleries known as *Scène Est* has emigrated and is showing the latest in new conceptualism. However, there still exist numerous *salons*, a hark back to the 19th-century tradition, although their participants are unlikely to cause ripples, as did their forerunners, the Impressionists. The **Grand Palais** hosts international exhibitions but the art affair of the year is the **FIAC**, a contemporary art fair that attracts galleries and collectors from all over the world every October. Its opening (*vernissage*) is the epitome of the Parisian art world: international, elegant, and pretentious.

►► Art Moderne de la Ville de Paris, Musée d' 50A3

Palais de Tokyo, 11 avenue du Président Wilson, 75016; tel: 01 53 67 40 00
Métro: Iéna
Open: Tue–Fri 10–5:30; Wed 10–8:30; weekends 10–6:45.
Admission: expensive

The monumental, colonnaded Palais de Tokyo standing high above the Seine was designed by Aubert, Dondel and Viard for the 1937 International Exhibition. It was intended to celebrate the progress of technology, but labor disputes meant that on the day of its official opening the President was rushed around an unfinished site. However, one brilliant survivor of this unfortunate period is Dufy's 197-foot by 33-foot mural dedicated to *La Fée Electricité*, colorfully intact and covering the walls of a mezzanine room. Four major paintings, *Rhythmes* (1938) by Robert Delaunay, invigorate the lofty main hall downstairs while another great mural, *La Danse* (1932) by Matisse, hangs in a room devoted to the artist. After years of neglect the museum has now come into its own. The permanent collection, built up over the years from private donations, gives the flavor of a museum of the 20th-century *Ecole de Paris*, yet a lively contemporary department consistently produces temporary exhibitions of outstanding quality and ambition, which help to keep this museum within an international sphere.

The core collection Start your visit downstairs, where the permanent collection kicks off with Utrillo, Rouault,

Modern art is still a going concern: a display at the Musée d'Art Moderne (left) and on the gates of a Paris school (above)

SUMMER ON THE TERRACE
Both the museum bookstore (limited in space but well-stocked) and the snack bar on the lower floor are worth investigation. The latter is particularly enticing in the summer months, when tables move outside on to the terrace dotted with Bourdelle's statues overlooking the river—but as always, avoid peak lunch hours when the lines are long.

PARIS' OLDEST HOUSE
The oldest house in Paris is at 51 rue de Montmorency, 75003, and was built by Nicolas Flamel in 1407. The house in nearby rue du Volta, reputed to be older, is in fact a 17th-century reconstruction. The smallest house, at 38 rue du Château d'Eau, has a facade measuring just over 3 feet wide and is 16 feet high.

AMERICAN IN PARIS
American-born James Whistler was just one of many American and English artists who moved to Paris seeking inspiration from the French Impressionists. Their works can be seen in Giverny's striking modern gallery, the Musée d'Art Americain, not far from Claude Monet's last home and famous garden (see pages 200–201).

Valadon, Bonnard, and Vuillard. Don't miss the latter's exquisite portraits of his contemporaries, Bonnard, Maurice Denis, Roussel, and Maillol. The next step is Fauvism (Matisse, Derain), Cubism (Braque, Picasso), and related contemporaries Metzinger, Lhote, Léger, Gromaire, Robert and Sonia Delaunay. Two works by R. Delaunay in particular are worth stopping at: his *Ville de Paris* (1911) and his *Rugby Players*. This burgeoning pre-war period, when Paris was an international hub, also encompasses Modigliani, Szenes, Foujita, Chagall, Soutine, all immigrant artists who contributed to creating the first *Ecole de Paris*. Less strong on Surrealism, the collection moves into Abstraction (Arp, Domela, Magnelli, Fautrier) and *nouveau réalisme*, a 1960s return to figuration and France's version of Pop Art.

The spacious galleries on the street level and second floor are reserved for temporary exhibitions, usually keeping a historical 20th-century figure parallel with avant-garde work by young artists of today.

▶▶ Arts et Métiers, Musée des *51D3*

60 rue Réaumur, 75003; tel: 01 53 01 82 00
Métro: Arts et Métiers
Admission: moderate

This extraordinary and much overlooked museum was set up under the Revolutionary government of 1794, based on a foresighted idea of Descartes who, a century earlier, had seen the need for conserving and exhibiting artisan machinery. Installed in a medieval priory, the museum encompasses a 13th-century church, and a section of wall is still crowned by two original towers of the same period.

Cars and curios The enlightening collection includes models and examples of early transportation (what other church nave accommodates parked Peugeots, Foucault's pendulum and Blériot's first flying machines?), astronomical equipment, clocks (including a decimal example for the Revolutionary calendar), automatons (mostly 18th-century rococo), energy, acoustics, glass (Daum, Lalique, Gallé, Murano), photography, and broadcasting. Modern inventions in the collection include an antiquated 1938 wooden washing machine and the first mass-manufactured car, made by Ford in 1908. The renovation has modernized facilities without destroying the museum's 19th-century charm.

▶ Astérix, Parc see pages 26–27

▶ Bac, rue du *50C3*

This mainly 18th-century street winds south from the Pont-Royal and crosses the boulevard St.-Germain before narrowing into a classy shopping street, ending at the vast department store **Au Bon Marché**—Paris' oldest. The name Bac goes back to the days when the Louvre palace was under construction and a boat (bac) ferried stone across the river to the site.

As you wander southward from the bridge you pass some of Paris' most prestigious antique shops, as well as the **Galerie Maeght** which, at No. 42 (courtyard), occupies the former Hôtel de Boulogne.

South of St.-Germain, the rue du Bac boasts anything from shoes to fine wines, and a branch of Hédiard. Its houses once sheltered literary *salons* and members of the 19th-century intelligentsia such as Chateaubriand (at No. 118–120), who was buried a few doors away from his home at the chapel of the **Missions Etrangères**.

After making a nice little profit selling a painting to the French government in 1893, the American painter James Whistler installed himself at No. 110. Cohorts such as Degas, Toulouse-Lautrec, Manet, and the writers Mallarmé and Henry James dropped by for no doubt animated discussions, while his child-models scandalized the concierge by frolicking naked in the garden.

At No. 136–140 the **Hôtel de la Vallière** houses the Chapel of the Filles de la Charité where, in 1830, repeated visions of the Virgin Mary finally led a nun named Catherine Labouré to glorious canonization. One million or so pilgrims come by every year to see her relics.

The garden of the Maison de Balzac (left), where Honoré de Balzac (below) went into hiding from his debtors

▶ Balzac, Maison de *10B3*

47 rue Raynouard, 75016; tel: 01 42 24 56 38
Métro: Passy
Open: Tue–Sun 10–5:40. Admission: moderate

Pursued by debtors, the writer Honoré de Balzac laid low in this pretty Passy house from 1840 until 1847, using an assumed name but nevertheless managing to pen *La Cousine Bette* and *Le Cousin Pons* in a creative flow that happened from midnight onward. This intimate museum contains portraits and caricatures of the writer and of his favorite mistress, alongside other memorabilia. A library devoted to his works and critical reviews of them completes the Balzacien picture.

▶ Banque de France *50C3*

rue Croix-des-Petits-Champs, 75002
It is not open to visitors

A Napoleonic initiative, the Bank of France (near Palais Royal) was founded in 1800 and soon moved to its present imposing quarters, conveniently down the road from the Bourse (stock exchange). The mansion was built in 1635 by François Mansart, but was rebuilt in the 19th century.

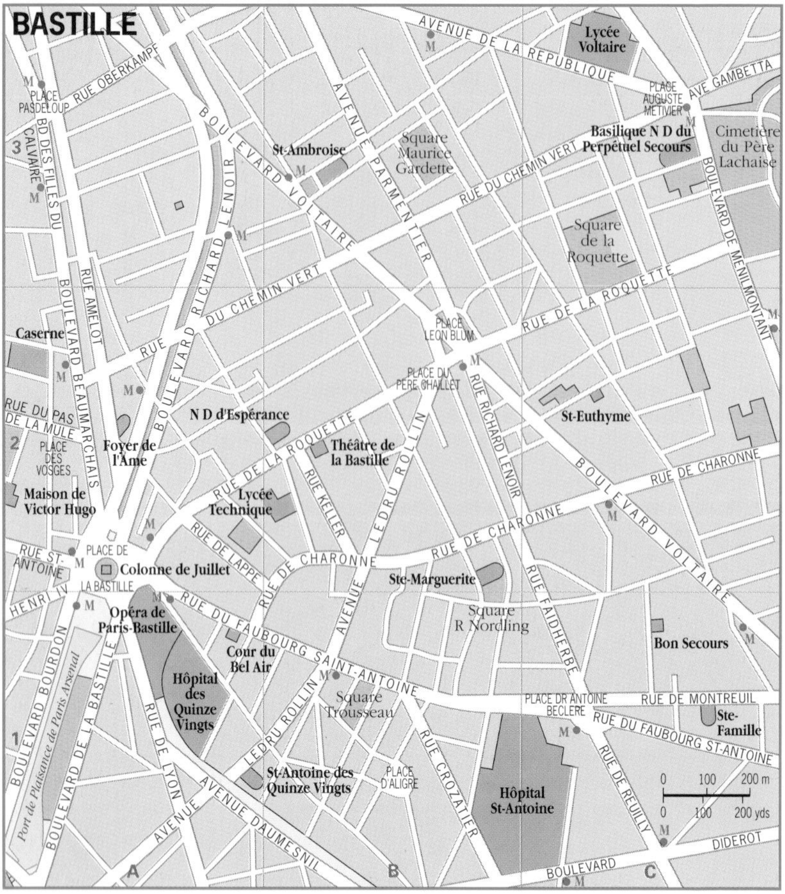

►► Bastille *72A2*

Métro: Bastille

Forever linked with the storming of its prison in 1789—the first violent uprising of the French Revolution—today's Bastille area is just as lively, though more dedicated to a hedonistic way of life. Designer bars, nightclubs, white-walled art galleries, a marina, and ethnic restaurants create its 21st-century character while its new symbol, the "people's" opera-house, towers over the main square.

A new look Only 20 years ago this was still a resolutely working-class district, full of specialized craftsmen's workshops often located in verdant courtyards or hidden passages. Artists were the first to move in, transforming derelict industrial spaces into spacious studios and homes. And where artists go, galleries follow, soon chased by appropriate watering holes. The **marina** terminating the Canal St.-Martin was redeveloped in the early 1980s, and soon after that the **opera-house** rose from the ground, vying for attention with the central column, the **Colonne de Juillet**, erected in 1840 to commemorate victims of the 1830 uprising.

PLACE DE LA BASTILLE

Nothing remains of the Bastille except a line of paving stones in the modern square marking the original site of Charles V's 1380s fortress, built to guard the eastern entrance to the city. During the reigns of Louis XV and XVI it housed political prisoners, including Voltaire and the Marquis de Sade, precipitating the storming of the fortress on July 14, 1789—today celebrated as a national holiday, Bastille Day.

Beneath the traffic circulating wildly around it are buried hundreds of citizens killed during the 1830 and 1848 uprisings.

Unique streets Today's main artery running northeast from the square is the **rue de la Roquette**: here you have your choice of hip bars, trendy clothes stores and the adventurous **Théâtre de la Bastille**. The perpendicular **rue de Lappe** has maintained a nocturnal reputation since the 1930s, when the Balajo dance hall attracted the likes of Mistinguette, Arletty, and Piaf. This street also has traditional connections with the Auvergne: a specialized grocery shop and a restaurant roofed with wooden clogs remain—but who knows for how long?

Other lively streets worth investigating are the **rue Amelot, rue de Charonne** and **rue Keller**, while the **Faubourg St.-Antoine** is traditionally lined with furniture stores, from kitsch to contemporary, part of its long-standing crafts tradition. To alleviate the tedium of this stretch, go into No. 56, the **Cour du Bel Air**, where you will discover a paradisical ivy-clad courtyard with a rare charm and the odd gallery.

Meeting of worlds North of the Faubourg you feel the strangely schizophrenic character of this area, still undergoing transformation. Street water pumps used by African immigrants stand in front of art galleries selling paintings for thousands of francs. Carpenters knock back their breakfast stimulants at a bar next to sleek young advertising executives. Many worlds meet at the Bastille but their universe is still without definition.

Looking to the future and commemorating the past: the Opéra de Paris-Bastille (top) and the Colonne de Juillet (above)

The Seine and its banks give as much flavor to the city as any monument. It runs a 452-mile course from Burgundy to the English Channel and joins both the Oise and the Marne just outside Paris. Named by Julius Caesar, it was described in 1862 by Verlaine as a "muddy old snake," with its cargoes of "wood, coal, and corpses." Today the river boasts cleaner water (much appreciated by local anglers), new cargoes of sightseers, houseboats, and riverside expressways speeding traffic along this essential artery.

BOATING ON THE SEINE
The *bateaux-mouches*, which sail along the Seine night and day, can be boarded at the Pont de l'Alma and during summer run every half-hour from 10 AM–11:30 PM (tel: 01 42 25 96 10). At the Pont d'Iéna, you can catch a *bateau parisien* (tel: 01 44 11 33 44), traveling east to the Ile St-Louis and west as far as the scaled-down version of the Statue of Liberty. All trips provide a multilingual commentary and last about an hour.
For smaller rivercraft, go to the tip of the Ile de la Cité at Pont-Neuf for the Vedettes du Pont-Neuf (tel: 01 46 33 98 38).

With the city divided between Rive Gauche (Left Bank) and Rive Droite (Right Bank) and monuments lining both banks, the Seine can never be ignored. Sensitive to winter rain, it often reaches menacing levels, leading to the closure of its lower banks (*berges*) and creating ensuing havoc in the Parisian traffic flow. However, the Seine blossoms into its own in the warmer months, sprouting contented anglers, rows of *bouquinistes*, idle students, snoozing tramps, starstruck lovers, and various forms of sunworshipers. When you tire of retracing Parisian history, chasing the latest architectural feats or fox-trotting traffic, this should be your destination.

River history Until the 14th century the banks of the Seine remained a web of towpaths and specialized ports. The first *quai* to be structured was the **quai des Grands Augustins** in 1313, but it was the Rive Droite which developed fastest under Henri IV, soon becoming a continuous stretch from the **Tuileries** to the **quai des Célestins**. Louis XVI was the savior of the Rive Gauche and built up the embankment leading from the **quai St. Bernard** through **St.-Michel** and the **quai des Grands Augustins** as far as the **Invalides**. Following the pattern set by the construction of the **Pont-Neuf** in 1604 (now the oldest bridge in Paris), other bridges were gradually cleared of houses and stores, and under Napoleon the last watermills disappeared, leaving an unimpeded view along the river. Haussmann is once again to be thanked for the trees that line long stretches of the *quais* and provide essential summer shade.

River road Scandal broke out in the 1960s when part of the precious Rive Droite was developed into an expressway; public outcry was such that the equivalent Rive Gauche project was abandoned. However, one of the great nocturnal experiences to be had is driving through the Rive Droite tunnel from Concorde and emerging at river level with a glittering view across to the **Ile de la Cité** and the floodlit turrets of the **Conciergerie**.

River walks For a historic riverside promenade, you could do a lot worse than choose the central Rive

Droite stretch, accessible from beside the **Pont des Arts**, which runs as far as the **Pont Alexandre III** next to the **Grand Palais**. A leisurely walk here will take you past a string of monuments across the river (**Institut de France, Beaux-Arts, Musée d'Orsay, Assemblée Nationale**), as well as some imaginatively decked out houseboats and, in summer, an army of bronzing bodies.

For pure romanticism nothing can beat the *quais* of the **Ile St.-Louis**, while, on the Rive Gauche, you can now walk unimpeded from the **Pont-Royal** (beside the Musée d'Orsay) right through the center as far as the **Pont d'Austerlitz** in the east, past St.-Michel in the Latin Quarter, to emerge eventually at the **Jardin des Plantes**.

Down by the river again, within view of **Notre Dame**, the route moves into a more upscale stretch with houseboats and a contemporary sculpture garden. This part is also characterized by joggers and amateur painters having a go at the superb back view of Notre-Dame and of the elegant mansions lining the **Ile St.-Louis** opposite.

Riverside reading If you want to dig out obscure magazines, second-hand and antiquarian books, prints, or postcards, don't forget to investigate the *bouquinistes*. Most are concentrated on the Rive Gauche between the **quai de la Tournelle** and the **quai Malaquais** (opposite the islands); their green stands are an inimitable fixture of the riverside landscape.

Two ways to see the river: by bateau-mouche *or just by sitting on the banks*

Thirty-six bridges span the Seine along its 8-mile flow through Paris; the oldest, dating back to 1604, is the Pont-Neuf. Tramps sleep below them, lovers are entwined atop them, suicides throw themselves off them, and poetry is written about them. From the two-tiered Pont de Bir-Hakeim, with its art nouveau pillars and métros rattling across the top, to the idyllic planked footbridge, the Pont des Arts, idolized in the songs of Georges Brassens, the bridges of Paris are all part of the city's cultural and physical landscape.

For centuries the city only had two bridges: the **Grand Pont** and the **Petit Pont**, which linked the Ile de la Cité with both banks. It was only in the late Middle Ages that three more wooden bridges appeared, the **Pont Notre-Dame**, the **Pont au Change,** and the **Pont St.-Michel**, none of which were solid constructions, and so frequently bowed to high waters, ice, fires, or collisions by rivercraft. However, their commercial viability was underlined in 1414 by a letter from Charles VI which authorized the building of houses on the Pont Notre-Dame "for the good, the decoration and the increased revenue of the town." **The Pont au Change** (opposite Châtelet) was so named for its continuous rows of money-changers' shops, and when the **Pont-Marie** was built in 1635 it still carried an overload of real estate.

Bridges boom Things changed with the farsighted minister Colbert who, in 1716, created an official institution, the **Ponts et Chaussées**, which led to the feverish construction of 21 new bridges. Existing bridges were being cleared of their cumbersome houses, and by the time Napoleon came along new materials such as cast iron created the uncluttered spans that we see today. Paris' 36th bridge, the **Pont Charles-de-Gaulle**, was built between 1993 and 1996 to link the fast-developing 12th and 13th *arrondissements* in eastern Paris.

Pont-Neuf Paris' oldest bridge, the Pont-Neuf, is also its most famous. Built to facilitate the King's journey between the Louvre Palace and the abbey of St.-Germain-des-Prés, its innovative, houseless design was controversial.

Flamboyant as ever, Henri IV inaugurated it in 1604 by galloping across on his charger; today his equestrian statue still dominates the stretch (an 1818 replacement of an earlier statue, melted down during the Revolution). For years this was the site of a permanent funfair, which attracted jugglers, acrobats, and street-sellers; painted by Turner, the Pont-Neuf was also ceremoniously wrapped up by the land-artist Christo in 1985.

Pont-Neuf, the city's oldest bridge

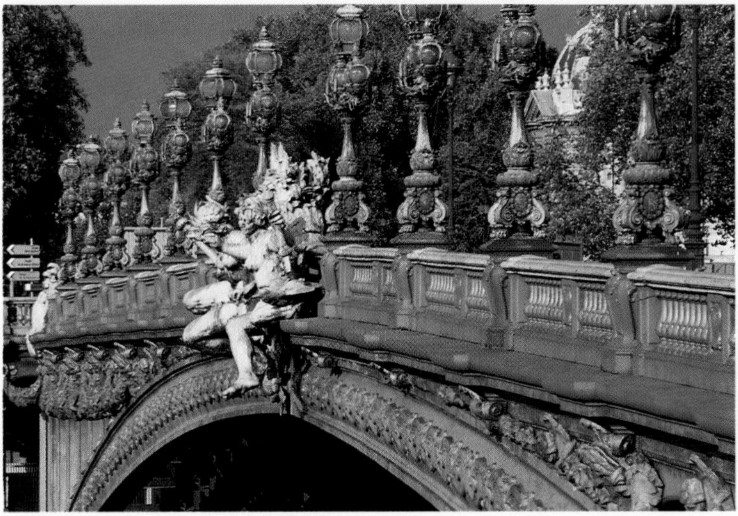

Belle Epoque architecture at its most ornate: Pont Alexandre III

Pont-Marie The 1635 Pont-Marie joins the Ile St.-Louis with the Right Bank. Named after the property developer of the Ile St.-Louis, a certain Mr Marie, this bridge nearly had a very short 20-year life. It was top-heavy with three-story houses (all the more *écus* to the developer), until the spring thaw of 1658 caused a powerful flood, and half of these homes, stores, and their occupants toppled into the Seine.

Pont Royal Slightly more youthful, the Pont Royal, which joins the Tuileries to the rue du Bac, was entirely financed by Louis XIV and built in 1689 by Gabriel after Mansart's design. This time the object was to make life easier for nobles visiting the Palace from the exclusive Faubourg St.-Germain. The pure classical style of its graceful stone arches has never been modified, and on each end pillar there is a hydrographic scale showing historic high-water levels.

❑ A bridge you may not discover easily is the romantically curved footbridge from which Arletty murmured "*Atmosphères, atmosphères*" in Marcel Carné's classic film, *Hôtel du Nord*. This is no figment of cinematographic imagination but actually spans the Canal St.-Martin, a 3-mile canal running from the Bastille to the Canal de l'Ourcq. ❑

Pont Alexandre III In complete contrast, the wildly ornate Pont Alexandre III flashes its gilt and bronzed cupids in the setting sun. Symbolic of the optimism of the Belle Epoque, it was built for the 1900 Exposition Universelle and dedicated to a new alliance between Russia and France. The first stone was laid by the Tsar in 1896, and the facades bear coats of arms of the two countries. Over 15 artists worked on this wedding-cake bridge to create winged horses, gilded cupids, garlands, and various other Greco-Roman artifices on every available ramp, balustrade, and corner.

Pont de l'Alma Commemorating a victory over the Russians by the Franco-British alliance in the Crimean War, the Pont de l'Alma was originally built in 1856 and replaced in 1974. Of the four symbolic statues of the participating armies only the Zouave soldier remains, acting as an official high-water marker.

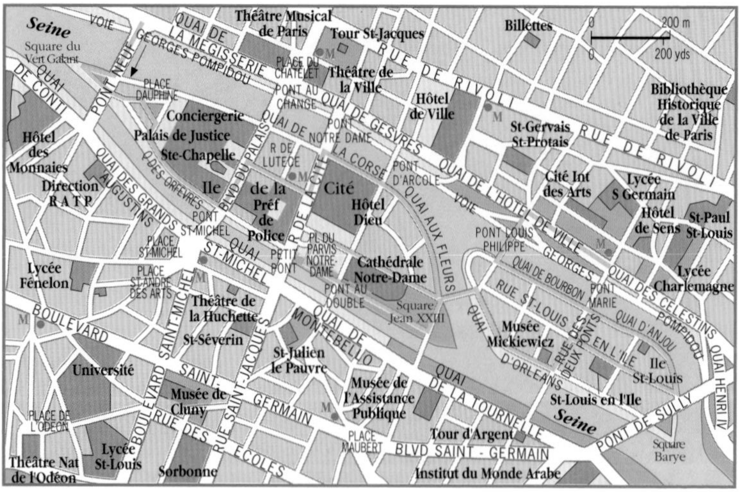

Walk

Exploring the city's islands

Start at Pont-Neuf. Cross to the statue of Henri IV where steps lead down to the island tip.
Here you can circle round the island tip, or take a boat trip.

Back up on the bridge, cross to enter the place Dauphine.
The **place Dauphine** is where Yves Montand and Simone Signoret both used to live.

In front of the Palais de Justice, turn right, then left along the quai des Orfèvres to the Pont St.-Michel. Turn left here.
The route now takes you past the courtyard of the **Palais de Justice**.

Immediately after the Préfecture, turn right into the rue de Lutèce.
The **rue de Lutèce** leads through the flower market to the **rue de la Cité**.

Go left at the rue de la Cité and turn right along the quai de la Corse.
The **quai de la Corse** continues into the **quai aux Fleurs** and has a view north of the **Hôtel de Ville** and east toward the **Ile St.-Louis**.

Circle round back to Notre-Dame.
At this point you are walking among Paris' oldest medieval streets.

Walk round Notre-Dame and through the gardens on the south side; cross the little bridge onto the Ile St.-Louis.
Once the home of wealthy financiers and magistrates, the island remains remarkably conserved; keep an eye open for superb courtyards, wrought-iron details, and sculpted heads.

Follow the quai d'Orléans past some magnificent 17th-century town houses to the rue des Deux Ponts. Turn left here then right into the rue St.-Louis-en-l'Ile.
Pass Paris' best ice cream maker, **Berthillon,** and the island's richly decorated church. The corner **Hôtel Lambert**, at No. 2, is reputed to be the finest mansion of this period in Paris, designed by Le Vau in 1640.

Turn left along the quai d'Anjou.
Both Baudelaire and Théophile Gauthier once lived at **No. 17**, a town house with an exceptional balcony. **No. 19 quai de Bourbon** is the magnificent mansion where Camille Claudel lived and worked.

Cross the Pont Louis-Philippe, with its stunning view along the Seine.

Throwing the light on glassware: the Musée Baccarat boasts over 1,200 masterpieces, including entire services designed for royal courts of Europe

► Baccarat, Musée 51D4

30 bis rue de Paradis, 75010; tel: 01 47 70 64 30
Métro: Château d'eau
Open: Mon–Sat, 10–6. Admission: inexpensive

A visit to this glass museum and showroom will take you into a street packed with porcelain and crystal outlets. The best example has got to be the wonderful 1900s ceramic facade of No. 18. Baccarat, however, has remained the king here ever since 1828, when he became supplier to royalty and heads of state and subsequently moved his company to the present site. The museum exhibits anything from chandeliers to perfume bottles.

Beaubourg see pages 80–81

Beaux Arts, Ecole Nationale Supérieure des 176B3

14 rue Bonaparte, 75006; tel: 01 47 03 50 00
Métro: St Germain
Open: Mon–Fri, 8–8; library 1–6. Admission free

Once a convent, now Paris' art school, built between 1820 and 1862, this imposing facade glowering across the river at the Louvre is the hub for Parisian art students. Its entrance at 14 rue Bonaparte leads into the main courtyard, which still contains a selection of architectural features salvaged by the archeologist Lenoir from destructive Revolutionary fervor. Look inside at the rather dilapidated central hall and galleries, feel the dust, then compare the recently restored Chapelle des Petits-Augustins (1608), in which plaster casts, Renaissance reproductions and the real thing nonchalantly rub shoulders. The exhibition halls opening on to the *quai* sometimes hold interesting shows.

►► Belleville IBCC5

Métros: Belleville, Ménilmontant

Rising almost as high above central Paris as Montmartre, and with corresponding panoramic views, the northeastern quarter of Belleville is a colorful, eclectic mixture. Its traditional working-class character combines with an immigrant population and errant artists to animate its streets, bars, and restaurants, though real-estate promoters have already wrought patchy havoc.

BACK STREETS OF BELLEVILLE

If you explore the side-streets leading off the rue de Belleville, rue de Ménilmontant, and the rue des Pyrénées you'll come across some surprises: look for the passage de la Duée (3 feet wide) or the atmospheric passage des Soupirs. And if you yearn for a vast choice of Asiatic or North African cuisine, this is where to head for.

▶▶▶ Beaubourg *142A3*

Centre national d'art et de culture Georges Pompidou, place Georges Pompidou, 75004 Paris; tel: 01 44 78 12 33
Métros: Rambuteau, Hôtel de Ville, Châtelet
Admission free (Forum, Library); Galleries: moderate/expensive; free first Sunday of the month)

This factory-like museum and free-wheeling cultural center is a landmark of high-tech style right in the middle of historic Paris. It stands out as a symbol of democratized culture. The building has been given a welcome facelift to celebrate 20 years of popular success. Refurbished by Renzo Piano (who, with Richard Rogers, was one of the original architects), it reopened on the first day of the new century to a rapturous reception by record crowds. Sculptor Constantin Brancusi's workshop has been reconstructed on the Rambuteau side of the piazza and the musical research center (**IRCAM**) considerably expanded. The handsomely revamped spacious interior is organized on eight levels (–1, 0, and 1 to 6), starting with an auditorium and cinema in the basement. The escalator extending across the exterior is now no longer a free ride, and is accessible only to ticket holders.

MNAC/CCI (Musée National d'Art Modern et Centre de Création Industrielle)▶▶▶ The permanent collections of the modern art and industrial design museum now occupy the beautifully lit Levels 4 and 5 with a gain of 43,000 square feet. The historic collections will be displayed on Level 5 and the contemporary collections on Level 4. Together they represent a remarkable artistic itinerary through the 20th century from Fauvism (1905) through Cubism, Dada, Surrealism, Abstraction, Pop Art, Minimalism, and today's Conceptualism. Matisse is extremely well represented; cubist works by Picasso, Braque, and Juan Gris are shown with abstract works by Picabia, followed by Léger's visions of the mechanical world, Calder's ethereal mobiles, and paintings by Miró, in striking contrast with conceptual art represented by artists such as Joseph Beuys. The collections are continually extending: recent acquisitions include a surrealist sculpture by Giacometti, works by Pierre Chareau, Chagall, Vlaminck, Per Kirkeby, Alechinsky, Man Ray, as well as drawings and models by contemporary architects including Jean Nouvel and Renzo Piano. Above the permanent collections, Level 6 will be used for temporary exhibitions with considerable gain of space (10,760 square feet). There is also a handsome new restaurant.

Other attractions With improved services including special facilities for visitors with disabilities, the new three-level Forum starts in the basement (Level –1) with halls for music, dance and poetry recitals, and **Cinema 2▶** for experimental films. Besides information and ticket offices, the first floor (Level 0) has a bookstore and special areas for children. On the mezzanine's Level 1 are a giftstore, café, **Cinema 1▶**, which shows seasons of rare international movies, and the entrance to the vast, and well-equipped **reference library▶** (Bibliothèque public d'information, BPI). Its books, documentary films, C.D.s, C.D.-Roms and Internet facilities occupy Levels 2 and 3.

A POPULAR VENUE
Decried by many, Beaubourg's worst failing is in fact its great popularity, unimagined by architects Piano and Rogers when it opened in 1977. In its first 14 years of existence over 90 million visitors crossed the threshold—so expect long lines in the summer when it reopens.

Opposite and below: the show goes on inside and outside the high-tech Beaubourg, ranging from street theater to Surrealism and cabaret artists to Cubism

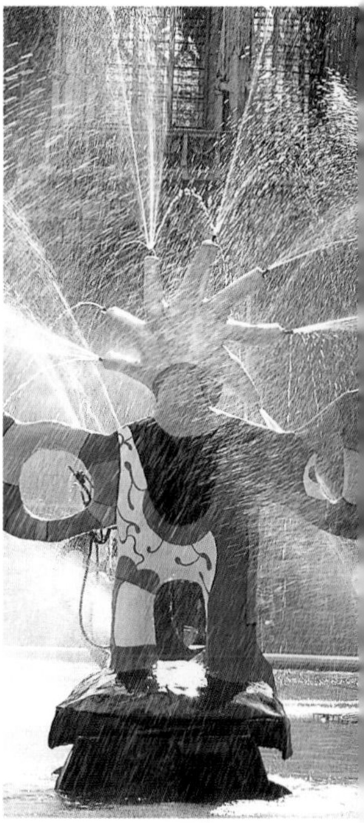

As the city's face changes with the transience of the seasons, so does its fun. Numerous events are held year in, year out at the same date, the most famous being Bastille Day on July 14, a great opportunity to witness boisterous street partying. The Office de Tourisme (127 Champs Elysées, 75008; tel: 01 49 52 53 54) publishes an annual guide every October; below are some of the regular highlights.

PARIS IN THE SPRINGTIME
Paris has always had strong associations with spring. A surprisingly large percentage of Paris' annual 20 million visitors come during springtime when blossoms flourish and the sidewalk cafés come alive after the long winter. Spring is the season of fairs, concerts, and flower shows, particularly spectacular at the Bagatelle Gardens and the Parc Floral. As an incentive, many hotels offer special spring weekend packages.

Winter

Epiphany: the Russian Orthodox version of Christmas on January 6 and 7 is celebrated at the **Saint Alexandre Nevsky Cathedral** (12 rue Daru, 75008). For the French, January 6 becomes the **Fête des Rois**, and is memorable for its pâtisserie, *galette des Rois*, an almond cake ring that contains a hidden bean. The lucky cruncher of the bean dons a gold foil crown and chooses his consort.

Chinese New Year: between late January and early February Chinatown comes into its own. Make sure you are in the 13th *arrondissement* between the avenue d'Ivry and the avenue de Choisy for this colorful event (for information tel: 01 45 20 74 09).

Spring

Foire du Trône: France's largest funfair sets up from March to May at the **Porte Dorée**, next to the Bois de Vincennes. Candyfloss and dodgems replace what was originally a medieval fair during Holy Week.

May Day: May 1 is Labour Day, still taken very seriously, with marches organized by most trade unions, shops and museums closed, and no newspapers. Buy a posy of symbolic lily-of-the-valley from a street seller and join in the crowds.

Celebrations for Bastille Day, July 14, a national holiday throughout France

The month of May includes **Ascension** and **Whitsun** which add two further opportunities to *faire le pont* (i.e. join a midweek holiday to a weekend for four or five days' break).

Roland-Garros: the French Tennis Open is held late May to early June and is now a fashionable event at which to be seen.

Theoretically, tickets for outside courts can be bought on the day but black marketeers have wrapped up this trade. Otherwise apply in writing to Stade Roland-Garros, 2 avenue Gordon Bennett, 75016 Paris (tel: 01 47 43 48 00).

Summer

Exposition de Roses: against the bucolic background of the **Parc de Bagatelle** in the Bois de Boulogne, an international rose competition is held on June 21 and the rose garden remains open till October. The **Orangerie** also hosts the **Chopin Festival**, which is held from late June to July (tel: 01 45 00 22 19).

Fête de la Musique: midsummer night is now loudly celebrated all over Paris with free concerts. Key sites (including **Palais-Royal**, the **Bastille**, **République**) resound to amplified rock or world music into the small hours.

Course des Garçons de café: over 500 professional waiters and waitresses career around the streets of Paris, each bearing aloft a tray laden with bottle and glasses. The fastest non-spilling participant wins. Starting and finishing at the **Hôtel de Ville**, it takes place in late June.

Bastille Day: the action really takes place on the evening of July 13 with *bals populaires* pulling in pulsating crowds to every square or fire station. Beware of firecrackers, which are freely chucked around. Fireworks and the ubiquitous *merguez* (barbecued spicy sausages) complete the ambience. On July 14 a surprisingly pompous military parade passes down the **Champs-Elysées** accompanied by an impressive fighter-jet flypast.

Tour de France: the grand finale of this wildly popular bike race pedals manically along the *quais* of the Rive Droite before crossing the finishing line on the Champs-Elysées. Third week in July.

Autumn

Festival d'Automne: the city's most avant-garde cultural festival sets the ball rolling after the long summer break. Held in various venues over Paris, its dance, theater, and music program is always worth investigating (tel: 01 53 45 17 00).

Fête des Vendanges à Montmartre: Montmartre's biggest yearly splash takes place for the harvesting of its tiny vineyard on the first Saturday in October.

Prix de l'Arc de Triomphe: this is the equestrian event of the year opening the racing season in early October at the **Hippodrome de Longchamp**.

FIAC: a social event disguised as an international art fair, the FIAC (Foire International d'Art Contemporain) opens the art season in October in the Espace Eiffel Branley along the Seine.

A NEW WINE

On the third Thursday in November the race is on to get the first bottles of the year's Beaujolais Nouveau to Paris. Never regarded as a serious wine, it can be overly acid or fruity, but the tradition of who gets there first has spread all over the world. On that revered Thursday afternoon, Paris stops work, bars spill out into the street and endless vociferous opinions on this year's vintage float away into the night air.

THE NATIONAL LIBRARY
The Bibliothèque Nationale contains 12 million printed books, 15 million prints and photos, 1 million records, 600,000 maps, 800,000 coins and medals, and 350,000 periodicals. Every year a further 80,000 books are added.

The Bibliothèque Nationale's former reading room in the Richelieu building

▶ Bercy — *51E1*

Métro: Bercy

Once nostalgically known for its wine warehouses, which formed a self-sufficient village of their own in eastern Paris, Bercy is now an area undergoing intensive development. Already the site for the **Palais Omnisports** (which plays a double act of accommodating sports activities and rock concerts) and the mammoth **Ministry of Finance**, Bercy spreads east from the **Gare de Lyon** through a maze of new office and apartment blocks. Frank Gehry's daring new design for an American Cultural Center closed down after financial troubles. It is due to reopen in 2002 as the new **Musée du Cinéma**. However, not all is concrete in Bercy. At the heart of these sites lies a freshly landscaped park, the **Parc de Bercy**, which has preserved some of the old wine warehouses from destruction by the bulldozers, so allowing some remnants of its past to linger on.

▶ Berryer, Cité — *50B3*

25 rue Royale, 75008
Métro: Madeleine

Once an open-air market, this alleyway leading off the rue Royale recently attained the distinction of "historical monument." In fact more a lunchtime haunt for local office workers, it is at its best in the summer months when restaurants and wine bars invade the sidewalk.

▶ Bibliothèque Nationale de France — *51E1*

11 quai François-Mauriac, 75013; tel: 01 53 79 53 79
Métro: Bibliothèque François-Mitterrand, quai de la Gare

Lack of room forced France's mammoth National Library to take its 12 million books across the Seine to more spacious premises in the redevelopment riverfront area of Tolbiac. Named after François Mitterrand but known as the BNF, the edifice with its corner towers like four open books, has taken over the books that were previously housed in Cardinal Mazarin's palace over on the Right Bank. The public also has access to the Internet and an excellent audio-visual section of video cassettes, D.V.D.s and C.D.s.

▶ Bibliothèque Nationale-Richelieu — *50C3*

58 rue de Richelieu, 75002; tel: 01 47 03 81 26
Métro: Bourse, Palais Royal

The charming old National Library is being transformed into a research library of art history and architecture. It still houses prints and photos and holds temporary exhibitions in the Galerie Mansart and Galerie Mazarine. See also the **Cabinet des Médailles et Antiques**▶, curious antiquities mostly from ancient Greece and Rome.

▶▶ Bois de Boulogne — *IFCA4*

Métros: Porte Dauphine, Maillot, d'Auteuil

Over 2,000 acres of park and playground make up western Paris' lungs, well frequented at weekends by the better-heeled inhabitants from nearby Neuilly and the 16th *arrondissement*. A favorite medieval hunting-ground, in the 18th century it became an aristocratic leisure ground. Finally Napoleon III and Baron Haussmann gave the park the form it has today and

Landscaped romance from the 18th century: the Jardin de Bagatelle in the Bois de Boulogne

made it public. It is awash with lakes, waterfalls, follies, winding paths, and open spaces, with two racetracks: Auteuil and Longchamp. Its nocturnal users (transvestites, prostitutes) had to move out, leaving the solitude of the morning hours to jogging office workers.

Make for one of the high spots, the **Parc de Bagatelle▶**, where a small château (built in 1775) overlooks a romantic park originally laid out by the landscape gardener Thomas Blaikie. Rose bushes abound (over 700 varieties) and a restaurant with open terrace overflows on summer nights. Farther south, the **Pré Catalan** is another well laid-out garden, with a gigantic copper beech as its main feature. Here there is another upscale gastronomic halt overlooking a small lake. Adjoining it is the **Jardin Shakespeare**, so called because of its open-air theater and vegetation inspired by the bard's botanical references.

Children's pursuits If your children-in-tow are tiring, head for the **Jardin d'Acclimatation▶** on the far north edge (*métro*: Sablons) where amusements await them–from toy trains to puppet shows, an "enchanted river" and a small zoo. This section of the park is open 10–5 daily, 10–6 in summer with special events on Wednesdays and on weekends.

● **Stroll** For a dream and a stroll, go to the **Serres d'Auteuil** at the southern point of the Bois (*métro*: Porte d'Auteuil). Here the tropics await you in some superb 19th-century greenhouses. If you are here in late May walk a little farther and you'll come to **Roland-Garros**, where the famous French Tennis Open takes place.

JOGGING IN THE PARK
The best jogging track in the Bois de Boulogne surrounds the Lac Inférieur, an idyllic expanse of water punctuated by two islands, where you can rent rowing-boats or bikes.

SHAKESPEARE & CO
At No. 93 place Edmond-Rostand, next to the Luxembourg *métro* station, is the house which sheltered the American bookstore owner Sylvia Beach (founder of Shakespeare & Co, an American literary landmark in prewar Paris) from the Nazis for two years.

▶ Boulevard Saint-Michel *50C2*

Traditionally thick with students and tourists, the boulevard Saint-Michel had its heyday during the 1968 student riots, when barricades outnumbered cafés and confrontations with the forces of order carried on deep into the night. In Roman times it was one of the two roads leading south from the Ile de la Cité, lined with baths, a theater, and the forum.

Today its bookstores and movie theaters are interspersed with an increasing number of cheap clothes stores and fast-food joints. Although it is the symbolic heart of the Latin Quarter, the boulevard is really only of passing interest, as the architectural and historical high points lie in its sidestreets.

Nightlife At its northern starting-point by the Seine, the Fontaine St.-Michel, designed by Davioud in 1860, is a favorite nocturnal gathering point for street artists, buskers, and other hangers-out. The nearby *métro* entrance is one of the few remaining Hector Guimard art nouveau originals. Cafés and movie theaters are buzzing into the early hours and if you're short of reading matter or cigarettes at this time, here is where to go. In the daytime you are more likely to see students escaping to the cafés from long lectures at the Sorbonne or the Ecole de Médecine.

● **Stroll** If you take a stroll starting on the corner of the boulevard St.-Germain you cannot miss the superb **Musée de Cluny▶▶▶**, floodlit at night, a forceful presence by day. As you head uphill you pass the **place de la Sorbonne**, a small square lined with trees and café-terrasses, even at chillier times of the year. The **place Edmond-Rostand**, crowned by an inevitable fountain, ends the slope and the animated section of the boulevard, opening out on to the **Jardin du Luxembourg** to the west and with an impressive vista of the **Panthéon** to the east.

▶ Bourbon, Palais *50B3*

33 quai d'Orsay, 75007; tel: 01 40 63 60 00
Métro: Assemblée Nationale
Admission: expensive (guided tours only by appointment)

Hiding behind the imposing facade of this 18th-century mansion are the halls of French power: its central parliament, the Assemblée Nationale. Elected every five years, its 577 deputies come and go, and are usually more absent than politically present, a habit which has led to some scolding in recent times by the powers above.

The mansion's history Originally constructed for the Duchess of Bourbon in 1722, the building passed through the hands of the Condé family and Louis XV before Revolutionary confiscation. In 1807 Napoleon, with an astute eye for aesthetics, insisted on a new neo-classical facade (by Poyet) to mirror that of the Madeleine, directly opposite across the Seine and the place de la Concorde.

Today visitors (in limited numbers) can observe heated debates from the gallery overlooking the vast crimson and gold embellished chamber.

DELACROIX'S MASTERPIECE
A tour of the Palais Bourbon includes the sumptuous library ceiling painted by Delacroix in 1838–1847 with his version of the history of civilization (*Guided tours* every Sat at 10, 2, and 3 unless the National Assembly is sitting. *Admission free*; proof of identity is required).

▶ La Bourse 50C3

Place de la Bourse, rue Vivienne, 75002
Métro: Bourse
Open: Mon–Fri, tours between 1:30 and 4 PM
Reservations should be made in advance; tel: 01 40 41 62 20
Admission: moderate

Every major city has its money-spinning hub and in Paris it all happens at the Bourse, another neoclassical Napoleonic invention.

Built on the site of a convent between 1808 and 1826, it was remodeled in 1902–1907, when two wings were added (giving the building the shape of a cross), and is now the meeting point for commodity traders, setting the tone for the surrounding streets, full of money-changers and restaurants called L'Ecu or the Stock Exchange Luncheon Bar (1878).

Inside the Bourse you can watch brokers haggle and bonds change hands at a frenetic pace through a glass window. You can learn all about price-indexing and the importance of the Stock Exchange in France's economy from the public gallery, with the help of specially prepared audiovisual presentations and documentary films.

▶ Bricard de la Serrure, Musée 142B3

1 rue de la Perle, 75003; tel: 01 42 77 79 62
Métro: Saint Paul
Open: Tue–Fri 10–12, 2–5; Mon 2–5. Admission: moderate

An eccentric collection of door decorations—locks, keys, knockers, handles, and plaques—is housed in a magnificent 1685 mansion, built by the architect of the Hôtel des Invalides, Libéral Bruant, for his own personal use.

Eugène Bricard, who lived in the 19th century, gathered together these unusual objects from all periods and countries, displayed in five lofty rooms. The name Bricard still exists as a lock manufacturer.

Money and security: the Bourse (above) and the Musée Bricard de la Serrure (below)

Paris has for a century rested on the green laurels of Haussmann's two woods (Vincennes and Boulogne), three parks (Montsouris, Monceau, and Buttes Chaumont) and two gardens. There are few other real breathing spaces.

The architectural renaissance of the 1980s has, however, woken up to arboreal needs and seen a renewal of the garden tradition, previously buried under a will to kill anything green in the urban mosaic. The **Parc de la Villette**, on the northeastern perimeter, whatever its overall design shortcomings, provides canals and vast lawns—good for local frisbee experts—as well as "conceptual" gardens.

But gone are the 19th-century days of romantic artificial lakes and hills, exemplified by the Buttes Chaumont, a fantastic project which transformed a city rubbish dump into a hillocked mini-paradise complete with grotto, waterfall, and colonnaded temple. Today architects and landscape gardeners have to impose their abstract concepts on available structures, missing out completely on escapist naturalism.

Of the recent park projects the **Parc André Citroën** is perhaps the most ambitious. On the site of the old Citroën factories in southwestern Paris, nearly 35 acres of land have been landscaped to lead directly down to the river, burying embankment traffic in their wake. Two gigantic high-tech greenhouses reign over a garden with more geometric precision than a Swiss watch. If this Cartesian approach touches your soul, don't miss the even more recent **Parc de Bercy** (see page 84), which follows a more classical pattern to match the lay-out of its former village of warehouses. A lucky bonus here is the existence of centennial trees—otherwise parks take decades to assume any form.

The Jardin du Luxembourg, at the heart of the Rive Gauche, is the most popular park in Paris

Parks of the past Step back a century or so and you can rest in relative bucolic peace in any one of Paris' classic parks. The **Jardin du Luxembourg**, saved from Haussmann's ambitions by a petition of 12,000 signatures, remains a symbolic expanse. Creating a natural southern limit to the Latin Quarter and its itinerant students, it is also a favorite haunt of chic Montparnasse residents and their offspring. Its fountains, statues, kiosks, tennis courts, chess and card-players, and book-reading habitués give it an unchanging atmosphere, strengthened by endless literary and celluloid links. Remember the struggling Hemingway who at low points would drop by to pick up a pigeon for dinner, or numerous *Nouvelle Vague* scenes with existentially oriented actors staring morosely into the pond.

Arty park Farther to the south, the **Parc Montsouris** belies its granite quarry past and instead lives up to its 1920/30s arty character, the days when the nearby artists' studios were actually inhabited by brush or

BIRTH OF THE FORUM DES HALLES

Developers were presented with a gaping hole when the 19th-century Baltard pavilions, site of the central fruit and vegetable market, were demolished. The hole remained for years, until one bright spark thought of filling it with a shopping center. Thus the Forum des Halles was born and an adjacent garden laid out. After years of neglect, the gardens have been cleaned up and expanded, new trees planted, graffiti removed from the sculpture, and most of the panhandlers have moved on.

pen-wielding luminaries (Braque, Derain, Salvador Dali, and Henry Miller were all neighbors). Today swans, joggers, and child-minders are by and large the chief users of the park, joined by a brass band during the summer months (see page 151).

Back on the Right Bank, the revamped **Tuileries**, conveniently laid out between the Seine and the rue de Rivoli, remain a centuries-old favorite. Otherwise a great park classic is the **Parc Monceau**, originally planted in English style by Thomas Blaikie in 1783. Picturesque ruins of columns, a pyramid, tombs, Ledoux's rotunda and statues complete a peaceful setting perfect for local nannies and their wards.

Over in Boulogne (*métro*: Porte de St.-Cloud) a curious and little known garden gives an overview of different botanical styles, from a Japanese garden to a Vosges-type forest. The **Jardins Albert-Kahn** were laid out at the beginning of the century by a horticulturally obsessed philanthropist who also founded a rare documentation center about nature all over the planet. Ultimately, though, you cannot beat the **Bois de Boulogne** or the **Bois de Vincennes** for bucolic escapism.

Relaxation among the flowers in the Parc Monceau—small, peaceful, and elegant—Paris' answer to St. James's Park, London

José-Maria Sert's 1925 ballroom in the Musée Carnavalet—a magnificent room in this, the first privately owned Renaissance mansion in Paris

THE MARQUISE DE SÉVIGNÉ

The famous writer Marie de Rabutin-Chantal, Marquise de Sévigné, leased the Hôtel Carnavalet from 1677 until her death in 1696. Here she wrote a collection of 1,500 letters to her daughter, today considered one of the great chronicles of 17th-century high-society Paris.

▶▶▶ Carnavalet, Musée *51E3*

23 rue de Sévigné, 75003; tel: 01 42 72 21 13
Métro: St.-Paul
Open: Tue–Sun 10–5:40. Admission: moderate

Two adjoining mansions in the Marais house the museum of the history of Paris from prehistory through to the 20th century. Exemplary in its presentation, it juxtaposes visions of Paris through the eyes of painters, documents, the decorative arts, and period rooms. Descriptive panels are in French only.

Entrance is through a beautifully sculpted courtyard of the 16th-century Hôtel Carnavalet, much transformed in 1660 by François Mansart before the arrival of its most celebrated resident, the writer Madame de Sévigné. The collections exhibited here take you from the origins of Paris through to the Middle Ages. The splendors of the Renaissance are evoked in four vast first-floor rooms, while Madame de Sévigné's possessions and furnishings on the second floor give a rounded view of Louis XIV's era. Sizzling heights of decoration from Louis XV's and XVI's reigns are displayed in paneled interiors, while the richly painted and gilded woodwork (1656) from the Hôtel Colbert de Villacerf is a superb example of Louis XIV ornateness.

Next door, the collections installed in the sleekly renovated Hôtel Le Peletier de Saint-Fargeau (1690) take you on through the Revolution to the 19th century and finish in the early 20th century. Look out for the keys of the Bastille prison, Hubert Robert's paintings, made in and out of prison in the 1790s, and Le Sueur's unusual comic-strip account of this period. Anything and everything was decorated with revolutionary slogans—fans, plates, clocks, furniture. Napoleon's favorite campaign picnic-case (110 pieces) introduces you to the Empire and to the Second Empire with the elaborate cradle of the Imperial prince (1856). Reconstructed interiors include Proust's corklined bedroom and brass bed, Henri Sauvage's Café de Paris and the ballroom from the Hôtel de Wendel, painted by José-Maria Sert in 1925.

► Cartier, Fondation *50C1*
261 boulevard Raspail, 75014
(see page 122)

►► Catacombes *50C1*
1 place Denfert-Rochereau, 75014; tel: 01 43 22 47 63
Métro: Denfert-Rochereau
Open: Tue–Fri 2–4; Sat–Sun 9–11, 2–4. Admission: moderate
Over six million slumbering skeletons hide out here in the world's largest deposit of human bones. During World War II this underground network of 102 miles of tunnels was used as a secret meeting place for Resistance fighters; today urban potholers regularly slip into them for chilly and chilling explorations. Visitors tour in groups to view the macaber remains. Remember to take a flashlight and sweater and be prepared to climb hundreds of stairs.

►►► Chaillot, Palais de *50A3*
Place du Trocadéro, 75016; tel: 01 44 05 39 10
Métro: Trocadéro
This colonnaded mammoth, commanding a stunning perspective of the Eiffel Tower and the Champ de Mars directly across the Seine, was built for the Exposition Universelle of 1937; its curved wings are dotted with glittering bronze statues and the wide terraces overlook a fountain-ridden garden. It housed no fewer than four museums, a theater, and a movie theater until a fire seriously damaged the east wing in 1997. As a result, the **Cinémathèque Française** (tel: 01 56 26 01 01), founded in 1936 by Henri Langois, has moved to new premises along the *grands boulevards* (42 boulevard de Bonne-Nouvelle, 75010) where it continues to show a fantastic program of film classics. In the basement, between the two wings, is the **Théâtre National de Chaillot** (tel: 01 53 65 30 00), whose postwar director, Jean Vilar, democratized the theater and later founded the Festival d'Avignon.

(Continued on page 94)

THE CATACOMBES
The Catacombes were originally channeled out in Roman times to provide stone and plaster; it was only after a campaign orchestrated by Voltaire in 1785 that the occupants of the pestilential cemeteries above ground were moved below.

The impressive colonnaded wings of the 1937 Palais de Chaillot, a vast cultural center, frame the Eiffel Tower perfectly

Mountains of fruit and veg, hundreds of varieties of cheese, strings of saucisson, clouds of perfumed herbs ... food markets are part and parcel of Paris life. Then there are books, stamps, flowers, birds; and antiques and bric-à-brac change hands as if industrialization had never existed.

FLEA MARKETS

The Paris flea market was first set up in a no-man's-land in north Paris around 1880. In 1920 Romain Vernaison, a property owner, installed stalls and let them to antique dealers (Marché Vernaison) and the Marché Biron soon followed suit, in 1925. Today the flea market at the Porte de Clignancourt covers 74 acres and has over 1,500 shops and 1,400 licenced stalls.

Of over 80 permanent markets in Paris, the market at rue Mouffetard is one of the oldest and most popular

A stroll around a French food market is a gastronomic education in itself. When you see a stallholder squeezing Camemberts, pressing avocados, or pinching melons you'll be witnessing a precise and incontestable philosophy in action. Parisians shop daily, as produce is fresh and the timing of its consumption must be perfect. Keep that Camembert too long and it will walk off the table; eat it too soon and you miss out on its very essence.

Apart from the circulating markets, which set up on sites and days all over the city, there are permanent daily street markets such as the **Marché d'Aligre**, the **rue Poncelet, rue Montorgueil, rue Mouffetard** (closed Mon, Wed, Fri, and Sun), and the **rue de Buci**. These unveil their wares around nine in the morning and pack up towards seven, not forgetting a very provincial lunchbreak between one and four. Sunday afternoons and Mondays finally give market workers time to recuperate from the weekend onslaught, when even the most ardent restaurant-goers indulge in a serious return to their culinary sources.

The art of shopping Every market has its historic boulangerie or cheese shop—often with fantastically ornate interiors worthy of a château—that proves the level of attention and pride bestowed on mere foodstuff. Amid the sea of outdoor stalls, these five-star landmarks can usually be spotted by their lengthy lines—Parisians are tremendously faithful, gastronomically at least. Cafés are, of course, another integral part of market shopping.

The market operation being a lengthy and concentrated business (each purchase requires at least five minutes, depending on the stall's popularity or the holder's garrulousness), it merits a drink and quick exchange of wit at half-time.

One of the most picturesque street markets, the **rue Mouffetard**, has also, unfortunately, become one of the most well-known to tourists. It still has its charm however, as does the **rue de Buci** in St.-Germain-des-Prés, another crowd-puller, due to its convenient central location.

But make sure you go to a typical local market such as the **rue Poncelet** (17th *arrondissement*), the **place d'Aligre** (12th), which doubles up as a bric-à-brac market and is also strong on North African specialties, or the **rue du Poteau** (18th), on the slopes of Montmartre, with its inimitable "old Paris" character.

Famous fleas Flea markets (*marché aux puces*), are judiciously sited around the city perimeter. Their eclectic and often dusty and/or exotic goods never lose their pull, whether for well-heeled tourists and residents or for the poorer inhabitants.

The world famous **Porte de Clignancourt** flea market is rightly known as a tourist trap, yet its alleyways, covered markets and stalls always come up with something for everyone—the sheer bulk of goods plus the laws of probability see to that. From old buttons to recycled clothes to Louis XV mirrors to 1950s coffee-pots—it's very difficult not to find your own particular joy among these varied offerings.

Diametrically opposite the Porte de Clignancourt on the Paris map, the flea market at the **Porte de Vanves** has recently become a favorite with young trendies; there is little of great value but plenty of eccentricities, art deco and 1950s furniture, a smattering of exotica and quite a wide selection of old prints.

Not as popular nor as interesting as it used to be, the **Marché de Montreuil** in the east of Paris is gradually being taken over by bargain household-goods stalls, leaving little space for the junk; however, secondhand clothes remain a specialty and Yves St. Laurent jackets have even been known to be found, in perfect condition, so ... keep looking.

For those looking for secondhand books, if the *bouquinistes* (dealers) don't suffice, spend your weekend hours at the **Parc Georges Brassens** (15th), where you will find an unrivalled array of antiquarian and secondhand books.

BIRDS AND FLOWERS

For a market with color, go to the Marché aux fleurs (held daily on the Ile de la Cité in front of the Préfecture), replaced on Sundays by a bird market. Or try the stamp market held on Thursdays and weekends on the corner of the avenue Matignan and the Champs-Elysées.

MUSÉE DE L'HOMME
There is an excellent bookstore in the Musée de l'Homme, as well as the ultimate restaurant-with-a-view, the Totem.

MUSÉE DU CINÉMA
After a fire in its premises below the palace, the prestigious cinema museum's collection of over 3,000 items is being transferred to Frank Gehry's building, originally designed for the American Center and now scheduled to reopen in 2002 (see page 84). The collections include the Lumière brothers' photorama and Edison's kinetoscope of 1894 alongside set models by Eisenstein, photographs, costumes (worn by the likes of Valentino and Garbo), and actual sets from *Metropolis*.

(Continued from page 91)

Housed in the east wing and also damaged in the fire is a rather odd museum, created in 1882 by the architect Viollet-le-Duc. The **Musée des Monuments Français** is a museum of full-scale copies of architectural features from pre-Roman times to the 19th century. It is a good opportunity to see a panorama of this field in one fell swoop. Closed for reconstruction, the museum is due to reopen in the course of the year 2003, under the name of **Cité de l'Architecture et du Patrimoine**, and will hold collections ranging from the middle ages to the 20th century.

In Chaillot's west wing, there is a choice of two museums, the **Musée de l'Homme** (*Open* daily 9:45–5:15; closed Tue), or the **Musée de la Marine▶** (*Open* daily 10–6; closed Tue). Predictably, the latter, one of the largest maritime museums in the world, set up by Charles X in 1827, concentrates on French naval history and displays ship models, marine instruments, paintings (including 13 of *Vernet's Ports de France*, executed between 1754 and 1765), and sculpture. Don't miss the Emperor's barge (built in 1811 for Napoleon) or a cross-section model of the glittering transatlantic liner *Normandie*, the floating 1932 palace of decorative arts destroyed by fire during World War II. The **Musée de l'Homme** (tel: 01 44 05 72 72), although rather shabby and in need of a window cleaner, houses fascinating anthropological and ethnographical displays. Mental travel is possible from the Pacific to Africa with detours around Asia and, particularly strong, South America. Look for the life-size "shark-man," King Béhanzin and the medieval frescos from Abyssinia, both in the rich African section. On the top floor, in the Salon de la Musique, 500 or so world instruments are displayed with background sound. Live concerts are a regular feature.

An exhibit from the Palais de Chaillot's Musée de la Marine, portraying French Maritime history from the 18th century to the present day

Cyclists in the Tour de France speed along the Champs-Elysées. The avenue is guarded by the Chevaux de Marly (below)—but only by copies; the originals are in the Louvre

▶▶ Champs-Elysées *50B3*

The broad pavements and wide expanse of this avenue, which sweeps majestically down from the Arc de Triomphe to the place de la Concorde, somewhat run down in recent years, have had a welcome facelift and the Champs-Elysées can now fulfil its role as one of the places dreamed about by visitors to Paris. It is lined with elegant sidewalk cafés, a maze of revamped shopping malls, the prestigious French mecca of hi-fi and video, and a string of large-scale movie theaters showing latest releases, hard to beat for their comfort (or their lines).

You can thank Marie de Médicis, wife of Henri IV, for turning it into a fashionable driveway in 1616. Then thank the landscape designer, Le Nôtre, for the gracious alleys of trees and gardens leading from the Concorde which by 1707 had earned the avenue its name: Elysian Fields. It was in 1824 that the avenue became structured with sidewalks and fountains, soon crowded with cafés and restaurants and a very chic clientele. Various Universal Exhibitions helped to increase its popularity, particularly in 1900, when the **Grand Palais** and **Petit Palais** sidled up together.

Center of ceremony Having lost none of its appeal, the Champs-Elysées remains the central Parisian stretch for official processions and celebrations. Catch it on July 14 (Bastille Day) and most of the French army rolls past with a jet accompaniment flying exceedingly low overhead. Later in July you may find yourself here for the last leg of the Tour de France bicycle race, an event deeply rooted in the French psyche. You can catch the setting at its best around Christmas, when every tree glitters with festoons of elegant white lights—then try New Year's Eve for size. The lower half of the avenue boasts a few select restaurants nestling below the chestnut trees: **Ledoyen, Cercle Ledoyen** or **Le Pavillon Elysée**—all have hefty prices but make a nice indulgence with their garden terraces. Otherwise avoid any eating establishment on this avenue—everything is geared toward unsuspecting tourists—and explore side streets for better value.

GREAT PROCESSIONS

In 1989 the Bicentenary celebrations culminated in Jean-Paul Goude's spectacular procession moving and dancing down to the Concorde, where Jessye Norman sang La Marseillaise. De Gaulle's triumphal Liberation march took place here in 1944, as did the silent procession in 1970 paying tribute to him after his death. Victor Hugo's funeral parade made its way along the avenue du Champs-Elysées in 1885.

Where else did Lenin, Sartre, Picasso, Modigliani, Apollinaire, James Joyce, and Trotsky cultivate their genius but in Parisian cafés? Not to speak of the intellectuals of the Revolution, who plotted France's future in the watering holes of the Palais Royal. The café tradition lives on, and Parisian thinkers still hatch ideas or chew the cultural cud in public rather than in their often minuscule abodes. Time was when cafés were part of the Great French Pick-up tradition, but lone women are nowadays as much at ease here as they are at home.

The Parisian habit of people-watching includes fashion comparisons, or attention to *le look*. Where better to indulge it than from a shady *café-terrasse* in the summer months, or a warm, noisy, smoky interior during winter? Unfortunately the majority of Paris' 6,000 or so cafés reek of *croque-monsieurs* (grilled ham and cheese sandwiches) and resound to sounds of pinball machines, so shrewd selection is essential.

Many of the favorites are in upscale Saint-Germain, although the well-loved **Café de Flore**, which rose to fame when Sartre and Simone de Beauvoir set up literary shop there, has now sadly closed. However, a few doors along is the equally famous **Les Deux Magots**, named after the statues of two corpulent Chinamen astride their strongboxes. *Magot* also means a hoard of money, and this is what you'll spend if you succumb to the menu of 25 different brands of whiskey. But think of the ghosts of Mallarmé, André Breton, Hemingway, André Gide and Sartre and, as in every historic café, beware the prices! Tourists and Middle Eastern businessmen abound, and the odd native publisher or movie star still slips in.

CAFÉS BRANCHÉS
Internet cafés are now as prolific in Paris as they are in the rest of the world. However, the current crop of *café branchés* (trendy cafés) that are springing up, represent a further testiment to the modern lifestyle. Catering to chic, environmentally-conscious Parisians, this is where customers can recharge their electric scooters while recharging their own batteries with a cup of coffee.

Historic haunts For a more down-to-earth café, head down to the corner of the rue de Seine and the rue Jacques-Callot. Here you can plunge into the less monied and eccentric **La Palette**, with its comfortable and noisy back room and idyllic summer terrace. La Palette is a favorite with art students, artists and gallery owners. Its walls are plastered with good and bad art, and its head-waiter-cum-proprietor is a classic: quick-witted or scowling, he's unforgettable.

Back in an increasingly characterless Montparnasse, an institution not to miss is **La Coupole**. Built in 1926 by an astute waiter working at Le Dôme across the street, its majestic art deco splendour is hard to rival, despite recent remodeling. The main hall is a world-famous brasserie whose ghosts include pre-war Americans in Paris such as Hemingway (he got everywhere), Man Ray and Henry Miller, backed up by locals Matisse and Kiki de Montparnasse. Across the road, the rival **Le Sélect** dates from the same period and still attracts a heterogeneous crowd late into the night.

Right Bank landmarks In the heart of the Rive Droite's commercial quarter, Opéra, stands another Parisian landmark café, the **Café de la Paix**. Although mainly frequented by exhausted tourists, its interior demands a visit. Designed by Charles Garnier (responsible for the neighboring opera-house), the murals, moldings and chandeliers are a shrine to the glorious excesses of mid-19th-century décor. However many famous cafés litter the centre of Paris, you will doubtless come across your own finds, rich in local characters and decorative idiosyncrasies. Don't miss out on the latest *fin de siècle* café, **Café Beaubourg** on the square outside the Centre Pompidou. Here, in Christian de Portzamparc's postmodernist setting, you can watch Rive Droite intellectuals go by. If you really want to be with it, pop into the **Web Bar**, one of the trendiest of the latest generation of Parisian night haunts, the modern version of the literary cafés of the 18th and early 19th centuries (32 rue de Picardie, 75003; *métros*: République, Temple); in addition to providing the most up-to-date cyberspace, this fashionable establishment offers its customers a varied cultural programme including poetry readings, concerts, art exhibitions and dance performances.

Le Zinc To some, it is the traditional Parisian zinc café that epitomizes the city's café culture. The **Café de l'Industrie**, on rue St-Sabin near the Bastille, is a typical example, with its zinc-lined counter-top and an authentically atmospheric smoky interior. Alternatively, try **Le Cochon a l'Oreille**, a tiny café at 15 rue Montmartre, once renowned for serving onion soup at dawn.

LE PROCOPE
The first café to open its doors in Paris was Le Procope (which still exists but as a restaurant), in 1686, run by a Sicilian who soon attracted most of the political and literary élite to his tables. Voltaire had a daily habit of drinking 40 cups of mixed coffee and chocolate there, and the young artillery officer Napoleon Bonaparte once had to leave his hat as a deposit while he went off to search for funds.

CAFÉ MARLY
The latest designer café, the Café Marly, was conceived by Olivier Gagnère to slip effortlessly into a wing of the Louvre. It attracts an elegant crowd and in summer offers unbeatable views of the pyramid.

Spoilt for choice at one of Paris' many cafés

In the early days, brasseries only sold beer. Today, high ceilings echo with clattering plates and chattering voices, mirrors double the people-watching scope, carved wood and etched glass partitions protect your privacy and waiters in full-length white aprons swing trays of oysters or choucroute *between the tables.*

IN SEARCH OF OYSTERS
For the best oysters, try Le Bar à Huîtres in the Marais, L'Huîtrier in the Chaillot quarter, the cheerful Bistrot du Dôme in Montparnasse or nearby La Cagouille which boasts one of the finest shellfish platters in town.

An invention which arrived from Alsace in eastern France, wholesome brasserie fare usually includes sausages piled high on *choucroute* (sauerkraut), ham, sausage and anything else that can be concocted from a pig—all drowned in pitchers of beer. Many specialize in seafood, so if you're in Paris during the "r" months (September to April) when oysters are at their optimum, indulge. Most brasseries are open on Sundays and last orders carry on well after midnight, making them ideal for late eaters.

The world famous brasserie chain **Flo**, which includes **Flo**, **Julien,** and **Terminus Nord** in the 10th, the **Vaudeville** in the 2nd and more recently **La Coupole** in the 14th, is hard to beat for atmosphere, value, and spectacular settings. The **Brasserie Flo** itself remains a Parisian favorite, tucked away in a courtyard and inevitably packed out, whereas **Julien**, more visible on the Faubourg, has a higher tourist concentration. Bang opposite the Stock Exchange, the patronizing **Vaudeville** waiters serve traders sweating over the *Financial Times*

La Coupole, one of the celebrated Flo chain of brasseries, frequented by artists and intellectuals since it opened in 1927

at lunchtime and a mixed glamorous bunch in the evening. The elegant **Terminus Nord**, the only jewel in the dubious *quartier* of the Gare du Nord, has an easy-going atmosphere.

La Coupole is, of course, La Coupole. Josephine Baker and her pet lion cub are not the only celebrities to have sat on its brown velvet seats under its soaring art deco ceiling. Despite its recent, much criticized renovation, the famous pillars painted by artists (in exchange for meals) such as Chagall, Léger, Juan Gris, Delaunay, and Soutine remain. Othon Friesz's dynamic murals have been restored and 600 seats are still available. Actors, artists, models, business executives and plain ordinary people all mix in at this nonstop party.

Paris' star brasserie, the **Lipp**, is centrally situated on the boulevard St.-Germain, where all celebrities seem to tread. Once ruled by a man with an iron glove, Roger Cazes, who was quick to decide whether you were worthy of a first-floor table or were to be relegated upstairs, it now has a less disdainful management. Long a favourite with politicians (from de Gaulle to Pompidou and Mitterrand) it is also a great haunt for authors. Idiosyncrasies prevail: no soup on Sundays, roast pork on Monday, cassoulet on Thursday ... and nonstop *choucroute*. No reservations; pot luck and the shape of your face decide your destiny.

First draughts One of Paris' oldest brasseries (1864), and apparently the first to serve draught beer, the **Bofinger** thrives in a sidestreet off the Bastille, another Flo acquisition. With its ornate glass dome, marquetry and gracefully framed mirrors, it is a delight to dine in.

Less opulent but serving the same basic fare minus the shellfish, the **Brasserie de l'Ile Saint-Louis** boasts the best brasserie terrace in Paris. A south-facing view over the Seine, Notre-Dame a few yards away and Berthillon ice creams: its credentials are impeccable. Inside, the stuffed stork perched on the bar is about the same age as the 1913 expresso machine, and the bartender has pulled draught beer here since the 1950s. Crowded and cramped, its backroom restaurant remains a firm favorite with tourists and eccentric locals.

Pigalle, too, has its *choucroute* institution, namely the venerable **Brasserie Wepler** on place Clichy. Better value than the central establishments and just as accommodating in size, its oyster bar is outstanding. The vast, brassy décor is not the most discreet, but its eclectic clientele fills out the corners comfortably.

A sign of good taste: the still flamboyant Bofinger serves excellent shellfish, grilled meats, and choucroute

Gabriel's imposing Ecole Militaire in the Champ de Mars, where Napoleon trained to become an officer

"AN EXCELLENT SAILOR"
Thanks to a new tax on playing-cards and the lottery, funds were found for the colonnaded and domed Ecole Militaire, completed in 1773 and considered to be Gabriel's masterpiece. Thus the 18th-century gamblers inadvertently financed the grooming of France's military cadets, one of whom was none other than Napoleon. He entered the academy aged 15, in 1784, considered fit "to be an excellent sailor."

► Champ de Mars *50A2*

Originally laid out for army maneuvres, whence the name, which refers to Mars, the Roman god of war, the green lawns of the Champ de Mars stretch from the Eiffel Tower down to the Ecole Militaire. It was the site where the Roman invaders battled it out with the Parisii in 52 BC to obtain supremacy over Paris and where the Parisians later beat off the Vikings. The Champ de Mars has witnessed many an official celebration, horse-races, and ballooning experiments by the intrepid Montgolfier brothers. It is a favorite with children of chic local residents.

Dominating the area is the Ecole Militaire, designed as a military academy by Gabriel (also responsible for Versailles' Petit Trianon), who was commissioned by Louis XV and his mistress, Madame de Pompadour.

Chartres see pages 194–5

► Chasse et de la Nature, Musée de la *142B3*

Hôtel de la Guénégaud, 60 rue des Archives, 75003; tel: 01 42 72 86 43
Métros: Rambuteau, Hôtel de Ville
Open: Wed–Mon 10–12:30 and 1:30–5:30. Admission: moderate

Definitely one of Paris' more curious museums, filled with rooms of hunting weapons and stuffed animals. Housed in a Marais mansion, the Hôtel Guénégaud, which was built in 1650 by François Mansart, it possesses a tiny yet perfectly manicured garden, visible from the rue des Quatre Fils. The museum collection itself covers hunting arms used from prehistory until the 19th century (knives, crossbows, swords, airguns, rifles). On the second floor big-game hunting comes to the fore (with souvenirs of the museum's founder, Monsieur Sommer). A rich collection of relevant paintings and decorative arts include hunting and animal scenes depicted by François Desportes, the court artist employed by Louis XIV at Versailles, alongside Chardin, Oudry, and Carle Vernet.

Since 1895, when Louis Lumière held his first cinematographic projections in a basement room of Le Grand Café, at No. 14 boulevard des Capucines, Paris has remained a world center of movies. A century or so later, there are now over 300 movies showing at any time of the day or evening, from old Hollywood classics to recently released European avant-garde efforts—and almost all foreign language films are shown in their original version (these are labeled VO).

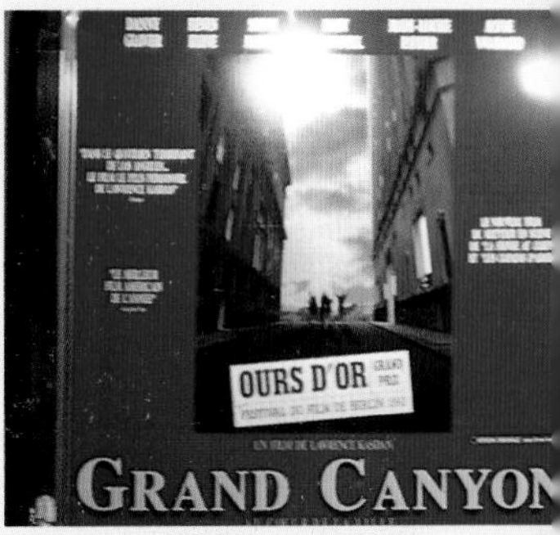

City images Many French movie-makers are inextricably linked with the atmosphere of Paris, not least being the directors of the 1930s and 1940s. Born in Les Halles and a pupil of the famous Lycée Louis-Le-Grand, René Clair showed Paris for the first time on screen in *Paris qui dort* (1923) and soon after in *Sous les toits de Paris*. Yet however authentic they look, his charming, animated old streets, rattling omnibuses, and smoking chimney-pots were all studio-built.

A decade later, Marcel Carné, another Parisian born and bred in Batignolles, focused on the rough, industrial life of the *faubourgs*, encapsulating Montmartre and Jean Gabin in the *Quai des Brumes* and the Canal St.-Martin in *Hôtel du Nord*, which starred the legendary Arletty and Louis Jouvet. *Les Enfants du Paradis* poetically interpreted the street underworld around the Cour des Miracles in a classic Parisian fresco.

The other side of the Parisian coin was reflected in Jean Renoir's *La Règle du Jeu* (1939). Here was the elegant, muted, bourgeois world of Proust and the 16th *arrondissement*, rife with barely disguised jealousies.

Classic venues To see such Parisian classics go to the **Vidéothèque** (see page 183), the **Cinémathèque** (see page 91), the **Cinéma 1** at Beaubourg (see page 81); all specialize in reruns, as do certain Rive Gauche cinemas. For these programs, which often change daily, check one of the weekly listings magazines (*Pariscope* and *L'Officiel des Spectacles*), published on Wednesdays. But for real audience comfort go to any of the following: **Kinopanorama** (15th), **Max Linder** (9th), **Le Grand Rex** (2nd). These are now supplemented by the new multiplex movie theaters such as the Ciné Cité chain at Les Halles and Bercy, or **MK2 Quai de Seine** at La Villette.

Mass-release movies are shown in a string of Champs-Elysées movie theaters

At the crossroads: place du Châtelet sits over the largest métro *station in the world, a veritable subterranean labyrinth*

▶ Châtelet, place du *166B4*

A hectic central crossroads, the place du Châtelet lies between the Pont au Change, which crosses to the Ile de la Cité, and the boulevard de Sébastopol. Once the site of an imposing fortress, Châtelet is known today for its vast underground métro station, where all lines and all buskers seem to meet. Two important theaters flank the square and in its center the sphinx-endowed fountain, erected in 1808, commemorates yet another Napoleonic victory, the Egyptian campaign.

Both identical theaters were built by Davioud in 1862 but now lead separate and even rival existences. The **Théâtre Musical de Paris** concentrates mainly on opera and classical music, with occasional ballet, and usually has a rich program of international performers. It now has an annexe in Les Halles, the Auditorium, where more unusual or obscure music is performed.

The modernized interior of the **Théâtre de la Ville**, previously named the Sarah Bernhardt, has preserved for posterity the diva's dressing room. Audiences flock here to see the top names of contemporary dance or innovative French theater. Early evening concerts of jazz or world music have recently been programed to give home-bound office workers a chance to unwind.

TOUR ST.-JACQUES
Just north of the place du Châtelet lies a 175-foot-high tower in the flamboyant Gothic style, all that remains of the 16th-century Church of St. Jacques-la-Boucherie—once a meeting point for pilgrims setting out to St. Jacques' shrine at Compostela

▶ Chinatown *IBCB2*

Following world tradition, Paris now has its very own Chinatown in the 13th *arrondissement*, spreading south from the place d'Italie through the rue de Tolbiac to the Porte de Choisy. Asiatics are now said to constitute 10 percent of the population of this *arrondissement*, and China is by no means the only country of origin. Squeezed between high-rises, pagoda-like storefronts crammed with Chinese curios jostle with a fantastic variety of eateries on all scales, from Hong Kong-style canteens to more intimate Laotian, Cambodian, and Vietnamese places. Clubs, dance halls, and gambling dens also contribute to the atmosphere but these are usually out of bounds to westerners, as the fortunes changing hands are illegal.

DRAGONS IN THE STREETS
The best time of the year to visit Chinatown is during Chinese New Year (late January), when dragons take to the streets.

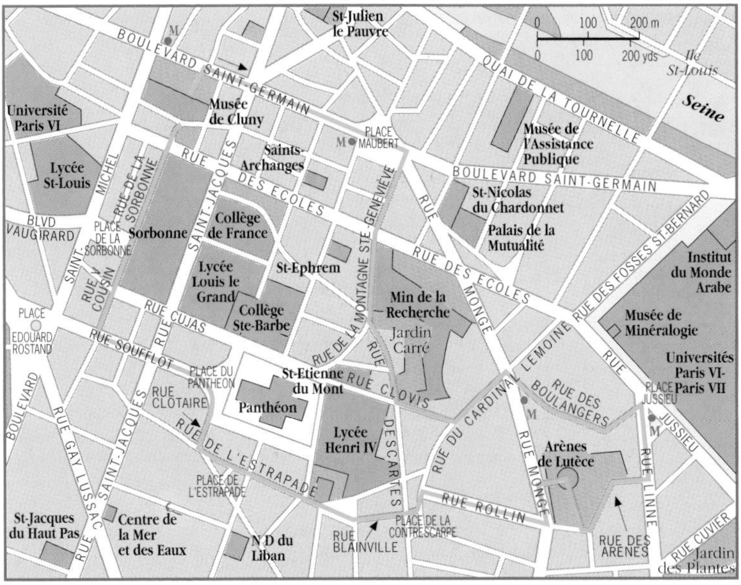

Walk

A circular walk from the Musée de Cluny

Start in front of the Musée de Cluny. Walk east along boulevard St.-Germain to the place Maubert. Turn right behind the vast police station and walk up the steep rue de la Montagne Ste.-Geneviève.
Named after the patroness of Paris, the **rue de la Montagne Ste.-Geneviève** was part of the Roman road linking Lutetia with Italy, and for centuries was lined with colleges and schools. Some remain today.

At a fork, turn up the rue Descartes.
The route now passes what was once the famous **Ecole Polytechnique** and is now a ministry (its delightful gardens are open to the public).

Turn left into the short rue Clovis.
The **rue Clovis** was named after the king of the Franks who defeated the Romans and founded France. Near **No. 5** is a section of medieval city wall.

Walk downhill towards the place du Cardinal Lemoine and take the second narrow turning on your right down the rue des Boulangers, right up the rue Linné and right again into the rue des Arènes.
Here, you enter the ruined Roman amphitheater, **les Arènes de Lutèce**, now used for boules.

Exit onto the rue Monge, turn left then right into the rue Rollin, which crosses the animated place de la Contresçarpe and becomes the rue Blainville.
The **rue Blainville** was the site of Paris' first public library.

Follow this street into the rue de l'Estrapade, turning right down the rue Clotaire to confront the illustrious Panthéon. Walk down the gracious rue Soufflot.
Below the **rue Soufflot** are the ruins of a Roman forum.

Turn right down rue V Cousin, which leads to the rue de la Sorbonne, symbolic heart of French learning.
Pass **Ste.-Ursule-de-la-Sorbonne** (1642), where Richelieu is buried, before returning to the Cluny.

MUSEUM OF THE MIDDLE AGES
Between 1500 and 1843, when it became a museum of the Middle Ages, the Hôtel de Cluny housed the likes of Mary Tudor, widowed at 16 after a three-month marriage to Louis XII; James V of Scotland, and, in the 17th century, various cardinals including Mazarin.

►►► Cluny, Musée de (Musée du Moyen Age) *166A2*

6 place Paul Painlevé, 75005; tel: 01 53 73 78 00
Métros: Cluny-la-Sorbonne, Odéon, St.-Michel
Open: Wed–Mon 9:15–5:45. Admission: moderate

Once a pied-à-terre for a wealthy order of Benedictine monks from Cluny in Burgundy, the former Hôtel de Cluny stands on and beside Paris' oldest Roman baths, the ruins of which can still be seen on the corner of boulevard St.-Michel and the boulevard St.-Germain. Built between 1485 and 1500, the mansion is one of France's finest examples of domestic Gothic architecture. Sold off after the Revolution, in 1833 it entered the hands of art collector Alexandre du Sommerard, whose rich finds form the basis of the museum today.

Although 8,000 Renaissance works were recently transferred to the museum at the Château d'Ecouen, the Cluny vaults contain another 20,000 objects, rarely displayed. However, those that are visible are superb. From the mutilated heads of statues from Notre-Dame (more Revolutionary decapitation) unearthed in 1977 in a bank vault, to a series of 15th-century tapestries, to dazzling displays of jewelry, manuscripts, and stained glass, this is a collection of inspiration.

MUSEE DE CLUNY

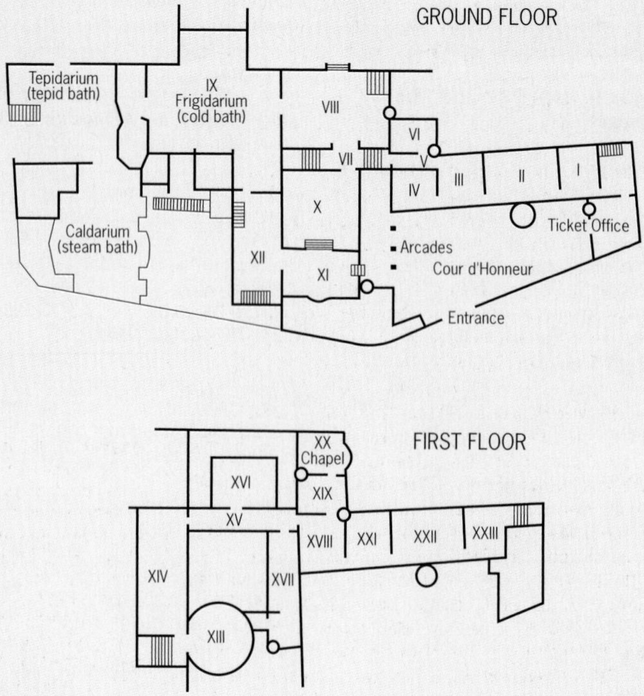

La famille Jouvenel des Ursins *(1445–1449), one of the tapestries in the Musée de Cluny—indisputably one of the finest collections of medieval art and crafts in the world*

Roman baths On the lower floor the late 2nd-century baths are a reminder of the sheer strength of Roman architecture. The vaulted ceiling of the Frigidarium (cold bath) rises over 46 feet with 21-foot-thick walls. In one corner stands the *Pilier des nautes*, Paris' oldest sculpture. Leading off from here, a vast network of Roman vaults has recently been restored and can be toured.

Back on the first floor, you enter the museum via displays of medieval costume and accessories (including 14th-century winklepickers), Byzantine, Coptic and European textiles, and a series of tapestries. One series, *La Vie Seigneuriale*, shows the life of a noble household.

On the second floor a rotunda-shaped room houses one of the museum's great splendors, the six allegorical tapestries of *La Dame à la Licorne*. Exquisitely woven, probably in the southern Netherlands for the Lyonnais family of Le Viste, their delicate tones represent flora and fauna as a graceful background to the central feminine figure. Each tapestry shows her acting out a sense—sight, touch, smell, taste, sound—while the enigmatic sixth work presents her in front of the motto *A mon seul désir* (to my only desire). Is this freedom from the senses or mastery of all five? Your guess is as good as anybody's over the last five centuries.

Jewels and crowns Room XVI presents a treasure trove of goldwork and jewelry: Gallic, Barbarian, and Merovingian examples include belts, buckles, bracelets, the sublimely fashioned "Rose d'Or,' six Visigoth crowns and two 13th-century double gold crosses.

Apart from the stained-glass windows removed from Ste. Chapelle and St. Denis, the most striking church relic is the glittering gold altar frontal (1015) from Basel cathedral, made for the Emperor Heinrich II (Room 9).

At the back of the top floor don't miss the Abbot's Chapel with its flamboyant vaulting fanning out from a central pillar. Twelve niches contain statues of the Amboise family (Jacques Amboise rebuilt the mansion in 1500) and tapestries depicting the life of St. Stephen carry on into adjoining rooms.

MISTAKEN IDENTITY

The 21 mutilated heads from Notre-Dame, displayed in Room VIII, actually represented kings of Judea and Israel, but were assumed by the stampeding revolutionary mob to be kings of France—hence their sorry fate. These 13th-century heads, all without noses, were discovered during excavations at the Hôtel Moreau in 1977.

THE GUILLOTINE
The guillotine is not such an anachronism: it was last used in 1977, after nearly 200 years of loyal service and capital punishment was abolished in 1981.

► Collections Historiques de la Préfecture de Police, Musée des 166B2

1 bis rue des Carmes, 75005; tel: 01 44 41 52 50
Métro: Maubert-Mutualité
Open: Mon–Fri 9–5; Sat 10–5. Admission free

If you feel like checking out Charlotte Corday's statement about murdering Marat in his bathtub, this is where to go. Situated at the back of the *commissariat* (police station) in the 5th *arrondissement*, this macaber little collection of exhibits covers many of Paris' great criminal moments from the 16th century to the present day. A particularly graphic representation shows the ghastly punishment meted out to the murderer of the Duc de Guise in 1563: he was tied to four horses and quartered. Other niceties include orders for the arrest of Docteur Guillotin in 1795 and a book splattered with the bloodstains of the assassinated President Paul Doumer. An array of weapons runs the gamut of knuckledusters, garrottes (strangling cords), variously concealed knives (one in a lady's fan), and a guillotine blade.

The Théâtre Français – home of the Comédie Française, founded in 1680, and still Paris' most famous national theater company

► Comédie Française 50C3

2 rue de Richelieu, 75001
Métro: Palais-Royal

A monument to French classical theater, the building named the Théâtre Français is actually a 1900 remodeling job of the original 1790 Doric-style edifice, mostly destroyed in a fire. It has been home since 1799 to the Comédie Française company, founded by Louis XIV in 1680 with members of Molière's troupe. The playwright himself died on stage seven years earlier while performing in *Le Malade Imaginaire*; the armchair which cushioned his fall when illness struck can still be seen in the foyer along with busts and statues of dramatists: Carpeaux's Dumas, Rodin's Mirabeau, Clésinger's Georges Sand, and Houdon's sedentary Voltaire. Although the basic repertoire of the Comédie-Française remains a string of Molière, Racine, Corneille, and Marivaux classics, a recently appointed director has opened up the field. And nobody will forget the spirit of Sarah Bernhardt, the great tragic actress who played many of her finest roles here.

Phone 01 44 58 15 15 for information on the rare guided tours.

AN INFAMOUS CRIMINAL
One of Paris' most celebrated murderers was the infamous Landru who recruited his victims through small advertisements suggesting marriage. He killed 11 women in total, using a gruesome assortment of weapons including a rolling pin and curling tongs. He was finally executed in 1922.

French furniture and objets d'art *are well illustrated by the rich collection at the Musée des Arts Décoratifs, whose 20th-century department is due to reopen by 2002 (see page 64). From the organic curves of art nouveau, French design moved effortlessly into a more sober art deco style that was exemplified by the Exposition Internationale des Arts Décoratifs in 1925.*

The great *couturier* **Poiret** bankrupted himself with his three converted barges decorated by Dufy; Parisian design then moved resolutely into geometric modernism. After **Dunand**, **Chareau**, **Ruhlmann,** and **Le Corbusier** the next French designer to open up a new style was **Jean Prouvé**, master of 1950s' curves.

New life After decades of remaining dormant, French design underwent a major renaissance in the 1980s. Stimulation came from the **Mobilier National**, which since 1964 had acted as an inspiring go-between for designers and furniture manufacturers and the newly created government agency **VIA**, which supported and promoted young designers. The VIA showroom, now in the **Viaduc des Arts** near Bastille, displays prototypes and manufactured items, all for sale, some more functional than others, though standards have dropped.

State style Design in the 1980s became such a cultural symbol that even the President commissioned new furnishings for the Elysée Palace, and some ministries have adopted a distinctly futuristic image. **Philippe Starck, Jean-Michel Wilmotte, Andrée Putman,** and **Garouste et Bonetti** are favorites in the official field, and their status is now firmly international, with Starck the uncontested leader. Another wave carries with it the names of **Martin Szekely, Sylvain Dubuisson, Olivier Gagnère, and Marie-Christine Dorner**. The **Galerie Néotu** (25 rue du Renard, 75004; tel: 01 42 78 96 97), which exhibits the latest in French design, was a precursor in this field.

For an overview of the current Parisian taste in furniture and object design, take a stroll along the rue du Bac, then dive into a network of streets (rue de Verneuil, rue de Lille, and the rue de Seine) to see examples of illustrations and antecedants.

Décor of the day To see examples of French design *in situ*, the most obvious relics of the 1980s in Paris are the interiors of the **Café Beaubourg** (see page 97) and **La Villa** (a hotel with a public bar and a jazz-club at No. 29 rue Jacob, 75006, designed by **Dorner**). The more classical **Café Marly** (at the Louvre) has retained its popularity into the new century.

A typically futuristic building in the design-conscious La Défense

Designs on the future? Although design is no longer the essential magic password that it became in the 1980s, its importance has smoothly infiltrated daily life—whether in sleekly renovated museums, dentists' waiting rooms, movie theaters, and industrial objects. And the appetite for new forms did not diminish with the turn of the century.

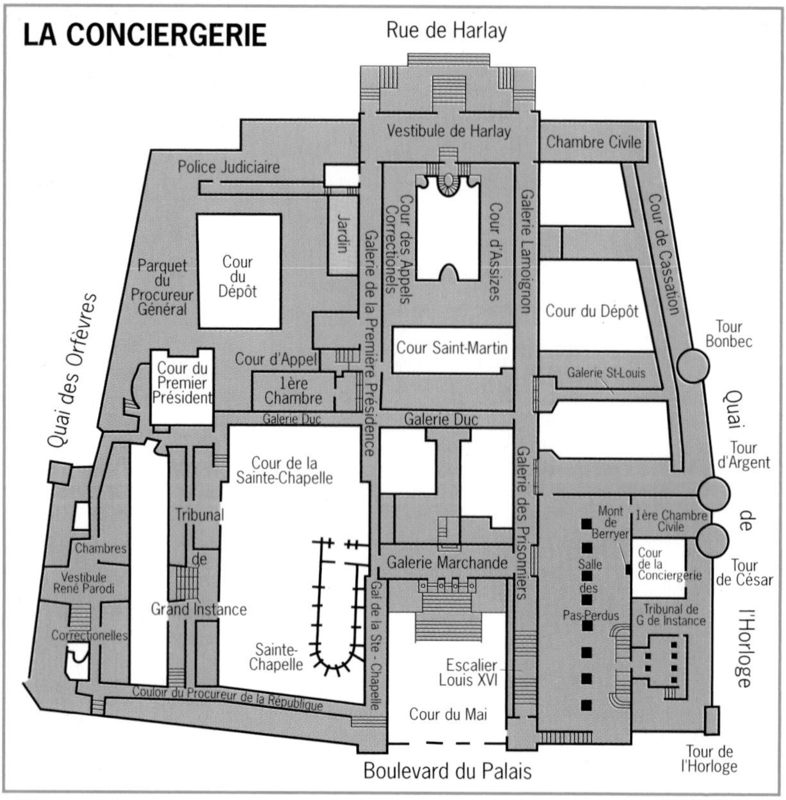

▶▶ Conciergerie, La *166B4*

1 quai de l'Horloge, 75001; tel: 01 53 73 78 50
Métros: Cité, Châtelet
Open: Apr–Sep, daily 9:30–6:30; Oct–Mar, 10–5; closed on national holidays. Admission: moderate; expensive for a combined ticket for the Conciergerie/Ste.-Chapelle

Rising above the roofs of the quai de l'Horloge on the Ile de la Cité, the twin towers of the Conciergerie struck horror into the hearts of thousands for over five centuries. Originally built to house Philippe-le-Bel's caretaker (concierge) and palace guards, by 1391 it was functioning as a prison and continued as such until 1914. Before entering, stop at the corner to look at the Tour de l'Horloge, which incorporates Paris' first public clock. Commissioned by Charles V in 1371, it is set against a constellation of gold fleur-de-lys; the surrounding sculptures of Law and Justice were added in the 16th century. A bell that rang for three days following the birth of any royal babe could not really toll for the Revolutionaries, so in 1793 a new silver bell was installed.

Grim history The prisons of the Conciergerie are best known for their hospitable role during the Revolution, although they had already housed and tortured thousands, including Ravaillac, murderer of Henri IV. During the Terror 4,164 citizens were held here, 2,278 of whom finished under the guillotine. The

"MADAME DEFICIT"
The Conciergerie's most celebrated inmate, Marie-Antoinette, was not France's most popular queen. Nicknamed "Madame Veto," "Madame Deficit" or simply "the Austrian," she was renowned for her extravagance. Her millinery bills alone would have kept an average French family for its entire life. Her favorite hairdresser, Léonard, once accomplished the dubious exploit of weaving 18 yards of ribbon into her hair. On her arrest in August 1792, legend goes that this same pampered hair turned grey overnight. The "simple" cell life had a disciplinary effect on her character and she behaved with dignity until her execution in October 1793.

best-remembered inmate is Marie-Antoinette, the extravagant Austrian wife of Louis XVI. Other guests included Charlotte Corday, Marat's assassin; Madame du Barry, mistress of Louis XV; and, when the tide turned, Danton and Robespierre.

Entrance is through the Salles des Gardes, a vaulted stone chamber plunged into shadow by the construction of the embankment outside the windows. This opens on to the equally gloomy Salle des Gens d'Armes, an astonishing hall measuring 230 feet by 88 feet. Said to be Europe's oldest surviving medieval hall, it was restored in the 19th century by Viollet-le-Duc. A spiral staircase at the back leads to the original kitchens. Four walk-in fireplaces big enough to roast a couple of sheep indicate the scale of medieval appetites.

Star-rated cells Back at the entrance to the Salle des Gens d'Armes, follow the rue de Paris, where less monied prisoners (*les pailleux*) snoozed on straw bedding. Three types of accommodations were available: the communal straw-strewn floor; a shared cell with beds; and for those with real pull and funds, a private cell complete with table for memoir writing. From this corridor you reach what was once the prison's most animated crossroads, the Galerie des Prisonniers, where lawyers, visitors, and prisoners came and went. On the left was the barber's cell, where inmates were shorn before their trip to the guillotine.

A narrow staircase leads up to displays of objects related to the Conciergerie's bloody history. The first musty room is the most striking: wall panels list all the 2,780 guillotined victims of the Revolution.

Downstairs you reach the Chapelle des Girondins, named after the 22 condemned Girondins (left-wing members of the 1791 Legislative Assembly) who celebrated their last night alive with true revelry here. What is now the altar was the site where Marie-Antoinette's cell formerly stood.

At the far end of the Galerie des Prisonniers, her cell has been re-created. None of its contents is authentic but the spartan furniture, peeling wallpaper and models of card-playing guards behind a screen give the sorry feel of Marie-Antoinette's last sojourn.

Floodlights now shine on to the grim facade of the Conciergerie

The city's first public clock, on the Tour de l'Horloge

DR. GUILLOTIN
Dr. Guillotin perfected his "philanthropic beheading machine" by trying it out on a miserable bunch of sheep in the courtyard of his home, No. 9, cour de Rohan.

THE OBELISK
The oldest monument in Paris, dating from the 13th century BC, was originally used as an astronomical instrument to measure the sunshadow in the Temple of Thebes. Dragged from the desert to the Nile, loaded onto a special barge and towed to Rouen by paddle steamer, it was then transported to Paris by French sailors and gunners. Its 19th-century pedestal illustrates the obelisk's remarkable journey.

The spacious, grandiose place de la Concorde, at the hub of Paris, is best viewed after rush hour

►►► Concorde, place de la *50B3*

Once a swamp, now Paris' largest square, throbbing with traffic and fumes, the Concorde was designed between 1755 and 1775 to accommodate an equestrian statue of the reigning king, Louis XV. It soon changed name and function when the guillotine was trundled out. As the place de la Révolution it saw over 1,300 heads roll, including Louis XVI, Marie-Antoinette, Danton, and Robespierre. The architect, Jacques-Ange Gabriel, also designed the two properties flanking the rue Royale, one of which survived the Revolution in the hands of the Comte de Crillon, and is now the **Hôtel Crillon**.

With the cooling of revolutionary passions in 1795 the square was renamed Concorde and soon acquired Coustou's *Chevaux de Marly* at the entrance to the Champs-Elysées. The next transformation came in 1833 under Louis-Philippe, when he was presented with a 75-foot-high, 3,000-year-old obelisk by Mohammed Ali, viceroy of Egypt (see page 158). Gabriel's eight stone pavilions, each topped by a statue depicting a French town in human guise, still remain.

►► Cour du Commerce St.-André (Cour de Rohan) *176C2*

59/61 rue St.-André-des-Arts, 75006
Métro: Odéon

A shopping mall with atmosphere and history: it seems to be a contradiction in terms. However, central Paris has 17 such places (see page 181) and the Cour du Commerce was the first. Built in 1776 on the site of a tennis court, it became a hive of revolutionary activity, with Marat printing his pamphlet *L'Ami du Peuple* at No. 8, Danton installed at No. 20, and the anatomy professor Dr. Guillotin at No. 9. At No. 4 you can see the remains of a 13th-century tower, part of the city wall, and the Renaissance courtyards of the Cour de Rohan are still picturesque. Today the passage houses a string of restaurants and tea-shops; it opens into the boulevard St.-Germain (at No. 130), opposite Danton's statue.

La Grande Arche, a window on new development in Paris, large enough to surround Notre Dame—the centerpiece of a striking, skyscraping business zone

►► La Défense *10A5*

RER: La Défense; tel: (La Grande Arche) 01 49 07 27 57
Admission: moderate

Paris' new 300,000-ton white marble symbol, La Grande Arche, is the western gateway to the capital and reigns over an urban development first mooted in the 1930s. World War II put a brake on all urbanistic projects, but by 1958 an astonishing edifice, the CNIT, had risen from the ground. Throughout the 1960s, wondrous and hideous architectural experiments sprouted in all directions, symbols of France's postwar mutation. Catastrophic in many cases, utopic in others, La Défense was intended as a new business and residential center. The oil crisis in 1973 slowed its momentum but had a positive effect too, forcing architects and developers to look more closely at what was fast becoming a nightmare knot of viaducts, tunnels, and unrelated forms.

Three successive Presidents examined three successive projects to complete *La Tête Défense* (head) and finally provide this labyrinth with a focal point. An unknown Danish architect, Otto Von Spreckelsen, was finally selected by Mitterrand to build his marble "window on the world," the disembowelled cube that has become La Grande Arche. Its symbolic measurements (100m by 100m) echo those of the Cour Carrée in the Louvre. Completed just in time for the Bicentenary celebrations in 1989, its unfortunate architect had by then abandoned the whole project in a huff and died before its inauguration.

The wide esplanade of La Défense has now assumed its own identity, with office workers happily lunching by the fountains or on café terraces. Numerous contemporary sculptures punctuate this concrete landscape, one of the most striking being François Morellet's *La Défonce*, a fine geometric construction which topples into the underground storerooms of the national contemporary art collection.

LA GRANDE ARCHE
Fast becoming a must on the tourist trail for its fantastic open-air panoramic views over Paris, La Grande Arche offers a ride to the roof in transparent shaftless lifts—vertigo sufferers beware! Beautifully designed galleries on the top floor house temporary exhibitions, as do the EPAD galleries buried beneath the forecourt outside (access to roof daily, 10–7).

Self-portrait, by Eugène Delacroix—one of a collection of paintings, drawings, letters, and photographs in his modest former studio

EUGENE DELACROIX
Although he yearned to be a pure classicist, Delacroix was the embodiment of romanticism. His wide knowledge of literature and his contact with the old masters of the Louvre gave him a rare imaginative breadth. The influence of classical legends and history is apparent in his early works: *Dante and Virgil crossing the Styx*, *Death of Sardanapalus*, *The Capture of Constantinople* (all at the Louvre). But it was a trip to Morocco in 1832 that left an indelible mark on his style, foreshadowing Impressionism. Prolific and talented in every field, from portraits to wild beasts, Delacroix was also an accomplished decorator; you can see his vigorous style in the Chapelle des Anges of St.-Sulpice or the royal salon and library at the Palais Bourbon.

►► Delacroix, Musée *176B2*

6 place Furstemberg, 75006; tel: 01 44 41 86 50
Métro: St.-Germain-des-Prés
Open: Wed–Mon 9:30–5. Admission: inexpensive

The apartment and studio where the great Romantic painter Eugène Delacroix (1798–1863) spent the last six years of his life is now a small but charming museum, freshly restored in 1991. The place Furstemberg has hardly changed over the last century and still has a provincial atmosphere, with its flowering trees and decorative streetlamps. Visiting this museum is more a chance to experience the calm and character of Delacroix's environment than to see his works, most of which are housed in the Louvre.

Personal effects The first of the three rooms was his bedroom and still contains some furniture, as well as his treasured tobacco pot. The dining room displays his intricate painting table and the central salon his desk. Other memorabilia, etchings, sketches, watercolors, and letters are displayed throughout, but look out particularly for a recently acquired painting, *La Madeleine au désert*. Delacroix manages in this compelling image to convey the enigmatic strength and aura of the saint with a typically luminous yet ambiguous treatment.

Continue outside down a wrought-iron staircase and across a tiny garden to Delacroix's studio, which he had built himself. The studio is a fairly ordinary building, though decorated with neoclassical bas-reliefs, and contains more studies, sketches, and a portrait of his redoubtable mistress, Jenny Le Guillou, who scared many a friend from his door in his later years. Lithography stones used to print his edition of *Hamlet* are presented, along with paintings by his disciples Riesener and Andrieu.

In recent years, a more liberal state approach has allowed "Gay Paris" to abandon its once outrageous self-assertive stance and to become a natural part of the urban landscape. Encouraged by a governmental decision in 1981 to destroy secret-service files on homosexuals, and by the lowering of the legal age for homosexual activity to 16, the gay population of Paris acquired a new identity virtually overnight and has now been assimilated into French society.

The headquarters of the gay community moved from the rather sleazy rue Ste.-Anne to the gentrified Marais *quartier*.

Since then, despite the tragic effect of A.I.D.S., Europe's first gay radio station, Radio FG (98.2FM), is still going strong and an exuberant Gay Pride Parade is held in Paris every June.

Changing attitudes A.I.D.S. has had an enormous influence on attitudes to gay and heterosexual life. Greater Paris has a population roughly equivalent to that of Greater London but has twice as many A.I.D.S. cases. Unlike the U.S., where cruising areas, saunas, and sex clubs were closed down, Paris has reacted more moderately, trying instead to change sexual behavior slowly, without putting a stop to it. However, the closing in 1992 of the Bois de Boulogne, known for the nocturnal sexual activities that took place within it, was a sign of major changes to come.

Areas known as gay meeting places include the Tuileries esplanade, overlooking the Seine, the riverbank opposite the Musée d'Orsay in the summer months, and the shady tranquility of the Père Lachaise cemetery. Sunday afternoon dancing at *Le Palace*, a decade-old tradition, attracts hundreds of men (3 cité Bergère. *Open* 5–10); while for other days of the week the hotspot is *Queen*, a predominantly gay disco accepting women, with extravagant theme parties, Seventies disco on Mondays and house music on other nights (102 avenue des Champs-Elysées, open from midnight). For a more low-key evening, Le Central's bar and coffee-house in the Marais have become the epicenter (corner of rue Vieille-du-Temple and rue Ste.-Croix-de-la Brétonnerie). From here it is a stone's throw to popular bars such as the Skeud (35 Ste.-Croix-de-la-Brétonnerie), and the very congested Le Quetzal (10 rue de la Verrerie).

An advice and information service in English is offered by FACTS-line (tel: 01 44 93 16 69) on Monday, Wednesday and Friday, 6–10 PM.

New legislation gives gay couples in France fiscal equality with heterosexuals

The "Queen of Paris" offers one of the most breathtaking views of the city, from its 905-foot viewing platform, and one of Paris' "top" restaurants

TEMPTING FATE

The Eiffel Tower has inspired much idiosyncratic behavior. Those who have plummeted from its peak include a moustachioed Icarus who, in 1912, plunged to his death when his wings failed to open. He turned out to be a bankrupt tailor escaping from his debtors. In 1928 a watchmaker tried out a new parachute—too innovative: it didn't open either and he rapidly met his maker. A luckier performer cycled down the steps from top to bottom to win a bet, survived, but was arrested for provocative behavior.

▶▶▶ Eiffel, Tour *50A3*

Tel: 01 44 11 23 23
Métro: Bir-Hakeim; RER: Champ de Mars
Open: daily 9:30–11; Jul–Aug, 9–midnight.
Admission: inexpensive

A "hollow chandelier," "staircase to infinity," "tower of Babel," or "aviary of the world," monstrosity or hallowed symbol of Paris, the Eiffel Tower has run the gamut of descriptions in its 100 odd years of existence. Built in a record two years by Gustave Eiffel for the 1889 Universal Exhibition, celebrating the French Revolution centenary, it was intended for demolition 20 years later. But by then it had as many artistic and intellectual fans as it had opponents when built, and it was saved for the utilitarian purposes of its broadcasting antennae. Thus the instincts of writers and artists such as Apollinaire, Dufy, Delaunay, Utrillo, and Pissarro were vindicated and the scandalized agonies of Garnier, Verlaine, Leconte de Lisle, Maupassant, and Zola relegated to history.

Standing a regal 985 feet high, weighing over 7,000 tons and composed of 15,000 iron parts, the "Queen of Paris" (*dixit* Cocteau) sways no more than 5 inches in high winds and shrinks or grows 6 inches according to temperature. For 40 years it remained the highest structure in the world until New York's Chrysler building usurped the title, although it acquired a further 65 feet in height in 1957 when television antennae were added to existing radio, telegraph, and meteorological apparatus. Mountaineers have scaled it, pilots have tried to fly through its pillars and in 1909 the Comte de Lambert circled 300 feet above it in a flying machine.

Public spectacle About four million people visit this extraordinary construction annually, so be prepared for a long wait at the lifts. Go to the fourth floor (at 905 feet) for Paris' most spectacular view which, on a clear day, can extend to 42 miles. Hardier folk can attempt the steps in the south pillar which lead up to the first and second platforms (respectively at 185 feet and 115 yards). Above all don't dismiss its nocturnal transformation. Even if you are not dining in one of the Tower's two restaurants, go to the top for a glittering visual feast or at least pass close by for an unforgettable vision of the 292,000-watt interior lighting system, illuminating the intricate structure against the night sky.

Towering figure The engineer Gustave Eiffel kept an office in his Tower until his death in 1923. Although this was the ultimate symbol of his skill and imagination, Eiffel left hundreds of other constructions all over the world. Born in 1832 in Burgundy of German stock, he was already working on the famous Bordeaux bridge at the age of 26.

Bridges soon became his specialty: iron and the hydraulic methods he used for installing their supports helped to build his reputation. Factories, churches, a synagogue (rue des Tournelles), shops (Le Bon Marché), banks and, over a period of 18 years, 31 railway viaducts and 17 major bridges all came within his creative sphere. Egypt, Peru, Portugal, Hungary, Bolivia, and Indo-China all have their Eiffel monuments, while the U.S. has its 150-feet-tall Statue of Liberty—a mere stripling beside the Tower.

Constructive contributions When his wife died at a young age in 1877 Eiffel threw himself heart and soul into his work, never remarrying. Shortly before the Tower commission he was involved in an imbroglio over the Suez Canal and was sued for not respecting a deadline. He untied himself from these potentially uncomfortable knots with the help of fellow Freemasons, a powerful pressure group in those days. After his masterwork was built he continued to produce marvels of engineering and contributed constructions to the 1900 Universal Exhibition. With the saving of the Tower from demolition in 1910, Gustave Eiffel must have been a satisfied man when he died at 91.

Gustave Eiffel—the bridge engineer who startled the world with his Eiffel Tower in 1889

HIGH-JUMP
Three hundred and eighty suicide victims chose this edifice to end their days. Protective shields, finally installed in 1971 on every outdoor platform, put an end to this tragic spin-off.

THE MAGICIAN OF IRON
The Eiffel Tower was without a doubt the pinnacle of Gustave Eiffel's lifetime achievements, for which he was nicknamed "magician of iron." He also used the tower for numerous aerodynamic experiments, working from Auteuil where he built the first aerodynamic laboratory.

► l'Elysée, Palais de *50B3*

55–57 rue du Faubourg St.-Honoré, 75008
Métro: Miromesnil, Champs-Elysées-Clemenceau
Not open to the public

This sumptuous residence has housed French presidents for over a century. Built in 1718, it was greatly altered in 1753 to suit the extravagant tastes of Madame de Pompadour. A radical volte-face came with the Revolution, when the Elysée turned into a public entertainment park, but under Napoleon it reverted to being a private residence—first for his sister, then for his wife Joséphine. Various other notables, including Wellington, Napoléon III (before becoming Emperor), and Queen Victoria, passed through its courtyard, garden, and grand staircase before 1873, when it assumed its role as the President's official residence.

Already greatly modified, modernized and enlarged, the Elysée continues to undergo the decorative whims of each President. Agam's pop-art works, commissioned by Pompidou, have since been moved to the Musée d'Art Moderne. Valéry Giscard d'Estaing left his mark above all for inviting in the local street cleaners for a chat on his return from a radical night out, and Mitterrand had many of the salon ceilings painted in a neoclassical style by Gérard Garouste.

Palais de l'Elysée, official residence of presidents since 1873 and the decision-making center of French politics. The French Government meets here every Wednesday

A hidden corner in one of the courtyards of the Faubourg St.-Honoré, one of many reminders of bygone centuries here

► Espace Montmartre-Salvador Dali *148C2*

11 rue Poulbot, 75018; tel: 01 42 64 40 10
Métro: Abbesses
Open: daily 10–6. Admission: moderate
The 1,200-square-yard black-walled surrealist interior of the Espace Montmartre is a fitting backdrop for over 300 of Dali's works (mainly sculptures and illustrations), some never seen in France before this fittingly weird exhibition opened in 1991.

► Faubourgs

Inextricably linked with the urban development of Paris, the faubourgs still possess an identity of their own. Faubourg means "fake borough" and refers to the extension of inner streets beyond specific city boundaries. Paris' first suburbs have been integrated into the fabric of the city center for centuries yet the word still has a pejorative ring: "he was born in the faubourgs" implies that someone's origins are not the most sophisticated. The queen of the faubourgs, Edith Piaf, nevertheless built her career on her modest beginnings in **Belleville**, making the faubourg accent chic in itself. Ironically the oldest faubourg, the **Faubourg St.-Honoré**, which extended the central rue St.-Honoré, is now the hub of Parisian wealth while the **Faubourg St.-Germain** area is a haven for the discreet residences of the bourgeoisie.

Historically the **Faubourg St.-Antoine**, running east from the Bastille to the place de la Nation, is "the crater from which revolutionary lava escaped most often." Today, more peaceful in spirit, its identity is still linked with the crafts of its former artisans.

The real atmosphere of the faubourgs is found in the area between the **Faubourgs Montmartre** and **Poissonière**. From the *grands boulevards*, the Faubourg Montmartre winds uphill toward Pigalle and Montmartre, carrying in its wake a colorful string of bars and cheap restaurants. Boasting some fine mansions but lacking in major sites, it is mistakenly overlooked by many visitors to Paris.

LE GENERAL
A caricaturist's delight, with his towering height and unmistakable nose, Charles de Gaulle was to some a hero, to others a tyrant: without doubt he was a unique and outspoken French President. His escape to London in World War II and organization of the Free French movement made him a symbol of liberty, but after the war he fell from political favor. De Gaulle's comeback in 1958 led to a new constitution and strengthened presidency. Age and narrow-mindedness brought his downfall; three years after the student riots and general strikes of 1968 he died at his home in Colombey-les-Deux-Eglises.

There's no better place than Paris to play at being a jetsetter. Steeped in a tradition of ostentation, its temples of pretension and luxury are legion. An important feature of the Parisian psyche is the ability to flaunt style which is often but not always necessarily linked with wealth. A fine line divides the B.C.B.G. (traditional chic) from the flashier and sometimes more imaginative displays of new money, but for outsiders this is not an essential factor. However a thick wad of 500 franc notes or a collection of credit cards is.

"SLOANES" IN PARIS
Although a recently coined term, B.C.B.G. (*bon chic, bon genre*) has firmly stuck as a label for the Parisian equivalent of London's "Sloane Rangers." Its subjects hide out in the prosperous 16th *arrondissement.* Passy and Neuilly shelter hordes of this well-groomed species clad in finely cut gray or navy suits (both sexes) and a touch of flamboyance symbolized by a Hermès scarf. Sleek discretion is the key. Weekend golf is the pastime.

Eating Glamorous gastronomy is no mean affair in Paris and the moment you enter the three- and four-toque category of the Frenchman's bible, the *Gault Millau*, you are guaranteed not only an elegant setting and sublime victuals, but also a sophisticated array of dining companions. Try the historic monuments, such as **Lucas-Carton, Le Grand Véfour, La Tour d'Argent, Taillevent**, and **Ledoyen**. Allow yourself to be pampered by sycophantic waiters and relax in sensual comfort. And for the grand panacea of Parisian cuisine, book a table (months ahead) at **Pierre Gagnaire**, where the roasted sweetbreads with fondue of chicory will guarantee your elitist election to paradise.

Drinking Whatever your liquid tastes, Paris will provide the appropriate watering-niche, from discreet *salons de thé* to shadowy nocturnal haunts. For the most elegant of breakfasts or teas, head for **Ladurée** in the rue Royale, where you'll wade through carrier bags marked Lanvin or Chanel to get to a table. Savor the coffee while enjoying the ceiling fresco of a cherubic pastry chef. In the nearby rue de Rivoli reigns the historic **Angélina's**, also straight out of the Belle Epoque, as are some of its regulars. As day turns to night head for **Le Forum** in the boulevard Malesherbes, where one of their 150 cocktails should put you in the right mood, failing which carry on to the bar of the **Hôtel George V**, where the champagne concoctions make up for the height of the bar stools. Still thirsty after midnight and on the Left Bank? Then go to Montparnasse's media mecca, **La Closerie des Lilas**, where tinkling piano music, polished wood, and a long history of illustrious drinkers generate a special aura.

Shopping For chic shopping stick to the Faubourg St.-Honoré, rue Royale, place Vendôme, and rue de la Paix. Have a shirt made to measure at **Charvet**, shoes at **Hermès** (by London bootmaker John Lobb), pick up a watch at **Van Cleef & Arpels**, indulge in a new haircut at **Carita's**, then stop for a snack at **Caviar Kaspia**. Short on household goods? **Lalique** in the rue Royale will supply a nice range of frosted crystal and **Christofle**, across the street, has the lobster forks. Need some new asparagus dishes? Then head

Hermès is an essential part of the B.C.B.G. look. Hermès window displays are considered to be among the world's finest

toward the place de la Madeleine where **Fauchon** is a haven for B.C.B.G. gourmets.

Sleeping For one of the world's best siestas go to the sparkling **Crillon** and stretch out in a spacious suite with its terraced view over the Concorde. Or book in at Paris' first "grand hotel," the gilded and chandeliered **Meurice**, which dates from 1815. Then try the **Raphaël** on the avenue Kléber for a quick transposition to a country château atmosphere, increasingly appreciated by the movie world. Or join the *crème de la crème* and ghosts of Proust and Chanel at the eternal **Ritz**.

Walking For a glamorous stroll you can strike off the Champs-Elysées. Instead, keep to the streets of stylish shopping (above) or, for more bucolic surroundings, the shady paths of the **Parc Monceau**.

Dancing If you can talk your way in (no mean achievement), **Castel's** and **Villa Barclay** remain Paris' glossiest nightspots, where a moneyed international set rubs shoulders on the dance floors. Or join the jetsetting business executives and top models at **Les Bains** on the rue du Bourg-l'Abbé, 75003.

PARC MONCEAU
At the heart of one of the wealthiest areas of Paris, surrounded by magnificent mansions, lies the exquisite late-18th century Parc Monceau, designed in the picturesque English style by Thomas Blaikie. The park offers a welcome respite from the rush of city life, scattered with interesting follies, grottoes, six Belle Epoque monuments dedicated to prominent French writers and musicians, and a delightful lake.

Fashionable drinking at Angélina's, one of the oldest salons de thé, *famous for its almond-coated croissants*

Paris is not solely reserved for the rich and famous, as many an impoverished writer or artist has found out. Its easy-going cafés make ideal focal points for struggling creators of all sorts and visitors on extra-low budgets. And you don't have to sleep under the bridges to survive.

TIPS FOR DRINKERS
For drinks and snacks remember that prices are almost 50 percent cheaper if you stand at the bar. Beer drinkers should ask for *une pression* or *un demi,* signifying draught beer, as opposed to the pricier bottled variety. *Café au lait,* or *café crème* and tea are big money spinners—try to convert to black coffee, *un café,* the cheapest possible beverage.

A typical backstreet brasserie with its small tables and chairs overflowing onto the sidewalks makes an ideal venue for a reasonably priced lunch

Locomotion Much of central Paris can be covered on foot but there are moments when a *métro* or bus ride is unavoidable—and welcome. Make sure you use either a *carnet* of 10 tickets (valid for all transportation within Paris) or a weekly card, a better deal than the tourist-oriented *Paris Visite,* which provides unlimited transportation for three or five days. If you're really dug in, buy a *carte orange,* which whisks you around for a month. All season tickets are available at *métro* stations and are pretty reasonable for a reliable and efficient service.

Accommodations Give the faubourgs a go! Enjoy the colorful life of a less central *quartier,* hang out in local cafés, sample its bistros and markets and you'll save yourself the price of a few more nights. One- and two-star hotels beyond the Bastille, around République, the Faubourg Montmartre or the Gare de l'Est, deep in Montparnasse or as far south as Chinatown, will come up with some surprisingly acceptable accommodations at (relatively) low prices.

Gastronomic survival If you're not developing the baguette-saucisson-and-cheap-plonk-in-the-hotel-bedroom technique, there are plenty of bistros that will supply you

with a copious feed for 60 francs or so. Lunchtime fixed menus, even in smarter areas, are invariably excellent value, as are the *plats du jour* in cafés and brasseries. Forget mineral water and order a free *carafe d'eau* or drink wine by the *pichet.*

Evening feeds prove more difficult, but not insoluble. Although much frequented by tourists, **Chartier** and its lesser known sibling, **Drouot,** provide good basic fare in extraordinary settings—but get there early. In the fifth *arrondissement* a multitude of Greek, Italian, Vietnamese, and even French restaurants (try the Bistrot de la Sorbonne) cater for a vast student population. Head up the steep rue des Boulangers where you can take your pick from a handful of bustling bistros. Alternatively, continue uphill to the rue Mouffetard, still a favorite despite being under touristic siege for a decade or so, and stop at **Le Pavé aux Herbes** for taramasalata and brochette.

In the sixth *arrondissement* there is no shortage either: at the **Polidor** you eat with the spirits of Verlaine and James Joyce, while **Le Petit Saint-Benoît** offers bland but ancient décor and solid French cuisine. The popular **Restaurant des Beaux Arts** is substantial and always fun. Off St.-Germain, the narrow rue Grégoire de Tours has a string of low-priced Greek and Italian haunts close to the action and you can't go wrong for atmosphere and budget if you dive into the hub of streets surrounding the rue de la Huchette: the odors of shish kebab announce an irresistible menu.

Don't forget Chinatown, in the 13th *arrondissement,* which feeds millions at low rates, while Belleville and La Goutte d'Or, although far from the madding crowd, have an insurpassable mixture of Oriental, Arab, and African restaurants, all very reasonable. Couscous makes an excellent cheap and balanced diet wherever you are in Paris.

Culture Entrance fees to museums mount up, so it may be worth investing in a *carte musées–monuments*, valid for one, three, or five consecutive days and providing unlimited entry to all monuments and museums, as well as avoiding the lines.

Otherwise Sundays, although sometimes crowded, are often half-price and in some cases free. Don't forget that private art galleries cost nothing (see pages 66–68), Parisian architecture and views are free and street artists provide itinerant amusement.

Shopping Apart from the flea markets, Paris has a good line in cheap supermarkets and stores such as **Prisunic** and **Monoprix**, where you can pick up household gadgets or fashion accessories for unbeatable prices. Fashion victims should seek out the *dépôt-vente* stores, where little-worn designer and *couture* gear is sold at a fraction of its original price.

Then there are the ubiquitous **Tati** branches (boulevard Rochechouart, rue de Rennes, République, and rue du Faubourg du Temple), where, if you fight through the crowds of concierges, you can kit yourself out for derisory amounts, although no one's guaranteeing the quality.

ETHNIC EATING

The very best in ethnic food in Paris can be found in restaurants, with cuisine from France's former colonies, in particular Vietnam and North Africa. North African restaurants serve delicious, spicy dishes, including couscous. The main area is Belleville, which abounds with small, inexpensive restaurants. For the best in Vietnamese and Chinese food, head for Chinatown in the 13th *arrondissement.*

For the cheapest lunch in Paris, look out for the many stands selling freshly-baked croissants, croque-monsieurs and crusty baguettes

Folies Bergère

The Folies Bergère, the oldest and best-known music hall in Paris, has recently turned to musical comedies such as Fame

GOBELINS TAPESTRY CENTER
Over 5,000 tapestries have been woven at the Manufacture des Gobelins, using a palette of almost 15,000 colors and including designs by Poussin, Boucher, Gromaire, Picasso, and Matisse.

ROYAL TAPESTRIES
When Jean Gobelin, discovered the secret of making a scarlet dye and founded a small family business in 1440, he would never have imagined that two centuries later it would develop into the royal tapestry centre. Today the internationally-renowned factory is government owned with every item commissioned by the state. It is possible to watch the weavers only in natural light as artificial illumination changes the appearance of the colours.

► Folies Bergère — 51D4

32 rue Richer, 75009; tel: 01 44 79 98 98
Métro: Cadet, Le Peletier Rue Montmartre

Tacky it may be, but the Folies Bergère still stands after 125 years. Its bar has been immortalized on canvas by Manet, and this was where the likes of Mistinguette and Josephine Baker thrilled the audiences of les *années folles*, while the acrobatic Tiller Girls swung along astride their merry-go-round horses under its dome. The Folies Bergère has today renounced its century-old vocation and is no longer a cabaret. Feathers, bare breasts, and sequins are a thing of the past, which only the name now evokes. However, traditions die hard and it continues to offer its customers the possibility of dining before the show, a popular musical comedy usually running for several weeks.

► Fondation Cartier — 152C1

261 boulevard Raspail, 75014; tel: 01 42 18 56 50
Métro: Raspail
Open: daily except Mon 12–8; Thur 12–10. Admission: moderate

Ten years ago the Fondation Cartier (of jewelry and watches fame) began an interesting experiment in corporate sponsorship by creating a sculpture park and contemporary art exhibition center in a lush park at Jouy-en-Josas. In spring 1994 it took up residence in central Paris on the former site of the American Center. Its new building is the work of the architect Jean Nouvel (famed for the Institut du Monde Arabe). Huge glass windows open on to a garden landscaped by artist Lothar Baumgarten, making nature over-obtrusive for the first-floor exhibitions. In the garden itself a small amphitheater offers dance and theater performances.

►► Fontaine des Innocents — 51D3

square des Innocents, 75001
Métro: Châtelet, Les Halles

Sheets of water have gushed down three sides of this

superb Renaissance fountain designed by Pierre Lescot and sculpted by Jean Goujon since it was erected in 1550. Now the focus of attention for the cruisers and bruisers of Les Halles, for centuries this square was the site of a cemetery, as well as being a meeting place for the food merchants of Les Halles. In 1786, when not much available soil was left, it was decided to transfer the two million or so rotting skeletons to the Catacombes (see page 91). The fountain, originally on the corner of the rue St.-Denis, was then shifted to its present central site and acquired its fourth side, carved by Pajou.

Jean Goujon's 16th-century Fontaine des Innocents

Fontainebleau see pages 198–199

▶ Furstemberg, place de *176B2/C2*

Métro: St.-Germain

Once the *cour d'honneur* of the abbot of St.-Germain's palace and named after Cardinal Furstemberg, who rebuilt it in 1699, this little square embodies everyone's dreams of Paris in the spring. Blessed with four generous, perfumed magnolia trees, and an unaffected architectural harmony, it makes a balmy evening's favorite for musicians and promenading couples. The corner houses at Nos 6 and 8, which include Delacroix's former apartment and studio, were once the palace stables.

Giverny see pages 200–121

▶ Gobelins, Manufacture des *51D1*

42 avenue des Gobelins, 75013; tel: 01 44 61 21 69
Métro: Les Gobelins.
Guided tours: Tue, Wed, Thu at 2 and 2:45.
Admission: moderate

This has been the official tapestry factory since the heyday of Louis XIV. Originally a dyeworks set up by the Gobelin brothers, then taken over by Flemish weavers, it soon attracted royal attention through the eyes of Colbert, Louis XIV's astute minister. By 1662 it became the royal tapestry center and rapidly expanded to include furniture and carpet workshops. Much of the interior decoration of Versailles was woven, carved, or inlaid here and even Marie-Antoinette deigned to visit the workshops. You can still see the centuries-old looms clicking away today, guided by expert weavers, who start training aged 16. The informative one-and-a-half hour guided tour also takes in the famous Savonnerie carpet workshops.

▶ Goutte d'Or *51D4*

Métro: Barbès-Rochechouart

Immediately east of Pigalle (west of Gare du Nord), the poetic-sounding Goutte d'Or (Drop of Gold) is a hive of cosmopolitan activity, where Arabs and Africans live, shop, lunch, dine, and hang out in an atmosphere straight out of Algiers or Abidjan. As with Belleville, the property developers are moving in fast, while the city council is working hard at "cleaning up" an area also notorious for drug dealers and squatters. If you're seeking a friendly, low-priced couscous joint, go there

A SUDDEN DEATH

One sunny day in 1610 Henri IV, traveling along the rue des Innocents, requested the coach's leather hood be lowered, despite earlier warnings from an astrologer that he would die that day. As he entered rue de la Ferronnerie a fanatic called Ravaillac stabbed Henri and he died later that day.

Shedding its light across the river: the Grand Palais' massive roof, designed by Charles Girault

on a summer evening when the locals congregate on doorsteps. This is not chic Paris and unfortunately it won't last.

►► Grand Palais 50B3

avenue Winston-Churchill, 75008 (entrance: avenue du Général Eisenhower); tel: 01 44 13 17 17
Métro: Champs-Elysées–Clémenceau
Open: Wed 10–10; Thu–Mon 10–8. Admission: moderate

Its soaring iron and glass domes visible from far along the river, the Grand Palais is another example of ambitious turn-of-the-century architecture. Built, together with the Petit Palais opposite, for the 1900 Universal Exhibition, it has since hosted hundreds of temporary fairs and art salons. Its west wing, which opens on to the avenue Franklin-Roosevelt, houses the Palais de la Découverte (*Open* Tue–Sat 9:30–6; Sun 10–7), a well-organized science museum with superb planetarium. The main halls on the east side, covering an area of 6,000 square yards, exhibit prestigious art retrospectives.

► Grand Véfour, Le 50C3

17 rue de Beaujolais, 75001; tel: 01 42 96 56 27
Métro: Palais-Royal, Pyramides

Ornately mirrored, gilded, and painted, the restaurant Le Grand Véfour is a living historic monument. Peep through the windows at its Restoration painted ceiling and glass-protected dancing walls: it is a seductive delight. Nestling in a neoclassical colonnade since the late 18th century, when the Palais-Royal was the heart of Parisian intellectual life, Le Grand Véfour has seen diners such as Napoleon, Victor Hugo, and Colette (who lived upstairs).

LES HALLES
Les Halles has seen better days. After only 25 years, the Forum has lost its luster, apart from a few picturesque enclaves like the rue Montorgueil and lively restaurants like Au Pied de Cochon and La Poule au Pot.

► Grévin, Musée 50C4

10 boulevard Montmartre, 75009; tel: 01 47 70 87 99
Métro: rue Montmartre
Open: daily 1–6 (school holidays 10–7). Admission: expensive

Founded in 1882 by a caricaturist, the Musée Grévin is the Parisian answer to London's Madame Tussaud's. Throngs of immobile figures beckon you through the city's history and plenty of blood and gore is assured in the Revolution section. Elsewhere, rock and movie stars are aligned with Presidents, artists and a myriad of other celebrities. Famous events are vividly recreated and there is a hall of mirrors and an area devoted to magic.

►►► Guimet, Musée (Musée Nationale d'Arts Asiatiques Guimet) *50A3*

6 place d'Iéna, 75016; tel: 01 56 52 53 00
Métro: Iéna, Boissière. Admission: moderate
This superb museum exhibits a remarkable display of Oriental antiquities, built up from the industrialist Emile Guimet's 1879 collection. Much of the Louvre's Asiatic department has been transferred here to widen the panorama of sculptures, carvings, paintings, and artifacts from Indo-China, China, Japan, Tibet, Afghanistan, Pakistan, and India.

Particularly stunning is the collection of Khmer art, which includes serene stone buddhas and Hindu gods (6th- to 12th-century) and the richly painted Tibetan and Nepalese tankas and intricate inlaid silverwork.

The Indian department includes early Mathura and Amarâvati carvings, south-Indian bronze deities and Moghul and Rajput miniatures. A rich Chinese department includes the Calmann collection, a wide-ranging display of porcelain. The museum has recently been closed for renovation. However, both China and Japan are also represented in a separate collection at the museum annexe (19 avenue d'Iéna), Le Panthéon Bouddhique (*Open* Wed–Mon 9:45–6), where buddhas of all periods, media, and sizes meditate for eternity.

►► Les Halles *51D3*

Métro: Les Halles
RER: Châtelet–Les Halles
The "belly of Paris" (*dixit*, Emile Zola) has undergone multiple transformations since the great days of the food market which started around 1100. Neatly delineated by the rue Beaubourg in the east, the rue du Louvre in the west, the northern rue Réaumur and southern rue de Rivoli, Les Halles functioned as a market until 1969. The grocers and butchers were then moved out to the suburb of Rungis and their superb 1860s Baltard pavilions were demolished (only one was preserved, now installed at Nogent-sur-Marne).

It took the city council and government ten years of wrangling to decide how to fill the gaping hole: although the result is aesthetically disastrous, Les Halles temporarily recovered its role as a central commercial and social hub. Venture below ground into the **Forum** (tel: 01 45 08 07 18) for shopping, movie theaters, swimming, billiards, videos, or concerts. Stay above ground for basic food and drink, hustlers, street-artists *et al*. The traditional 5 AM onion soup can still be consumed at **Au Pied de Cochon** but your fellow-suppers will be tourists, not market vendors. Yet a wander through the surrounding streets throws up atmospheric bars and restaurants which haven't changed for a century.

► Hammam *51D1*

La Mosquée, 19/39 rue Geoffroy-St-Hilaire, 75005
tel: 01 45 35 97 33. Métro: Censier–Daubenton
Open for women: Mon, Wed, Thu, Sat; for men: Fri, Sun
Admission: inexpensive to moderate
Sick of Parisian chic or lowlife? Then go to the Turkish baths at La Mosquée where, around a marble fountain sheltered by a tiled dome, you can mentally waft

THE PARIS MOSQUE
Hammam, home of the Grand Imam and spiritual center for the city's Muslim community, was built in Hispano-Moorish style during the 1920s. The grand patio was inspired by the Alhambra, with its decorative mosaics and fine cedar and eucalyptus woodwork. With an impressive 108-foot-high minaret and numerous ornately decorated domes, the mosque is considered to be a modern gem of European Islamic architecture.

Les Halles in its 20th-century guise—a traditional market venue for almost nine centuries, today Les Halles is one of the biggest shopping malls in Europe

The Musée de l'Histoire de France

yourself to Marrakesh. The steam of the 194°F sauna helps ... Allow three to four hours for the full relaxing benefit. Finish with a mint tea.

▶▶▶ l'Histoire de France, Musée de 51D3

Hôtel de Soubise, 60 rue des Francs-Bourgeois, 75003
tel: 01 40 27 61 78. Métro: Rambuteau, Hôtel de Ville
Open: Wed–Mon 1:45–5:45; weekends noon–5:45
Admission: inexpensive

Although some of the historic documents displayed here are fascinating, the principal interest lies in the museum's sumptuous architecture. It was mostly built by Delamair in 1709 for the Princesse de Soubise, by extending a 14th-century manor (whose double-towered entrance on the rue des Archives remains intact), and the interiors were decorated in the 1730s by Boffrand. The richness of this period accompanies you from the majestic Cour d'Honneur into the first-floor palace apartments, where Boffrand employed the talents of painters such as Boucher, Van Loo and Natoire. The ornate decoration continues throughout the Princess' second-floor apartments, where the museum documents are now displayed. Letters written by Charlemagne and Joan of Arc, the wills of Louis XIV and Napoleon and Marie-Antoinette's last missive before the chop are worth a read.

'NOTHING'
At the Musée de l'Histoire de France, look out for Louis XVI's classic diary entry for July 14, 1789, the day the Revolution broke out: he quite simply inscribed Rien ("nothing").

▶ Hôtel Hénault de Cantobre 142B2

82 rue François Miron, 75004; tel: 01 44 78 75 00
Métro: St. Paul, Hôtel de Ville
Open: Wed–Sun 11–8. Admission: inexpensive

This 18th-century private mansion, situated in the southern part of the Marais, was recently restored to house the **Maison Européenne de la Photographie** (European Photo Center). The permanent collections number more than 12,000 items and the center holds temporary exhibitions devoted to photographers such as Erwin Blumenfeld, Alexey Brodovitch, Irving Penn, and Robert Doisneau, as well as themed exhibitions.

▶ Huchette, rue de la 166B3

Métro, RER: St.-Michel

One of Paris' oldest streets, dating back to 1284, the rue de la Huchette is known today for its unadventurous gastronomy: it's souvlaki or souvlaki. At the heart of the Latin Quarter (southeast of place St.-Michel), students and tourists pile in here thinking they have discovered authentic Paris along its cobbled, narrow length. Two symbols remain of the 1950s, when this street experienced a real high: a minute theater and a basement jazz bar. Still running at the theater since the days when Ionesco first staged them are his plays *La Cantatrice Chauve* and *La Leçon*. Downstairs in the crowded caveau at No. 5, be-bop has hardly missed a note.

MODERN ARAB ARCHITECTURE
The remarkable architecture of the Institut du Monde Arabe combines modern materials with the spirit of traditional Arab architecture. The south facade consists of 1,600 identical metal light screens which electronically filter the sunlight as it enters the building. Their design is taken from the carved wooden screens called *moucharabiyahs*, often found on buildings from Morocco to southeast Asia.

▶▶▶ Institut du Monde Arabe 51D2

1 rue des Fossés St.-Bernard, 75005; tel: 01 40 51 38 38
Métro: Jussieu, Cardinal-Lemoine
Open: daily (except Mon) 10–6 (library 1–8)
Admission: moderate

Difficult to miss as you cross the Seine from the Ile St.-Louis, the Institut du Monde Arabe benefits from both its strategic location on the quai St.-Bernard and its sleek contemporary architecture. Founded in 1980, it moved into these custom-built premises in 1987, partly financed by the government and partly by 20 Arab states anxious to encourage cultural exchanges between Islam and the West. This aim is achieved through temporary exhibitions, a permanent museum collection, concerts, lectures, a library, and research facilities. Although budgets remain a thorny point—recent upheavals in the Middle East having stemmed the financial flow—and the museum is still sparsely filled, the Institute is an attraction for anyone interested in the Arab world and in contemporary architecture.

Before looking at anything else, notice the powerful aluminium and glass building designed by Jean Nouvel and the Architecture Studio. Apart from the light-sensitive diaphragm windows on the south facade, the transparent elevator shaft alone justifies the visit. Spirit yourself to the tenth-floor terrace, which provides magnificent views west along the river and north towards the Bastille. In the elegant, pricey restaurant enjoy the same views, along with baklava or shish kebab, or a juice on the terrace.

Design priorities continue on the three floors of the museum, where astrolabes vie for attention with display systems. From Spain to India, spanning the 9th to 19th centuries, the ceramics, bronzes, ivories, and carpets of this collection reflect the brilliance of this civilization.

HOME TO NAPOLEON
Number 10 rue de la Huchette reeks of Napoleonic lore. This was where Bonaparte languished for long months, despairing of his future, having fallen out with the authorities. In October 1795 he re-entered the political spotlight by dint of gunning down an insurgent mob; five years later he was gloriously installed at the Tuileries Palace across the river.

The striking facade of the Institut du Monde Arabe, which contains many Arab-Islamic treasures

Giving a definitive opinion about the best features in Paris is a hazardous enterprise. Seasons change, as do quality and popularity, all decisive factors in the enjoyment of certain places. Luckily, however, there are always unchangeables and these include the places that are listed below.

Café bests The best café with a view is an outdoor terrace in central Paris, 230 feet up on the sixth floor of the department store **La Samaritaine**, overlooking Pont-Neuf. Open only during the warmer months (generally May to October), it is a popular lunch spot for local office workers, but always has room at other times. The view due south and either way along the Seine of monuments within spitting distance is spectacular. A lookout point above displays an enameled "artist's impression" of Paris in 1900, good for comparing with today's horizon. A similarly central but more chic terrace with a view concentrating on the Ile St.-Louis and the Bastille, is on the tenth floor of the **Institut du Monde**

Best for refreshments with a panoramic view—La Samaritaine department store

Arabe. Its tea room is open 3–7 PM and Ziryab restaurant 12–2:30 and 7:30–10:30 PM.

Antique bests If you are looking for top-class antiques, don't go to the **Marché de Vanves**, Paris' best junk market (*brocante* in French). (*Open* Saturday and Sunday 7 AM–7:30 PM at the Porte de Vanves). It has now established itself among young couples as the place to go for finding the ultimate item of battered yet stylish furniture. Stall-holders are full of witty banter and always ready to "discuss" a price. Rainy days, although not the most enjoyable, do lead to the best bargains.

Oyster bar bests Although difficult to pronounce the best oyster bar, **Le Bar à Huîtres** (112 boulevard du Montparnasse) is without a doubt the most convenient. Oysters can be eaten in any quantity you like: on the sidewalk outside, or with more attention, seated at a barstool inside. *Belons, fines de claires* or *Marennes* are all superbly fresh and immaculately opened by friendly Bretons, and are best washed down with a pitcher of Sauvignon or a bottle of young Muscadet. **Montparnasse** is traditionally the seafood center of Paris because of its proximity to trains arriving directly from Brittany. Remember that oysters are best consumed during the "r" months (September to April).

Tea break bests In winter months *salons de thé* are easily the most accessible and comfortable places to recover from weary sidewalk- and museum-bashing, often graced with deep armchairs, reading matter and classical music: they are an alternative to the bright, noisy atmosphere of bistros and cafés.

A favorite in the Marais is **Les Enfants Gatés** (43 rue des Francs-Bourgeois). Convenient for the Musée Picasso, the Carnavalet, or the place des Vosges, it is a long-standing, unpretentious tea room, which serves delicious cakes, savory tarts and salads throughout the day *(Open* 12–8. *Closed* Mon and Tue).

Escapism bests If the slickness of central Paris restaurants and settings is becoming too much, head north of the center to the back streets of the faubourgs. In the suitably dilapidated surroundings of the passage Brady (*métro*: Château d'Eau, Strasbourg St.-Denis) you can indulge in Pakistani and Indian food in any of the countless budget restaurants which line this covered passage-way. In summer, candle-lit tables spill outside, spice levels run high and the odd errant rat only adds to the flavors of exoticism.

Studio bests For a fascinating view of how a late 19th-century artist lived, go to the best artist's studio-museum in Paris, the **Musée Gustave Moreau** (14 rue de La Rochefoucauld, 75009, tel: 01 48 74 38 50). Although the lower floors (his studio) have been open to the public for years, the upstairs apartment was only reconstructed and renovated in late 1991 and presents his rooms with the objects and decoration he chose.

Moreau himself (1826–1898) prepared the museum for posterity shortly before his death, and over 7,000 of his eerie symbolist works are exhibited in this elegant town house. At last the artist's wish has been fully accomplished.

Bakery bests After years of watching industrial baking methods turn the good old baguette into something bland, spongy, and characterless, many *boulangeries* have fought back and are once more producing that crispy golden crust and inimitably chewy interior. Recent winners of "best baguette of the year" are **Julien**, 75 rue St.-Honoré, and **Kayser**, 8/14 rue Monge. The bakers now also make more types of "biological" bread, in response to the phenomenal success of *Pain Poilâne*. Named after Lionel Poilâne, this loaf is now sold in cheese-stores and better supermarkets all over Paris, and airlifted to New York and Tokyo.

For your first experience go to the family bakery, 8 rue du Cherche-Midi, 75006, to savor this bread.

The Sun King's wounded soldiers were given a home at Les Invalides

The tomb of Marshall Foch in Les Invalides. Foch was overall commander of French, British and American armies toward the end of World War I

►► Les Invalides 50B2

Tel: 01 44 42 37 72
Métros: Latour–Maubourg, Invalides, Varenne
Admission: moderate/expensive

Pompous, severe, authoritarian, the 643-foot facade of the Hôtel des Invalides masks a masterpiece of French classical architecture. Designed by Libéral Bruant, it was completed in 1676 by Hardouin-Mansart, who later incorporated the impressive Eglise du Dôme (1706), a commission by Louis XIV to reflect the greatness of his reign. For once the Sun King was thinking of others, as Les Invalides was designed to house old soldiers, many invalided and reduced to dire straits. Six thousand once resided there; today under a hundred remain.

The main attraction for time-limited visitors is Napoleon's tomb, which presides gloriously over the crypt of the Dôme. Twenty years after his death on the distant island of St. Helena, Napoleon's body was returned to France and in 1861, like a Russian doll, it was encased in six layers of coffins crowning an immense granite base. Other military tombs fill the chapels of this superb baroque church, rich in painted cupolas, graceful arches, columns, sculptures, bas-reliefs, and inlaid marble floors. An ornate gilded, garlanded, and ribbed dome completes these glories.

Not to be confused with the Eglise du Dôme, the adjacent Eglise St.-Louis also concentrates on military memorabilia. Here numerous generals are buried, but more visible are the tattered remains of captured regimental banners hanging from the upper galleries.

On entering Les Invalides through its Cour d'Honneur you will be following in the footsteps of many a military hero, including de Gaulle and Churchill. For the ins and outs of military history head straight to the **Musée de l'Armée**► (*Open* daily 10–4:45; summer 5:45). One of the world's largest in this field, its extensive collections of weapons, armor, flags, uniforms, and paintings trace the evolution of warfare from prehistoric days to World War II. Inevitably Napoleonic relics abound (including his stuffed horse, "Vizier") but other periods such as the Second Empire and both World Wars are equally well-displayed. Nor is the Orient forgotten: one section specializes in the superbly crafted arms of the Middle and Far East. In the Musée des Plans-Reliefs (*Open* daily 10–6 PM; winter till 5. *Closed* for lunch), scale models of fortresses in France and near her borders form a collection which originated under Louis XIV in 1668 and for years remained a military secret.

▶ IRCAM *142A3*

1 place Igor Stravinsky; tel: 01 44 78 12 33
Métro: Hôtel de Ville. Admission: various—phone for details
Behind the dancing, clanking sculptures of the Fontaine Stravinsky, in the shadow of Beaubourg, stands an understated entrance. It leads to one of France's most important cultural laboratories: below ground lies a high-technology musical research center. The founder of IRCAM was composer and conductor Pierre Boulez; here, a team of electronic engineers and composers has unrivaled facilities for acoustic invention and experiment. Concerts and workshops are held in a futuristic auditorium, and visiting composers can try out the 4X, a digital sound processor which performs 220 million operations per second.

▶▶ Jacob, rue *176B3*

Métro: St.-Germain-des-Prés
Exuding what everyone expects the Rive Gauche to be, the picturesque rue Jacob (between rue des Saints Pères and rue Bonaparte) is crammed with galleries, antique shops, bookstores, and interior decoration stores. Stroll along this street watching out for the shadows of former residents Racine, Wagner, Mérimée, and Stendhal but keeping an eye open for ethnic jewelry, astrolabes, art deco curios, Chinese porcelain, architectural prints, and swathes of sumptuous fabric. Walk east and you'll end up in the Left Bank gallery mecca; go west and you'll eventually arrive at Les Invalides.

▶▶ Jacquemart-André, Musée *50B4*

158 boulevard Haussmann, 75008; tel: 01 42 89 04 91
Métro: St.-Phillipe-du-Roule
Open: daily 10–6. Admission: expensive
Once a prestigious private collection of 17th- to 18th-century European art and Italian Renaissance works, subsequently bequeathed to the nation, the Musée Jacquemart-André disappeared in a cloud of scandal when its curator was accused of appropriating funds. Result: the museum closed, but has now been renovated and reopened.

This elegant 1870 mansion displays works of art from the Italian Renaissance as well as paintings and drawings by Rubens, Rembrandt, Frans Hals, Van Dyck, Chardin, Boucher, Watteau, and Lancret, alongside Savonnerie carpets and Gobelins tapestries.

▶ Jeu de Paume, Galerie Nationale du *50B3*

place de la Concorde, 75001; tel: 01 42 60 69 69
Métro: Concorde.
Open: Tue–Fri 12–7, Sat–Sun 10–7 (Tue until 9:30 PM)
Admission: moderate
Reopened in 1991 after five years of renovation and internal transformation, the Jeu de Paume now turns a rejuvenated

PLACE IGOR STRAVINSKY
The charming place Igor Stravinsky with its modern eccentric fountain and pond of psychedelic sculptures, pays tribute to the great 20th-century Russian composer who made Paris the center for his new style of music, abandoning conventional harmony, rhythm, and form. Indeed the premier of his iconoclastic *The Rite of Spring* in 1913 at the Théâtre des Champs-Elysées led to rioting in the audience. Where better for the innovative IRCAM studios than alongside this unique and extraordinary square?

EXPERIMENTAL MUSIC
"Listen to your century"—slogan of the Ensemble InterContemporain, a group of contemporary instrumentalists based at IRCAM.

Galerie Nationale du Jeu de Paume, built by Napoleon III on the site of Henri IV's orangery in the Tuileries Garden and devoted now to contemporary art

face to the public. This is just another in a long string of mutations since its Second Empire origins as an indoor tennis court. Its collection of Impressionist paintings was transferred to the Musée d'Orsay in 1986. Today, its spacious galleries are used for temporary exhibitions of international contemporary art.

►► Judaïsme, Musée d'Art et d'Histoire du

71 rue du Temple, 75003; tel: 01 53 01 86 53
Métro: Rambuteau, Hôtel de Ville
Open: Mon–Fri 11–6; Sun 10–6. Admission: moderate
Housed in the handsome 17th-century mansion, Hôtel de St.-Aignan, the collections are devoted chiefly to the art and history of Jewish communities in France and North Africa. Exhibits cover the Middles Ages, Emancipation of the Jews after the French Revolution, intellectual and artistic achievement in the 19th century and the tragedies and triumphs of the modern era.

► Justice, Palais de *166B4*

2 boulevard du Palais, 75001; tel: 01 44 32 50 00
Métro: Cité
Open: Mon–Fri 9–5. Admission free
"Liberté, Egalité, Fraternité" is inscribed above the entrance at the top of the grand marble steps leading into France's symbol of civil authority. It is only since the Revolution that the palace took on its present function. Before that it played royal palace, with many transformations, from Roman times until 1358, when Charles V abandoned it completely. During the Revolution, summary judgments were passed here and prisoners left the Cour du Mai by the cartload, destined for the guillotine.

The main lobby (the 17th-century Salle des Pas-Perdus) is still thick with black-robed lawyers, judges, and plaintiffs. See the stunningly decorated blue and gold Première Chambre Civile, once possibly Louis IX's bedroom (he was an avid collector of holy relics) and later used by the Revolutionary Tribunal. It is possible to watch the action in most of the courts, if your French can cope with the animated repartee.

WHAT'S IN A NAME?
The Jeu de Paume, meaning "game played with the palm of the hand," was originally built during the Second Empire as a real or "royal" tennis court at the west end of the Jardin des Tuileries. However, when lawn tennis became more popular than real tennis, the court was used to exhibit artworks.

▶▶▶ Louvre *50C3*

Pyramide du Louvre, Cour Napoléon, 75001
Tel: (multilingual recorded message) 01 40 20 51 51; (information desk) 01 40 20 53 17; www.louvre.fr
Métro: Palais-Royal, Musée du Louvre; direct access
Open: Wed–Mon 9–6; Mon (part of the museum) and Wed (whole museum) until 9:45 PM. Admission: expensive (reduced after 3 and Sun. Free 1st Sun of every month)

The Louvre represents an astonishing historical continuum of French rulers from the Middle Ages to the present—and it is not over yet. Since 1981 this palatial museum has been in constant mutation, undergoing restoration and underground extension. Guiding these radical changes was the American architect I.M. Pei, whose transparent pyramid now crowns the Cour Napoléon. Nor have these transformations been without their archaeological surprises: medieval fortifications have been thrown up in the wake of the bulldozers.

How to visit To do the museum and your intellect any kind of justice, several visits should be planned, bearing in mind the late opening hours on Mondays and Wednesdays when rooms are less crowded. High points of the collections are well signposted and free plans are available at the entrance. Between 1992 and autumn 1993 (bicentenary of the museum opening) 10,000 works were shuffled around; by 2000, many, many more had changed place. Completion of the **Grand Louvre** project is promised for 2001.

To avoid waiting in line, buy your ticket in advance by phone (01 49 87 54 54), minitel (3615 Louvre), or at FNAC shops (reduced rate after 3 PM and on Sun; free for under-18s). Improvements include new facilities for disabled visitors (01 40 20 59 90), an army of benches for weary visitors, full air-conditioning in the Grande Galerie (989 feet long) and other rooms, new restaurants/ cafés, a picnic area, baby changing facilities, stroller-lending service.

History In the late 14th century, Charles V transformed Philippe-Auguste's fortress into a medieval castle. Nearly two centuries later, the wily Renaissance king François I instigated considerable rebuilding, mostly designed by Pierre Lescot in 1546. François I also initiated the Louvre collections, bringing the Mona Lisa and its creator, Da Vinci, to France. In 1578, Catherine de Médicis had a completely new palace built at the far end of the present Louvre, looking across the Tuileries Gardens. Henri IV had the riverside gallery built to link the Louvre and the Palais des Tuileries. Louis XIII set about extending the Cour Carrée and Louis XIV brought his architect Le Vau to complete his father's project before the court transferred lock, stock and barrel, to Versailles. The Louvre's golden days were almost over, as the last king to live in the palace was Louis XV and this was only while the Palais des Tuileries was being cleaned.

New Role Meanwhile, this vast building served other purposes (concert hall, art gallery, theater) and was invaded by tenants, some more desirable than others: *(Continued on page 136)*

THE "NEW" LOUVRE
The refurbished rooms are situated in some of the oldest parts of the Louvre which, over a period of 500 years, witnessed many historic events, including Napoleon's wedding. Famous artists worked on their decoration and many others had lodgings in the palace. The most important rooms now have illustrated panels relating various episodes of the Louvre's history.

THE TOUR DE L'HORLOGE
The extensive Palais de Justice complex decorates the *quais* of the River Seine with its many ornate ancient towers, including the unusual square 14th-century Tour de l'Horloge, featuring one of Europe's first public clocks. Beneath the clock face is the Latin inscription: "This clock which divides the day into twelve equal parts is a lesson that justice must be protected and the law defended."

LAST SUPPER LINK
Louis XIV used the Salle des Caryatides for an annual ceremony (common among European monarchs) in which he washed the feet of 13 paupers on Holy Thursday to recall the humility of Christ washing the feet of his Apostles.

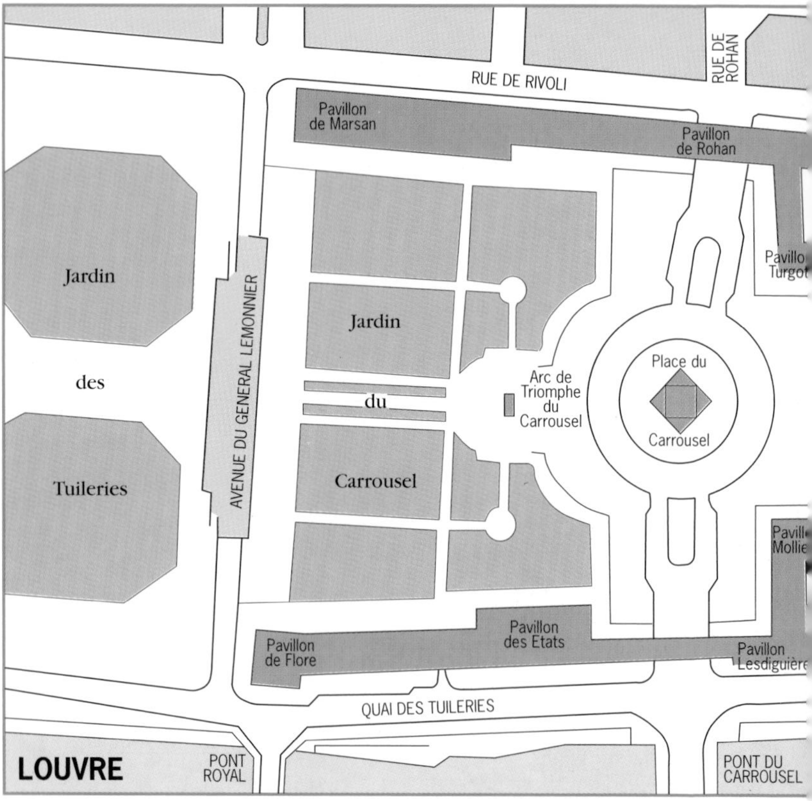
RUE DE ROHAN
RUE DE RIVOLI
Pavillon de Marsan
Pavillon de Rohan
Pavillo Turgot
Jardin des Tuileries
AVENUE DU GENERAL LEMONNIER
Jardin du Carrousel
Arc de Triomphe du Carrousel
Place du Carrousel
Pavill Mollie
Pavillon des Etats
Pavillon de Flore
Pavillon Lesdiguière
QUAI DES TUILERIES
LOUVRE
PONT ROYAL
PONT DU CARROUSEL

DID YOU KNOW?
When the Louvre was opened to the public the royal collection numbered over 2,500 works. Today there are over 30,000 exhibited. The Louvre's glass pyramid is cleaned monthly by a robot.

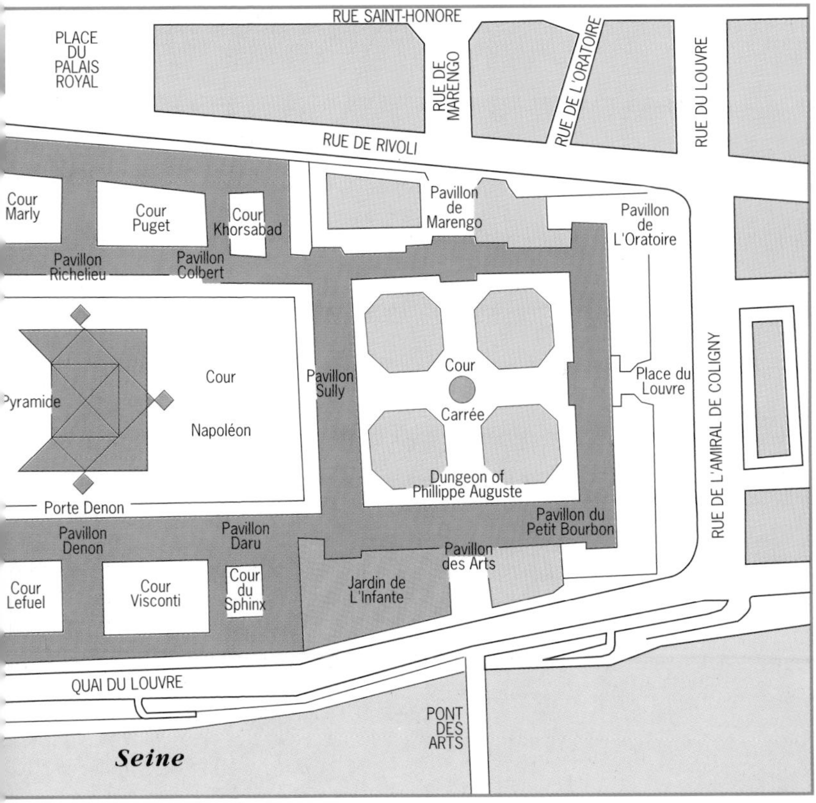

The Louvre—its old and new aspects. Its most recent addition, the glass pyramid entrance, was opened in 1989

(Continued from page 133)
artists, including Bouchardon and Boucher, squatters, "cabaret" artists and whores. It became such a slum that in 1750 it narrowly escaped demolition ... However, in 1793, during the Revolution, a museum was opened to the public in the Grande Galerie—the Musée Central des Arts. Revival came with Napoleon, who moved into the Palais des Tuileries—severely ransacked by the mob—and celebrated his marriage to Marie-Louise in the Louvre. Always ready to leave his mark, Napoleon set about creating a central courtyard dominated by the Arc du Carrousel, building a northern wing and adding floors. Equally important was Napoleon's contribution to the wealth of the museum, as at every one of his numerous victories ransoms and looting increased the Louvre stock. Under Napoleon III considerable extension finally united the Louvre and the Palais des Tuileries, although this union was short-lived: in 1871 the Tuileries palace was burnt to the ground by the Commune.

The museum Entrance to the Louvre is through the unmistakable glass pyramid, which leads down into a gleaming marble underworld of further entrances for each wing. A gigantic bookshop, a *chalcographie* (print) store, cafés, and restaurants all contribute to the animation of this crossroads, which also leads through to a vast shopping center and under the Carrousel, the **Centre de la Mode** for professional fashion shows. On the east side of the reception area, follow the Sully entrance to visit the impressive medieval remains of Philippe Auguste's dungeons (ca1200) and

BEHEMOTH
The Louvre is now the largest museum in the world, covering 720,000 square yards.

galleries exhibiting pottery and royal artifacts found during excavations.

Egyptian antiquities are on the first and second floors of the Sully wing, in a new display inaugurated in December 1997; the collections are presented thematically on the first floor, and chronologically on the second floor. The extensive Greek, Roman, and Etruscan Collections are situated in the Denon and Sully wings. Here you will find the eternally serene *Venus de Milo* and, in the corner staircase of the Denon wing, the soaring *Victory of Samothrace*, one of whose mutilated hands is exhibited in a case near by (it was excavated nearly a century later). In the southeastern corner of this wing is the **Salle des Caryatides**. This is the oldest surviving room of the palace built for Henri II and is named after the four monumental statues by Jean Goujon which support the end gallery.

The Orient The new galleries of Oriental Antiquities and Islamic Art are on the first floor of the Richelieu wing and in the Sackler wing of the Sully area. A highlight of this section is the Cour Khorsabad, a skylit courtyard displaying the massive sculptural facades of crowned and winged bulls from the Assyrian Palace of Khorsabad (ca713 BC).

The paintings For many visitors the Louvre means painting. Take the Denon entrance to the second floor,

allowing a quick detour through the 16th–19th-century Italian sculpture section on the first floor to look at, among the Bellinis, Della Robbias, and Donatellos, Michelangelo's two formidable *Slaves*. Above is the Grande Galerie full of Italian Renaissance masterpieces (Vinci, Raphaël, Titian); the *Mona Lisa* hangs in an adjacent gallery leading to another vast area where large-scale paintings by David, Gros, Géricault, and Delacroix are displayed.

French painting of the 18th and 19th centuries (Watteau, Boucher, Chardin, Fragonard, Robert, Ingres, Corot) is now concentrated on the third floor of the Sully wing. Flemish, Dutch and Northern schools complete the galleries of the magnificently renovated Richelieu wing on this floor while below, on the second floor, are exhibited the fabulous Trésor de St.-Denis and *objets d'art*.

GRAND ENTRANCE
On either side of the passage Richelieu leading into the Louvre from the Palais-Royal, two immense glassed-in courtyards display monumental French sculpture, including the original *Chevaux de Marly*.

The Louvre galleries contain one of the world's greatest art collections including the Venus de Milo *and Leonardo da Vinci's* Mona Lisa

▶ Luxembourg, Palais du 50C2

15 rue de Vaugirard, 75006
Métro: Odéon; RER: Luxembourg
Open: to the public only one day a year in September, 9–6 (tel: 01 42 34 20 60). Groups by appointment

Yet another symbol of the vagaries of French history, the Palais du Luxembourg and its famous gardens were originally commissioned by Marie de Médicis, the widow of the assassinated Henri IV. Bored with the Louvre, her idea was to build a palace that would remind her of her native Florence. After she had aquired the property from Duke François of Luxembourg in 1612, the architect Salomon de Brosse was given plans of the Pitti Palace for inspiration and work started in 1615. However, by the time it was completed in 1621 she had been forced into exile by her own son, Louis XIII. Following a reconciliation with the king, she was exiled by the powerful Cardinal Richelieu. She died penniless in exile in Cologne.

Many of the fabulous works of art commissioned for its interior have since been moved. The series of 24 allegorical paintings by Rubens (commissioned in 1621) depicting Marie de Médicis' life now hang in the Louvre. Major renovation undertaken by Chalgrin (who later designed the Arc de Triomphe) was rudely interrupted by the Revolution when the palace took on the role of prison (keeping out of trouble, among others, Danton, the De Noailles family, and Camille Desmoulins), before passing into the hands of the Directoire. Chalgrin's work resumed and by 1804 the palace was ready to receive the newly created Senate, which still meets here today. Delacroix added to the rich interior in 1847 by painting the Library ceiling with homages to Virgil, Homer, and Dante, while the

The monumental 17th-century Palais du Luxembourg—the first palace built in Paris during "the century of palaces"—houses the Sénat, France's upper parliamentary house

architect Alphonse de Gisors made major additions, including the fabulously decorated Salle des Conférences.

War and peace After almost a century of relative calm, during World War II the Palais du Luxembourg was occupied by the head of the Luftwaffe for the Western Front, and its gardens were soon riddled with underground air-raid shelters. Today its political role and promenading popularity have regained the upper hand. Don't forget to pay homage to the instigator of this palace at the shady Fontaine Médicis. Set in one of the few original Italianate features, the fountain sculptures (added later) depict a bronze cyclops, Polyphemus, glaring downward at the innocent marble lovers, Acis and Galatea. Leaving no stone untouched, the reverse side, facing the rue de Médicis, boasts a bas-relief of Leda and the swan (1807).

MADELEINE MUNCHIES
Gourmets come to the place de la Madeleine without even noticing that big church in the middle. They're heading for one of the two rival luxury grocery stores, Fauchon or Hédiard (see page 217), or the great restaurant Lucas-Carton (see page 278).

▶ Lycée Henri IV *166B1*

23 rue Clovis, 75005
Métro: Cardinal-Lemoine; RER: Luxembourg
Closed to the public
In the heart of the intellectual fifth arrondissement, the Lycée Henri IV is one of France's most prestigious high schools and claims Jean-Paul Sartre among its former teachers. It was built in 1796 on the site of an abbey devoted to Ste Geneviève, the patron saint of Paris, and a former basilica founded by Clovis, the man who beat the Romans in AD 486. Once the Revolution had swept by, only the Gothic Tour de Clovis, the refectory and some kitchens remained.

▶ Madeleine *50B3*

place de la Madeleine, 75008; tel: 01 44 51 69 00
Métro: Madeleine
Open: Mon–Sun 7 AM–7 PM; closed over lunch on Sun.
Admission free
Something of a white elephant, the Madeleine has had a checkered career, narrowly avoiding being transformed into a railway station, a stock exchange, a bank, a theater and yet another temple for Napoleon. Although building started on it in 1764, many ups and downs ensued before it at last regained its original function in 1842 and was completed as a church. The unmistakable Greek temple form, supported by 52 Corinthian pillars, commands a spectacular perspective down the rue Royale. A classic site for society weddings and funerals, the rose marble interior has seen the coffins of Chopin, Josephine Baker and, more recently, Marlene Dietrich.

A church disguised as a Greek temple: the Madeleine

▶▶ Maison de Verre *176A2*

31 rue St. Guillaume, 75007
Métro: rue du Bac
A temple to the purity of modernism, this extraordinary house was built between 1928 and 1931 by the art deco architect Pierre Chareau, contemporary of Le Corbusier. Walls of glass bricks with steel frames and an airy geometric interior are the innovations that replaced a 17th-century town house. Only one thing remained: a stubborn tenant in her top-floor flat.

MAISON DE VERRE
The exterior of Pierre Chareau's Maison de Verre (1932) is visible from the courtyard, but written applications are necessary to tour inside (31 rue St.-Guillaume 75007).

Malmaison see pages 202–203

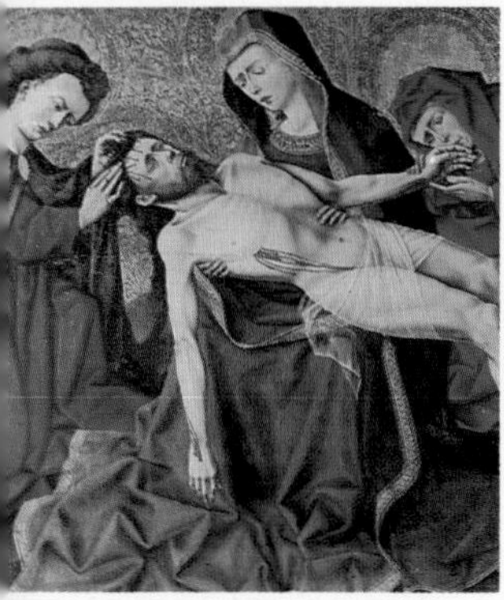

"Paris is well worth a mass," stated Henri IV before rapidly converting to Catholicism and bringing to an end the bloody Wars of Religion. Since then the Catholic faith has dominated Paris and the main concentration of Protestants lies in the south of France. As a visitor to Paris you may think the same as Henri IV and, whether religious or not, you may want to witness French church traditions for yourself. Or you may want to participate in the ceremonies of another faith. All is possible: Paris contains over a hundred parish churches and many a synagogue, temple, and mosque.

ST.-SULPICE
The 12th-century church of St.-Sulpice, built for local peasants banned from the monastic church, was completely remodeled in the 17th and 18th centuries, It is impressively vast inside and richly decorated.

Catholic Most churches are open from about 8 AM to 7 PM and hold morning, noon and evening services, stepped up on Sundays to at least five throughout the day. For an atmospheric Catholic mass, number one priority is **Notre-Dame**. Despite the hordes of fellow tourists it's hard to find a more inspiring setting (see pages 154–157). **St.-Germain-des-Prés**, an ancient Benedictine abbey, makes a similarly historic context, while the nearby church of **St.-Sulpice** (see page 174) has the sounds of France's largest organ, as well as murals by Delacroix.

For enthusiasts, **Sacré-Cœur** in Montmartre (see page 171) is a monumental basilica and has hourly services every morning, evening mass at 6 PM and sung mass at 11 AM on Sundays.

St. Etienne du Mont's arched rood-screen forms one of Paris' most striking church interiors

Other options Although slightly off the main tourist beat, a handful of other Parisian churches will supply rare historic settings. Instead of Sacré-Cœur, for example, go round the corner to one of Paris' oldest churches, **St.-Pierre-de-Montmartre** which has preserved much of its original 12th-century architecture. In central Paris, near Beaubourg, the **Eglise St. Merri** is a superb example of flamboyant Gothic, although it was not actually completed until 1612. A 1331 bell remains from the medieval chapel which previously occupied the site and, if you attend a midday service here, admire the superb 16th-century stained-glass windows and remarkable carved woodwork. The massive 17th-century organ was once played by Saint-Saëns and concerts are still held here (tel: 01 42 71 93 93 for details).

Another historic organ, one century older and particularly ornamental, remains in the church of **St.-Etienne-du-Mont**. The bizarre architectural mixture (Gothic, Renaissance, classical) is due to a long construction period stretching from 1492 to 1626. The delicately fretted rood-screen (unique in Paris), which forms an arch between the nave and the choir, must be seen. Both Pascal and Racine were buried here and Ste. Geneviève's relics can be seen in the south ambulatory.

Protestant There is a reasonable though more limited choice of Protestant churches. The neo-Gothic **American Church** on the quai d'Orsay is a classic, particularly for the expatriate American community, which organizes all sorts of fundraising activities. Services are at 11 AM on Sundays. Not to be confused with this is the **American Cathedral** in the avenue Georges V, of Anglican leaning, which holds two Sunday-morning services, one with a choir at 11am. Paris' best reputed voices can be heard at **St. George's English Church** near the Etoile in their 10:30 AM Sunday service. Presbyterians should make for the **Church of Scotland** in the rue Bayard or the Scots **Kirk Manse** in the rue Thimonnier.

Jewish At the heart of the Jewish quarter around the **rue des Rosiers**, there is a synagogue designed in 1913 by the art nouveau architect Hector Guimard, although its facade is hard to see in the narrow rue Pavée. Further north in the Marais, near another traditionally Jewish area, the Temple, is the synagogue in the rue Notre-Dame de Nazareth while the ninth *arrondissement*, which bristles with kosher restaurants, has a large religious center in the rue St. Georges and another synagogue, which can be found in the rue de la Victoire.

Islamic Despite the large percentage of Muslims in France, their worshipping needs are not the best catered to. The imposing central Mosque's minaret rises over the rue Geoffroy St. Hilaire opposite the Jardin des Plantes (Friday prayers at 12:30 PM are reserved for Muslims).

See also **Travel Facts** page 263.

ST.-ROCH
Creatively minded worshipers can head for the Eglise St.-Roch, which holds a special Sunday noon mass in honor of artists and musicians. Some artists even have studios in the upper reaches of the church, and Corneille's tomb honors all writers. As with many of Paris' central historic churches, concerts are regularly held here.

ST.-EUSTACHE
For some of the best church music in Paris, visit the massive church of St.-Eustache, parish church of Les Halles, unusually combining Gothic structure with Renaissance decoration. St.-Eustache has had a long musical tradition: Liszt and Berlioz directed premieres of their work here, and the choir, Les Chanteurs de St.-Eustache, are internationally acclaimed for their concerts on Christmas Eve and St. Cecilia's Day.

LE MARAIS
The winding streets of Le Marais boast what is considered to be the oldest house in Paris (ca1400), as well as a lively Jewish quarter dating from the 13th century.

▶▶▶ Le Marais *IBCB4*

Only 20 years ago, the Marais was a dilapidated, neglected corner of central Paris, a far cry from the fashionable *quartier* it has now become. Its Cinderella-like transformation was mostly due to André Malraux who, in 1962, pointed out the historic value of numerous crumbling monuments, and a restoration program was slowly embarked upon, soon followed by an invasion of smart boutiques, restaurants, and art galleries.

The background Stretching west to east between Les Halles and the Bastille and north to south from the République to the Seine, the heart of the Marais remains immediately west of its lung, the place des Vosges. Before Henri IV commissioned this symmetrical "place Royale" in 1605, the nearby rue St.-Antoine was already

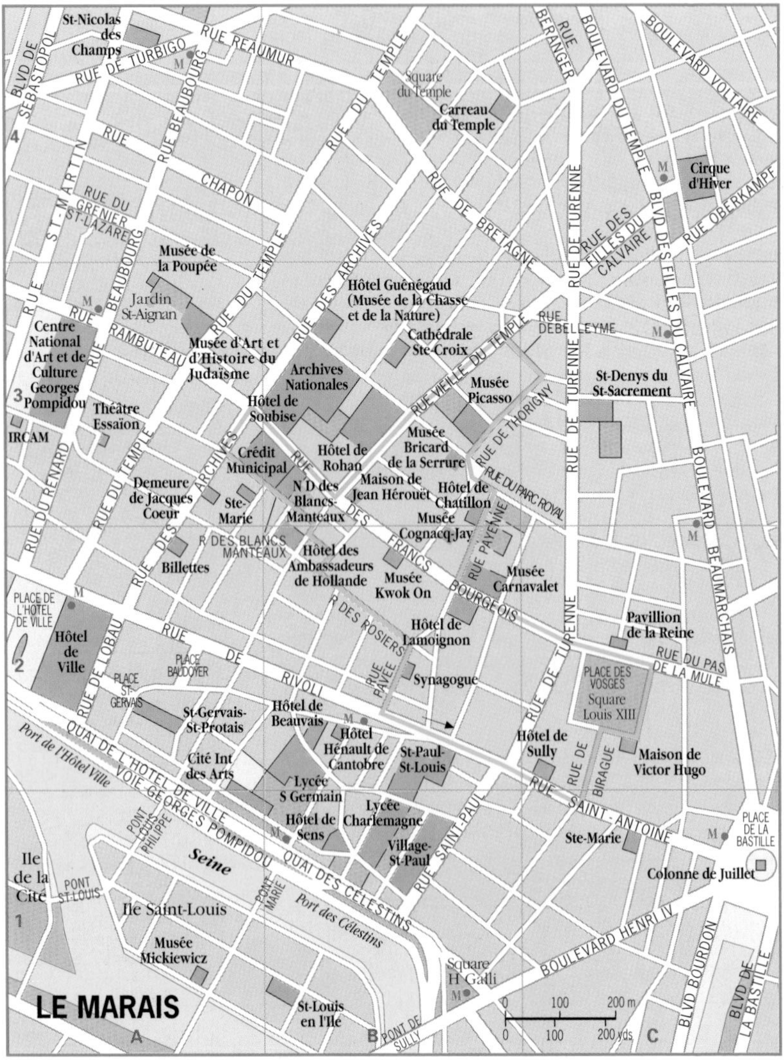

a popular axis for royal festivities, while for two centuries the northern section had been controlled by the powerful religious and military Ordre des Templiers (Knights Templar) until its brutal suppression in 1312. Even in Roman times this low-lying area was called Le Marais (the marsh).

But it was the 17th and, to a lesser extent, the 18th centuries that propelled the Marais to its zenith, with aristocrats vying to create the most elegant mansion, the most imposing courtyard or the most precious interior. Literary salons, philosophical debates, duels, love affairs, power struggles: the Marais rapidly became a hotbed for the likes of Madame de Sévigné, Voltaire, Molière, Racine, and Richelieu. With the Revolution, its aristocratic sun set and its glorious mansions were sold off to merchants and artisans.

Masterpieces It is impossible to wander around the Marais without stumbling across architectural masterpieces, even if you can only admire them from their courtyards. Don't miss the following: **Hôtel de Lamoignon**, 24 rue Pavée; **Hôtel de Sully**, 62 rue St.-Antoine (see page 178); **Hôtel de Rohan**, 87 rue Vieille du Temple; **Hôtel de Châtillon**, 13 rue Payenne; **Hôtel de Sens**, 1 rue du Figuier (see page 175); **Hôtel des Ambassadeurs de Hollande**, 47 rue Vieille du Temple; and the **Hôtel Salé**, housing the **Musée Picasso**; the **Hôtel Guénégaud** and its **Musée de la Chasse**; **Hôtel d'Avaux** or **St.-Aignan**; the **Musée du Judaïsme** (see page 132); and the **Hôtel Libéral Bruand**, which houses the **Musée Bricard de la Serrure** (see pages 164, 100, and 87 respectively).

Between the restored facades you'll also find plenty of 20th-century temptations, in the form of hundreds of contemporary art galleries, restaurants, bars, clothes, and

PLACE ROYALE
Henri IV, founder of the place Royale, missed its inauguration ceremony: he had been assassinated two years earlier.

Architectural detail in Le Marais, one of the oldest areas of Paris, dotted with ornate 17th-century mansions

Taking a break in the graceful place des Vosges—once the site of many jousting tournaments and duels

antiques shops. Yuppies have moved in with a vengeance, yet there's a small **Chinatown** around the rue Chapon, where crowded backroom workshops churn out goods. The wholesale costume jewelry and rag trades still monopolise much of the **rue du Temple** and its sidestreets. A unique combination of history, function, and trendy chic makes this one of Paris' favorite strolling areas.

Place des Vosges▶ Since 1612, when 10,000 spectators watched the spectacular celebrations to inaugurate the "place Royale," a stream of famous characters has inhabited its mansions and apartments. Princesses, duchesses, official mistresses, Richelieu, Sully, Victor Hugo, Gautier, Daudet, Bossuet, and, more recently, the painter Francis Bacon and the architect Richard Rogers (of Centre Pompidou fame) have all gazed at its perfect symmetry. Thirty-six red brick- and stone-faced houses with arcaded first floors and steep pitched roofs create the harmonious form of this square, which encloses a garden of fountains, plane trees and gravel paths. Before the square was built, it was the site of a royal palace, the Palais des Tournelles, abandoned and demolished by Catherine de Médicis when her husband Henri II was killed in a tournament here. The north and south façades retained the royal touch, as each has a larger, central house, respectively the queen and the king's pavilion. In 1800 the name "place Royale" was replaced by "place des Vosges" in honor of the first French district to pay its new taxes.

Literary echo Although restaurants, chic clothes stores, antiques dealers, and art galleries now line the place des Vosges, there remains one remnant of the square's literary past in the **Maison de Victor Hugo▶** at No. 6. Between 1832 and 1848 the great French writer penned many a manuscript here (see page 182). Maybe he witnessed one of the many duels which took place on the square, despite Richelieu's ban on them in the 17th century. This argumentative habit continued well into the 19th century, although the favorite dawn meeting place was transferred to the Bois de Boulogne.

Walk

A Tour of Le Marais

See map page 142.

Starting from the métro St.-Paul, walk east along the rue St.-Antoine.
Pass the **church** (1627–1641), and on your left, at No. 62, the magnificent **Hôtel de Sully**.

Turn left into the rue de Birague which leads into the spectacular place des Vosges.
Notice that the facades are painted in *trompe l'oeil* to resemble brick. Commissioned by Henri IV, the square was completed in 1612 and became home to luminaries such as Richelieu, Molière, and, at No. 6, Victor Hugo, in a house now devoted to his museum. Continue around the square past restaurants, galleries, and some eccentric stores, look into the garden entrance of No. 28, the discreet hotel **Pavillon de la Reine**, and stop for a drink at No. 19, **Ma Bourgogne**, which in summer spreads its tables under the arcades.

Continue to the rue des Francs Bourgeois.
Pass the **Musée Carnavalet**, built in 1548 and later home to the writer Madame de Sévigné.

Turn right along the rue Payenne.
The gardens on the right and courtyards on the left are typical of the 17th-century Marais style.

Follow the rue du Parc Royal to the left and then turn right into the rue de Thorigny.
Here you pass the **Hôtel Salé**, built in 1659, now the **Musée Picasso**.

At the end turn left along the rue Debelleyme, past some contemporary art galleries and left again down the rue Vieille du Temple.
Halfway down on your right at No. 87, you pass the carved gates of the **Hôtel de Rohan** and, on the corner of the rue des Francs Bourgeois, the

A boutique in Le Marais

picturesque 1510 turret of the **Maison de Jean Hérouët.**

Turn right here, past more elegant mansions and the Crédit Municipal (municipal pawnshop) at No. 55 on your left.
On the right is the impressive 1709 courtyard of the **Hôtel de Soubise**, now the national archives.

A short way down the rue des Archives turn left again into the rue des Blancs-Manteaux, which takes you back to the rue Vieille du Temple. Cut across to follow the rue des Rosiers.
This is the central Jewish quarter, full of specialist shops as far as the rue Pavée.

Turn right at the rue Pavée, past the synagogue designed by Guimard, to return to your starting point.

MUSÉE MAILLOL
In the former house of 19th-century novelist Alfred de Musset, at 59 rue de Grenelle, 75007, is a small museum dedicated to Aristide Maillol (1861–1944), one of Paris' most influential turn-of-the-century sculptors. It contains a private collection of Maillol's works donated by his former model Dina Vierny. Bronze figures by Maillol are also exhibited around the Jardin des Tuileries.

► Marly, Chevaux de *50B3*

Sculpted by Nicolas and Guillaume Coustou, these two groups of rearing white marble horses were salvaged from the Château de Marly (destroyed during the Revolution) and brought in 1795 to guard the entrance to the Champs-Elysées. Sixteen live horses were needed to pull their weighty mass. The originals are now preserved from pollution in the Louvre and copies stand in their place on the corner of the place de la Concorde.

►►► Marmottan Louis-Boilly, Musée *IFCA4*

2 rue Louis-Boilly, 75016; tel: 01 42 24 07 02
Métro: Muette
Open: Tue–Sun 10–5:30. Admission: moderate

Located opposite the discreet charm of the Ranelagh gardens, which still boast a hand-cranked merry-go-round, the Musée Marmottan is another of the 16th *arrondissement*'s hidden treasures. Although Paris' main concentration of Impressionist works is at the Musée d'Orsay, the Marmottan follows closely in the quality stakes.

The 19th-century town house originally contained a Renaissance and Empire collection bequeathed to the state by the historian Paul Marmottan, later extended by a generous Wildenstein donation of medieval manuscripts and finally by the magnificent Michel Monet donation. Son of the Impressionist Claude Monet, he left a collection essentially composed of 65 of his father's works executed toward the end of his life at Giverny. Thus clouds of irises, wisteria, and water lilies fill much of an underground gallery, backed up with works by Monet's contemporaries such as Renoir,

A fine collection of Monet's work is displayed at the Musée Marmottan including Impression—soleil levant *which gave its name to the Impressionist movement*

Pissarro, Sisley, Berthe Morisot, and Caillebotte. Another donation, made in 1987, extended this remarkable collection to include Gauguin and Corot. Don't miss Monet's seminal painting *Impression—soleil levant*, which gave the movement its name and was also one of a booty of nine paintings stolen from this museum in 1985 and recovered five years later in Corsica.

▶ Marronniers, Hôtel des *176B3*

21 rue Jacob, 75006; tel: 01 43 25 30 60
Métro: Mabillon, St.-Germain-de-Prés
Nature-lovers should try to stay at this hotel in the heart of St.-Germain—its obsessive decorating style is nearly entirely based on vegetation, fruit, birds, and flowers, while two superb chestnut trees dominate the garden. Declared a national monument, the oak-beamed rooms and superb vaulted cellars (converted into lounges) combine to create an atmosphere of special charm.

▶ Mémorial du Maréchal Leclerc de Hauteclocque et de la Libération de Paris et Musée Jean Moulin *152B2*

dalle-jardin Atlantique, 75015; tel: 01 40 64 39 44
Métro: Montparnasse-Bienvenue
Open: Tue–Sun 10–5:40. Admission: moderate
Two perspectives on World War II; one through the life and times of a great soldier, the other via the Resistance leader Jean Moulin against a background including the Free French forces, the Allies, and Resistance groups.

▶ Meurice, Hôtel *50C3*

228 rue de Rivoli, 75001 (south of place Vendôme)
tel: 01 47 42 25 49. Métro: Tuileries
Once a favorite with the moustachioed Salvador Dali, who made the Royal Suite his Paris base for 30-odd years, the Meurice still claims a good percentage of the world's rich and famous. Opened in 1816, it was Paris' first "grand hotel." During World War II it had the doubtful honor of becoming Nazi headquarters and in August 1944 witnessed the surrender of Von Choltitz to the Allies. Retaining its aristocratic, old-world atmosphere the Meurice makes an elegant setting for tea.

▶ Monnaie, Hôtel et Musée de la *176C3*

11 quai de Conti, 75006; tel: 01 40 46 55 53
Métro: Pont-Neuf
Open: Tue–Fri 11–5:30; Sat and Sun 12–5:30.
Admission: moderate
Another of the dignified facades lining the Left Bank of the Seine, La Monnaie was once the national mint. This elegant building was designed by Antoine in 1770 (he lived in his creation until his death in 1801), replacing the 17th-century Hôtel de Conti. Today the workshops (*ateliers*) still produce commemorative coins and guided tours will explain the techniques (tel: 01 40 46 55 35. *Guided tours* Sun only, 3 PM).

A series of lofty salons overlooking the Seine are used for temporary exhibitions; the main museum is situated at the back of the courtyard. Here the history of coins and medals is traced from 300 BC to the present. A museum store opens on to the rue Guénégaud.

ANCIENT RELICS
The rue de Nevers, which runs parallel to the rue Guénégaud off the quai de Conti, is one of Paris' oldest streets, and hasn't changed its skinny width since the 13th century. Once marking the boundary between a convent and a town house, it contains a section of the Philippe-Auguste city wall. The arch over the entrance (constructed at a later date) is engraved with part of Claude le Petit's 17th-century poem satirizing the Pont Neuf (directly opposite) and its imminent collapse; the author finished at the stake.

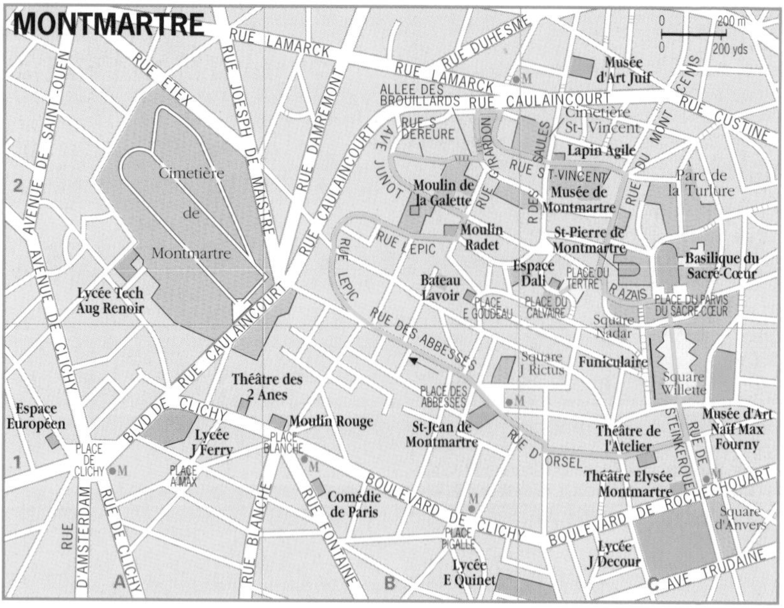

▶▶▶ Montmartre *11D4*

High on its northern hill overlooking Paris, Montmartre was long linked with the artistic community that scraped a living there. Toulouse-Lautrec immortalized the can-can-kicking Jane Avril, the Moulin Rouge, and singer-poet Aristide Bruant, and no doubt frequented the local hot cabaret, Au Lapin Agile. Meanwhile, Cubism was born in the draughty Bateau-Lavoir studios, which housed no lesser figures than Picasso, Juan Gris and Braque. Today little is left of this burgeoning creative community: the "painters" on the place du Tertre can hardly swing a brush and real-estate values are high enough to keep any impoverished artist at bay. Yet as you wander through its back streets you can't help but be affected by the charm of this neighborhood, perfectly revealed in its romantic tree-lined steps, squares, gardens, and individually designed houses.

The Mill The landmark most associated with Montmartre is, of course, **Le Moulin Rouge**, located on the tacky boulevard de Clichy at the bottom of the hill in Pigalle, best known for its sex shops and hustlers. But why a mill? In fact there were once over 30 windmills in Montmartre, which ground silex from the underground gypsum quarries riddling the hill, but by the early 19th century the quarrying and mills were abandoned to save the hill from collapse.

Following closely in the symbol stakes is **Sacré-Cœur**, the white marble wedding-cake basilica crowning the hill. When it was completed in 1910 (it took 35 years to build) its architect was heavily criticized for its Romanesque-Byzantine style, but no one realized how many millions would flood to see it. The main reason for its popularity is the view across Paris: on clear days it stretches a spectacular 18 miles.

Le Moulin Rouge, opened in 1889 and made famous by Toulouse-Lautrec through his many studies of cabaret artistes

Paris at dusk, from Montmartre—a romantic view of the capital from the steps of the Sacré-Cœur

Presenting the past To get a better idea of the history of this area, go to the **Musée de Montmartre▶** at 12 rue Cortot (*Open* Tue–Sun 11–6). This 17th-century house and its pretty garden once belonged to a member of Molière's theater troupe and was later inhabited by Renoir, Utrillo, and Dufy. Locally made porcelain, a reconstructed interior of a 19th-century bistro, caricatures of local eccentrics by Daumier, drawings by Toulouse-Lautrec ... it is an interesting if not extensive collection.

Fruit of the vine Back in the land of the living, don't miss Montmartre's **vineyard** (opposite the historical cabaret) on the rue des Saules. Every October the grapes are harvested and 500 or so bottles of *Clos Montmartre* are filled. Lastly, whichever street you take you can't miss the **place du Tertre**: at least you can truthfully say what a tourist trap it is.

MOULIN DE LA GALETTE
The Moulin de la Galette, one of only two mills remaining at Montmartre, was built in 1622. During the 1814 Siege of Paris, the mill owner, Debray, was crucified on its sails for trying to stop the invading Cossacks. In the late 19th century, the Debray family converted the mill into a popular open-air dance hall, providing inspiration for many artists, including Renoir and Van Gogh.

Walk

A circuit of Montmartre

See map page 148.

Start at Abbesses métro *station.*
This station boasts one of the original 1900s Guimard entrances.

Follow the rue des Abbesses, west till the road branches. Turn right up the rue Lepic.
Number 54 is where Van Gogh and his brother Theo once lived.

Follow the curve until you see the Moulin de la Galette on your left.
The **Moulin de la Galette** was once a dance hall, frequented by Renoir.

Turn left and left again into the avenue Junot.
At No. 13 lived the artist Poulbot, inventor of the ubiquitous wide-eyed urchin image. Next door at No. 15 is the Dadaist Tristan Tzara's house, designed by Adolf Loos.

Turn right along the rue S. Dereure and on to the Allée des Brouillards.
The Allée leads to an 18th-century mansion, once a dance-hall and home to the poet Nerval.

Follow the raised path beside the gardens to the rue Girardon, where you can either turn left down the steps to visit the Cimetière St. Vincent or go along the rue St.-Vincent to the rue des Saules.
The **Maison Rose** restaurant on the corner was painted by Utrillo and today provides an ideal terrace for lunch. Opposite is Montmartre's **vineyard**, harvested annually on the first Saturday in October.

Follow the rue St.-Vincent, passing the famous Au Lapin Agile. At the rue du Mont Cenis, turn right and climb the steps.
En route, pass Berlioz' former apartment and the pretty **rue Cortot**, which contains the local museum.

Go straight on to the place du Tertre.
Patachon is a tea room with a superb view; walk round the back of it to the **place du Calvaire**.

Returning to the entrance to the place du Tertre, follow the rue Azaïs to the front of Sacré-Cœur.
Here you can climb to the top of the bell tower or take the modernized Montmartre *funiculaire*.

At the bottom go straight on down the rue de Steinkerque, past a lively string of stores selling cheap fabrics, then turn right into the rue d'Orsel.
On your left you pass the charming **Théâtre de l'Atelier** (1822).

Return to the place des Abbesses.

Place des Abbesses métro *station*

► Montsouris, Parc *IFCD2*

Métro: Porte d'Orléans; RER: Cité Universitaire
Open: dawn to dusk

Another of Baron Haussmann's creations, the site of the Parc Montsouris was once peppered with windmills, relics of its granite quarry past. By the turn of the century this pocket of landscaped green had become a favorite hideaway for artists and literati escaping the intellectual overkill in nearby Montparnasse. The Belle Epoque restaurant, suitably called Jardin de la Paresse (Garden of Laziness) on the rue Gazan, is a superb example of architecture of the period, and claims such illustrious diners as Trotsky, Mata Hari, and Sartre. At the top of the hill is a replica of the Tunisian palace of Beys built in 1867 and recently extensively restored.

► Mosquée, la *51D1*

place du Puits-de-l'Ermite, 75005; tel: 01 45 35 97 33
Métro: place Monge
Open: Sat–Thu 9–noon, 2–6. Admission: inexpensive

One of the Left Bank's best surprises, the Paris Mosque was built in 1926 with French funds as thanks for North African military support during World War I. Strongly faithful to ornate Moorish architecture, its roofs are green tiled, fountains pink marbled, and doors carved, while the *salon de thé* whisks you to Cairo. The worshiping area can be visited with a guided tour.

AFRICAN DELIGHTS
For a little exoticism, the African section of the Marché Mouffetard, near the rue de l'Arbalète, has a bright array of smoked fish, handwoven baskets, and sandals.

►► Mouffetard, Marché *166B1*

Métro: Place Monge, Censier-Daubenton
Open: Tue–Sat 8–1, 4–7 and Sun morning

Thronging with tourists, the Marché Mouffetard is nevertheless one of Paris' most picturesque and colorful central markets. This is the land of gastronomic fantasies, where the products available probably outstrip any mental invention. It is best to visit late in the morning, when shoppers elbow past piles of fruit and vegetables and the stall-holders' desire to sell is peaking volubly. Stop for an aromatic coffee and succulent homemade croissants at the **Café Mouffetard** at No. 116. The colorful murals at the Italian grocer **Chez Facchetti** (No. 134) should not be missed.

Fruits de mer at the Marché Mouffetard, a colorful market on one of Paris' oldest streets

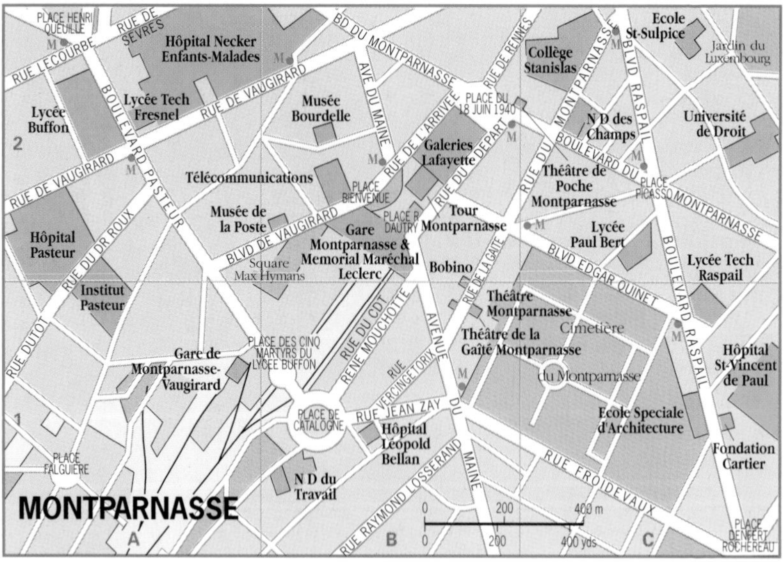

THE CEMETERY AT MONTPARNASSE
Notable former residents of the area lie in the Montparnasse cemetery, accessible from the boulevard Edgar Quinet, where you can pay homage to Sartre, de Beauvoir, Baudelaire, Maupassant, Saint-Saëns, and car-lovers' hero, André Citroën.

THE CEMETERY AT MONTMARTRE
This vast cemetery, laid out in 1795 and covering 25 acres, is one of the best known in Paris. Here you will find the graves of composers Delibes, Berlioz, and Offenbach (who wrote the famous cancan tune immortalized in Paris cabarets); painters Dégas and Fragonard; writers Heine, Dumas, Stendhal, and Zola; film director Truffant; Russian dancer Nijinsky, and the playwright Sacha Guitry.

► Montparnasse *50B1*

Although its sun set long ago, Montparnasse is so evocative of early 20th-century cultural history that it is hard to miss out. Legendary meeting places still exist, haunted by shadows of literary and artistic gurus of the 1920s and 1930s, yet its main boulevards have lost much of their charm, sacrificed to the whims of consumerism.

Tour Montparnasse► Symbolic of this transformation, the heart of the area is towered over by the 690-foot-high **Tour Montparnasse**, an architectural *faux pas* erected in 1973 to crown a vast commercial center. It does, however, offer unbeatable panoramic views from its 59th floor. Across the windy esplanade is the modernized Gare Montparnasse, still confusing and badly designed despite the addition of the TGV Atlantique terminus. Behind this gigantic structure is a *quartier* that has undergone 20 years of hectic redevelopment, replacing atmospheric narrow streets with uninspired apartment blocks. Ricardo Bofill's neoclassical designs are perhaps the most interesting.

High points But despair not! Some corners are worth searching out such as No. 16 rue Antoine Bourdelle, where you can visit the **Musée Bourdelle►** (*Open* Tue–Sun 10–5:40); the picturesque garden, house, and overflowing studios of this sculptor, student of Rodin, are fascinating. Near by, at 15 rue Falguière, stand the newly built offices of France's most respected daily newspaper, *Le Monde*, while farther south is another institutional landmark, the **Institut Pasteur**.

Pursuit of pleasure Back to the east of the Tower, follow the boulevard Edgar Quinet to the **rue de la Gaîté**, Montparnasse's answer to the rue St.-Denis. Its traditional pleasure-seeking character survives among the sex stores and a number of small theaters and

Paris mapped out from the Tour Montparnasse, one of the tallest office buildings in the world

cabarets; here, too, floats the ghost of the modernist dancer Isadora Duncan, who performed at No. 26 and lived at No. 4.

Heart of the matter The pulse of Montparnasse remains centered along the stretch between the boulevard Raspail (reigned over by Rodin's statue of Balzac) and the rue du Montparnasse. Between fascinating specialist stores, restaurants, the architecture of the rue Vavin, and, finally, Montparnasse's living symbol, **La Coupole** restaurant—once the "hang out" of Paris' intellectual class—visitors may at last experience something of the area's past ebullience.

TOUR MONTPARNASSE
After the completion of Montparnasse's skyscraping eyesore, President Georges Pompidou, who had authorised its construction, took a helicopter tour of the neighborhood to survey the finished job. "That's enough," he ruefully told his urban planners, "we stop right there." Then he turned his attention to building highways along the foot paths beside the river Seine.

Cabarets and theaters can be found among the sex stores on the rue de la Gaîté

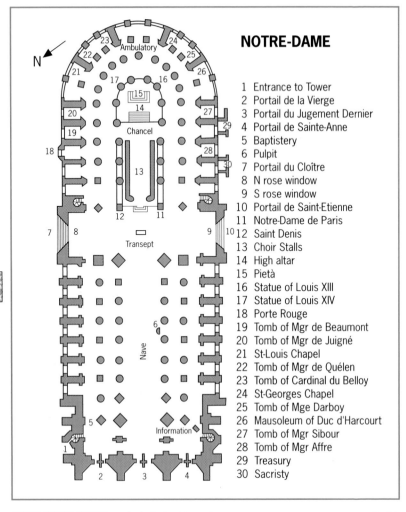

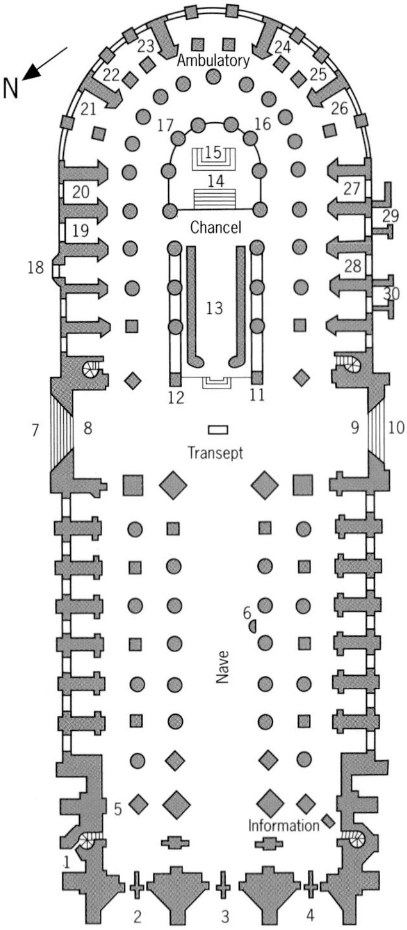

NOTRE-DAME

1 Entrance to Tower
2 Portail de la Vierge
3 Portail du Jugement Dernier
4 Portail de Sainte-Anne
5 Baptistery
6 Pulpit
7 Portail du Cloître
8 N rose window
9 S rose window
10 Portail de Saint-Etienne
11 Notre-Dame de Paris
12 Saint Denis
13 Choir Stalls
14 High altar
15 Pietà
16 Statue of Louis XIII
17 Statue of Louis XIV
18 Porte Rouge
19 Tomb of Mgr de Beaumont
20 Tomb of Mgr de Juigné
21 St-Louis Chapel
22 Tomb of Mgr de Quélen
23 Tomb of Cardinal du Belloy
24 St-Georges Chapel
25 Tomb of Mge Darboy
26 Mausoleum of Duc d'Harcourt
27 Tomb of Mgr Sibour
28 Tomb of Mgr Affre
29 Treasury
30 Sacristy

THE PLACE DU PARVIS NOTRE-DAME
A bronze star on the sidewalk in the Place du Parvis marks the official geographical center of France, where all French national highways begin. The name Parvis is believed to originate from "paradisus" (heaven on earth), the name given to the view of the west front of a medieval cathedral, traditionally the most ornate side, from the open space fronting the building.

►►► Notre-Dame *51D2*

tel: 01 42 34 56 10. Métro: Cité
Admission free; (Towers) moderate; (Treasury) inexpensive
"Each side, each stone of the venerable monument is a page not only of the history of the country, but also of the history of science and of art." Victor Hugo's words—written in 1831 as part of his voluminous historical novel *Notre-Dame de Paris*, which introduced the famous hunchback, Quasimodo—ring as true as the bells of this twin-towered cathedral. Notre-Dame occupies a site that goes back to early Roman times, when *Lutetia* was concentrated on the Ile de la Cité, the heart of the city. Further proof of Notre-Dame's importance is the fact that it is used as point-zero for measuring distances from Paris.

Soon after the Romanesque abbey of St. Denis, just north of Paris, was completed (1144), Bishop Maurice de Sully decided that Paris needed its own cathedral, and construction started in 1163 with foundations laid by Pope Alexander III. The choir was completed in 1182 and the west front and twin towers between 1200 and 1250. It was only in 1345 that the original plans were realized, thus making it an edifice of transition, between the Romanesque and the Gothic.

As a work of the people, Notre-Dame was built by guilds of carpenters, stone-carvers, iron forgers, and glass craftsmen who all labored in the pure medieval spirit of a communal religious effort. For years it remained a meeting place for trade unions as well as a dormitory for the homeless. Its adjoining cathedral school was renowned throughout Europe and eventually gave birth to the Sorbonne.

Unfortunately, the structure of Notre-Dame suffered over the centuries, and by the time Napoleon came to crown himself emperor in 1804, it was in a sorry state of disrepair. Victor Hugo's vehement criticism in 1831 finally goaded the government into action, led by the architects Lassus and Viollet-le-Duc, who enthusiastically set about remedying the damage of centuries. It took over 20 years.

According to Hugo the culprits were threefold: time; political, and religious evolution; and, worst of all, the vagaries of fashion. He was virulent about the absence of countless statues from both the facade and the interior (many toppled during the Revolution), the clear glass

One of the classic views of Notre-Dame—seen at its best from the riverside promenade or from a bateau-mouche on the river

FRANCE'S LARGEST ORGAN
The 7,000 or so pipes of the massive 1730 organ make it one of France's largest, fit to inspire the 6,500 music lovers who flock to free recitals held every Sunday at 5:45.

The impressive buttressed structure of Notre-Dame. Closer inspection reveals finely carved statues and gargoyles, many the work of Viollet-le-Duc

(Louis XV had decided that stained glass was out of date and replaced most rose windows), the replacement of the old Gothic altar with a heavy marble sarcophagus, and the amputation of the spire in 1787 by an architect of "good taste." Much of Hugo's ranting was well heeded: the Gallery of Kings was reproduced (some of the originals were excavated in 1977, and are now at the Cluny) and a 295-foot spire erected, but it was not until after World War II that the stained-glass windows were remade. Viollet-le-Duc also modestly added a statue of himself amongst the Apostles.

West facade Crowned by two 225-foot towers are three imposing, asymmetrical portals representing (left to right) the Virgin Mary, the Last Judgment, and St. Anne, Mary's mother. In the Middle Ages when the statues were painted, these served as a Bible for the illiterate, and it is well worth looking closely at each portal.

Apart from the lintels of the central portal, the sculptures of the tympanums and arches are all original. On the left the Coronation of the Virgin dominates the Resurrection and the Assumption, surrounded by kings, angels, prophets, and zodiac signs. The middle of the Last Judgment was much tampered with by Soufflot in 1771, and the statue of Christ is 19th century. The sculptures of St. Anne on the right date mostly from 1165–1175, showing scenes from her life, the childhood of Christ and, in the tympanum, Mary proffering Jesus to a kneeling King Louis VII (who consecrated the church), seen on the right and the founder, Bishop Sully, on the left.

The towers, originally intended to be surmounted by spires, make a strenuous climb (225 steps to the summit of the north tower, and another 125 to the top of the south tower). In the south tower hangs the famous 13-ton bell "Emmanuel," recast in 1686, evoking memories of a tormented Quasimodo. The fantastic range of gargoyles—grotesque stone figures of demons, birds, and weird beasts—are again the work of Viollet-le-Duc, serving to keep evil spirits at bay.

North and south facades These sides present three distinct, receding storys with bold flying buttresses. Look at the magnificent north porch, the *portail du cloître*, built in 1250 by Jean de Chelles. The statue of the Virgin is original, and the tympanum relates the story of Theophilius, a monk who, after signing a pact with the devil was saved in *extremis* by the Virgin. Immediately to the east is the red door (*porte rouge*), a superb sculpted work by Pierre de Montreuil (1260). Here the tympanum shows the crowning of the Virgin Mary, and the arches portray episodes from the Crucifixion and Resurrection of Christ.

Regally facing the Left Bank, the south porch is dedicated to St. Stephen and was started by Jean de Chelles in 1258. Most of the arch statues are copies, but the tympanum relating the life of the saint and the medallions of student life are all original. The garden at the back of the cathedral was entirely filled with houses and chapels until the 1831 uprising, which destroyed most of this church property.

The southern rose window, depicting Christ surrounded by saints and angels is 69 feet high and still contains some of its original 13th-century stained glass

Interior Entering this awesome cathedral, notice the difference in light between the nave, the transept and the chancel—thanks to the gradual cleaning of the interior.

The traditional Gothic layout consists of a nave of ten bays flanked by double aisles which continue around the choir. The walls are lined with 37 chapels altogether, added during the 13th and 14th centuries. Amongst the traditional annual offerings by the goldsmiths' guild are those adorning the first two chapels to the right, by Le Brun, and in the transept, by Le Sueur.

At the crossing of the transept you can admire the three rose windows, to the north depicting Old Testament figures surrounding Mary (almost totally original glass) and, to the south, Christ in a crowd of angels and saints. The choir, much altered under Louis XIV, also attracted Viollet-le-Duc's untiring attention: over half the original stalls remain, as well as some bronze angels (1711). Numerous tombs of bishops lie below the choir and around the ambulatory. The sacristy (*Open* 9:30–6) on the south side of the choir, houses the treasure of Notre-Dame, which consists of medieval manuscripts, ecclesiastical plate, and reliquaries. The famous crown of thorns and piece of the True Cross are brought out on Fridays during Lent and Good Friday.

Big ceremonial moments are, of course, marked at Easter and on Christmas Eve, but the cathedral, this "vast symphony in stone," radiates an extraordinary power at any time. The cathedral is closed over Saturday lunchtime.

A 3,300-year-old needle: the Obelisk, in the place de la Concorde was once used to measure the sun's shadow at the Temple of Thebes

►► Obelisk *50B3*

place de la Concorde, 75001
Métro: Concorde

Like Cleopatra's Needle in London, the Obelisk is the city's oldest monument—about 3,300 years old. For once it is not a result of colonial grabbing, as it was actually donated in 1833 to King Louis-Philippe by Mohammed Ali Pasha, Viceroy of Egypt. The place de la Concorde has been a central symbol since the removal of Louis XV's equestrian statue during the Revolution, and the 230-ton pink granite Obelisk, after a lengthy journey from Luxor, ended the ongoing polemics.

► Olympia *50C3*

28 boulevard des Capucines, 75009; tel: 01 47 42 25 49
Métro: Opéra

Still a favorite venue for solo performers of variety, old-time pop and sometimes jazz since the days of Piaf, Aznavour, Charles Trenet, and Yves Montand, the Olympia possesses that rare quality in an old concert hall—comfort in spite of complete renovation.

► Opéra Comique *50C3/C4*

5 rue Favart, 75002; tel: 01 42 44 45 46
Métro: Richelieu-Drouot

This strangely oriented theater is tucked down a side-street with its back firmly turned to the boulevard des Italiens. Originally built in 1780 (and rebuilt since after several major fires) to house the Comédie-Italienne, it was constructed in this way to distinguish it from the numerous "popular" theaters springing up along the boulevard. Often called the Salle Favart, the Opéra Comique long specialized in Italian opera and operetta and recently extended to classical music and ballet.

► Opéra de Paris-Bastille *72A1*

120 rue de Lyon, 75012; tel: 01 44 73 13 00
Métro: Bastille

This prestigious architectural operation, instigated by President Mitterrand, was a case of "watch the controversy grow." From day one, when a design by an unknown and relatively inexperienced architect (Carlos Ott) was inadvertently selected, all hell broke loose. Heavily criticized for its ungainly volume and exorbitant cost, the Opéra-Bastille finally overcame most teething problems (including last-minute changes in musical director) and by 1990 creaked into operatic action. Technically sophisticated and highly flexible it has about 3,000 seats in the main auditorium and wonderful acoustics.

►►► Opéra de Paris-Palais Garnier *50C4*

place de l'Opéra, 75009 Paris; tel: 01 40 01 17 89
(Tour Information: 01 40 01 22; Museum: 01 47 42 07 02)
Métro: Opéra
Open: Museum, daily 10–5; summer 10–6. Admission: moderate

The sumptuous and prestigious Palais Garnier was inaugurated in 1875, 15 years after the 35-year-old Charles Garnier's riotous design had been officially accepted. A fittingly lavish epitaph to the manic architectural activities of the Second Empire, it was once the largest theater in the world (13,156 square yards).

Since the opening of the Opéra Bastille, the Palais Garnier has become almost exclusively devoted to ballet. Although the quality of the Ballet de l'Opéra de Paris is internationally renowned, its repertoire tends to remain on the traditional side of contemporary dance. Previously directed by the fiery Rudolf Nureyev, who disappeared in 1990 in a cloud of controversy, the company is now enthusiastically run by the youthful *danseur étoile* Patrick Dupond.

Even if you don't see a performance here, make sure you look at Garnier's marble and gilt Grand staircase, the equally baroque Grand Foyer and the auditorium ceiling by Chagall. Outside, keep an eye open for Carrier-Belleuse's provocative lamp-bearing statues and the copy of Carpeaux's sculpted group *La Danse* to the right of the front arcade: the original is now at the Musée d'Orsay.

IMMENSE PROPORTIONS
The Opéra de Paris' immense stage can accommodate 450 performers, watched by 2,200 spectators under a domed ceiling painted by Chagall (1964).

►►► L'Orangerie 50B3

place de la Concorde, 75001; tel: 01 42 97 48 16
Métro: Concorde
Closed for renovation work, which is scheduled for completion in August 2001.

Echoing the Second Empire architecture of the Jeu de Paume, its Tuileries twin, the Orangerie was originally the greenhouse for the Tuileries Palace, before becoming an exhibition center in the early 20th century. Home to the extensive Walter-Guillaume collection, which ranges from the Impressionists to the 1920s (Cézanne, Renoir, Sisley, Rousseau, Derain, Matisse, Soutine, Modigliani, Picasso, Van Dongen) it offers a pleasant, uncrowded art tour. Although airily displayed, the 144 works are patchy in quality and do not always represent the best of these masters. However, the high point is Monet's eight gigantic panels of *Water Lilies*, painted for the Orangerie's two oval basement rooms, which were presented to the museum in 1927, a year after his death. Go to Giverny to see his original inspiration, but make sure you see these glorious reflections and the depth of their multiple tones.

L'Orangerie, in the Tuileries Garden, was originally a greenhouse but now contains an important collection of Impressionist paintings

MUSEE D'ORSAY

GROUND FLOOR UPPER LEVEL MIDDLE LEVEL

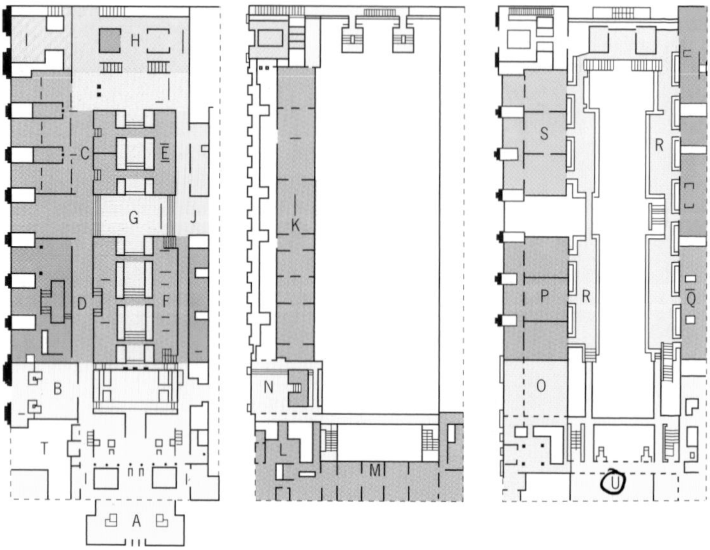

Painting

Sculpture

Architecture

Art Nouveau

Decorative Arts

Special Exhibitions

A Main Entrance
B Bookshop
C Impressionism before 1870
D Realism and the Barbizon School
E Symbolism before 1870
F Academism, Romanticism and Classicism 1850–1880
G Sculpture 1840–1875
H Salle de l'Opéra
I Architecture and Town Planning 1850–1900
J Decorative Arts 1850–1880
K Galerie des Hauteurs-Impressionism after 1870
L Les Salles d'Angles-Neo-impressionism and Pastels
M Galerie Bellechasse-Pont-Aven school and the Nabis
N Café des Hauteurs
O Painting and Sculpture of the Third Republic
P Symbolism and Naturalism 1870–1914
Q Early 20th-century painting
R Sculpture 1870–1914
S French and International Art Nouveau
T Gift Shop
U Restaurant

►►► Orsay, Musée d' 50C3

1 rue de Bellechasse, 75007; tel: 01 40 49 48 14 (Recorded information: 01 45 49 11 11). Métro: Solférino Open: Tue–Sun 9–6 (Thu 9am–9:45pm); winter 10–6 Admission: moderate

Yet another example of Parisian metamorphosis, this building was originally a palace and subsequently a hotel and train station. It opened in 1986 as a museum of the fine and applied arts (1848–1914), and it is infinitely rewarding and accessible.

Ground floor: to the right of a central sculpture passage are paintings by Ingres, Gérôme, Delacroix, and the academics of the period. Symbolism is represented by Puvis de Chavannes, and Gustave Moreau, along with early works by Degas. The galleries on the other side present the pre-1870 teething days of Impressionism in Manet's superb *Olympia, Le Balcon* and *Déjeuner sur l'Herbe,* Bazille, Renoir, Fantin Latour, and several seminal works by Monet. Toward the front of this floor are grouped realist works, many of them by Courbet.

Top floor: to follow the collection chronologically, go straight to the top floor using the front escalators. Here you move into the Ecole de Pont-Aven (Gauguin, Emile Bernard, Sérusier), the mysterious world evoked in Odilon Redon's pastels, Toulouse-Lautrec, Henri Rousseau, and finally Seurat. Then starts the heart of the Impressionist collection, devoted to Cézanne, Van Gogh, Monet, Renoir, Degas, Sisley, Whistler, Mozirot, and Pissarro.

Middle level: overlooking the entrance below, the middle level concentrates on the sculpture and painting of the late 19th century until 1914. In the superbly renovated ballroom are paintings by Bouguereau, *La Naissance de Vénus,* and Gérôme's *Tanagra* alongside monumental sculptures. Through Naturalism (Dalou, Cormon) discover more Symbolist works with foreign parallels such as Burne-Jones and Böcklin. Most striking here are Rodin's sculptures (the powerful *Balzac*, busts, *The Thinker*) and those of his followers Camille Claudel, Rosso, Bourdelle, Bernard, and the familiar rounded forms of Maillol.

In the galleries to the right are the Nabis (Bonnard, Vuilland, Roussel, Denis, and Vallotton). This floor also displays some superb applied arts, concentrating on art nouveau furniture and objects.

A REMARKABLE TRAIN STATION

The original hotel and train station comprising what is now the Musée d'Orsay were erected in an astonishing two years, to be completed for the Exposition Universelle in 1900. Victor Laloux was the architect responsible for its soaring glass and iron roof, together with a wildly ornate Belle Epoque restaurant and ballroom, all still intact. Conversion into a museum came in the early 1980s, masterminded by Gae Aulenti, who created a structure of imposing presence.

CAFÉ DES HAUTEURS

The striking Café des Hauteurs, on the top floor of the Musée d'Orsay, has an unusual view across Paris through the face of the enormous station clock.

Space and style in the Musée d'Orsay

THANKFUL RECOVERY
The Panthéon was Louis XV's way of thanking Ste. Geneviève, patron saint of Paris, for his recovery from gout.

A SCIENTIFIC EXPERIMENT
The interior of the Panthéon's soaring dome was used in 1849 by the scientist Foucault to prove, with a pendulum, the rotative movement of the earth.

MUSÉE EDITH PIAF
Edith Piaf, brought up in the working-class east end of Paris, began her career as a singer here in local bars and cafés before achieving international acclaim in the 1930s. A visit to the tiny museum, crammed with Edith Piaf memorabilia, is worthwhile if only to hear her original records (5 rue Crespin du Gast, 75011; tel: 01 43 55 52 72. *Open* by appointment only Mon–Thu 1–6). *Métro*: Ménilomontant.

► Panthéon 51D2

place du Panthéon, 75005; tel: 01 44 32 18 00
Métro: Cardinal-Lemoine; RER: Luxembourg
Open: Apr–Sep 9:30–6.30; Oct–Mar 10–6:15; closed public holidays. Admission: moderate

Necropolis for the outstanding citizens of France, the Panthéon shelters luminaries such as Voltaire, Rousseau, Victor Hugo, Zola, Louis Braille (inventor of braille), Jean Jaurès, and the Resistance martyr Jean Moulin, as well as a shrine containing the heart of left-wing hero Gambetta. Originally commissioned by Louis XV in 1744, the Panthéon was only completed at the Revolution.

By this time its architect, Soufflot, had died and his neoclassical edifice, based on the form of a Greek cross, was subsequently finished by one of his students. In 1791 its windows were bricked up and its function changed from that of church to Temple of Fame. In 1885 it again changed to become the lay temple it remains today.

The austerity of this monument is slightly alleviated by late 19th-century paintings, the most famous being those by the Symbolist Puvis de Chavannes, depicting the life of Ste. Geneviève.

►► Pavillon de l'Arsenal 51E2

21 boulevard Morland, 75004; tel: 01 42 76 33 97
Métro: Sully-Morland
Open: Tue–Sat 10:30–6:30; Sun 11–7. Admission free

Inaugurated in 1988 as a window on the city's architectural evolution, the Pavillon de l'Arsenal is proof of Paris' growing awareness of its museum-like role. A permanent exhibition on the first floor, *Paris: la ville et ses projets*, retraces through drawings and photographs the historic projects that have etched the face of the city. These are arranged around a spectacular 60 square yards laser-activated scale model. Temporary exhibitions on the upper mezzanines of this luminous, skylit building cover architectural projects and competitions, often in an international context. All in all it is well worth a detour.

►► Père Lachaise 11E3

boulevard de Ménilmontant, 75020; tel: 01 43 70 70 33
Métro: Gambetta, Père Lachaise
Open: daily 8–5:30; summer 8–6. Admission free

The strange fascination of this vast cemetery stems partly from its illustrious incumbents and partly from the fantastic variety of tomb designs. Laid out in 1803 on the slopes of a hill in Ménilmontant to echo a peaceful English-style garden, the cemetery is full of twisting paths, unexpected views, swaying trees, and, above all, some ornate sculpture, altogether making it far from lugubrious.

Pay homage at the Mur des Fédérés to the 147 last defenders of the 1870 Commune, executed here and buried in a common grave, or to any number of political and cultural figures. Buy the plan sold at both entrances, which will lead you to the tombs of Abelard and Héloïse, Chopin, Haussmann, Modigliani, Edith Piaf, Proust, Delacroix, Oscar Wilde, Alice B. Toklas, Jim Morrison, Simone Signoret, and Yves Montand.

▶ Petit Palais 50B3

avenue Winston-Churchill, 75008; tel: 01 42 65 12 73
Métro: Champs-Elysées-Clémenceau
Open: Tue–Sun 10–5:40,Thu 10–8. Admission: moderate

When you tire of the aggressive sights of the Champs-Elysées, this is where to take refuge. Rarely crowded, unless a popular exhibition is on, the museum offers an exceptional patchwork collection of mainly 19th-century French works: Delacroix, Ingres, Courbet, Carpeaux, the Impressionists, and Postimpressionists. Examples of the Dutch school and two private donations complete this eclecticism.

▶ Photographie, Centre National de la 50B4

Hôtel Salomon de Rothschild, 11 rue Berryer, 75008
tel: 01 53 76 12 32. Métro: George V
Open: Wed–Mon 12–7. Admission: moderate

Having recently moved into the renovated Hôtel Salomon de Rothschild, situated just off the rue du Faubourg St.-Honoré, the Centre National de la Photographie now presents monographic exhibitions of contemporary photography which are usually of a high quality. The center also publishes a three-monthly brochure known as *Le Journal*, distributed by art galleries specializing in photography, and was co-producer, with the Beaux-Arts, of the *Première Biennale de l'Image*, the first biennial exhibition devoted to "pictures."

TWINS
Like its twin, the Grand Palais, the Petit Palais' glass and iron domed building was constructed for the 1900 Universal Exhibition, not as a permanent fixture.

Nineteenth-century works are displayed in the Petit Palais. This smaller twin of the neighboring Grand Palais boasts an exquisitely presented collection of French paintings and furniture

►►► Picasso, Musée 51E3

Hôtel Salé, 5 rue de Thorigny, 75003; tel: 01 42 71 25 21
Métro: Chemin-Vert, St Paul
Open: Wed–Mon 9:30–6; winter 9:30–5:30
Admission: moderate

The grand opening of this museum in 1985 signaled the end of 11 years of legal wrangling over Picasso's potentially astronomical death duties. The difficulty for the French government lay in establishing just how much work he had hoarded away: he had an annoying habit of shutting one château and moving on to the next when it was full. Finally, one quarter of his collection was accepted from his heirs in lieu of death duties. Thus this superb, expensively renovated 17th-century mansion with fixtures designed by Diego Giacometti contains over 200 paintings, 158 sculptures, 1,500 drawings, and numerous other creations, as well as 60 or so works by mentors and contemporaries such as Cézanne, Miró, Braque, and Matisse.

A must for anyone remotely interested in 20th-century art, it is arranged chronologically, taking the visitor from Picasso's youthful early 1900s Classicism through years of Cubist experiments with Braque to the high points of the 1930s and beyond. The many women in his life figure strongly—including Dora Maar, Françoise Gilot, and Jacqueline, who survived him but eventually committed suicide. But above all, the collection gives a vivid sense of the freshness and inventiveness which permeated every medium he touched—and they were many—throughout his long and creative life.

ZOO FOOD

When set up in 1793 the "people's democratic zoo" displayed survivors from the royal menagerie at Versailles. Although popular throughout the 19th century, with exotic animals donated from far afield, it was obvious prey for hungry citizens in the 1870–1871 Prussian siege. For months, better connected Parisians regaled themselves with the equivalent of *éléphant bourguignon* and *blanquette de girafe*.

Buste d'une femme *(1931), part of the excellent collection housed in the Musée Picasso*

► Pigalle IBCA5

Métro: Pigalle

The mere name sets many a bell ringing. Renowned *quartier* of the low-life since the last century, when local painters Renoir and Toulouse Lautrec would scout around the place Pigalle looking for models among the dancers, it now flourishes in a blatant sex trade. Lining the boulevard Rochechouart and surrounding streets are sleazy bars, sex stores, peep shows, "live sex", and far more. Pimps, hookers, transvestites all ply their trade here and rows of tourist buses ensure the right balance of payments. But don't be put off by the sleaze, as the area also has some of the hippest nightclubs and bars in town, frequented by respectable trendies who enjoy the early-hour downhill crawl home (see pages 230–233).

► Plantes, Jardin des 51D1

Zoo tel: 01 40 79 37 94; Museum tel: 01 40 79 30 00
Métro: Gare d'Austerlitz, Jussieu, place Monge
Admission: moderate

This spacious garden, which runs down to the Seine from the Montagne Ste.-Geneviève, is composed of a mosaic of carefully tended horticultural experiments (*Open* daily dawn to dusk). Presiding over this botanical paradise is the gigantic **Musée d'Histoire Naturelle** (*Open* Wed–Mon 10–5; summer weekends 10–6) and some ageing tropical greenhouses.

On the Jussieu side, France's oldest public zoo (*Open* daily 9–6; winter 9–5) still survives, although habitat conditions for its animals are unfortunately rather pathetic.

Few other cities in the world have embraced the visual arts in the same way as Paris. The countless artists attracted to the city have left an unusual heritage of custom-built artists' studios and new ones are still being built. Although one of the most famous, Le Bateau Lavoir, went up in smoke, many other historic ateliers remain, sheltered islands in a city increasingly prone to gentrification and less and less accessible to "Bohemians."

Even before the Revolution artists were pandered to and some were given studios in the Louvre Palace; ironically they were booted out so that the museum could be installed. The 19th century saw a rapid increase in the artist population and many of Haussmann's boulevards in Montparnasse, Montmartre and around Monceau incorporate studios, their high windows north-facing to benefit from the unchanging light.

❑ Celebrated paintings of the atelier include *Hommage à Manet* (Fantin-Latour, 1869), showing many of the artist's contemporaries, and *Atelier du peintre* (Courbet, 1855). ❑

Creation to conservation Some of the more bourgeois artists' studios have since become museums: the **Musée Henner** (43 avenue de Villiers, 17th); the **Musée Gustave Moreau** (14 rue de La Rochefoucauld, 9th); the **Musée Delacroix** (see page 112); **Musée Bourdelle** (see page 152); and the **Musée Bouchard** (25 rue de l'Yvette, 16th). Meanwhile the likes of Rousseau, Degas, and Van Gogh moved from one miserable garret to the next, proof that creation is not dependent on comfort.

Working studios Most of the community studio complexes which flourished at the turn of the 20th century are still inhabited, so if visiting them be discreet. Most famous is **La Ruche**, in the passage Dantzig, south of Montparnasse, where Soutine, Chagall, Léger, and Diego Rivera gathered in the 1920s, heating themselves with vodka and using a communal water pump in the garden. Conditions were rough, but from this emerged *l'Ecole de Paris*. Equally verdant, the **Cité Fleurie** in **the boulevard Arago** is the queen of studio communities and recently only just escaped redevelopment.

Survivors At No. 31 rue Campagne Première in Montparnasse stands an exceptional block of ateliers built in 1911, while farther south around the Parc Montsouris, the creative hub of the 1920s survives in the **Villa Seurat**, rue Braque and adjoining rue Gauguet. Here struggled no lesser figures than Salvador Dali, De Staël, Le Corbusier, Braque, Derain, Foujita, and, recording it all for posterity, Henry Miller.

The Musée Delacroix is a former atelier in the place Furstemberg

THE PONT AU CHANGE
The Pont au Change or "Money Changers' bridge" was set up near the Latin Quarter in the 14th century by King Philippe le Bel—the only place in Paris where foreigners could change their money into French currency.

►► Quartier Latin *IBCA3*

For centuries Paris' intellectual heart, the Latin Quarter still thrives on its literary and artistic reputation. As you wander past Roman ruins (above all the Cluny) along its boulevards and sidestreets, you will experience a distinctly relaxed and youthful atmosphere compared with the Right Bank's frenetic, business-oriented pace. Here, the cliché of artists and students lingering for hours in cafés is actually true. No other area of Paris claims so many bookstores or schools, while historic churches, movie theaters, jazz clubs, and narrow streets peppered with a cosmopolitan range of restaurants prevent any terminal tedium.

The university The founding of the Sorbonne university in 1257 (see page 178) led to an animated influx of European students and professors; labeled "Latin" because students had to speak Latin, even outside classes, the area formed a Catholic city-within-a-city right up until the Revolution. In the 15th century its

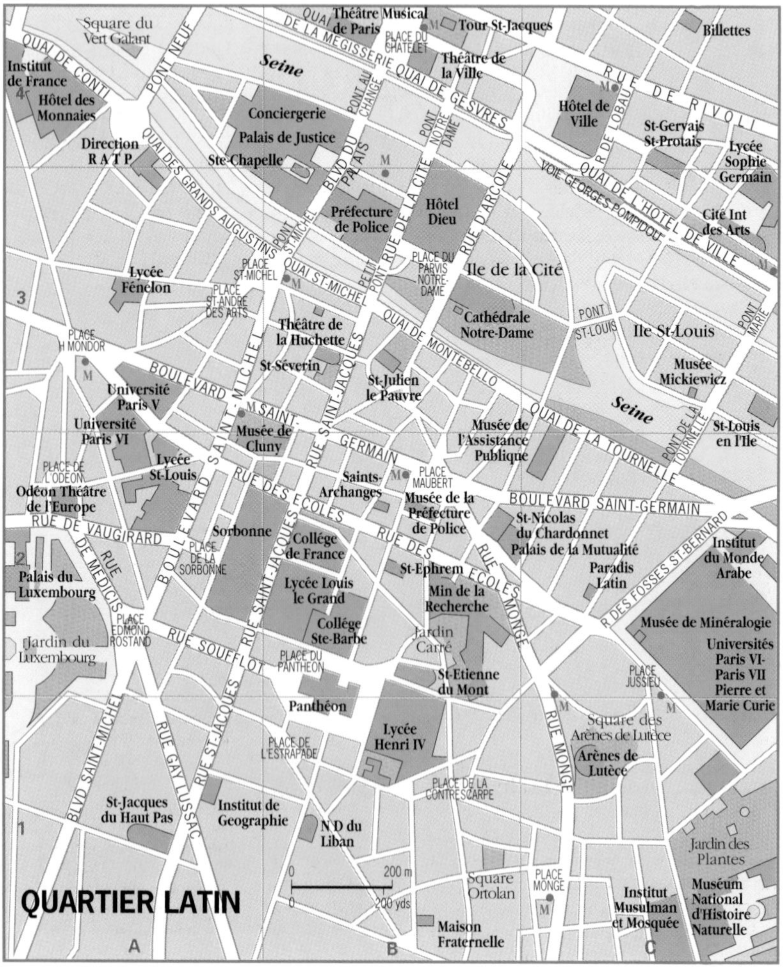

intellectual life was further extended by the proliferation of printing presses, which soon made the rue St.-Jacques France's publishing headquarters.

In the Latin Quarter people really do discuss life and the universe in cafés and brasseries

Wild reputation However, the area fast acquired a reputation for its undisciplined and Bohemian inhabitants, making it fertile soil for the Revolution. Nearly 200 years later in May 1968, the same characteristics of the Latin Quarter again hit the headlines when the students took to the streets, raised barricades and gave the riot police hell. Demands for university reforms combined with a general refusal of consumer-society values with such vehemence that the government was brought down and de Gaulle forced to resign.

Out with the old Unfortunately, much of the authentic Latin Quarter has disappeared behind the interchangeable facades and interiors of Greek restaurants, which have a particularly high profile between the **rue de la Huchette** and the **rue de la Harpe**. This is tourist land *par excellence*, although highlights such as the neighboring **Square René Viviani** with **St.-Julien-le-Pauvre** and **St.-Séverin**, are not far. Keep heading east into the sidestreets off the *quais* and you'll discover a wonderland of small specialty stores along winding streets redolent of the Middle Ages. Bookstores monopolize much of the trade. Farther south, off the rue des Ecoles and within spitting distance of the **Sorbonne** and the **Collège de France**, you can plunge into the heart of academia and probably find a café once frequented by Latin Quarter intelligentsia such as Verlaine, Sartre, and Camus.

ST.-JULIEN-LE PAUVRE
Considering the *gyros* and *souvlaki* restaurants all around, this exquisite early Gothic church completed in 1225 very appropriately belongs to the Melchior sect of the Greek Orthodox Church. When the doors open, its incense wafts out to compete with the fragrant barbecue smoke of neighboring establishments. Many visitors prefer its chamber and organ recitals to the bouzouki music blaring out next door.

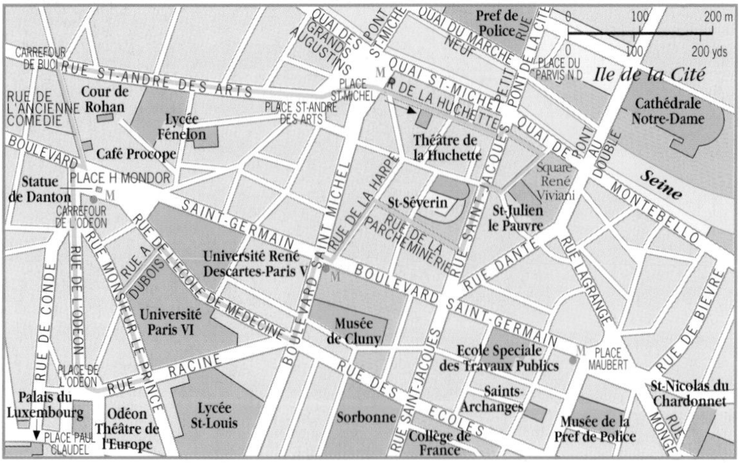

Walk

Tracing the Latin Quarter's streets

Start at the place St.-Michel and turn down the rue de la Huchette.
Cross the rue St.-Jacques and continue straight on to the square René Viviani.
Honored by an acacia tree reputed to be the oldest in Paris, this square is the setting for the partly Gothic church of St.-Julien-le-Pauvre.
Circle back to the rue St.-Jacques, passing St.-Séverin. Cut through the narrow rue de la Parcheminerie to reach the medieval rue de la Harpe, which, to the left, leads to the boulevard St.-Germain. Walk up the boulevard St.-Michel to the rue de l'Ecole de Médecine on your right.
The radical Marat was stabbed in his bath by Charlotte Corday in this street.

Turn left up the rue André Dubois to reach the rue Monsieur le Prince.
The **rue Monsieur le Prince** closely follows Philippe-Auguste's city wall; sections are embedded in Nos. 41 to 47. Today it is packed with cheap restaurants, including the historic Polidor at No. 41.

Go uphill and turn into the rue Racine leading to the place de l'Odéon.
The 18th-century **Odéon Théâtre de l'Europe** dominates this area.

Wander down the rue de l'Odéon to reach Odéon métro.
Across the boulevard St.-Germain is the rue de l'Ancienne Comédie. Pass Paris' oldest café, **Le Procope**, now a restaurant, on your right before you reach the Buci crossroads.
At the crossroads turn sharp right into the rue St.-André-des-Arts.
This street is thick with pizzerias, buskers, and cafés.

This leads you back to St.-Michel.

The square René Viviani

► Raynouard, rue *IFCB4*

This long street running parallel to the Seine takes you through the residential heart of Passy past the quaint **Musée du Vin** housed in 14th-century vaulted cellars (rue des Eaux, 5 square Dickens. *Open* Tue–Sun 10–6; wine tasting included) toward Auteuil. Apart from Balzac, who lived at No. 47 (see page 71), other illustrious inhabitants included the philosopher Jean-Jacques Rousseau, the songwriter Béranger, and Benjamin Franklin. Numbers 51 to 55 are the work of innovative architects Auguste and Gustave Perret, who built this block for their agency and apartments (1929).

LET THERE BE LIGHT
The first lightning conductor ever seen in France was erected by Benjamin Franklin on the roof of his house in rue Raynouard.

► Rivoli, rue de *50C3*

It is easy to forget that Rivoli is an Italian town, scene of the Napoleonic thrashing of the Austrians in 1797. In homage to this victory the long, colonnaded street was designed by the Emperor's architects, Percier and Fontaine in 1811, but only completed in 1835. Today its gracious arcades shelter rows of tourist shops interspersed with smarter joints such as the **Hôtel Meurice**, the *salon de thé* **Angélina,** and the bookstore **Galignani**. On its south side are the **Tuileries gardens**, the **Musée de la Mode et du Textile**, the **Musée des Arts Décoratifs** and, finally, the **Louvre**.

Elegant apartments in the heart of Passy. This was once just a simple village inhabited by woodcutters, but is now one of Paris' most chic residential districts

►► Rohan, Hôtel de *142B3*

87 rue Vieille du Temple, 75003; tel: 01 40 27 60 09
Métro: Chemin Vert, Rambuteau. Admission: inexpensive

Yet another Marais mansion enlisted to house the extensive Archives Nationales, the Hôtel de Rohan can only be seen during temporary exhibitions. Designed by Delamair in 1704 for the son of the Prince of Soubise, whose neighboring Hôtel (see page 126) was built at the same time, it was inhabited by a string of fast-living cardinals. Their apartments are examples of the ornate yet delicate mid-18th-century style.

►►► Rodin, Musée *50B2*

Hôtel Biron, 77 rue de Varenne, 75007; tel: 01 44 18 61 10
Métro: Varenne
Open: Tue–Sun 9:30–5:45; winter 9:30–4:45; park closes 6:45.
Admission: moderate (garden—inexpensive)

Even if not invited to the Elysée Palace or the Hôtel Matignon, at least you can experience the pleasures of

A TERRORIST ATTACK
Jo Goldenberg's, the most famous delicatessen and restaurant on the rue des Rosiers, was the tragic scene in 1982 of a terrorist attack, when gunmen killed six customers.

Musée Rodin. Some of Rodin's finest works have spread beyond the mansion where he spent his last nine years into the delightful rose gardens

Paris' third largest private garden, which surrounds the Hôtel Biron. Originally built for a prosperous wigmaker in 1730, the harmonious mansion of columns and pediments was eventually bought by a dedicated horticulturalist, the maréchal de Biron, who proceeded to indulge his gardening passion until dragged off to the guillotine.

Changing faces Subsequently a dance hall, convent, and school, the Hôtel Biron was in 1908 yet again transformed, this time into artists' studios. In moved the redoubtable Rodin, who stayed until his death in 1917, paying his rent with works. His fellow inmates included Rainer Maria Rilke (working as Rodin's secretary), Isadora Duncan, Cocteau, and Matisse. On Rodin's death the house became the Musée Rodin.

The gardens The blissful rose gardens are one of Paris' greatest hidden treasures, containing several of Rodin's most important pieces: *Le Penseur*, permanently meditating, *La Porte de l'Enfer*, and *Les Bourgeois de Calais* eternally dragging their chains. A former chapel housing temporary sculpture exhibitions and an outdoor café, open during the summer months, complete its attractions.

The house Inside the elegant, airy house you can follow Rodin's evolution chronologically, from his early academic sketches and paintings to his vigorous water colors. His lyrical power and technical breadth are as apparent in the passionate white marble *Kiss*, the nude John the Baptist, the spiritual *Main de Dieu*, or *Eve and L'Age d'Airan*, each of which is displayed in the rotundas. Busts of contemporaries such as Puvis de Chavannes, Mahler, Carrier-Belleuse, Lady Sackville-West, and the suffragette Eve Fairfax reveal his penetrating approach to humanity, particularly evident in his paunchy nude studies of Balzac on the second floor. Works by contemporaries include his tragic model, muse and mistress, Camille Claudel, Eugène Carrière, Munch, Renoir, Monet, and Van Gogh.

►► Rosiers, rue des *142B2*

This ancient street runs the length of Philippe-Auguste's famous city wall and some remnants remain, hidden behind recent facades. It was already known in 1230 under its present name, probably thanks to numerous rose gardens, but today street odors tend more toward Middle Eastern falafel. Heart of the Jewish quarter, the street houses a noisy, animated community with numerous take-out Mediterranean specialties and Jewish stores.

►►► Royal, Palais 10/1/01 *50C3*

Métro: Palais Royal

From heaven to hell, the Palais Royal has run the full gamut of social status. Designed by Lemercier for the wily Cardinal Richelieu, who died there in 1642, the palace became royal when the Regent Anne of Austria moved in with her young son Louis XIV. His horizons being wider, Louis XIV eventually settled into the more

spacious Versailles, leaving the Palais Royal to his brother, Philippe d'Orléans, who turned it into a lively meeting place for the wits and fashion victims of the day. The houses and galleries surrounding the gardens were added in the 1780s and soon sheltered gambling dens, cafés, and brothels; one visitor described it as possessing "every kind of luxury, dirt, and magnificence imaginable." Since the police were banned, its cafés became a fermenting ground for revolutionary ideas.

Current occupation Today the magnificent palace buildings are occupied by the Ministry of Culture and the Conseil d'Etat, while the stores display a bizarre mixture, from stamps and medals to contemporary design, antique porcelain, and books. The garden offers clouds of brilliant color and its restaurants, *salons de thé* and benches are notorious summer crowd-pullers. A recent landmark is Buren's columns, which, in their black-and-white striped splendor, with underground waterways and nocturnal airport lighting, provide endless photo opportunities.

▶ Royale, rue *50B3*

Métro: Madeleine, Concorde

Haunt of luxury goods-hunters, the 18th-century rue Royale joins the Concorde to the Madeleine. Its most famous establishment must be Maxim's, at No. 3, where high society flocked during the Belle Epoque, while at No. 21 once stood the famous literary café, the Café Weber.

▶▶ Sacré-Cœur *51D4*

tel: 01 53 41 89 00. Métros: Abbesses, Anvers
Admission: inexpensive (dome and crypt); Basilica free

It is often forgotten but the Sacré-Cœur was commissioned as atonement for the 58,000 dead of the 1870–1871 Franco-Prussian war. Even today priests work in relays to keep the prayers going continuously 24 hours a day. This extraordinary neo-Romanesque-Byzantine edifice has a strong tourist pull, mainly for its hilltop site overlooking Paris. Climb the dome (*Open* daily 9–6; summer 9–7) for one of Paris' most spectacular views.

Sacré-Cœur—the highest point in Paris—affords 30-mile views from its dome

AUGUSTE RODIN (1840–1917)
Rodin supported himself for years molding and chiseling before creating a scandal with *L'Age d'Airan*, in 1877. By 1900 he was established in the official cultural community and enjoyed a public fame greater than any of his contemporaries. His works often caused violent quarrels among the critics; he despised outward "finish" and was mistakenly categorized with the Impressionists.

SACRÉ-CŒUR
A public subscription was opened to finance the Sacré-Cœur, a method which contributed to its lengthy construction period—35 years.

Spectacular stained glass in Sainte-Chapelle creates a blaze of light and color beneath the ornate star-studded roof

▶▶▶ Sainte-Chapelle

166B4

boulevard du Palais, 75001; tel: 01 53 73 58 51
Métro: Cité, St.-Michel.
Open: daily 10–5 in winter; 9:30–6:30 in summer.
Admission: moderate

Despite being one of Paris' oldest and most significant monuments, the Sainte-Chapelle is hidden in a courtyard behind the Palais de Justice, modestly holding back its charms. Built in under three years, its spire soars 245 feet above ground, unimpeded by flying buttresses—a daring architectural feat for the time. Proof of the intelligence of its design is that nothing has cracked over its 700-year existence, although there was a serious fire in 1630. But the most astonishing feature of this chapel is the ambitious range, color, and intricacy of its stained-glass windows; 1,134 biblical scenes are illustrated.

Simple style Most castle chapels of the early Middle Ages were as architecturally straightforward as the fortifications themselves and built on two floors, to accommodate the master and his family above, with retainers banished to the lower floor. In France the real development of castle chapels came with Louis IX (later canonized), who employed Pierre de Montreuil to build the Sainte-Chapelle, his private chapel, completed in 1248. St. Louis' aim was to have a shrine worthy of various relics acquired during the Crusades, including what was reputed to be the Crown of Thorns, pieces of the cross and drops of Christ's blood. These he had obtained, at an exorbitant cost, from the Emperor of Constantinople.

PRECIOUS RELICS
During the Revolution, St. Louis' ornate and valuable reliquary was melted down and the chapel itself narrowly escaped demolition, but the relics were saved and today they are kept in Notre-Dame, brought out only on Good Friday.

The front of the chapel is given relief by two porches, above which rises an immense rose window, rebuilt under Charles VIII in 1485, surmounted by a *fleur de lys* balustrade. Entrance through the portal takes you into the somber lower chapel. The decorative paintwork here is a product of the mid-19th century, when attempts were made to reproduce the medieval style. It was badly damaged during the Revolution, when it was used as a flour warehouse, and Haussmann's medievalists (in particular Viollet-le-Duc) were only too happy to go to town on this exceptional monument.

The upper chapel A narrow spiral staircase leads to the upper royal chapel: here a visual shock awaits you. Instead of walls you have luminous, unmitigated color—the concentrated effect of 739 square yards of the oldest stained-glass windows in Paris. Surmounted by delicately sculpted gables, the structure of the vaults unfortunately recedes behind more 19th-century paint; however, the main interest lies in the windows.

The windows Starting immediately to your left, you can follow the biblical narrative from Genesis through the Crucifixion to the Apocalypse (the rose window), taking in St. Louis himself on the way. Each window should be read left to right, bottom to top, apart from certain scenes in the choir apse.

Beginning with the first bay these are the main themes:

1 Genesis, Adam and Eve, Noah, Jacob
2 Exodus, Moses on Mount Sinaï
3 Exodus, the Law of Moses
4 Deuteronomy, Joshua, Ruth, and Boaz
5 The Judges, Gideon, Samson
6 Isaiah, the Tree of Jesse
7 St. John, the Virgin, Christ's childhood
8 Christ's passion
9 St. John the Baptist, Daniel
10 Ezekiel
11 Jeremiah, Tobias
12 Judith, Job
13 Esther
14 Kings, Samuel, David, Solomon
15 St. Helena and the True Cross, St. Louis and the Relics
16 The Apocalypse—a rose divided into 86 panels

Leaning against each pillar is a statue of an Apostle but few are originals, and all are heavily restored. Damaged originals are displayed at the Cluny.

In front of the altar stands a wooden canopied platform which once displayed the famous relics. The open spiral stairs leading to it (only the left-hand one is original) were often used by St. Louis in a ceremonial inspection of his treasure.

Acoustic advantages Concerts are regularly held in the chapel, taking advantage of its fantastic acoustics, but as these are in the evening you will not have an opportunity to admire the stained-glass windows (the oldest in Paris).

ARCHITECTURAL HIGHLIGHTS
Features to look out for include 12 medieval wooden carvings of the Apostles, the niches reserved for the royal family on both sides of the chapel in the third bays, and St. Louis' oratory, which Louis XI added in the late 14th century so that he could watch Mass unobserved through a small angled grille near the door. His escape route back to the adjoining palace was via a gallery leading off from the second bay.

ITALIAN BAROQUE
One of rue St.-Jacques' best kept architectural secrets is the splendid 17th-century church of the Val-de-Grace (No. 277 bis. *Open* daily 1–5). Tucked away in the grounds of a military hospital, the edifice built for Louis XIV's mother Anne d'Autriche is an exquisite and, for Paris, rare example of almost pure Italian Baroque. St. Peter's in Rome inspired both the dome and the bronze baldaquin canopy above the main altar.

► St.-Denis, rue *51D4*

This idiosyncratic street was named after the martyr St. Denis, who apparently accomplished the astonishing feat of staggering headless from where he was decapitated in Montmartre to the site of the future basilica of St.-Denis. The long Roman rue St.-Denis was once the processional route for French royalty arriving for coronation and departing for burial; today it presents a very different face, one of prostitutes, sex stores, and, at the Les Halles end, fast-food joints. Despite this sleazy appearance there are a few picturesque old-world bars squeezed between the new-world tack and a wander north toward the ornamental 1672 **Porte St.-Denis** can be amusing.

St.-Germain see pages 176–177

► St.-Honoré, rue *50A4–C3*

Like the rue St.-Denis it runs off the central area of Les Halles, yet the rue St.-Honoré is quite a different, well-mannered world. Lined with respectable clothes, food, and antiques shops it is also one of Paris' oldest roads: Jeanne d'Arc was wounded here, Molière was born here and Marie-Antoinette was transported to the guillotine along it. It takes in the baroque **Eglise St.-Roch**, skirts around the **Comédie Française** and crosses the **place du Palais-Royal** behind the massive **Louvre des Antiquaires**, a costly antiques market. On the western side of the rue Royale it becomes the rue du Faubourg St.-Honoré which, along with the avenue Montaigne, provides the greatest concentration of luxury clothes stores in the capital.

► St.-Jacques, rue *166A1*

Apart from its status as Paris' oldest street (another Roman feat), the steep rue St.-Jacques at last makes clear the origin of the delicious scallop dish, *coquilles St.-Jacques*. With a street named after the crusader St. Jacques, Paris became the starting point for the pilgrimage to the shrine of St. James the Apostle in Compostela, Spain. Pilgrims wore the saint's symbol, a scallop shell.

► St.-Jacques, Tour *51D3*

Métro: Châtelet
The flamboyant Gothic tower still standing in this square dates from the early 16th century, once part of the church of St.-Jacques-La-Boucherie, which was demolished in 1797. It is now a meteorological station.

►► St.-Sulpice, Eglise de *176B1*

tel: 01 46 33 21 78. Métro: St.-Sulpice
Open: 7:30 AM–7:30 PM and during services on Sunday
Apart from housing one of the world's largest organs, St.-Sulpice is a remarkable example of a public edifice, that took 134 years to build and was left with two strangely asymmetrical towers. Don't miss Delacroix's murals in the first chapel on the right as you enter, and look for a bronze meridian line stretching from the south to the north transept, which at winter solstice reflects sunbeams onto an obelisk, and onto a metal plate at equinoxes—a true tribute to France's 19th-century scientific spirit.

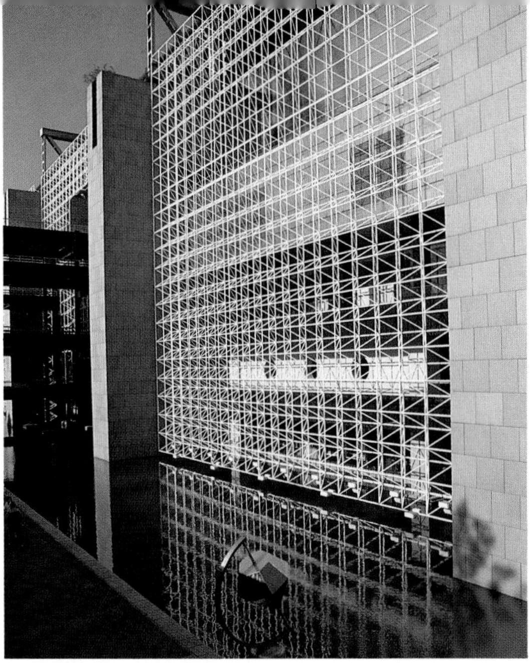

Cité des Sciences et de l'Industrie—a giant science and technology museum with over 7 acres of hands-on displays

▶ Sciences et de l'Industrie, Cité des *11E5*

30 avenue Corentin Cariou, 75019; tel: 08 03 30 63 06
Métro: Porte de la Villette
Open: Tue–Sat 10–6, Sun 10–7. Admission: expensive

Set in the far northeast of Paris in the vast Parc de la Villette, the futuristic Cité des Sciences attracts young visitors to participate in its spectacular displays of science and technology. Life is never the same again after visiting their "inventorium" or "Explora," which whisks you through 35,880 square yards of "space, life, matter, and communication," the very spacey Planetarium or the Cité des Enfants.

▶▶▶ Sens, Hôtel de *142B1*

1 rue du Figuier, 75004; tel: 01 42 78 14 60
Métro: Pont-Marie
Open: Tue–Fri 1:30–8, Sat 10–8:30
Admission free, temporary exhibitions inexpensive

It is well worth a special trip to see this mansion overlooking the Seine, Le Marais' greatest medieval building dating from 1475 to 1507. Built for the archbishops of Sens, it was later inhabited by Henri IV's first wife, Queen Margot. Her taste for young lovers created deadly rivalries, culminating in her ordering the beheading of one unfortunate victim on the mansion steps. Today, less dramatically, the building is used as an applied arts library, the Bibliothèque Forney.

▶ Sèvres, Musée de la Céramique de *10A2*

place de la Manufacture, 92310 Sèvres; tel: 01 41 14 04 20
Métro: Pont de Sèvres
Open: Wed–Mon 10–5. Admission: inexpensive

A leading name in world porcelain, this rich collection covers several centuries of Sèvres production, as well as European pottery of the Middle Ages, Islamic and Chinese ceramics, and Italian majolica.

A SPHERICAL MOVIE THEATER

Across the moat outside the Cité des Sciences et de l'Industrie stands the spherical Géode movie theater, which presents special wide-angle films in its hemi-spherical interior (booking essential; tel: 01 40 05 12 12).

A VISIT TO THE SEWERS

The Sewers (*egouts*), Pont de l'Alma, quai d'Orsay (tel: 01 47 05 10 29. *Open* Sat–Wed 11–5; winter 11–4) have, for some bizarre reason, become a popular tourist destination. One of Haussmann's greatest accomplishments, this vast 1,305-mile underground network—which also contains telephone wires and electricity cables—can be seen on a guided tour which includes a film and photographic display.

THE BOUQUINISTES
The history of these green bookstands lining the Seine dates back three centuries to when second-hand booksellers piled up their wares on the river-bank prior to carrying them across the river in wheelbarrows.

►►► St.-Germain-des-Prés 50C2

tel: 01 43 25 41 71. Admission free

Tranquilly cradled at the heart of Paris, St.-Germain remains eternally magnetic for the visitor and resident alike. Modern incursions are rare and the atmosphere still has something of the Paris of history, literature and cinema. The pace seems more leisurely than on the other side of the river, cafés still play their traditional role and backstreet bistros whisk diners back half a century or so. Aproned waiters and waitresses scold as they are reputed to, and the residents still include a fair share of eccentrics and/or intelligentsia.

Origins Symbol of its genesis, the **Eglise St.-Germain-des-Prés** dates from the late 10th century, when it was part of a Benedictine monastery that replaced a 6th-century abbey. By the 14th century it was surrounded by a fortified wall, which disappeared with the age of enlightenment to make way for housing—and the new

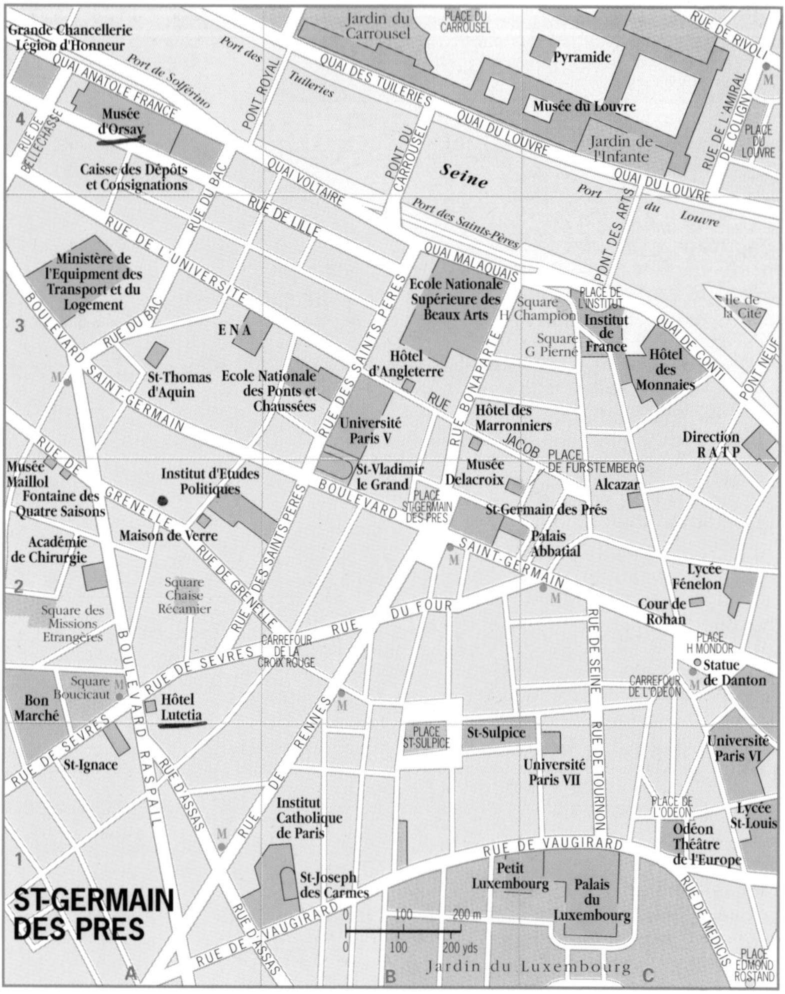

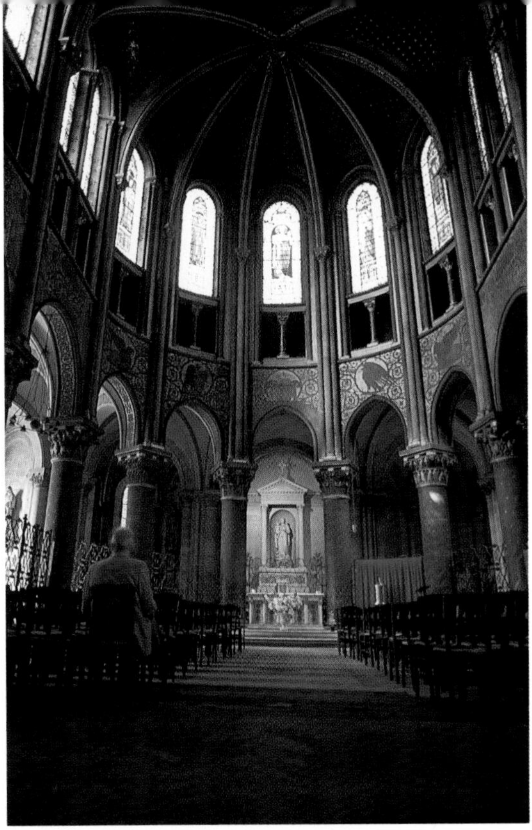

The Church of St.-Germain-des-Prés, the oldest church in Paris. Its eventful history dates back to a 6th-century abbey founded here by King Childebert

BOULEVARD ST.-GERMAIN
The lively cafés of boulevard St.-Germain—the rendezvous of the literary elite—include the Café de Flore, once frequented by Jean-Paul Sartre, and Café les Deux Magots, former haunt of Ernest Hemingway. Brasserie Lipp was one of former President Mitterrand's favorites.

nobles of the Faubourg St.-Germain to the west. Badly damaged during the Revolution, only one of its original three towers remains but the massive flying buttresses of the choir (12th century), remain intact. The 19th century brought much retouching and the nave and the choir contain murals by Flandrin from that period.

The living heart of St.-Germain is, of course, the **boulevard**, which runs west from the Latin Quarter to join the staid government buildings and bourgeois mansions of the 7th *arrondissement*. North of the boulevard, toward the Seine, remains an essentially arty district, crowded with small movie theaters, galleries, antiques stores, the national art school (see page 79), and the Mint (see page 147). In the shadows of its narrow streets you can make your own discoveries of stores, restaurants, or hidden courtyards, all finished with a veneer of affluence. It is a *quartier* in limbo, which cannot decide whether it is part of the forward-looking new capital or clinging to its prewar intellectual days.

South of the boulevard the streets widen and the atmosphere changes. From the church of St.-Sulpice to the Jardin du Luxembourg, through the shopping streets of the rue Bonaparte, rue de Sèvres, and rue de Grenelle, this is the St.-Germain of fashion and publishing. Chic bars replace crowded cafés and furniture design stores line the boulevard Raspail, leading up to the crossroads of Sèvres-Babylone, which is dominated by the renovated art deco **Hôtel Lutetia** and Paris' first department store, **Au Bon Marché**.

Seat of learning: La Sorbonne, the University of Paris, with its oldest building, the domed Church of St.-Ursule, dating from 1635

► La Sorbonne 51D2

45–47 rue des Ecoles, 75005; tel: 01 40 46 22 11
Métro: Cluny-La Sorbonne. Admission: moderate

Symbol of France's great spirit of learning, the Sorbonne was founded in 1257 and for centuries maintained an independent attitude to the state, recognizing the English Henry V as King of France, condemning Joan of Arc, later fiercely opposing Protestants (Henri IV) and the 18th-century "philosophers." The student revolts in 1968 gave the state its first opportunity to allow police to enter these premises. Richelieu was responsible for the rebuilding of the dilapidated college in 1642, although Lemercier's domed chapel, where the Cardinal lies in splendor, is all that remains: today's amphitheaters and endless corridors all date from the late 19th century. You can enter the imposing courtyard off the rue de la Sorbonne and ask for permission to see Puvis de Chavannes' mural in the "Grand Amphitheatre."

►► Sully, Hôtel de 142C2

62 rue St.-Antoine, 75004
Métro: St.-Paul

All was not sweetness and light in the heyday of Le Marais, as the gambling owner of this superb 1630 mansion is said to have lost his fortune overnight. He left a richly decorated home which was soon bought by Henri IV's former minister, the Duc de Sully. The courtyard is a particularly impressive example of Louis XIII, and the recently restored interior boasts some ornate ceilings and paneling. In the garden an Orangerie is used for temporary exhibitions and the bookstore of the Caisse Nationale des Monuments Historiques at the entrance has useful information on guided tours and monuments. (The garden is open daily. *Guided tour* of hotel at weekends; tel: 01 44 61 20 00 for times.)

Synagogue 142B2

Métro: St.-Paul

Although the architect Hector Guimard is best remembered for his fanlighted *Métropolitain* entrances, he was also prolific between 1895 and 1910. His synagogue in the heart of the Jewish quarter in Le Marais was built in 1913. He continued working until 1930, but distressed by the rise of fascism, Guimard emigrated with his Jewish wife to the U.S., where he died in 1942.

▶ Tristan Tzara, Maison 148B2

15 avenue Junot, 75018
Métro: Abbesses
Closed to public
In one of Montmartre's select streets stands the only house in Paris designed by the Austrian architect Adolf Loos. Opponent of the "decorative" art nouveau and defender of a pure rationalist style, Loos settled in Paris in 1923 and soon designed this house for the monocled writer Tristan Tzara, at the time deeply involved in bringing about the death-rattle of Dadaism.

▶▶ Trocadéro, place du 50A3

Métro: Trocadéro
Another landmark Parisian square, the Trocadéro is actually laid out in a semicircle facing the wings of the **Palais de Chaillot** and beyond that, in a direct line, the **Eiffel Tower**. Named after an Andalusian fort occupied by the French in 1823, it was not given its present shape until 1858, when a first **Palais de Chaillot** was built. The 1937 Exposition Internationale replaced the palace with the present monumental buildings, that house several museums (see pages 91 and 94). Around the area are well-frequented cafés and restaurants, including the *salon de thé* Carette, a regular on the Passy agenda.

▶▶▶ Tuileries, Jardins des 50C3

Métro: Tuileries
Open: daily 7:30 AM–7:30 PM; summer 7 AM–9 PM
Admission free
The famous Tuileries gardens were originally laid out Italian-style to complement the palace built for Catherine de Médicis in 1564. Corneille described them as "the land of the beautiful people and of gallantry," where balls, concerts, and fireworks provided constant animation. In 1649 Louis XIV stepped onto the scene with his minister Colbert and commissioned major

The Trocadéro Gardens sloping down toward the Seine from the Palais de Chaillot, are dotted with unusual sculptures and fountains

Jardins des Tuileries—60 acres of beautifully landscaped gardens at the very heart of the city

Messing about with boats in the Jardins des Tuileries

MAILLOL IN THE TUILERIES GARDENS
A series of sculptures by Aristide Maillol (1861–1944) decorates the lawns of the Tuileries gardens. This admirer of Gauguin and the Nabis exclusively sculpted nude female figures whose sensuous forms are reminiscent of Renoir's work. More of his work can be seen in the Musée Maillol, 61 rue de Grenelle, 75007 (*Open* 11–6. *Closed* Tue). *Métro*: rue du Bac.

changes by his favorite landscape gardener, the prodigious André Le Nôtre (also responsible for the immaculate gardens at Versailles, Chantilly, and Vaux le Vicomte). Two lateral esplanades were built up and the central alley which led away from the château laid out. At the time the gardens were considered among the best kept in Europe and was a fashionable promenading area. Although the royal residence went up in serious smoke at the hands of the Communards in 1871, the gardens survived, changing their appearance little over the next century.

Spruced up After years of neglect and pollution, the gardens have been replanted and relandscaped to match the renovation of the Louvre. Indeed, the terrace linking museum and gardens was designed by the Pyramid's architect, I.M. Pei. Carefully aligned fountains, ponds, terraces, lawns, and flowerbeds have been completely renovated, and two new restaurants added. Statues by Maillol and Paul Belmondo (father of film actor Jean-Paul) are shown to much better advantage.

Regained role Opposite the Pyramid, the Arc du Carrousel has regained its original role as a gate to the garden. The last stage of the project includes the Passerelle Solférino, a footbridge linking the gardens to the Musée d'Orsay, and the renovation of the Orangerie Museum at the Concorde end of the garden. The main area has kept its basic form but with numerous improved facilities (including children's playgrounds and bowling areas), and vastly regenerated and replanted vegetation. However, a quarter century is estimated as necessary for the full impact of new plantations.

If caught in Paris on one of its rare rainy days—March showers being the rule—head for the 2nd and 9th arrondissements, where a network of covered passages creates a sheltered itinerary full of surprises. Relics of pre-department store days, these passages were the fashionable shopping malls of early 19th-century Paris.

Almost 30 survive out of the original 140 passages: many have been heavily restored, others are dusty, partly derelict reminders of an age past, but all have traders in the strangest of domains.

Start with one of the most picturesque, hardly touched since it was built in 1826, the **Galerie Véro-Dodat**, which runs between the rue Jean-Jacques Rousseau and the rue Croix des Petits Champs. Named after two butchers, it was one of Paris's first streets to be illuminated by gas. Today its black and white tiled floor, window-boxes, and carved wood moldings make a shadowy, harmonious setting for an old-world restaurant, antiques stores, and galleries, including a wonderful antique doll store.

High fashion A few streets away, beyond the place des Victoires, is the **Galerie Vivienne**, perhaps the most fashionable of these passages, built in 1823 and decorated with mosaics. Home to one of Paris' best wine-merchants, Legrand, an extraordinary toy store, a unique bookstore established in 1826 (Nos 45 and 46), and a chic *salon de thé*, whose tables spill out under the lofty skylights, the Galerie Vivienne should not be missed. Running parallel and off it is the over-restored **Galerie Colbert**, that houses some interesting stores and galleries, all belonging to the Bibliothèque Nationale, as well as a brasserie, the Grand Café Colbert.

Head north up the rue Vivienne past the Bourse and you will find a passage with a strange past: the **Passage des Panoramas**. It was built in 1800 by an American who came to France to propose various inventions to the new Directoire, among which were a torpedo and a submarine. To earn a few bucks while waiting, he built two towers containing panoramas at the boulevard end of his passage. Today the passage is a mass of specialty stores (look for the card-engraver, Stern) with some unusual eating places, including a teashop installed on the site of an old chocolate factory, and an Italian trattoria that could be straight out of Rome.

The Galerie Vivienne

Other options Across the boulevard Montmartre the passages continue (**Passages Jouffroy and Verdeau**), each one revealing its own unique character to the inquisitive visitor with time to explore them.

FREQUENTED BY THE FAMOUS
Residents of the place Vendôme have included Chopin, who died at No. 12, and Anton Mesmer, the founder of the theory of mesmerism, who held experiments at No. 16.

► Vendôme, place *50C3*

Métro: Opéra, Tuileries

Supreme symbol of Parisian chic, the place Vendôme is densely populated by jewelry stores and anything else that can approach the same level of quality and price tags. The **Ritz Hotel** is an example, and its guest books include the names of Proust and Chanel. The square's facades were designed in 1685 by Hardouin-Mansart as an aptly gracious setting for an equestrian statue of Louis XIV by Girardon. This effigy did not outlast the energies of the mob during the Revolution and it was duly felled, to be replaced by the present bronze column. This was initially crowned by a figure of Napoleon as Caesar; in 1814 a statue of Henri IV took over but after several more changes, including the toppling of the column by the Communards, a copy of Napoleon's original statue resumed its post. The bronze itself came from canons captured at the Battle of Austerlitz.

► Vert Galant, square du *166A4*

Métro: Pont-Neuf

The pointed western tip of the Ile de la Cité is named after Henri IV, Paris' first regal town planner, who commissioned both the Pont-Neuf and the place Dauphine immediately across from his fine equestrian statue. This little garden has a wonderful view west along the Seine. Boat trips leave from the quay here.

ARTIST'S EXILE
Juliette Drouet became Victor Hugo's devoted mistress and accompanied him on his self-imposed exile to Guernsey (in furious reaction to Napoleon III's *coup d'état*), where they remained from 1852 to 1870.

Versailles see pages 210–213

►► Victor Hugo, Maison de *142C2*

6 place des Vosges, 75004; tel: 01 42 72 10 16
Métro: Bastille, St.-Paul
Open: Tue–Sun 10–5:40. Admission: inexpensive

This is one of Paris's most characteristic museums, giving a rounded view of the great writer's many talents and his changing residences, which included the second floor of this town house from 1832 to 1848. Displayed on the second floor are numerous pen and ink drawings by Victor Hugo, alongside occasional temporary exhibitions. Upstairs the rooms are laid out to give the atmosphere of his diverse abodes and include a surprising *salon chinois* and furniture from actress Juliette Drouet's room in Guernsey, all carved and/or decorated by the writer himself. Other Hugo memorabilia include a bust of him by Rodin.

Maison de Victor Hugo: the salle à manger chinoise *from Hugo's villa in Guernsey has been reproduced here, with most of the oriental style carving executed by Hugo himself*

► Vidéothèque de Paris *51D3*

2 Grande Galerie, Forum des Halles, Porte St.-Eustache, 75001
tel: 01 47 04 24 24. Métro: Les Halles
Open: Tue–Sun 12:30–8:30; Thu 10 PM
Admission: inexpensive

Another underground destination of Les Halles, the Vidéothèque is a must for anyone interested in both film and Paris. Since opening in 1988, this municipal video library has built up a stock of over 3,500 videotapes covering anything that has ever been put on celluloid concerning the capital—from the Lumière brothers in 1896 to the present—including TV documentaries, commercials, and feature films. You can either watch the excellent thematic programs shown daily on the large screen or use an individual monitor to view your own choice of movie(s). Entrance costs less than a movie theater seat.

►► La Villette, Parc de *IBCC6*

Métro: Porte de la Villette, Porte de Pantin

Nearing completion, the multipurpose Parc de la Villette is one of Paris' most important cultural projects of the 1980s. Stretching around the northeastern perimeter of the city, this amazing 136-acre park has been developed since 1979 by architect Bernard Tschumi to offer a concentrated range of cultural and leisure activities.

MUSÉE DE LA MUSIQUE
The latest addition to the Cité de la Musique complex, this museum (*Open* Tue–Thu 12–6, Fri–Sat 12–7:30, Sun 10–6) exhibits some 900 musical instruments from the 16th century to the present time, out of a stock of 4,500. The audiovisual tour, interactive areas, and demonstrations of instruments make this a lively sound experience as well as a visual delight.

Parc de la Villette—the extensive urban park created in a previously run-down area, combining arts and sciences with nature

Facilities and follies A major integral part of the project, the **Cité des Sciences et de l'Industrie** (see page 175), sits in its moat beside the canal, faced by a spherical movie theater, **La Géode►** (both designed by Fainsilber), but many of the surrounding walkway structures and red metal "follies" are cumbersome and apparently aimless. A survivor from 1867 is the original slaughterhouse, **La Grande Halle**, which in a renovated form now accommodates temporary events, from trade fairs to exhibitions to concerts. In front, dominating the Porte de Pantin park entrance, is the recently completed **Cité de la Musique**, designed by Portzamparc in a neo-1930s style, which gives music students modern facilities, and a superb public concert hall. Another concert hall, **Le Zénith**, conceived specifically for rock concerts, stands on the eastern edge of the park. Scattered between these landmarks are numerous children's facilities, cafés, gardens, a submarine, and the Inventorium, where you can "build" a house or program a computer.

The checkered history of the Château de Vincennes as a former royal residence, prison, porcelain factory, and arsenal makes a fascinating family day out

ALL THE FUN OF THE FAIR

The Bois de Vincennes plays host to the Foire du Trône, the largest funfair in France, from Palm Sunday until the end of May on the Reuilly lawns. The other main fair in Paris is held twice a year (summer and Christmas) in the Tuileries Garden. Its big wheel affords spectacular views of central Paris. Near the Sacré-Cœur and at the Forum des Halles are old-fashioned carousels.

► Vincennes, Château and Bois de *11F2*

Tel: 01 48 08 31 20. Métro: Château de Vincennes

Before its many reincarnations, the sturdy medieval castle commanding the east of Paris arose in the 14th century and was completed under Charles V. The symmetrical Pavillon du Roi and Pavillon de la Reine were added to the southern end by Le Vau while Cardinal Mazarin ruled the roost in 1652, but were badly damaged in 1944 when the Germans were abandoning Paris.

Although Louis XIV spent his honeymoon here, Vincennes was soon supplanted by Versailles (completed ca1680) and thus started its string of transformations. Successively a prison, a porcelain factory (which then moved west to become the famous Manufacture de Sèvres), a military school, an arms factory, and, under Napoleon, an arsenal, Vincennes became a fortress under Louis-Philippe in the 1830s and an ammunition depot during the German Occupation. For over a century, starting with the fanatical medievalist Viollet-le-Duc, intermittent restoration has been carried out.

Entrance to the château (*Open* daily 10–5; summer 10–6) is through the Tour du Village, a powerful 138-foot-high tower which leads into the central courtyard. On your left is a strange museum, with even stranger opening hours (tel: 01 49 57 32 00) dedicated to the history of hunting. The keep is closed for restoration till 2005, but the chateau's exterior and chapel are open to visitors.

The chapel The royal chapel dominating the courtyard, although in 14th-century Gothic style with a superb rose window, was completed in 1552 under Henri II, and its gracefully vaulted interior is well worth entering. The stained-glass windows in the choir are unusually toned Renaissance scenes of the Apocalypse, much restored in the late 19th century.

The keep Opposite the chapel, within in a walled area, the square turreted tower is one of the finest in France. Inside, the first floor once housed the kitchen and has now gained a door rescued from the Temple prison, where Louis XVI was imprisoned. A spiral staircase leads to the upper floors, where resident royalty, including Henry V of England and Charles IX, and later prisoners of state, once enjoyed a panoramic view of Paris.

The royal courtyard, accessible through another gateway and closed at the southern end by the monumental Tour du Bois, is flanked by the royal pavilions, closed to the public apart from a small section containing yet another idiosyncratic museum, the Musée des Insignes. Le Vau's Classical structure was inhabited by various minor royalty, as well as Cardinal Mazarin, who died there.

Bois▶ Landscaped at the same time as the Bois de Boulogne by Baron Haussmann, the Bois de Vincennes traditionally served the working-class population of eastern Paris. It possesses no fewer than three lakes, the Parc Floral, a race course, a zoo, a tropical garden, a Buddhist center, a theater complex and, at the Porte Dorée entrance, the Musée des Arts d'Afrique et d'Océanie (see page 63). Like Boulogne, it too was once rich royal hunting ground, sectioned off by another of Philippe-Auguste's walls in the 12th century. By Louis XV's reign it had become a popular promenading area and the woods were replanted.

The Zoo▶ Near the Lac Daumesnil, France's largest zoo (*Open* 9–5; summer 9–6) houses over 600 mammals and 200 species of birds in a fairly natural, spacious environment. The best time is had by mountain goats, careering up and down their 230-foot-high artificial rock. Avoid Wednesday afternoons and weekends, particularly in summer, as lines are long.

Nearer the château, the **Parc Floral** (*Open* summer 9:30–8; earlier closing in winter) provides an exceptional floral display renewed every season. Special sections exist for dahlias, water lilies, medicinal plants, irises, orchids, tulips, rhododendrons, and azaleas, and there is also an exhibition hall and a children's playground. Row boats and bicycles can be rented at the lakes. Vincennes also houses, adjacent to the Parc Floral, the famous collective theater, the **Théâtre du Soleil** at La Cartoucherie (a former munitions factory), founded by Ariane Mnouchkine in the late 1960s.

"GIVE ME BACK MY LEG"
High points in Vincennes' history include La Fayette heroically saving it from destruction by the mob in 1791, the Duc d'Enghien savoring his last dinner in the splendor of the Pavillon du Roi before facing Napoleon's firing squad at midnight, the peg-legged General Daumesnil refusing to surrender the castle to the Allies in 1814 with the cry "First give me back my leg" (he had lost it at the Battle of Wagram), and the execution of the tantalizing spy Mata Hari in 1917.

A BOILED KING
Macaber legend has it that on his death Henry V's body, rotten with dysentery, was boiled in the château kitchens.

Contemplating life as residents of the Bois de Vincennes zoo

Parisians seem to have an innate knack of staying chic. Even though 66 percent of French women now work full-time and often cope with children too, they seem never to have a hair out of place or an uncoordinated accessory. Not to speak of the men who swing along the boulevards or stub out their Gitanes with a flourish that is unmistakably Gallic.

FASHION SHOWS
Paris' fashion show season starts in January and July with the *haute couture* shows at the Cour Carrée du Louvre and a few other select venues. Tickets are virtually impossible to obtain. However, to attend a private *couture* show, call the *haute couture* houses one month prior to the show to reserve a ticket.

Wine can be ordered and delivered from any of the Nicolas chain of stores

So what is their eternal and annoying secret? Self respect (sometimes called egocentricity) is one good reason. And this means taking good care of oneself, pampering one's ego and one's outer shell.

Body beautiful Alexandre de Paris (3 avenue Matignon, 75008, tel: 01 42 25 57 90) is perhaps Paris' most famous hairdresser for men and women and also offers massages and facials. Service is suitably sycophantic and meals are also served during what can be time-consuming treatments. **Carita** (22 rue de Sèvres, 75007, tel: 01 42 22 75 70) now specializes in both sexes, and its three floors of clinical-looking individual booths cater for manicures, pedicures, massages, facials, and (the specialty), hair treatments. Phones and snacks are all part of the service. Now you will understand how Catherine Deneuve remains eternally youthful.

For skin care only, it is hard to beat the time-honored **Guerlain** (68 Champs-Elysées, 75008, tel: 01 45 62 11 21, and 2 place Vendôme, 75001, tel: 01 42 60 68 61). Elegant private salons in their original 1828 premises contrast with the frayed Champs-Elysées outside. In a similar vein the **Laboratoires Payot** (10 rue de Castiglione, 75001, tel: 01 42 60 32 87), founded by a Russian émigrée in 1919, has a timeless salon that specializes in body massages and, above all, facial care using its own excellent products. You can also buy the Institut's Pavlova perfume created for the great ballerina.

If the pores of your body really need liberating, head for the **Hammam** at the Mosquée where the steam and dry baths will cure most ills (see page 125).

Clothes beautiful To be impeccably turned out is another criterion for Parisian chicness. All Parisians make sure their clothes are clean and well-pressed before stepping out. For clothes alterations and more than perfect mending go to **Mermoz Retouches** (21 rue Jean Mermoz, 75001, tel: 01 42 25 73 36); prices and quality are both high. Most dry-cleaners also offer mending services. If you spill foie-gras or champagne on your *haute-couture* evening dress, opt for **Delaporte Star** (62 rue François I, 75008, tel: 01 43 59 82 11), much used by neighboring boutiques such as Dior and Balmain. Their prices are monstrous but service is excellent. For really top-class old-fashioned laundering, make for **Pouyanne** (28 avenue Franklin-Roosevelt

75008, tel: 01 43 59 03 47), who calls himself the "clothes' doctor" and looks after your delicate garments, kimonos, and furs! Deliveries are part of the friendly service.

Down at the heel? Then make sure you see a *cordonnier*. There are plenty of old-fashioned cobblers in every neighborhood, but you can always rely on the delivery service of **Claraso** (34 rue Godot-de-Mauroy, 75009, tel: 01 47 42 49 79). Repairs take at least a week.

Missing a tuxedo or a chic cocktail dress for an occasion you didn't anticipate? Then go to **Beral** (2 rue Caulaincourt, 75018, tel: 01 43 87 72 37) for the former and **Latreille** for the latter (62 rue St André-des-Arts, 75006, tel: 01 43 29 44 10).

Debauve et Gallais: chocolates with a chic label from the original 18th-century store in St.-Germain

Be chic to others How to thank your Parisian dinner hostess without arriving under a veritable forest of flowers? The answer is to have said forest delivered, and buy the best. **Lachaume** (10 rue Royale, 75008, tel: 01 42 60 57 26) remains the incontestable king, established in 1845. Although prices are astronomical, your hostess will appreciate the label. However, each district has its choice of worthy, if more modest establishments, that create the most imaginative, artistic bouquets.

Bottles clanking up the stairs never create a suave entrance, so why not have some of your chosen elixir delivered in advance? Any branch of the wine store chain **Nicolas** (8 avenue de Wagram, 75008, tel: 01 42 27 22 07) takes phone orders and delivers, for a flat charge of 60 francs on orders under 1300 francs, otherwise free.

Finally, a discreet box of fine chocolates never goes amiss, but again make sure it has the right label: choose from specialty suppliers **Christian Constant**, **Debauve et Gallais,** or **Dalloyau.**

ROYAL CHOCOLATES
Hot chocolate was served three times a week to the Sun King at Versailles. The first chocolate store opened in Paris in 1659 and Voltaire was reported to drink 12 cups a day in his old age. In the early 19th century Debauve et Gallais opened their store, still in the rue des Saintes-Pères today, to promote chocolate's therapeutic qualities.

Week's itinerary

Day one

St.-Germain-des-Prés. Besides the church, explore the art galleries, cafés, and antiques stores along the **rue Jacob, rue Bonaparte, rue de Seine** and the **rue de Buci** street market.

Visit the church on the **place St.-Sulpice**; then continue to the **Jardin du Luxembourg**. By the river go to the **Musée d'Orsay**. Cross the bridge and walk through the Tuileries to finish beside the **Orangerie**.

Day two

Saint-Honoré. Start at the **Louvre**, not missing the **Cour Carrée**; cross to the **Palais Royal**, entering the gardens beside the **Comédie-Française**. Explore this area and see the **Bibliothèque Nationale** before continuing to the **Opéra**.

Walk through the **place Vendôme**, past the **Ritz**, to the **rue de Rivoli**. Visit the **Jeu de Paume** and walk around the **place de la Concorde** to the gardens of the **Champs-Elysées**.

Day three

Le Marais/Bastille. Start exploring the islands, **Notre-Dame** and **Sainte-Chapelle**. Pass the **Hôtel de Ville** and go to **Beaubourg,** then walk through **Le Marais**. Visit the **Hôtel de Soubise**, the **Musée Picasso**, walk through the **place des Vosges** to the **Bastille**. Walk up the rue de la Roquette or take a bus to **Père Lachaise** at the top. Dine in **Belleville**.

Day four

Trocadéro. Start at the **Tour Eiffel**. Cross the bridge to the **Palais de Chaillot** and museums. Go to the **Porte de la Muette**, the **Jardin du Ranelagh** and the **Musée Marmottan** then head for the **Arc de Triomphe**. Take the *RER* to **La Défense** and visit **La Grande Arche**.

Day five

Spend the day in **Versailles**. Or drive to **Fontainebleau** and **Vaux-le-Vicomte**. Dine in **Montparnasse**.

Day six

Latin Quarter. Start at the **rue Mouffetard** market and nearby streets.

Tea at the **Mosquée**, a stroll in the **Jardin des Plantes**, then to the Roman **Arènes de Lutèce** and the **Institut du Monde Arabe**.

Follow the *quais* to **Saint Séverin** and finish at the **Cluny** museum.

Day seven

Montmartre. If Saturday or Sunday, start at the **Marché aux Puces**, Porte de Clignancourt.

Explore Montmartre, climb the dome of **Sacré Cœur**. *Métro* from **Pigalle** to **Monceau**; stroll in the park and then visit the **Musée Nissim de Camondo** (*Open* Wed–Sun 10–5) to view its collection of 18th-century decorative arts.

Buy presents at **Galeries Lafayette**!

The sweeping views of the city from the North tower of Notre Dame make the 387-step climb very worthwhile

Weekend's itinerary

The following is designed for visitors on their first trip to Paris.

Day one

Start at the **Louvre**, at 9 AM. On leaving don't miss the **Cour Carrée** behind the pyramid. Then stroll along the rue de Rivoli to **Angélina's** tearoom or the adjoining luxury **Hôtel Meurice** for a drink. Turn right along rue Castiglione to the **place Vendôme** and the **Ritz**, past the glitziest jewelers. At the place de l'Opéra take the rue Auber past the **Opéra** to the *RER* express *métro*. Take line A to **La Défense**. From the roof of **La Grande Arche** survey Paris.

Return by *RER* to **Les Halles** for lunch. Walk due east to the **Centre Pompidou (Beaubourg)** then enter **Le Marais** following the rue des Francs Bourgeois. A short detour takes you to the **Musée Picasso**; alternatively, go straight to the **Musée Victor Hugo** on the **place des Vosges**, a good spot for a coffee. Cross the rue St.-Antoine and take the rue St.-Paul through the antique market, the **Village St.-Paul**, towards the **Hôtel de Sens**. Cross the Pont Marie, explore the lower *quais* and spend your evening on the **Ile St. Louis**.

Day two

Start in **Montmartre**, exploring the backstreets, and Sacré Cœur. Return to the boulevard below by taking the lively market street, the rue Lepic. The **Moulin Rouge** is to your right at the bottom. Take the *métro* from **place de Clichy** to Varenne and the **Musée Rodin** with its pleasant café and gardens. Walk or take a taxi past **Les Invalides** to the **Champ-de-Mars** dominated by the **Tour Eiffel**.

Continue the afternoon in the **Latin Quarter**, going first to the **Cluny** museum. Explore the surrounding narrow streets before crossing to the **Ile de la Cité** to see the dazzling **Sainte-Chapelle**. Finish at **Notre-Dame** (free Sunday concerts at 5:45 PM). Return to the Left Bank, following the *quai* west to the **Hôtel de la Monnaie**. Turn into the mass of streets leading to the charming **place de Furstemberg**, past the church of **St.-Germain-des-Prés** and start your evening at the elegant **Brasserie Lipp**.

THE GEOGRAPHY OF PARIS
The Paris city boundary is roughly marked out by the ring road or *Périphérique*. Within this area, Paris is divided into 20 districts or *arrondissements*, beginning at the Louvre with the 1st *arrondissement*, then working outward in a clockwise spiral. When touring the city, use the main landmarks for instant orientation: Sacré-Cœur is to the north, Montparnasse Tower to the south and the Eiffel Tower to the west.

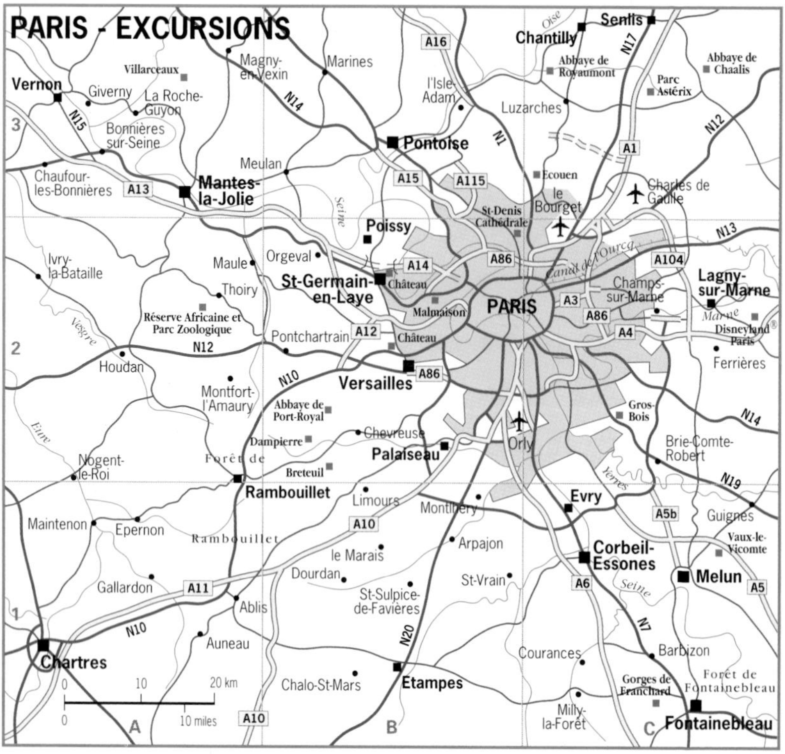

Opposite: the Horseshoe Staircase at Fontainebleau Palace

If the charms of one of the world's most romantic and historic capitals are occasionally overcome by the noise, the traffic, and, in the height of summer, the heat, then the surrounding countryside of the Île-de-France provides the perfect antidote and some excellent excursions.

A surfeit of the city's great cultural monuments and museums (or merely having children in tow) might result in a trip to the east of Paris to discover the fun of fantasy at Disneyland Paris or, alternatively, north to Parc Astérix. To the south west France Miniature at Elancourt offers a Gulliver's-eye view of the country where you will find scaled down monuments and typical village scenes.

Both history and the lush scenery of the Île-de-France can be enjoyed on a trip to one of the great châteaux such as Rambouillet, Fontainebleau, Vaux-le-Vicomte, and Chantilly. A car (rental details on page 249) will enable you to take in some of the sights and small towns along the way: the Le Nôtre landscaped park of the Château de Courances is worth a detour on a journey to Fontainebleau, and so too is a stop at the well-preserved Abbaye de Royaumont just south of Chantilly.

Closer to the center of Paris and therefore more convenient to reach by public transport are the châteaux of Ecouen, Gros-Bois, Malmaison, St.-Germain-en-Laye and, of course, the impressive big brother of them all, Versailles.

Excursions

▶▶▶ EXCURSION HIGHLIGHTS

The 19th-century version of the Château de Chantilly

►► Chantilly 190C3

Chateaux (Musée Condé), 60631 Chantilly; tel: 03 44 62 62 62.
Open: Wed–Mon 10:30–12:45, 2–5; summer 10–6.
Admission: expensive
Musée Vivant du Cheval; tel: 03 44 57 40 40.
Open: Wed–Mon 10:30–5:30, Sat–Sun 10:30–6.
Admission: expensive
By car: Autoroute du Nord, A1 to Survilliers exit (25 miles)
By train: from Gare du Nord to Chantilly-Gouvieux (30 min).

Due north of Paris is the classy epicenter of French horses and riding fanatics. Over 3,000 trusty steeds are stabled in the forested area surrounding Chantilly, and anything connected with horses is a semipermanent talk of the town; both the local horse museum and the race course attract the relevant crowds. The 19th-century château contains a stunning art collection, and the surrounding canal-crossed park is a pleasure to explore.

Chantilly was originally founded by a Roman named Cantilius, but it was the famous head of the French army, the constable Anne de Montmorency, who in 1528 built a Renaissance château on the present site on his return from valiant battles in Italy. Montmorency brought in some of the greatest artists of the period: François Clouet, Bernard Palissy, and Jean Goujon all participated. Soon after, the architect Jean Bullant was commissioned to build a small neighboring château, the Capitainerie, which still survives today.

Change of hands After the Montmorencys the château passed into the hands of the Condé family, powerful nobles who from 1643 to the 1830s made Chantilly their family seat. The prince known as the Grand Condé soon called in the great landscape designer Le Nôtre; he transformed the gardens and added lakes and canals, helping to make Chantilly one of the era's favorite partying places. Famous literati invited to the fashionable gatherings included La Fontaine, Fénélon, Bossuet, Racine, and Molière. It was also during this period that the resident chef invented *crème chantilly*.

During the 18th century the magnificent stables were erected, intended to accommodate 240 horses and over 400 hounds for stag and boar hunts. (Today these stables are devoted to a horse museum and dressage displays.) The Revolution, however, soon left its inevitable mark: most of the château was pillaged and demolished—except for the Capitainerie. Around 1840 the last of the Condé family bequeathed the property to the Duc d'Aumale. This was the man responsible for undertaking the rebuilding of the château (1876–1883), which produced the Renaissance pastiche that we can visit today.

The main château On the first floor, the Musée Condé displays some magnificent works and furnishings, from the Italian and French Renaissance through to the 19th century. The *pièce de résistance* is the illuminated medieval manuscript *Très Riches Heures du Duc de Berry* (only its reproduction is displayed). Look out for Poussin, Delacroix, Raphael, Van Dyck, Corot, and the remarkable Cabinet Clouet, which displays 16th-century portraits painted by the Clouet brothers. The same fraternity designed the stained-glass windows in the nearby Galerie de Psyche, made in 1542 for the Château d'Ecouen. In Le Santuario are exhibited major works such as Raphael's *Trois Grâces*, Filippino Lippi's *Esther et Assuérus*, and Jean Fouquet's 1455 miniatures for a book of hours. The Cabinet des Gemmes exhibits further miniature portraits, porcelain, a rare collection of fans, and a copy of the famous *Diamant Rose*. A large octagonal room called the Tribune houses masterpieces by Watteau, Delacroix, Ingres, and Philippe de Champaigne.

A guided tour of the apartments leads to the Capitainerie, which, apart from its superb restaurant (tel: 01 44 57 15 89), contains some fascinating features such as panels painted by Huet in the main bedroom and the superb carved wood paneling of the music room. The balustrade of the main staircase leading to the chapel took 30 craftsmen a year to complete. Gobelins and Beauvais tapestries, inlaid furniture, a room entirely decorated with paintings of monkeys—Chantilly is not short of interest.

Park Allow an hour or so to wander around. Take in the Hameau, an aristocratic version of rustic living built in 1774, similar to that used by Marie-Antoinette at Versailles. Follow Le Nôtre's canals, in particular La Manche, which leads you to an amphitheater-shaped lawn on either side of which are the *allées des philosophes*, where the thinkers of the day cogitated in bucolic surroundings. Finish your tour by going through the English-style garden with its temple, island, and waterfall.

Detail from the Château de Chantilly

SENLIS
Combine a trip to Chantilly with a visit to the neighboring town of Senlis—a maze of picturesque narrow streets dominated by the 12th-century Cathédrale de Notre Dame, one of France's oldest cathedrals. Its soaring spire is considered by many to be the most elegant in France.

SWEET AND SOUR
Chantilly has two culinary claims to fame—*crème chantilly* (whipped cream), served on hot waffles at the château gates, and the Condé family's great but rather nervous master chef, Vatel. When Louis XIV and a retinue of 5,000 courtiers arrived for a three-day stay in 1671, Vatel had neither enough roast meat for the first dinner nor fresh fish for the second. He sadly committed suicide.

The majestic cathedral of Notre-Dame de Chartres boasts world-famous stained-glass windows, the widest nave and the largest crypt in France

DON'T FORGET THE TOWN!
Take an organized trip to Chartres from central Paris with Cityrama (tel: 01 44 55 60 00) or Paris Vision (tel: 01 42 60 30 01), who arrange half-day excursions to Chartres including a guided tour of the cathedral.
If you have time, visit the Musée des Beaux Arts, a former bishops' palace, housing a fascinating collection of 17th- to 19th-century French furniture and paintings.

DRUID CONNECTIONS
Even before the Christian era, Chartres was famous for its Druid temple, and many scholars believe it was actually the Druid capital of the Carnutes described in the famous Latin text, Caesar's "Gallic Wars."

►► Chartres 190A1

By car: take the A10 from the Porte de St.-Cloud
By train: from Montparnasse

Rising above the wheat fields of Beauce are the two extraordinary mismatched spires of Chartres cathedral, "the very idea of the Middle Ages rendered visible" (Emile Male).

Notre-Dame de Chartres is the Virgin Mary's cathedral *par excellence*, built to house the precious relic of her *sacra camisia* (tunic), still displayed in the Treasury in only slightly frayed form after 2,000 years. King Charles the Bald donated the valuable relic in the late 9th century and it rapidly attracted streams of fervent pilgrims (many come on foot from Paris even today). Fires burned no fewer than five successive churches on the site, culminating in the devastating flames of 1194.

Miraculously, Mary's tunic survived unsinged, which led to a revival of religious fervor and a strong motivation for rebuilding. From the king to the lowliest farm worker, everyone offered money or physical labor, and the new cathedral was erected in a record 25 years.

Chartres today Centuries later, Chartres remains a remarkably homogeneous example of the transition from Gothic to Romanesque. The lower half of the facade, surviving from the earlier church, is pure 12th-century Romanesque. Its main entrance, the Portail Royal, illustrates the life of Christ, and the central tympanum shows him surrounded by the Evangelists and the Apostles. The door to the right is dedicated to

Mary. The left-hand door focuses on the Ascension. The right-hand octagonal spire, which crowns the 345-foot south tower, is original, but the north tower was decapitated by lightning and rebuilt in the early 16th century. The latter can be climbed, but be prepared for 378 steps. From the outside, admire the flying buttresses, the two magnificently sculpted porches, and the 14th-century chapel in the garden at the back.

The 176 stained-glass windows cover an area of 2,990 square yards: the three crowning the facade escaped the 1194 fire, while most others are 13th-century. The three rose windows represent the Apocalypse, the Virgin Mary, and the Last Judgment; *Notre-Dame de la Belle Verrière,* in the south choir, is reputedly the oldest window.

The circular labyrinth on the nave floor is a unique medieval survivor symbolizing good and evil with its centre representing paradise. Pilgrims used to crawl around all 306 yards of its pattern on their knees. The choir, one of the widest in Europe, is surrounded by a magnificent lace-like wall of stone sculpture incorporating 200 statues. Behind the choir is the staircase leading to the Treasury in the Chapelle Saint-Piat. Below the cathedral is the impressive 9th-century crypt; guided tours start from the Maison des Clercs.

Chartres makes a charming spot for a day's wandering, as the lower part of the town boasts more historic churches. The river provides a picturesque backdrop for old public washhouses and drying lofts, while in Vieux Chartres some fabulous architectural features await discovery.

ORNAMENTAL RESIDENCE

For a touching and astonishing spiritual monument go to the Maison Picassiette (22 rue du Repos, tel: 02 37 34 10 78).

In a nondescript suburb a local street sweeper, Raymond Isidore, spent his entire life decorating his house with fragments of china and glass.

He started in 1938 on the interior and finished his garden tomb in 1962.

Not even his wife's sewing machine escaped his mania for decoration.

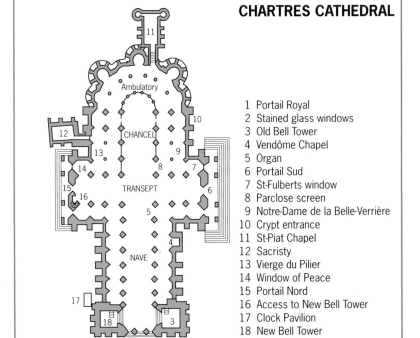

CHARTRES CATHEDRAL

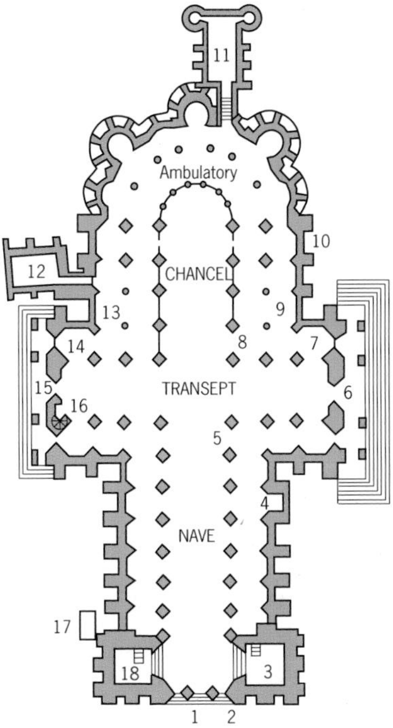

1 Portail Royal
2 Stained glass windows
3 Old Bell Tower
4 Vendôme Chapel
5 Organ
6 Portail Sud
7 St-Fulberts window
8 Parclose screen
9 Notre-Dame de la Belle-Verrière
10 Crypt entrance
11 St-Piat Chapel
12 Sacristy
13 Vierge du Pilier
14 Window of Peace
15 Portail Nord
16 Access to New Bell Tower
17 Clock Pavilion
18 New Bell Tower

▶ Disneyland Paris 190C2

Central Reservations Office/BP 100, 77777 Marne-la-Vallée, cedex 4; tel: 01 60 30 60 00 (recorded information 01 60 30 60 30; from the U.K.: 0990 03 03 03). Admission: expensive
By train: RER line A. By car: autoroute A4

Disneyland Paris, a mega project started in 1988, opened in April 1992 with a huge publicity campaign.

Situated 20 miles east of Paris in the bleak countryside of Marne-la-Vallée, Disney's fourth world resort (after California, Florida, and Tokyo) was, at first, beset by financial problems. Not so surprising perhaps, considering that the project budget was comparable to even the greatest of Louis XIV's extravagances at Versailles. The French were not very enthusiastic at first and did not flock to the park in great numbers, but the impact made by this foreign cultural invasion gradually wore off, the number of visitors steadily increased and, six years after it opened, Disneyland Paris had achieved a well-deserved success. It makes for a fun day away from the city.

New attractions are regularly being opened. As a concession to French culture an area of the park called Discoveryland has been inspired by Jules Verne's visions of the future, and the summer of 1994 saw the inauguration of the "Mystères du Nautilus" underwater trip (based on *20,000 Leagues Under the Sea*). Space Mountain, when it opened in 1995, was hailed as a technological feat and the greatest thrill in any of the Disney resorts.

Six hotels (five of them grouped around an artificial lake and each corresponding to a different American regional style and visitor's budget) together with a wooded campground complete with log cabins (remember Davy Crockett?) make up the accommodations on offer. Many of the hotels have slashed their prices to attract more visitors; they now compare more favorably with their Parisian counterparts.

Numerous restaurants, shops, water sports, and a golf course offer alternatives to the seemingly endless round of rides and attractions; however, it might be difficult for the visitor to escape the beaming Disney smiles of the myriad "cast members." Originally numbering 12,000, employed from all over Europe to aid visitors and maintain the squeaky-clean image, their numbers have been reduced, but there are still enough to be found on every corner.

As soon as they set foot inside Disneyland, your offspring can at last meet all of those characters who were previously reserved for the movie or television screen—Mickey, Minnie, Goofy, Pluto, and their diverse fairy-tale comrades are all here. Divided into five distinct areas or "lands," it has as its centerpiece the impressive and elaborately turreted Sleeping Beauty's Castle.

On entering Disneyland visitors find themselves projected into an idealized turn-of-the-century America on Main Street, with ragtime piano tunes, horse-drawn trolley cars, and "ye olde" stores and houses. Steam trains and boats leave here for a trip through Frontierland, with its fake canyons, gold mines, and rivers.

Sleeping Beauty's Castle, Disneyland Paris

DISNEY RESTAURANTS
Disneyland Paris eateries range from snack bars and fast-food joints to waitress-service restaurants. Reservations are recommended for most sit-down restaurants, many of which have recently relaxed their no-alcohol policies. All six Disney hotels have restaurants open to the public. Alternatively try the Key West Seafood, steak house or even the "Buffalo Bill" dinner-theater at Festival Disney, an enormous pleasure dome near the main Disney complex.

You never know who might be joining you on a Disneyland Paris ride

Fantasyland Inside the 15-story castle you enter Fantasyland, where Disney classics and European folklore are relived, with Sleeping Beauty the out-and-out winner. Make-believe becomes reality and young children squeal approval. Other top attractions include the delightfully poetic Peter Pan's Flight and the enchanting Pays de Contes de Fées, a canal cruise through miniature scenes from classic fairy-tales.

Adventureland This, on the other hand, is geared more to a slightly older age group as here swashbuckling adventurers fight it out in a tropical setting. A 92-foot-high "tree" created to be climbed brings visitors to the rustic dwelling of the Robinsons, while the island of the hidden treasure is ferociously guarded by Long John Silver and Captain Hook look-a-likes.

Discoveryland This final stopover is completely inspired by Jules Verne's and other visionaries' images of the future. Boasting its spectacular Star Tours—a flight simulator that whisks visitors onto an interplanetary journey—it also projects a circular movie, *Circle-Vision 360*, which draws visitors into themes of the future. Meanwhile, Starjets whizz above during the day and fireworks light up the sky at night.

►►► Fontainebleau, Château de *190C1*

77300 Fontainebleau; tel: 01 60 71 50 70
By car: take A6 from the Porte d'Orléans or N7 from Porte d'Italie
By train: from the Gare de Lyon
Open: Wed–Mon 9:30–12:30, 2–6 (winter 2–5)
Gardens open dawn to dusk. Admission: expensive

A magnificent vast forest of 42,000 acres, once royal hunting ground, surrounds the marshy terrain of the château, number two in the French royal domain stakes after Versailles. Apart from touring the imposing palace, visitors can indulge in horseback riding, cycling, rock-climbing, or simply walking in the forest. Only a few miles to the north lies Barbizon, famous for its mid-19th-century school of landscape painters.

A former hunting lodge dating from the 12th century, the château was transformed into a major royal residence by François I in the 16th century; he brought the best of Italy's Renaissance artists and craftsmen to

The Château de Fontainebleau, once a hunting lodge and a palace, now draws crowds of tourists. Napoleon disliked Versailles and therefore established his imperial seat here. The Napoleon Museum, in the Louis XV wing, recounts the story

decorate its lofty interior and laid out the garden with lakes and canals. Le Nôtre stepped in during the mid-17th century to redesign the garden, and the palace itself underwent numerous modifications and additions over the years before being finally adopted by Napoleon as a suitably majestic base.

The château Entrance is through the famous Cour des Adieux, where the Emperor bade farewell to his Imperial Guard in 1814 before being exiled on Elba. The famous horseshoe-shaped staircase was built by Du Cerceau for Louis XIII in 1634. In the Galerie François I, the original Renaissance frescos painted by the Florentine Rosso remained hidden behind other paintings, only coming to light in the 19th century.

The highlight of the interior, however, is the **Salle de Bal**, the ceremonial ballroom which hosted many a glittering occasion. Dazzlingly furnished and decorated with original frescos and wood paneling, it was commenced under François I, the last elegant gilt touches being added under his successor Henri II.

Napoleon's apartments occupy the wing built under Louis XVI, overlooking the Jardin de Diane and running parallel with the Galerie François I. His bedroom idiosyncratically contains a camp bed and some richly inlaid Boulle commodes. The **Salle du Trône**, created by Napoleon in 1808, is a decorative mixture of Louis XIII, XIV, and XV in the same way as the Queen's Apartments, the Chambre de la Reine, reveal the passage of every queen from Marie de Médicis to the Empress Eugénie. Adjoining this is the **Salon du Jeu** or **Boudoir de la Reine**, beautifully decorated thanks mainly to the luckless Marie-Antoinette, who commissioned Rousseau to paint its murals.

The most brilliant of 18th-century decoration can be seen in the **Salle du Conseil**, built under François I but entirely reworked under Louis XV, who commissioned the fabulous ceiling paintings by Boucher.

Further apartments can be toured but only with guides; enquire at the ticket desk. Otherwise, head outside to the gardens and the Tiber—the square central pond in Le Nôtre's formal Grand Jardin. Facing the Cour de la Fontaine is the Fountain of Ulysees, which in its turn fronts the peaceful expanse of a carp pond. On the other side of this aquatic area, immediately to the right of the Cour des Adieux, stretches the English-style garden relandscaped by Hurtault in 1812.

Barbizon The illustrious village of Barbizon is now characterized by upscale restaurants and tourist galleries. Between 1848 and 1870 it attracted a group of painters who were the first to practice outdoor painting, thus creating their own movement, the Ecole de Barbizon, and paving the way for the Impressionists. Corot, Millet, Rousseau, and Daubigny all worked here, spending their days dabbling on canvas and their evenings at the Auberge du Père Ganne. The inn exhibits some touching memorabilia, as do the houses of Millet and Rousseau (both on the Grande Rue). Don't be surprised to encounter traffic jams of tourist buses here.

SPORT IN THE FOREST
If the forest surrounding Fontainebleau is beckoning, go to the Office de Tourisme (31 place Napoléon Bonaparte, tel: 01 60 74 99 99) for information on horseback riding or bike rental. If you come by train, you can hire fairly basic bikes at the station. If you have a car, then the 5 miles to the village of Barbizon will be easy.

Barbizon, where art moved outdoors, away from the studio, paving the way for Impressionism

The magnificent garden provided Monet with constant inspiration during the last years of his life

▶▶▶ Giverny 190A3

Fondation Claude Monet, 27620 Giverny; tel: 02 32 51 28 21
By car: autoroute A13, exit at Vernon, take D5 to Giverny
By train: from St. Lazare to Vernon, then taxi or bus
Open: Apr–Oct, Tue–Sun 10–6. Admission: house and museum—moderate; gardens—inexpensive

Situated on the banks of the Seine as it flows northwest through Normandy, Giverny is famous for only one reason—Claude Monet. This charming village was where the painter lived from 1883 until his death in 1926, tending his famous garden which became as important to him as the works it inspired. Each month is characterized by a dominant color, but the most striking is perhaps May/June, when apple trees blossom, rhododendrons flower around the lily pond, and the wisteria tumbles over the Japanese bridge. However, any of the summer months will provide a ravishing vision of a discreetly controlled, color-coordinated Nature.

Entrance is through the vast studio that Monet had built, which now unfortunately only houses reproductions of his works and a souvenir shop. Monet's simple two-story house dominates the gardens, which slope down to the Japanese section. The pink house with its green shutters is pure delight for the colors of its interior which was thankfully extensively restored in the late 1970s after decades of neglect. Deep blue dominates the kitchen, brilliant yellow the dining-room, while Monet's vast Japanese print collection is hung throughout the house exactly as it was in his time. Upstairs, his bedroom has a superb view extending across the garden and beyond to the valley.

Oriental influence The opening up of Japan to the West in the late-19th century stimulated artists' imaginations, and Monet was no exception: his Japanese garden stands as proof and memorial. When prospering finances allowed him to purchase this plot of land, Monet set about diverting the River Epte to create a pond. This was soon crossed by an arched bridge and surrounded by bamboo and other vegetation reminiscent of the Orient. Monet spent the rest of his life capturing in canvas the essence of its shadows and light, mottled tones, wisteria, and water lilies.

Claude Monet (1840–1926) Brought up in Normandy, the youthful Monet soon moved to Paris to study painting. Here he met Bazille, Lepic, Renoir, and Sisley, with whom he associated at the Brasserie des Martyrs. Monet and Bazille spent Easter near Barbizon, painting like Millet and Daubigny in the open air; the same year, Monet discovered Manet. By 1870 he was following the fate of a *peintre maudit*, with his work refused by the official Salon.

After a trip to London where he discovered the works of Turner, Monet returned to Paris and settled in Argenteuil, on the Seine just north of Paris. Here, like Daubigny, he installed his studio on a boat, capturing the changing light of the river as he traveled. Artistically Monet always remained faithful to water, from his origins on the Channel coast to the banks of

MUSÉE AMERICAIN
The building along the road from Monet's house is the Musée Americain, showing the work of American artists who flocked to Giverny in the wake of Monet.

the Seine and eventually, of course, Giverny. In 1874 the Impressionist group was finally able to exhibit together, and it was Monet's 1872 painting entitled *Impression: soleil levant* that gave the group their identity. Success, however, did not come easily, and Monet's dire financial straits were only alleviated by friends like Manet who bought his paintings.

In 1879 Monet's wife died, just a few years before he finally achieved recognition as the high priest of a radically new movement in painting. By 1882 critics were at last favorable, and the following year he moved to "Le Pressoir" in Giverny, together with his two sons, his mistress Alice Hoschedé (whom he later married) and her six children. Other Impressionists such as Renoir, Sisley, and Degas all visited him there over the years, and Cézanne actually moved into the local inn for a period.

In 1897, with the maturing of the adjoining Japanese garden, Monet started on his famous water-lily series. He later had a studio specially built in the garden to accommodate his large-scale paintings. When Clémenceau asked him for a gift to the nation, Monet, by then in his 80s, set about painting a series of panels for the Orangerie, which he completed just before his death.

Monet's Japanese garden —a shimmering palette of changing colors—was the inspiration for his water-lily paintings, vast canvases which epitomize Monet's final period

MEMORABILIA
Right next door to Malmaison stands the late 17th-century Château de Bois-Préau (Open Thu–Sun 12:30–6; 6:30 in summer), bought by Josephine in 1809 to house her doctor, ladies-in-waiting and guests (avenue de l'Impératrice Joséphine, 92500 Rueil-Malmaison; tel: 01 41 29 05 55). Today it is a memorial museum for Napoleon. Souvenirs ranging from the grandly kitsch to the absurdly intimate include portraits of Napoleon on his deathbed, his campaign bed, boots, hairbrushes, and his death mask.

►► Malmaison, Château de *190B2*

avenue du Château de Malmaison, 92500 Rueil-Malmaison; tel: 01 41 29 05 55
By car: N13 from La Défense towards St.-Germain-en-Laye
By train: RER line A to La Défense. Bus 258
Open: 9:30–12:30, 1:30–5:15 (summer 1:30–5:45); joint ticket with Château de Bois-Préau. Admission: expensive

This 17th-century manor with its unassuming front is the most elegant and luxurious surviving example of Napoleonic (Empire) decoration in France. Bought by the young general in 1799 as a present for his bride Josephine—Paris' most celebrated, though hardly most virtuous, beauty of the time—it was from the start more her domain than his. When Napoleon divorced Josephine in 1809 to marry Marie-Louise of Austria, he magnanimously allowed Josephine to keep the château, along with her imperial title and retinue.

Little was done to the exterior by Napoleon's architects, who merely added a canopied entrance in the form of a Roman tent, but the interior was entirely remodeled. The columned vestibule recalls a Roman atrium, its style perfectly reflecting Napoleon's love of grandeur and his imperial ambitions. Haughty busts of the Bonaparte family now line the walls. To the right are the billiard room, the *salon doré* and the music room. The wall colors and hangings are a faithful recreation of the original décor, while the furnishings and bronze candelabra are Empire originals from Malmaison itself or other imperial palaces. In the music room, that in Josephine's time had a picture gallery extension, were once displayed some of the greatest pictures in Europe, from Rembrandt to Rubens, many looted by Napoleon's armies in Italy.

On the left of the entrance hall is the dining room which contains a remarkable 125-piece gilded silver service. The delicate wall paintings of muses and "Greek" motifs recall the decoration of ancient Pompeii. In Napoleon's council room next door the walls and ceiling in striped silk create the illusion of a Roman military

tent. The emperor's library boasts the most elaborate wall paintings as well as his famous mechanical desk brimming with secret drawers.

Upstairs are the emperor's bedroom, dressing room and sitting room decorated with portraits of the family. The central rooms are devoted to painting and memorabilia: David's celebrated *Napoleon Crossing the Alps*, Napoleon's toilet case, swords and captured weapons from the Egyptian campaign, and a rare Sèvres porcelain tea set with Egyptian motifs. An album of hand-painted flower prints by Redouté evokes Josephine's passion for exotic flowers, once extended to the Malmaison hothouses and gardens, the richest in Europe, which boasted plants and also animals specially imported from South America, Africa and Asia.

Beyond lies Josephine's private apartment. In her "official" bedroom the magnificent canopied bed decorated with gilded swans is the centerpiece of the room. This glamorous "imperial" style was redecorated the year of Josephine's divorce as a gesture of defiance to the new empress Marie-Louise. Next door is Josephine's smaller, more modest real bedroom painted in subtle colors. The exquisitely painted boudoir has a much lower ceiling and two fireplaces, making it the warmest room in Malmaison. This was where Josephine retreated in winter, her childhood in Martinique having left her with a lifelong aversion to cold weather.

In the attic rooms are Josephine's wardrobe and that of her daughter Hortense. Always coquettish, Josephine—much to Napoleon's annoyance—spent fortunes on clothes and jewelry and was the most luxuriously and best-dressed woman of her time. The dozens of pairs of shoes, parasols, day and court dresses with richly embroidered trains testify to this passion. Paintings and other memorabilia in these rooms illustrate the appearance of the Malmaison gardens and park under Josephine and trace the history of her descendants by Napoleon, including the future emperor, Napoleon's great-nephew Napoleon III.

The Château de Malmaison—Napoleon's gift to Josephine. Her apartments exhibit bills for her extensive wardrobe. She died owing a colossal 3 million francs

Malmaison Park contains a replica of Josephine's rose garden, Napoleon's summer-house/study and a coach house containing state carriages

Louis XIV's place of birth at St.-Germain-en-Laye—a fine Renaissance château which today houses the Musée des Antiquités Nationales with exhibits dating from prehistory to the Middle Ages

► Saint-Germain-en-Laye *190B2*

Tel: (château) 01 39 10 13 00
By car: Autoroute de l'Ouest (A13), exit at Versailles-Ouest–St.-Germain-en-Laye;
By train: take the RER line A1. Admission: moderate/expensive

In under half an hour you can reach this rather chic suburb, once the home of kings of France, from François I to Louis XIV. Its popularity and clean air were such that in 1847 the Baron de Rothschild personally financed a connecting railroad with Paris. Often overlooked by tourists, it is nevertheless a continuing favorite with Parisians. The atmosphere is unlikely to project you into provincial France, and on Sunday mornings most shops are open to accommodate the day-trippers—so be warned.

The main attraction remains the formidable fortress originally erected in 1122 to protect the west of Paris but substantially rebuilt by François I in the 16th century. One of its splendors is the Sainte-Chapelle, a 13th-century Gothic masterpiece, ten years older than its Parisian counterpart, although minus the stained glass, and with its rose window obstructed by one of François I's constructions. Notice the sculpted heads crowning each arch, which are portraits of St. Louis and his family.

Sun King's setting It was in this château that Louis XIV was born, where he took refuge during the popular uprising known as the Fronde (1648–1653), and altogether spent more time than at Versailles later in his life.

Once Versailles was fit to move into, he graciously left the use of St.-Germain-en-Laye to the exiled James II of England, who died there in 1701 (his mausoleum stands in the church across the square from the château).

Le Nôtre created the impressive esplanade high above the Seine; a stroll along here and back to base covers 3 miles. The view from the terrace across the valley of the Seine inspired the Impressionist painter Alfred Sisley.

Since 1867 the château has housed the **Musée des Antiquités Nationales** (*Open* Wed–Mon 9–5:15). This unique and fascinating archeological collection ranges from prehistory to the Middle Ages. Superb examples of silver and gold Merovingian jewelry, weapons, and glass are displayed alongside Gallo-Roman ceramics, images of Celtic and Roman divinities and funerary objects. The most astounding exhibit, going back 24,000 years, is the first known representation of a woman's face, **La Dame de Brassempouy**. Somewhat younger is the superb Bronze Age helmet with an engraved gold band from Amfreville. An entire room is devoted to a replica of the wall paintings of bulls from Lascaux's caves in the Dordogne.

The other landmark to head for in St.-Germain-en-Laye, the **Musée du Prieuré**, is a short walk away (go past the church across from the château and turn left down the rue au Pain, until you reach the rue Maurice Denis). A former 17th-century hospital, this building is devoted to the painter Maurice Denis, who died in St.-Germain-en-Laye (*Open* Wed–Fri 10:30–5:30; Sat and Sun 10–6:30). Symbolism, the Nabis, and Post-impressionism are the movements represented in the posters, paintings, and sculpture of his contemporaries Bonnard, Vuillard, Vallotton, Maillol, and Paul Sérusier. Denis tried to revive the tradition of sacred art; one example of his efforts is the chapel decorated by him, which adjoins the museum.

Maurice Denis (1870–1943) When still a precocious art student aged 18, Denis was already helping to form the group of Nabis. Sérusier, who had just spent the summer in the company of Gauguin at Pont-Aven in Brittany, shared the new theories with Denis and showed him the *Talisman*, an arrangement of pure colours on a wooden box lid painted under Gauguin's guidance. By 1890 Denis had published a manifesto of what he called neotraditionalism, outlining the formula that subsequently influenced much modern painting, a vindication of pure and autonomous painting: "Remember that a picture before becoming a warhorse, a nude woman or any kind of anecdote, is essentially a flat surface covered with colors arranged in a certain order."

While borrowing certain elements from Impressionism, the Nabis were also interested in contemporary influences such as the newly popular Japanese print, equally visible in Gauguin's use of flat planes of color. Their art was intimate, an art of domestic interiors such as in Vuillard's and Bonnard's works. Denis was the main exponent of its spiritual qualities, which he linked with nostalgia for the primitive and for nature.

ROYAL BIRTHPLACE AND RESTAURANT
Don't miss the Pavillon Henri IV in the gardens, the only remaining element of the Château Neuf where the Sun King was born and which the future Charles X gaily started to demolish in 1777. It is now a rather exclusive hotel-restaurant.

The Grande Terrace, Château de St.-Germain-en-Laye, designed by Le Nôtre with magnificent views across the Seine Valley

ROYAL FURNISHINGS
A tapestry workshop was set up in nearby Maincy to produce the necessary hangings for the château. This later became the celebrated Manufacture des Gobelins. However, Louis XIV took it over in 1662 and employed the best craftsmen including over 250 Flemish carpet weavers to furnish his new palace at Versailles. Traditional weaving methods are used today at the Gobelin factory, with guided tours three times a week.

A RUTHLESS MAN
Nicolas Fouquet, the ruthless powerful Minister of Finance, had quite a widespread reputation. As a result, the word "squirrel" or "*écureuil*" became known in local dialect as "*fouquet*." Throughout the château, there are squirrels painted by Le Brun, a cunning reference to Vaux's megalomaniac owner. The castle also contains an exhibition, illustrating Fouquet's rise and fall with life-size wax figures.

►►► Vaux-le-Vicomte, Domaine de *190C1*

77950 Maincy; tel: 01 64 14 41 90
By car: Autoroute A6, exit at Melun-Sénart
By train: from Gare de Lyon to Melun, then bus or taxi
Open: Apr–Oct, 10–6; mid-Nov–Feb by appointment, tel: 01 64 14 41 90. Admission: expensive
Fountain displays Apr–Oct, second and last Sat of the month, 3–6

Near Melun, 32 miles southeast of Paris, lies Vaux-le-Vicomte, one of France's great baroque châteaux. Its colourful history is so extraordinary that it needs to be known beforehand.

The land itself was bought in 1641 by Louis XIV's power-hungry Minister of Finance, Nicolas Fouquet. Superintendent of finances under Mazarin, Fouquet was also a great patron of the arts and passed on some of his immense fortune to the likes of Molière, La Fontaine, and Madame de Sévigné. His family motto *Quo non ascendet*? (roughly, "the sky's the limit") was particularly relevant to his tastes in decoration.

In 1656, Fouquet assembled the most talented artists and craftsmen of the time to create the ultimate symbol of his power and what was to become the first example of the Louis XIV style. Thus Louis Le Vau was appointed as architect, the painter Le Brun brought in for the interiors, and André Le Nôtre for the landscaping of the enormous park. For five years, an army of 18,000 workers slaved away in the construction of a château whose proportions were equaled only by the rate of embezzling Fouquet was reputed to have indulged in to pay his bills.

The party Finally, on a warm summer night in 1661, Fouquet threw a house-warming party that was to become legendary. The famous chef Vatel supervized the ovens, La Fontaine and Molière the cultural entertainment. Dishes of solid gold crowned dozens of buffet tables set out in the garden, while jewel-studded elephants lined the alleys of orange trees and Chinese fireworks were shot off from the ponds (there were over 1,000 fountains and waterspouts). Never had Parisian society seen a social event quite so extravagant. Nor had the 23-year-old Louis XIV, who had recently come of age to rule in his own right. Two weeks later Fouquet was arrested by the famous D'Artagnan, imprisoned, his possessions confiscated, and at his trial found guilty of embezzlement. Thus his dream ended in a dank cell, where he remained until his death. Meanwhile, his talented craftsmen found new employment working on the king's new residence at Versailles—directly inspired by Vaux-le-Vicomte.

Although spared during the Revolution, the château nevertheless fell on hard times. Only seven paintings, six statues, and two tables remained when a wealthy industrialist, Alfred Sommier, bought it in 1875. Today the interior and the grounds have been magnificently restored by his descendants, while installed in the stables is a Musée des Equipages (horse-drawn carriages and accessories). Its historic collection includes the carriage Charles X used to escape from Paris in 1830.

The interior In the château itself, after entering through the hall with its 12 doric columns, don't miss the Salon des Muses, with Le Brun's painted ceilings illustrating nine different muses. Here Molière and his troupe acted *L'Ecole des Maris* for the first time, with Queen Henrietta-Maria of England and Fouquet as audience. The intimately scaled Cabinet des Jeux possesses another Le Brun masterpiece on its ceiling, this time *Le Sommeil*. It is hardly surprising that the artist spent two years closeted in the château accomplishing his marvels, which continue in the Salle des Buffets and upstairs in Fouquet's bedroom. Another highlight is the Chambre du Roi—which of course never hosted the King—used as a model for Versailles and subsequently imitated throughout Europe. Try to tour the château during one of its breathtaking candlelit evenings (*Tours* May–mid-Oct, Sat 8:30–11 PM): over 1,000 candles flicker away, conveying the atmosphere of Fouquet's time.

The monumental gardens of Vaux-le-Vicomte are Le Nôtre's first masterpiece. A succession of terraces, lawns, fountains and ponds, lined with statues and neatly sculpted bushes, lead away from the château down toward an impressive canal, hidden until your footsteps bring you to its edge. You can continue into the woods on the other side.

IN THE GARDENS
Le Nôtre's perfectly manicured gardens at Vaux-le-Vicomte make a pleasant afternoon's stroll. Within the grounds the Musée des Equipages contains state carriages, saddles, and a smithy. Twice a month on Saturday afternoons there is a spectacular fountain display.

Vaux-le-Vicomte, built for finance Minister Nicolas Fouquet, made Louis XIV so jealous that he built the palace at Versailles in response

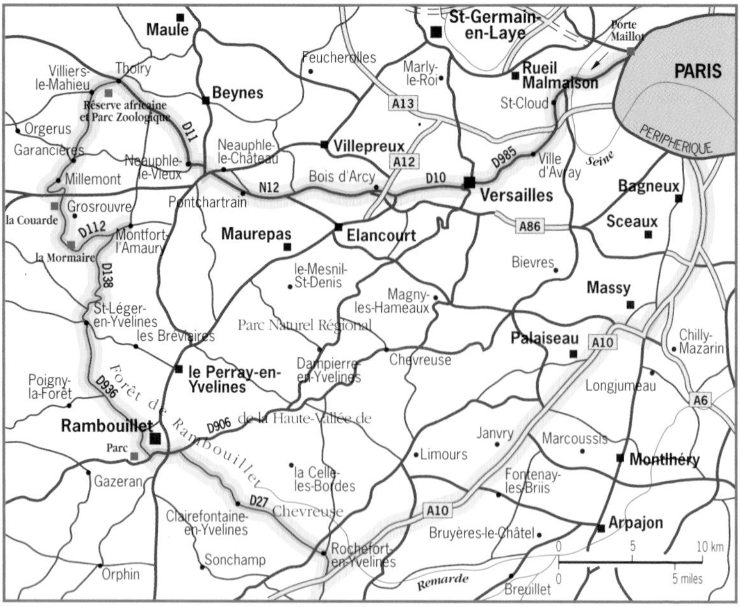

Drive

Parks and châteaux

Leave Paris from the Porte Maillot, taking the D985 through the Bois de Boulogne and across the Seine toward Suresnes. Follow it through St.-Cloud and into the park.
A perfect combination of water and forest, the **Parc de St.-Cloud** was laid out by Le Nôtre, although the château was burned down during the 1870 Franco-Prussian War.

Continue along the D985 through Ville d'Avray to Versailles.
Stop to visit this remarkable architectural and landscaping feat. The town itself has some charm, particularly the small quartier of **St.-Louis**, near the royal kitchen garden.

Take the D10 and soon, at a rather complex series of intersections, turn onto the N12, leading to Neauphle-le-Château. Follow this road through a mixture of rolling countryside and far-flung suburban developments to the village of Pontchartrain.
Here there stands a pink and white 17th-century château, now a school of agriculture, in a perfectly composed perspective. Although it is not open to the public, drive down through the curtain of trees to enjoy its setting. Continue through the village of **Neauphle-le-Vieux**, with its 13th-century church, once part of a Benedictine monastery.

Follow the D11 past the Forest of Beynes to Thoiry.
This is the perfect destination to appease restless young spirits, as the Renaissance château is set in a zoological park (*Open* daily 10–5, 6 in summer).

Immediately beyond the park on the D11 the road forks: turn left toward Villiers, where you pass another private château, and continue south to Garancières. At Millemont take the D197 and then the D199, turning right through Grosrouvre; a detour to the Château la Couarde is possible en route.
The **Château de la Mormaire** soon appears in this pretty agricultural

The President's retreat: the Château de Rambouillet, once a royal residence

landscape, where you join the D112 toward **Montfort-l'Amaury**, one of the most charming towns in the region. Once home to the powerful counts of Montfort (the 13th-century Simon de Montfort being the most notorious), the ruined castle remains at the top of the hill, as well as elements of former fortified walls. Don't miss the Gothic-Renaissance cemetery in the village center, which belongs to the church of St.-Pierre.

Leave Montfort by the D138 to St-Léger-en-Yvelines, a village built up around a 12th-century church. Near by stands an ancient menhir, a half-mile walk from the village.

Taking the D936, you soon come to the harmonious town of Rambouillet, The château of **Rambouillet**, once favored by kings and aristocrats, is now the President's official weekend and summer retreat. When he is not in residence it is open to the public; don't miss the extensive grounds. This *parc à l'anglaise*, with its follies, canals and islands, was bought by Louis XVI for Marie-Antoinette and a dairy was built to keep her amused. The château was mainly rebuilt in the early 18th century and its superb woodwork is only rivaled by Versailles. The bulky Tour François I testifies to the Renaissance king's presence here; this is where he died.

Leave Rambouillet by the D906, turning immediately right along the D27, which takes you through the forested Vallée de la Chevreuse to Rochefort-en-Yvelines and joins the A10 motorway leading back to Paris.

Stained-glass windows in St.-Pierre church, Montfort-l'Amaury

The Château de Versailles, seen from the south Parterre. It is the largest palace in Europe, capable of housing 20,000 people, and was the crowning glory of the Sun King, Louis XIV

▶▶▶ Versailles, Château de *190B2*

Tel: 01 30 83 78 00
By car: take autoroute A13, then follow signs
By train: RER line C to Versailles Rive-Gauche (closest) or main line from Saint Lazare to Versailles Rive Droite
Open: State apartments Tue–Sun 9–6:30; winter 9–5:30; Grand and Petit Trianon 12–5. The park is open daily 7 AM to dusk. Every Sun from May–Sep the fountains play from 3:30–5. Admission: (Palace) expensive; (Grand Trianon) inexpensive; (Petit Trianon) inexpensive

More than a palace, the Château of Versailles, Louis XIV's greatest creation, was conceived as a world unto itself. Seat of government, permanent residence of the royal family, and the cream of French nobility, it also functioned as a permanent exhibition of French grandeur and sophistication. The endless grounds were tamed into a geometry so perfect that even nature seemed to obey the Sun King's commands. Surrounding the palace and its formal gardens were the largest kitchen gardens in the kingdom, the only zoo, the largest artificial lake, acres of game-filled forest, a new town catering for the needs of the court, and two weekend retreats with their own grounds, the Trianons.

The original château, built by Louis XIII in 1631, was a modest hunting lodge. In 1661 Louis XIV announced his intention of moving his court to this deserted swamp 10 miles southwest of Paris, an astute way of isolating the nobility and his ministers while keeping an eye on his not-too-distant capital. Building hardly stopped until the king's death in 1715.

Three majestic avenues lined with trees and mansions converge on the great place d'Armes in front of the courtyard. Facing the square are the monumental stables built by Jules Hardouin Mansart, the second Versailles architect.

The first architect, Louis Le Vau, built around the original lodge on three sides, smartening up the old brick front in the center of the courtyard with urns, busts, and a wrought-iron balcony for the king's bedroom. Louis XIV's last addition to the palace was the magnificent baroque chapel behind the north courtyard block, finished in 1710.

Garden facade It is the garden facade that best epitomizes the Sun King's ambitions. Faced in stone, lined with Ionic columns, and capped by an ornamental balustrade and carved trophies, the central section is part of the original "envelope" designed by Le Vau. In 1678 Mansart filled in the terrace to create the Hall of Mirrors and added two lengthy blocks to the north and south, which make the garden front of Versailles the longest (801 yards) in Europe.

Royal apartments The central royal apartments are divided into two sections. Access to the Grands Appartements is from entrance A next to the chapel in the courtyard. The Petits Appartements (guided tour only) are reached from the south side of the courtyard. The Grands Appartements, laid out in the 1670s by the king's chief painter, Charles Le Brun, were the public rooms. Grand, luxurious, and draughty, they were used for official court assemblies and lavish entertainments.

Preceding the apartments is the king's private entrance to the chapel, laid out on two levels, the upper for the royal family and highest nobility, the first floor for the rest of the court. The vaulted ceilings are painted in the illusionist Italian manner.

The **Grands Appartements** themselves are dominated by colored marble, gilded bronze, sculpture, illusionist painting, velvet, and silk. Each salon is dedicated to an Olympian deity symbolizing a royal virtue or duty. Apollo, closely linked to the cult of the Sun King, lends his name to the throne room.

What most visitors come to see is the Hall of Mirrors. Flanked on either side by the ornate salons of War and Peace, it is the largest, most magnificent and last to be completed. It once boasted—apart from the 17 great mirrors—crystal chandeliers, precious furniture and

MOB RULE
On October 6, 1789, Versailles was invaded by a Parisian mob, led by the women of Les Halles. They massacred the bodyguard and attempted to break into Marie-Antoinette's bedroom. She fled to the king's rooms and remained safe until morning when she was removed forcibly to the Tuileries. The palace remained empty for over two years.

Versailles was the ultimate symbol of royal grandeur, from the symmetry of its facade to the Apollo Fountain, a story of divinity for a king who believed in his own glory

vases, gilded candelabra, damask curtains, potted orange trees, and a silver throne. The painted ceilings, Le Brun's masterpiece, depict the King himself. It was here that Bismarck proclaimed the unification of Germany in 1871 and that the Treaty of Versailles, ending World War I, was signed in 1919.

From the Hall of Mirrors, you enter the queen's official apartment. Hard to miss is the queen's bedroom, with the famous feather-canopied bed where all the royal babies were born in public view. Redecorated for Marie Leszinska, wife of Louis XV, the paneling is in the delicate rococo style, a welcome relief from the monumental grandeur of the Louis XIV salons.

Beyond the queen's apartment begins a series of dull picture galleries devoted "to the glories of France." Undoubtedly the greatest picture is David's huge *Distribution of the Eagle Standards* and a copy of his *Coronation of Josephine* (in the Louvre), both painted for Napoleon.

The **Petits Appartements** were the living quarters of the royal family and, of course, the king's mistresses. Built around dark inner courtyards, they aimed for privacy and an escape from court etiquette. They provide the finest and most priceless examples in France of 18th-century paneling and decoration.

The gardens The 247-acre Versailles grounds, the largest palace gardens in Europe, are the epitome of the French formal style. Laid out by Le Nôtre along a central axis leading to the Grand Canal in the park, the severe symmetry is relieved by hundreds of statues, follies, and

fountains. The most stunning are those of Latona and Apollo, illustrating the story of the Sun King's favorite god. The monumental Orangerie south of the palace is by Mansart. From the great Neptune Fountain (Bassin de Neptune) on the north side, stroll back to the center and past the Apollo Fountain (Bassin d'Apollon) till you reach the canal, where row boats and bicycles can be rented and a pleasure boat or mini-train taken to the Trianons, or you can walk along the avenue de Trianon.

The Trianons The Grand Trianon was built for Louis XIV as a love-nest and an escape from palace routine. Its delicate pink marbled architecture is a welcome contrast to the official grandeur of the palace. The garden, planted with flowers all year round (a million pots), was the most luxurious in France.

The Petit Trianon, built for Louis XV's mistress, Madame du Barry, was later presented to Marie-Antoinette by Louis XVI. Often described as the absolute jewel of French neoclassical architecture, its grounds were entirely transformed by her into a romantic "English" park with a make-believe village (Hameau), where the Queen could lead the "simple" life.

JAM-TASTING AT THE ROYAL KITCHEN GARDEN
Don't miss the gastronomic tour of the Potager du Roi (the royal kitchen garden). Open from April to mid-November, it can be toured with resident experts, culminating in vegetable and jam-tasting (Guided tours daily except Mon and Tue at 2:30 PM from the gate, 6 rue Hardy, tel: 01 39 24 62 62).

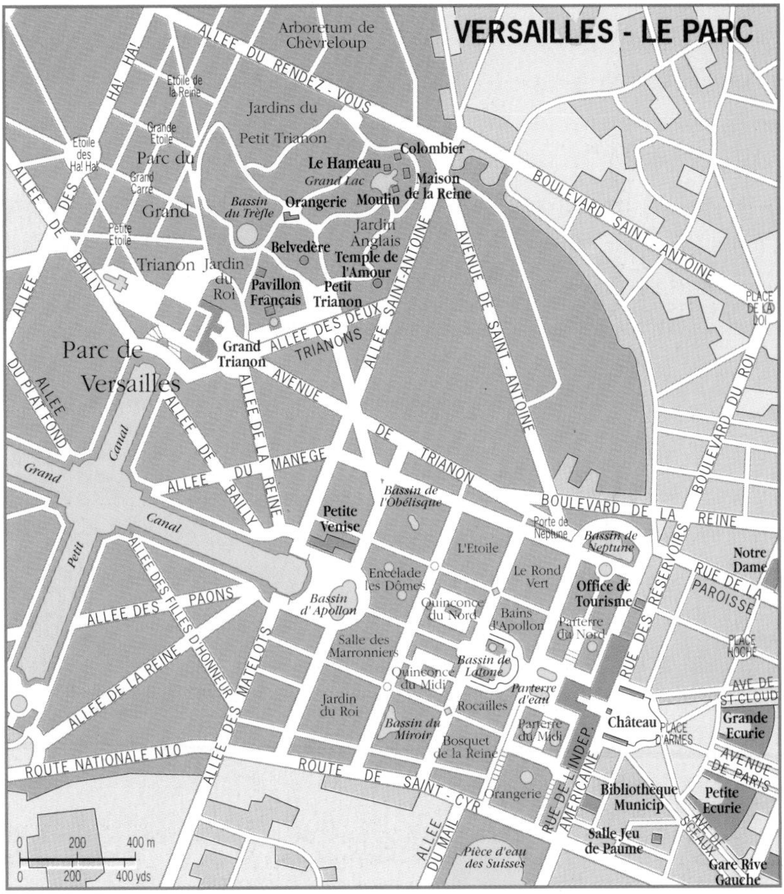

WINE STATISTICS
Wine was originally brought to the south of France by the Phoenicians and Greeks in the 6th century BC. In 1989 France produced over 6,081,800 tons and the French drank an average 16 gallons a head, down from 26 gallons per head in 1965.

SALES
It is not always easy to find a bargain in Paris with so many smart stores. However some stores offer reduced goods just before Christmas, otherwise the best sales, called *soldes*, are held in January and July. Look out for clothing marked stock, sold at stock price or *dégriffe*, meaning marked-down designer labels. Clothes marked *fripes* are second-hand.

Shopping

Whether *foie gras* or shoes, Parisian goods just beckon customers, totting up small fortunes on credit-card bills. But that is part of what this city is about, and nobody should leave with empty hands. Lovers of clothes and stylish accessories should window-shop in streets like rue des Francs-Bourgeois (affordable shoes, accessories, clothes), rue de Grenelle (designer clothes and shoes), rue Etienne Marcel (the mecca of young designers), place des Victoires (successful designers) or Faubourg St.-Honoré (luxury). Both the rue de Rennes and boulevard St.-Germain are good stretches for reasonably priced boutiques. For gourmets the choice is similarly enticing, and for everything one of the greatest pleasures is the perfect packaging, making even a modest purchase look royal.

Accessories

Annick Goutal, 14 rue de Castiglione, 75001 (tel: 01 42 60 52 82), *métro*: Concorde. Delicate, sensuous scents, oils, and lotions, beautifully packaged, make a pleasant change from the usual mass-produced couture perfumes.

Charles Kammer, 14 rue de Grenelle, 75007 (tel: 01 42 22 91 19), *métro*: La Tour Maubourg. Branch off place des Victoires. Smart shoe designs with imaginative details and almost possible prices.

Fabrice, 33 and 54 rue Bonaparte, 75006 (tel: 01 43 26 57 95), *métro*: St.-Germain. Very Rive Gauche accessory store: colorful jewelry, decorative headbands. Certainly not understated.

Lancel, 8 place de l'Opéra, 75009 (tel: 01 47 42 37 29), *métro*: Opéra. Branches all over Paris. Classic, good-quality bags, wallets, luggage.

Madeleine Gély, 218 boulevard St-Germain, 75007 (tel: 01 42 22 63 35), *métro*: rue du Bac. Astonishing selection of over 400 walking-sticks (cigarette-holder canes, watch-canes) and umbrellas of all shapes, designs, and sizes.

Marie Mercié, 56 rue Tiquetonne, 75002 (tel: 01 40 26 60 68), *métro*: Etienne-Marcel. Also at 23 rue St.-Sulpice, 75006. Paris' whackiest hat designer who also produces some seductive, very wearable designs. Look for the bargain bin in this tiny, very feminine boutique.

La Maroquinerie Parisienne, 30 rue Tronchet, 75009 (tel: 01 47 42 83 40), *métro*: Havre Caumartin. Vast choice of cut-price leather goods and luggage. Some top brands are available here.

Réciproque, 95 rue de la Pompe, 75016 (tel: 01 47 04 30 28), *métro*: Pompe, Victor-Hugo. Not strictly accessories but an excellent address for picking up second-hand couture and designer clothes abandoned by fickle ladies of 'the 16th *arrondissement*. Large accessory department stocks some real finds.

Sacha, 15 rue de Turbigo, 75002 (tel: 01 45 08 13 15), *métro*: Etienne-Marcel. Branches all over Paris. Young, fun shoes at accessible prices.

Stephane Kélian, 6 place des Victoires, 75002 (tel: 01 42 61 60 74), *métro*: Bourse. Branches in the Marais and

Champs-Elysées. Some sensational designs (matched by prices) at one of Paris' top shoe designers. Beautifully made, last for ever.

Books and records

FNAC, Branches at Forum-des-Halles, rue de Rennes and avenue des Ternes. Chain of large-scale book and record stores, also stocking camera, computer, and hi-fi equipment.

Galignani, 224 rue de Rivoli, 75001 (tel: 01 42 60 76 07), *métro*: Tuileries. Well-stocked, old-fashioned bookstore. Helpful bilingual service. Range of English-language books.

Virgin Megastore, 52 Champs-Elysées, 75008 (tel: 01 49 53 50 00), *métro*: Franklin-Roosevelt. FNAC's rival as *the* Parisian record store. Particularly popular with the younger crowd, keeping up with the fast-changing music scene.

Children

Agnès B Lolita, 10 rue du Jour, 75001 (tel: 01 45 08 49 89), *métro*: Les Halles. Ineffably Parisian, simple, and stylish cotton-knit and jersey clothes that don't come cheap.

Au Nain Bleu, 406/410 rue St.-Honoré, 75008 (tel: 01 42 60 39 01), *métro*: Concorde. The oldest toy store, illustrious, magical, unforgettable with toy soldiers galore, puzzles, dolls, and their houses, soft toys.

Le Ciel est à Tout le Monde, 10 rue Gay-Lussac 75005 (tel: 01 46 33 21 50), *RER*: Luxembourg. The sky is for all the world but this store is especially delightful for children. Boomerangs, kites of all descriptions, puppets, and pocket money toys.

Du Pareil au Même, 15–17 rue des Mathuruns, 75008 (tel: 01 42 66 93 80), *métro*: St.-Lazaire. Fashionable clothes at affordable prices; several branches in Paris.

Pom d'Api, 13 rue du Jour, 75001 (tel: 01 42 36 08 87), *métro*: Les Halles. Also at 28 rue du Four. Adorable hip miniature footwear. Doc Martens for toddlers, made in France.

Si Tu Veux, 68 Galerie Vivienne, 75002 (tel: 01 42 60 59 97), *métro*: Bourse. Charming toy store with teddy-bear branch and party dressing-up/games department.

Department stores

Au Bon Marché, 22 rue de Sèvres, 75007 (tel: 01 44 39 80 00), *métro*: Sèvres-Babylone. Founded in 1852, the oldest in Paris and the only Rive Gauche department store. Less crowded than the boulevard Haussmann stores, more genteel, more courteous. Good for household goods, lingerie, and children's wear. Basement bookstore is excellent.

Au Printemps, 64 boulevard Haussmann, 75009 (tel: 01 42 82 50 00), *métro*: Havre-Caumartin. An old classic. Wide-ranging clothes and accessories, good household and furniture departments—watch out for own-range Primavera. Quality not always up to its neighboring rival (Galeries Lafayette) but prices often lower. Own-label goods, Sélection Printemps, are good value.

BHV (Bazar de l'Hôtel de Ville), 52 rue de Rivoli, 75004 (tel: 01 42 74 90 00), *métro*: Hôtel de Ville. For kings and queens of do-it-yourself. The basement is a paradise of

CHEESE STATISTICS
France produces more varieties of cheese than any other country in the world. From Normandy to the Alps, cows', goats', and lambs' milk is syphoned off to create those miraculous odorous objects displayed in Parisian cheese stores – just a few pounds of the 160,000 tons produced annually. The French consume 46 pounds per year (the Americans a mere 22 pounds) per person.

✓ **AU BON MARCHÉ**
Au Bon Marché was originally built in 1852 on the site of an asylum, located at the junction of rue du Bac and rue de Sèvres. It was expanded by Eiffel in 1867. Since then it has maintained its chic image, particularly famous for its antiques and oriental rugs, and it houses an excellent food hall, the "Grande Epicerie."

A treasure-house of consumer goods: the Galeries Lafayette

MANNERS AND RULES
At business lunches, many smart Parisian executives still consider it impolite to talk business before the dessert arrives. When asking you to dinner a Paris host or hostess may make the invitation more tempting by telling you about the other guests, but will never talk about the menu. The French trust their own palates and so are easy-going about ordering red wine with fish or white wine with meat.

every imaginable tool, gadget, hardware, etc. Forget the fashion and stick to paint stripping; materials on fifth floor. Assistants are employed by brand names, so are supremely unhelpful.

Galeries Lafeyette, 40 boulevard Haussmann, 75009 (tel: 01 42 82 34 56), *métro*: Chaussée d'Antin. Spectacular glass-domed store, luxurious, often pricey but also stocks more economical, own-label goods. Two floors devoted to fashion. Every top designer has an outlet here selling latest designs. First-floor accessory department is excellent for presents. There is a smaller branch of Galeries Lafayette at Montparnasse at the base of the tower.

La Samaritaine, 19, rue de la Monnaie, 75001 (tel: 01 40 41 20 20), *métro*: Pont-Neuf. Labyrinthine multi-building department store which sells everything if you can find it. Usually helpful service. Most useful is Magasin 2 for *parfumerie*, do-it-yourself, household goods, furnishings, and, surprisingly, some designer clothes. La Samaritaine is not as crowded as BHV (see page 215). Roof-top tearoom.

Marks & Spencer, 35 boulevard Haussmann, 75009 (tel: 01 44 61 08 00), *métro*: Havre-Caumartin. British chain store, clothing and well-stocked quality food department, now a favorite with chic Parisians. No concessions to French taste. New branch on the rue de Rivoli, *métro*: Châtelet and at La Défense.

Food and wine

Cheese

Androuet, 41 rue Arsène-Haussaye, 75008 (tel: 01 42 89 95 00), *métro*: Liège. Encyclopedic range of aromatic French cheeses, perfectly ripened. Famous old restaurant and shop, delivery in Paris.

Barthélémy, 51 rue de Grenelle, 75007 (tel: 01 45 48 56 75), *métro*; rue du Bac. If you fancy a cheese meal why not try one of the take-out cheese-boards with its accompanying wine.

Tachon, 38 rue de Richelieu, 75001 (tel: 01 42 96 08 66), *métro*: Palais-Royal. Fabulous range of goat's cheeses, not forgetting the cow's, in atmospheric old store. Friendly professional advice.

Gourmet groceries

A la Mère de Famille, 35 rue du Faubourg-Montmartre, 75009 (tel: 01 47 70 83 69) *métro*: Le Peletier. Superb 18th-century grocery store with shelves full of ornate and colorful sweets, biscuits, and jams. Friendly, old-fashioned service.

Comptoir de la Gastronomie, 34 rue Montmartre, 75001 (tel: 01 42 33 31 32), *métro*: Etienne-Marcel. Old-fashioned store selling products from southwest France: goose and duck *foie gras*, truffles, dried *cèpes* (mushrooms), snails.

Fauchon, 26 place de la Madeleine, 75008 (tel: 01 47 62 60 11), *métro*: Madeleine. Over 20,000 exotic and luxury products from spices to fruit, tea, *charcuterie*, cakes. Too famous for good service, and the prices are outrageous.

Hédiard, 21 place de la Madeleine, 75008 (tel: 43 12 88 88), *métro*: Madeleine. Fauchon's main rival has branches all over Paris. Freshly roasted coffee, spices, expensive wines.

Izraël, 30 rue François Miron, 75004 (tel: 01 42 76 66 23) *métro*: St.-Paul. Colorful souk of North African and Oriental products. Sacks of grains, bottles of spices, piles of African baskets.

La Maison du Miel, 24 rue Vignon, 75009 (tel: 01 47 42 26 70), *métro*: Madeleine. Offers countless types of honey (tasting possible) in pretty tiled interior. Established in 1908.

Legrand Filles et Fils, 1 rue de la Banque, 75002 (tel: 01 42 60 07 12), *métro*: Bourse. Renowned wine and fine

A feast for the eyes and the taste buds: Fauchon, place de la Madeleine

THE BEST BOULANGERIE
The most famous bakery in Paris is L'établissement Poilâne in the Montparnasse district, renowned for its wholewheat "Poilâne" bread. Indeed no other *boulangerie* can boast bread known by the name of its baker. There is often a line outside the shop at 8 rue du Cherche-Midi, 75006, especially at around 4 PM when the fresh loaves come out of the oven.

grocery store founded in 1890. Outstanding range of wines, helpful service. Situated in the delightful Galerie Vivienne.

Maison de la Truffe, 19 place de la Madeleine, 75008 (tel: 01 42 65 53 22), *métro*: Madeleine. Unbeatable for luxurious truffles, caviar, and foie gras—the ultimate in gourmet delicacies.

Marché Biologique, Raspail Market, boulevard Raspail, 75006, *métro*: Rennes. Only the freshest organically reared or grown produce is sold at this market every Sunday morning.

Pâtisseries and chocolates

Brocco, 180 rue du Temple, 75003 (tel: 01 42 72 19 81), *métro*: République. One of Paris' top pâtisserie shops/tearooms. Delicious *Cérisette* or Brazilian mocha cakes.

Christian Constant, 37 rue d'Assas, 75006 (tel: 01 53 63 15 15), *métro*: rue du Bac. Tantalizing fruit tarts and rich cakes like Macao, Kalinka, or Pont Royal.

Debauve et Gallais, 30 rue des Saint-Pères, 75007 (tel: 01 45 48 54 67), *métro*: St.-Germain-de-Prés. Ask for Marie-Antoinette's chocolates! Original 18th-century shop selling tea, coffee, divine chocolates, and vanilla.

Dalloyau, 99/101 rue du Faubourg St.-Honoré, 75008 (tel: 01 42 99 90 00), *métro*: St.-Philippe-du-Roule. Pastry-maker for Napoleon. Exquisite macaroons and Mogador cake. Branches in 6th and 15th.

Lenôtre, 61 rue Lecourbe, 75015 (tel: 01 42 73 20 97), *métro*: rue du Bac. World-famous desserts, cakes, chocolates, and ice creams. Try an *opéra* or a *concorde*. Main branch in 16th.

Fashion

Designer clothes (women's)

Agnès B, 6 rue du Jour, 750091 (tel: 01 45 08 56 56), *métro*: Les Halles. A young Parisian classic. Smart, sporty clothes at reasonable prices. Branches all over the world.

Alaïa, 7 rue de Moussy, 75004 (tel: 01 42 72 19 19), *métro*: St.-Paul. The inventor of the much-copied skin-tight dress. Follow Grace Jones' example if you can.

Beretta, 24 rue St.-Sulpice, 75006 (tel: 01 43 26 99 30), *métro*: St.-Sulpice. Feminine, elegant clothes, often with original details.

Barbara Bui, 23 rue Etienne Marcel, 75001 (tel: 01 40 26 43 65), *métro*: Etienne-Marcel. Gossamer silk fabrics, drapey designs. Up-to-the-minute femininity. Expensive.

Cacharel, 5 place des Victoires, 75001 (tel: 01 42 33 29 88), *métro*: Bourse. Good quality designs for middle-of-the-road tastes. Last year's collection is sold off at Stock, 114 rue d'Alésia, 75014 (tel: 01 45 42 53 04).

Claudie Pierlot, 1 rue Montmartre, 75001 (tel: 01 42 21 38 38), *métro*: Châtelet-Les Halles. Chic little dresses which are stunningly simple.

Emmanuelle Khanh, 2 rue de Tournon, 75006 (tel: 01 46 33 41 03), *métro*: Odéon. Very Rive Gauche style, sharp yet fluid cuts, superb blouses.

Irié, 8 rue du Pré-aux-Clercs, 75007 (tel: 01 42 61 18 28), *métro*: rue du Bac. Cheerful, brightly colored designs in supple, inventive fabrics. A former designer with Kenzo. Reasonable prices.

Issey Miyake, 5 place des Vosges, 75004 (tel: 01 48 87 01 86), *métro*: St.-Paul. There are other boutiques on the Left Bank, but this one is stunning. Now legendary sculptural designs beautifully displayed.

Jean-Paul Gaultier, 6 rue Vivienne, 75002 (tel: 01 42 86 05 05), *métro*: Bourse. Witty, irreverent clothes in a soaring futuristic boutique. Questionable prices.

Kenzo, 3 place des Victoires, 75001 (tel: 01 40 39 72 00), *métro*: Bourse. King of zappy fun clothes. Huge boutique displays collections and accessories at high prices.

Studio Lolita, 2 bis rue des Rosiers, 75004 (tel: 01 42 74 42 94), *métro*: St.-Paul. Bargains from Lolita Lempicka's sexy fashion collections, especially last season's.

Tehen, 5 bis rue des Rosiers, 75004 (tel: 01 40 27 97 37), *métro*: St.-Paul. Stylish but comfortable jersey and knitwear coordinates in wide range of colors. Reasonable prices.

Les Trois Quartiers, 23 boulevard de la Madeleine, 75001 (tel: 01 42 97 80 12), *métro*: Madeleine. Most of the great names of fashion can be found in this shopping center at the heart of the chic Faubourg St.-Honoré.

Un Après-Midi de Chien, 32 rue Étienne-Marcel, 75002 (tel: 01 40 28 00 20), *métro*: Étienne-Marcel. Latest teen styles, embroidered blouses, pastel colors. Reasonable.

Menswear

Autour du Monde, 12 rue des Francs Bourgeois, 75003 (tel: 01 42 77 16 18), *métro*: St.-Paul. Safari image copied from surplus clothing. Timeless, ageless, good prices.

Daniel Hechter, 146 boulevard St.-Germain, 75006 (tel: 01 43 26 96 36), *métro*: Odéon, Mabillon. Branches all over Paris. Relaxed classicism, well-cut, beautifully color-coordinated range. Not cheap, but not outrageous either. Women's range too.

Façonnable, 9 rue Faubourg St. Honoré, 75008 (tel: 01 47 42 72 60), *métro*: Madeleine. Parisian view of British style at astronomical prices, but you can always stick to the silk boxer shorts.

Island, 4 rue Vide Gousset, off place des Victoires, 75001 (tel: 01 42 61 77 77), *métro*: Bourse. Casual sportswear and accessories, well-displayed, not overpriced.

Loft Design By, 12 rue du Faubourg St.-Honoré, 75008 (tel: 01 42 65 59 65), métro: Concorde. Revamped tweedy coats, oilskins, and casual separates at reasonable prices.

Household

Avant-Scène, 4 place de l'Odéon, 75006 (tel: 01 46 33 12 40), *métro*: Odéon. Furniture and lighting by contemporary French and European designers.

Etamine, 63 rue du Bac, 75007 (tel: 01 42 22 03 16), *métro*: rue du Bac. Vast home design shop, superb objects and fabrics imported from all over world, but always with a Parisian stamp of taste. Own fabric range.

Kitchen Bazaar, 11 avenue du Maine, 75015 (tel: 01 42 22 91 17), *métro*: Montparnasse-Bienvenue. Everything for the kitchen, including contemporary design and retro-style accesories. Bathroom Bazaar near by.

La Maison Ivre, 38 rue Jacob, 75006 (tel: 01 42 60 01 85), *métro*: St.-Germain-des-Prés. Tablecloths and handmade pottery from various regions of France including brightly colored items from Provence.

MINI COUTURE
"Mini couture" is the name given to clothing produced by top Paris designers for children. For the best-dressed baby in town, shop at Baby Dior, Kenzo Bébé, Sonia Rykiel Enfant or Caddie which carries a wide range of designer labels.

Food and drink

Although Napoleon apparently proudly claimed to complete his meals in under 18 minutes, you will rarely be able to do this in Paris and nor will you want to. Although trends toward more efficient eating have reduced traditionally endless lunches to more sprightly affairs, often wolfed down at the counters of bars and bistros, Parisians still enjoy their fodder, and still give it a lot of their time and money. Equally important is the liquid refreshment which in the 1990s gave rise to a growing number of *bars à vins* (wine bars), where numerous nectars are served by the glass and accompanied by very reasonably priced *plats du jour*.

Restaurants In Paris lunch is generally served from noon till 2 or 2:30, after which you should head for a brasserie which serves all day. Dinner is usually served from 7:30, although no self-respecting Parisian dines before at least 9 PM, and orders usually stop between 10 and 11 PM, after which diners will happily linger into the small hours. For avid post-midnight eaters the area to head for is **Les Halles**, where old favorites such as **Au Pied du Cochon, Au Chien qui Fume,** or **La Poule au Pot** remain open very, very late (the first all night and the last till 6 AM). Near by, **L'Epi d'Or** in the rue J. J. Rousseau and **Aux Crus de Bourgogne** in the rue Bachaumont continue the local tradition. Reservations are essential in more select restaurants, even if made in the afternoon for the evening.

Beware of Sundays, a favorite closing day, which leaves some *quartiers* deserted and recovering from the excesses of Saturday night. However as Paris is Paris, you will not starve: head for one of the popular brasseries or the famous and chic **Café Drouant** near the Opéra, where the annual literary prize, the Prix Goncourt, is awarded. If in the 16th, go to the bustling

AU PIED DU COCHON
As the name suggests, this colorful lively brasserie serves pigs' trotters from 5 AM onward, washed down by delicious onion soup. Formerly a popular haunt for high society, there to watch the workers in the market, today it is extremely popular with tourists and locals.

Food is a form of art in the French capital and almost as famous as Paris fashion

Brasserie Stella; in the 7th, indulge in the rich specialties of the southwest at **Thoumieux**. Near the Arc de Triomphe? Walk downhill to **Le Bœuf sur le Toit** in the rue du Colisée and join the fun. On the islands? Go to **Nos Ancêtres les Gaulois**, which, despite being a favorite tourist haunt, makes a warm, boisterous retreat on a winter Sunday evening. Want a change from French cooking (unlikely)? **Darkoum** in the rue Ste.-Anne, has a spectacular Moorish interior, impeccable service, and delectable couscous and tajines.

Budget eating Choosing where you eat in Paris depends very much on budget, although if this is relatively unimportant the city is at your feet. Without going to the ruinous top restaurants such as **Taillevent, Pierre Gagnaire**, or **Lucas-Carton**, you can still dine divinely in a growing number of serious restaurants which now offer a "menu" in the evening. Previously this budgeting method (an all-in three-course meal at a fixed price, wine excluded) was only available at lunchtime, but, many chic destinations are now using it to drum up more evening business.

Even if your pocket does not stretch to *haute cuisine*, you can try the more affordable bistros of the top chefs Michel Rostang (**Le Bistrot d'à côté**) or Guy Savoy (**Bistrot de l'Etoile**), both of whom opened these more affordable establishments as a welcome alternative to their renowned temples of gastronomy nearby. The 17th *arrondissement* running into the 8th, is the heart of Parisian gastronomy, and has a heavy concentration of celebrated chefs and their restaurants. Reservations sometimes have to be made months in advance but if you want to spend anything approaching 1,000 francs for one admittedly divine dinner, it is worth thinking ahead.

If you are looking for a more intimate tête-à-tête at a price that will allow you a taxi back afterward, then head for **Le Marais** whose backstreets are full of wonderful surprises. The rue des Rosiers, the Jewish quarter, specializes in both North African and Eastern European restaurants, while surrounding streets such as the **rue des Ecouffes** (try the trendy vegetarian **Piccolo Teatro**), **rue des Francs-Bourgeois, rue Vieille du Temple,** and the **rue Ste-Croix de la Bretonnerie** all harbor an interesting selection. The junction of the latter two streets specializes in gay bars.

For more classic cuisine, go to the place des Vosges, where **Ma Bourgogne** reigns supreme on summer nights with tables spilling out under the arcades. Although there is nothing special about its basic dishes, prices are reasonable and the setting is unique. As this *quartier* thrives, the number of restaurants grows, and it is worth investigating the nearby **rue des Tournelles** (try the delicious *menu du marché* at **Baracane**) and the **rue de Birague**, without forgetting a charming little square, the place du **Marché Ste.-Catherine**, which has several reasonably priced restaurants. Back toward St.-Paul, the **rue François Miron** has some old favorites, while the **rue du Pont Louis-Philippe** will take you down to a string of interesting restaurants lining the *quai* by the Seine. Here **Le Trumilou** serves basic fish dishes in a provincial-style atmosphere.

REGAL RESTAURANTS
Many restaurants offer palatial settings which make the food seem irrelevant. Le Grand Véfour, in the Palais-Royal, is a magnificent example of sumptuous decoration from the 1820s, although the establishment itself dates from before the Revolution. On the rue de Rivoli the *salon de thé* Angélina is unrivaled for its early 1900s classical style, complete with Mediterranean landscape murals. Art deco reaches its zenith at La Coupole in Montparnasse; and the most over-the-top example of turn-of-the-century opulence is to be found in the extraordinary restaurant at the Gare de Lyon overlooking the platforms, Le Train Bleu.

LE FROG ET ROSBIF
Drop in at Le Frog et Rosbif (116 rue St-Denis, 75002; tel: 01 42 36 34 73) for the best English breakfasts in town or to enjoy an enormous brunch on Sunday mornings while browsing through the newspapers. A truly English-pub atmosphere with quiz nights, live bands, and home-brewed beer, it is popular with French and English alike.

Le Pub Renault, on the Champs-Elysées, adds French style to a British institution

COUSCOUS
Couscous restaurants can be found in every *quartier*. The word "couscous" refers to the wheat grain (semolina) which, ideally, is heaped in a moist, buttery pile and mixed with a fresh vegetable stew. Completing the dish is the meat you have chosen; the best bet is nearly always *brochettes d'agneau* (lamb kebabs) or *méchoui* (a piece of roasted lamb). The other mainstay of Moroccan, Algerian and Tunisian cuisine is the *tajine*. Baked in a clay dish, tajine is basically a meat stew but with a combination of exotic ingredients—olives, almonds, prunes, conserved lemons—and cooked slowly to create a delicious sauce.

St.-Germain-des-Prés Similar in style and budget are the numerous restaurants crowded into the narrow side streets of **St.-Germain**. Streets leading south from the *métro* Mabillon toward St.-Sulpice are packed with intriguing places, from Aux Charpentiers, an old classic full of carpenters' models or le Mâchon d'Henri, the yuppies' haunt, where you munch to live samba, to family-run pizzerias, or hangouts papered with old movie posters. Perfect for budgeting too, St.-Germain claims old favorites along the **rue Monsieur-le-Prince (Le Polidor)** or tiny little places lining the very narrow **rue de l'Echaudé**. This is not the haunt of high gastronomy (although **L'Echaudé St.-Germain** comes high in the candlelit dinner stakes), but you will emerge well fed without feeling totally fleeced. Continuing in the same direction, the **rue Dauphine** claims some reasonably priced, reliable restaurants, culminating at the bottom in one of Paris' best Indian restaurants, **Yugaraj**.

In the summer months this area is a delight to wander around. Try **Le Bistrot de Paris**, a sign of a return to traditional bourgeois cuisine. One of the city's best Vietnamese restaurants, **Tan Dinh**, is situated beyond the rue du Bac toward the Musée d'Orsay, and has a particularly impressive wine list. Finally, the ultimate in conditions for a *dîner à deux* can be found at **Lapérouse**, which still has ornately mirrored turn-of-the-century private rooms upstairs—although its cuisine is not what it used to be.

Le sandwich An unexpected craze has begun to sweep Paris at lunchtime. The English sandwich, white sliced bread and all, is now in such demand that Marks & Spencer are importing the bread daily from the U.K. and feverishly filling and packing sandwiches at the boulevard Haussman ready for the lunchtime rush. Now even French department stores are getting in on the act.

Wine bars *Bars à vins* are increasingly popular as relaxed lunchtime spots where quality wine accompanies a basic hot dish or even more copious "menu." Friendly, bustling places where some clients eat at the counter and others squeeze around small tables, they epitomize the Parisian character: fast, no frills, and with a quick patter. Those which come closer in style to bistros are open in the evenings, but the purist *bar à vin* usually closes around 9 PM. The 1st and 2nd *arrondissements*, where business executives are thick on the ground, have a wide choice, but try and go either before 12:30 or just after 2 PM if you want to get a table. An old favorite is **Le Rubis**, where plates of charcuterie or cheese help absorb varying amounts of wine. **Willie's Wine Bar**, opened and run by an Englishman, and its brother, **Juvéniles**, both serve thirsty stockbrokers from the nearby Bourse. In the same *quartier*, **Le Gavroche** is justifiably popular, while **Le Dauphin**, in the rue St.-Honoré, is a haven of traditional French cuisine.

In Le Marais, don't miss **Le Coude-Fou**, a narrow bistro often peopled by local eccentrics. **La Tartine** on the rue de Rivoli, is yet another old-timer, where nothing seems to have changed for at least 40 years. Beyond the Bastille, near the place d'Aligre market, is the traditional old favorite, **Le Baron Rouge**, where locals fill their bottles from the wine barrels. The atmosphere is particularly lively on a Sunday morning. Another Parisian monument, even farther afield, is **Jacques Mélac's** famous wine bar. The jovial moustachioed owner produces his own Parisian vintage, resulting in a rowdy wine-picking festival every September. During the rest of the year his bistro overflows with enthusiasts of the heavier end of French cuisine.

St.-Germain has its famous **Chai de l'Abbaye**, a popular but rather soulless wine bar near the rue de Buci market, but is better represented by **Le Comptoir du Relais** at the Carrefour de l'Odéon. Popular with the local fashion crowd is **Au Sauvignon**, which has a well-oriented terrace for improving summer tans. The chain of **L'Ecluse** wine bars (on the quai des Grands Augustins, in Les Halles or at the Madeleine) is excellent for sampling smooth Bordeaux, but their dishes are mainly cold platters.

Bastille Outside the tourist center, wine bars gain even more character, generally because of a faithful crowd of regular customers. Finish your long day or evening in style at the sleek, trendy **Café du Passage** in the rue Charonne, just east of the Bastille.

The spread of trendiness is only a recent phenomenon around the Bastille. Squeezed between the latest "in" places are numerous local restaurants serving basic fare, and many of the hotspots serve ethnic food. Here you can dine on Thai cuisine among low-flying parrots at the **Blue Elephant**, or dive into a mountain of couscous at the reputable **Chez Léon**.

A favorite with young trendies is the **China Club**, a red-lacquered restaurant and bar, more recommended for its cocktails than its fairly standard Chinese dishes.

In the same street, the rue de Charenton, but nearer the Opéra-Bastille, is a theatrical Italian restaurant serving regional specialties, **Sipario**, while between the two is a variety of young and friendly eating places. Turn into the avenue Ledru-Roblin and you can try out a

Parisian wine bars offer the chance to sample a wide range of good vins de terroir

WINE-TASTING
Most wine bars offer wine by the glass, however it is cheaper to order it by the carafe. Different sizes are referred to as a *quart* (25cl), a *demi* (50cl) or a *pichet* (equivalent to a 75cl bottle).

THE LEGENDARY JULES VERNE
Perhaps the hardest dinner reservation to get in Paris, and certainly the highest at 400 feet, is the exclusive Jules Verne Restaurant on the second level of the Eiffel Tower. Book two months in advance for a window table!

longstanding classic, **Le Bistrot du Peintre**. Across the place de la Bastille, you could go to **Café de la Bastille** if you really like people watching: it is now serving oysters and offers a set menu at lunchtime in a contemporary décor.

Chic eating Farther east of the Bastille, toward Faidherbe, is a new epicenter of trendy eating. Go to the fashionable and chic Moroccan **Le Mansouria** or to **Les Amoges**, a bastion of refined inventive French cuisine, in the Faubourg St.-Antoine. Visitors determined to remain firmly within the limits of Gallic cuisine should go a few steps farther to **Chardenoux**, an unpretentious Belle Epoque restaurant serving the best of traditional bistro food. Back in the heart of the Bastille in the rue de Charonne is a firm favorite with locals and visitors alike, **Chez Paul**, where booking is necessary despite its relaxed appearance. Still in the Gallic home-cooking mood, but situated in the uninspiring district around the Gare de Lyon, is a justifiably famous bistro, the elegant **Au Trou Gascon**, where fish is treated in unusually full-flavored ways and hot *foie gras* is dished up with asparagus.

There is still plenty of scope for serious foodies, despite the increase of fast-food eateries

If you find yourself up at **La Villette**, don't hesitate to stay there for lunch or dinner. On the main avenue **Jean-Jaurès** is a traditional Parisian restaurant complete with red benches and lace curtains, and **Au Cochon d'Or** serves generous portions of grilled meat dishes—at a price. For those more interested in fish, the next-door restaurant, **Dagorno**, is a local institution and its decorative Belle Epoque setting creates an elegant background.

Eating with a view Finally, for lunching or dining in bucolic splendor, the **Parc Montsouris**, the **Parc des Buttes-Chaumont,** and the **Bois de Boulogne** all oblige, each with reputable, chic and rather costly establishments. The greenhouse-styled **Pavillon Montsouris** now has an affordable menu and the view over the park will make up for any frustrations over service. **Le Pavillon Puebla** is, in fact, a Napoleon III pavilion, and its decorative style is suitably theatrical: here the cuisine is an astute mixture of traditional and new, served in a vast room overlooking the hillocky park. Queen of them all is **Le Pré Catalan**, housed in a small palace hidden in the verdant Bois de Boulogne.

Le Train Bleu restaurant in the Gare de Lyon

SALONS DE THÉ
Tea rooms in Paris are extremely popular, opening from noon until early evening. Ladurée at 16 rue Royale is particularly grand with Louis XIV décor and delicious pâtisseries. Angélina, near the Louvre, is famous for its hot chocolate with whipped cream. Alternatively the Café de la Mosquée near the Jardin des Plantes serves refreshing mint tea.

Parisian delicatessens are in a class of their own. Most serve delicious pâtés and quiches—ideal for a picnic

Here you can sample exquisite lobster, crab, or tender young rabbit, followed by divine desserts. If the weather is fine, few pleasures are greater than eating in this peaceful, romantic setting.

Ethnic eating Increasingly cosmopolitan, Paris now offers a vast selection of ethnic restaurants. Although **St.-Germain-des-Prés** is traditionally strong, and the streets near the Opéra such as the rue **Ste.-Anne** now cater almost exclusively to a growing Japanese business community, much enjoyment can be had by venturing out of the center to farther-flung *arrondissements*. Home to communities of French Asiatics, North Africans or West Indians, *quartiers* such as **Belleville** or the 13th (**Chinatown**) offer a wide spectrum. Good for tight budgets too, many of the Chinese/Vietnamese restaurants are excellent value, proof being the custom generated by Asiatic families. **Le Président**, a large establishment and the **New Nioullaville** all have endless menus, satisfying specialties and rapid service. Around the crossroads of the boulevard de Belleville and the Faubourg du Temple, you cannot go wrong. Venture farther up the rue de Belleville and you will find **Tai Yien**, another canteen, this time featuring an enormous carp aquarium.

LE FAST-FOOD
French chains have come up with their own response to transatlantic hamburger outlets by launching their own, more "typically French" fare: *La Croissanterie*, *La Brioche Dorée* or—top of the range—*Pomme de Pain* and its fresh baguette-style salad-filled sandwiches. Very often, they are strategically located next door to movie theaters.

Fish and seafood vocabulary

anguille	eel
bar	sea bass
bouillabaisse	fish and seafood soup
brandade de morue	creamed salted cod
brochet	pike
cabillaud	fresh cod
crabe	crab

coquilles St Jacques	scallops
crevettes	shrimps
daurade	sea bream
écrevisses	crayfish
hareng	herring
homard	lobster
huîtres	oysters
langouste	spiny lobster
loup	catfish
lotte	angler
maquereau	mackerel
merlan	whiting
morue	cod
moules	mussels
raie	skate
rouget	red mullet
saumon	salmon
sole	sole
thon	tuna
truite	trout

Meat and poultry vocabulary

agneau	lamb
andouillette	chitterlings sausage
bœuf	beef
brochette	kebob
caille	quail
canard /caneton	duck /duckling
cassoulet	meat and bean casserole
chevreuil	venison
choucroute	sauerkraut
contrefilet	loin steak
côte de bœuf	T-bone steak
côtelettes	chops
dinde	turkey
dindonneau	young turkey
foie	liver
gigot	leg of lamb
langue	tongue
lapin /lapereau	rabbit
lièvre	hare
oie	goose
perdrix	partridge
pintade	guinea fowl
porc	pork
poulet	chicken
poussin	spring chicken
saucisses	sausages
steak tartare	raw minced beef
veau	veal

Cooking methods

The French often have a partiality for undercooked meat, so if you want what is considered "rare" in an Anglo-Saxon country it is safer to say *à point*.

bleu	very rare
saignant	rare
à point	medium rare
bien cuit	well done (relatively ...)

See also pages 277–281.

Paris is a paradise for anyone who has a sweet tooth

SPECTATOR SPORTS
Highlights of the Parisian sporting calendar include the Roland Garros International Tennis Grand Slam tournament mid-May through early June, the Prix de l'Arc de Triomphe horse race in October, and the climax of the annual Tour de France bicycle race in July—along with numerous rugby and football internationals. The 24-hour car race at Le Mans every June is only 125 miles southwest of Paris.

Paris' best jogging circuits are in the Champs de Mars, the Bois de Boulogne and the Bois de Vincennes

Sports

If you're dying to sweat off some of the extra *foie gras* and Sauternes that your poor body has been assailed with, you can turn to the gymnasiums and swimming pools of the capital. But practicing sport in Paris is not easy. Although there are officially 97 gyms, 36 pools, and 57 tennis stadiums, the real picture is a different one, with inconvenient opening hours, far-flung locations, members-only policies and overcrowding the norm. Don't forget the big peripheral parks of Boulogne and Vincennes: both have good cycling and boating facilities as well as endless jogging potential. For information on municipal facilities and sporting events, contact **Allo-Sports** (tel: 01 42 76 54 54).

Cycling The excellent SNCF system of "Train + vélo" combines a train journey with renting a bike from the station at your destination, a perfect way to discover forests, châteaux, and villages. A list of stations is available at any mainline SNCF station. Otherwise you can rent them in Paris for confronting merciless city traffic.

Paris á vélo c'est sympa!: 37 boulevard Bourdon, 75004 (tel: 01 48 87 60 01).

Paris-Vélo: 2 rue du Fer-à-Moulin, 75005 (tel: 01 43 37 59 22).

How about a three-hour guided tour?

Paris Bike: 83 rue Daguerre. 75014 (tel: 01 30 51 87 64).

Gymnasiums Private chains have taken the lead over municipal gyms, which remain rather dusty, under-equipped affairs in comparison. It is usually possible to have a day pass or a book of 10 passes at a reasonable rate.

Gymnase Club is the biggest on the market and, ever expanding, it has now even taken over the Garden Gym chain. One of the best-equipped Gymnase Club gyms is at 17 rue du Débarcadère; 75017. Call for details (tel: 01 45 74 14 04).

Vitatop has two more exclusive, sophisticated gyms on the outskirts (tel: 01 40 68 00 21). The branch on the roof of the Sofitel Hotel offers a spectacular Parisian skyline from your jacuzzi.

Lastly, for those who have really overdone it in the restaurants, a vast and extravagant multisports complex could be the answer.

Aquaboulevard, 4 rue Louis-Armand, 75015 (tel: 01 40 60 10 00). Artificial nature brought to the périphérique of Paris. As well as a gym, there are indoor putting-greens, a wave pool, tennis and squash courts, and water sports (Open late; day pass available).

Swimming Most of the 30-odd pools in Paris are municipal, therefore affordable. But avoid Wednesdays and weekends when local school kids take over. Opening times are complicated, so phone direct or check Pariscope for details. Below are the more central pools.

Piscine d'Auteil, Bois de Boulogne, route des Lacs á Passy, 75016 (tel: 01 42 24 07 59). Ideally situated if you're thinking of spending the days in the Bois de Boulogne, jogging, boating, or cycling.

Boules or pétanque is a less strenuous sporting option, but it's taken just as seriously as any other

Piscine Buttes-aux-Cailles, 5 place Paul-Verlaine, 75013 (tel: 01 45 89 60 05). A tiled art deco gem of a 36-yard pool, another one outdoors, open in summer.

Piscine des Halles, Porte du Jour, Forum-des-Halles, 75001 (tel: 01 42 36 98 44), 55-yard underground pool, clean and bright with "tropical" garden.

Piscine Jean Taris, 16 rue Thouin, 75005 (tel: 01 43 25 54 03). Two 27-yard pools, favorites with local students, and one toddlers' pool. Built in 1978; water cleaned electronically, so no chlorine!

Piscine du Marché St.-Germain, 7 rue Clément, 75006 (tel: 01 43 29 08 15). Hidden beneath the St.-Germain market complex is a 27-yard pool with a special diving section.

Squash Club Quartier Latin, 19 rue de Pontoise, 75005 (tel: 01 43 54 06 23). A 36-yard pool with a distinct 1930s air. Solarium, squash courts, and sauna.

Piscine Saint-Merri, 16 rue du Renard, 75004 (tel: 01 42 72 29 45). Right next to Beaubourg, small indoor 27-yard pool with solarium.

Tennis Your best bet for a game of tennis is in the Bois de Vincennes, where 24 courts huddle in the Centre de tennis de la Faluère, a gigantic sports complex. The desirable, much-coveted public courts in the Jardin du Luxembourg are more central, but require reservations through a municipal club.

For details on joining local clubs contact **Allo-Sports** (tel: 01 42 76 54 54). Numerous private clubs exist, mainly at the *portes* of Paris, but membership is costly and is probably only worthwhile if you are staying for a long period.

PARISIAN PASTIMES

Typically Parisian sports include afternoon boating or horseback riding in the Bois de Boulogne or the Bois de Vincennes and *pétanque*—which Parisians claim to be their most popular sport—played on any shady stretch of gravel or earth in the parks. Golf is also becoming increasingly popular, with many clubs developing on the outskirts.

"IN" PLACES
Fickle as ever, Parisian *branchés* (plugged in, hip) float from one club to the next, making and breaking the fortunes of bartenders. Pigalle neon and fun tackiness remains a favorite: try Le Moloko for drinks, La Locomotive for a dance floor twirl or La Cigale for a rock concert. The Bastille is now firmly established, and the rue de Lappe never sleeps. Revel in the kitsch splendor of Le Balajo or join the crowd at La Casbah. Other streets like rue de Charenton or rue de Charonne are burgeoning with bars too. Les Halles and in particular the rue des Lombards are good for late drinks and music, but to really rub shoulders with Paris jetsetters head for Les Bains.

The boulevard de Clichy, similar to London's Soho with its fast-food joints, movie theaters, sex stores and "live' shows, is always a crowded nightspot

Nightlife

Parisian nightlife changes fashion as the proverbial snake does its skin. Old favorites are few and far between, often handed over to the destiny of tourist buses, while others sink in the wake of youth's fickleness. But a vast choice remains, and you will never find yourself at a loss for a drink or a swing round the dance floor in the early hours.

One warning: the price of drinks in clubs can be astronomical, so if quantities of alcohol are essential, stick to regular bars (though after 10 PM prices are uncontrolled everywhere).

Opening hours Action starts in the nightclubs well after midnight, continuing till 5 AM or so, while some of the jazz bars also carry on late. All clubs are closed on Mondays, and finding jazz is tricky, though not impossible, on both Sundays and Mondays.

Check the listings published in the weekly *Pariscope, Une semaine de Paris* or *L'Officiel des Spectacles* for detailed programs.

Feather clubs

Many visitors come to Paris for just that: the renowned cabaret shows that seem straight out of a time-warped Hollywood. All are virtually monopolized by ogling tourist parties. You can unload a small fortune on exorbitantly priced drinks.

If this is the kind of evening out you're looking for, the following selection might be useful.

The famous Folies-Bergère was considered to be the naughtiest cabaret in Paris when striptease was introduced as part of the show in 1894

Crazy Horse Saloon, 12 avenue George V, 75008 (tel: 01 47 23 32 32), *métro*: George V. Bare-breasted girls strut through their erotic routines, assuming seemingly impossible postures. Reputed to be the most professional.

Folies-Bergère, 32 rue Richer, 75009 (tel: 01 44 79 98 98), *métro*: Cadet, rue Montmartre. This Parisian institution, renowned for diamanté, feathers, breasts, and glitter, has now turned to staging musical comedies. It has retained the traditional dinner before the show.

Le Lido, 116 Champs Elysées, 75008 (tel: 01 40 76 56 10), *métro*: George V. Fantastic special effects alleviate an otherwise predictable show. The Bluebell Girls dance to a sea of regimented tourists.

Moulin Rouge, 82 boulevard de Clichy, 75018 (tel: 01 53 09 82 82), *métro*: Blanche. A thousand costumes, 100 girls, singers and acrobats, an aquarium, crocodiles. What is this? Just the delirium of a spectacular show in the classic venue.

Paradis Latin, 28 rue Cardinal Lemoine, 75005 (tel: 01 43 25 28 28), *métro*: Cardinal Lemoine. Not in the same league as the above, but a shimmering floor show.

Jazz bars

All Jazz Club, 7–11 rue St-Benoit, 75006 (tel: 01 42 61 87 02), *métro*: St.-Germain-des-Prés. Jazz concerts from 10:30 PM to 2 AM. Guest stars include the Al Copley Trio.

Au Duc des Lombards, 42 rue des Lombards, 75001 (tel: 01 42 33 22 88), *métro*: Châtelet. Comfortable, dark jazz lounge with average to good musicians. Nightly.

Baiser Salé, 58 rue des Lombards, 75004 (tel: 01 42 33 37 71), *métro*: Châtelet. Blues, funk, or jazz, with cocktails until 4 AM.

Café Rive Droite, 2 rue Berger, 75001 (tel: 01 42 33 81 62). High-decibel sounds by local musicians till dawn.

Caveau de la Huchette, 5 rue de la Huchette, 75005 (tel: 01 43 26 65 05), *métro*: St.-Michel. An old classic. Smoky, crowded basement bar and dancing for students and tourists.

JAZZ

All styles of jazz from Free-form to Dixieland can be heard in this jazz-crazy city, with venues ranging from pubs to concert halls. New Morning is one of the most popular clubs, along with Au Duc des Lombards and Le Petit Opportun. The Grande Halle de la Villette hosts a huge international jazz festival in July and the Paris Jazz Festival takes place every October.

HARRY'S BAR
This cozy, wood-paneled bar is the original Harry's Bar, named after its first bartender, Harry MacElkone. Harry bought the bar in 1923 and it soon became a regular haunt for Ernest Hemingway and F. Scott Fitzgerald. Today it is run by Harry's son.

American in Paris: Harry's Bar was opened in 1911 by American jockey Tod Sloane on the rue Daunou

Cavern Café, 21 rue Dauphine, 75006 (tel: 01 43 54 53 82), *métro*: Odéon, Pont-neuf. Indie rock, blues rock, jazz, funk.

Magique, 42 rue de Gergovie, 75914 (tel: 01 45 42 26 10), *métro*: Pernéty. Live jazz and rock concerts start at 10:30 PM.

Meridien, 81 boulevard Gouvion St.-Cyr, 75017 (tel: 01 40 68 30 42), *métro*: Porte Maillot. Rather staid hotel bar, but good jazz classics play here.

New Morning, 7–9, rue des Petites Ecuries, 75010 (tel: 01 45 23 56 39). *métro*: Château d'Eau. Paris' best. Has an excellent program of international jazz concerts.

Péniche Makara, quai de la Gare-BNF, 75013 (tel: 01 44 24 09 00), *métro*: quai de la Gare. Assortment of reggae, hip-hop, jazz, funk rock, Afro groove, jazz funk, on a barge near the BNF.

Petit Journal St-Michel, 71 boulevard St-Michel, 75005 (tel: 01 43 26 28 59), *métro*: Luxembourg. New Orleans style jazz until 2 AM in this favorite, though cramped, old venue. Restaurant/bar.

Le Petit Opportun, 15 rue des Lavandières-Ste-Opportun, 75001 (tel: 01 42 36 01 36). Well-established bar, good French jazz program in crowded basement.

Le Sunset, 60 rue des Lombards, 75001 (tel: 01 40 26 46 60), *métro*: Châtelet. Funky jazz cellar for Les Halles late-nighters. Restaurant and bar.

La Villa, 29 rue Jacob, 75006 (tel: 01 43 26 60 00), *métro*: St.-Germain. Chic jazz bar in designer-hotel.

Late-night bars

Bartok, 64 rue de Charenton, 75012 (tel: 01 43 45 25 53), *métro*: Ledru-Rollin. Low bar prices, late hours. Acid jazz as well as rock and jazz in the cellar.

Bilboquet, 13 rue Saint-Benoît, 75006 (tel: 01 45 48 81 84), *métro*: St.-Germain. Classic, straight-laced atmosphere. Restaurant and bar with live jazz.

Birdland Club, 20 rue Princesse, 75006 (tel: 01 43 26 97 59), *métro*: Mabillon. Friendly, late. Golden-oldie jazz records set the laid-back tone.

Café Charbon, 109 rue Oberkampf, 75011 (tel: 01 43 57 55 13), *métro*: Ménilmontant. A striking success in the latest trendy area for bar-crawling enthusiasts with good funk and house music.

La Casbah, 18/20 rue de la Forge-Royal, 75011 (tel: 01 43 71 71 89), *métro*: Faidherbe-Chaligny. Vast, imaginative Mauresque-art deco cocktail bar with dancing downstairs. Video screen and a team of fancy bartenders.

China Club, 50 rue de Charenton, 75012 (tel: 01 43 43 82 02), *métro*: Ledru-Rollin. Vast, shady, red-lacquered bar/restaurant with discreet upstairs cocktail lounge. Hip, crowded, buzzy. Near Bastille.

L'Entrepôt, 14 rue de Charonne, 75011 (tel: 01 48 06 57 04), *métro*: Bastille. Cheerful, popular cocktail bar guarded by bouncer. Smoky billiard room downstairs.

Harry's Bar, 5 rue Daunou, 75002 (tel: 01 42 61 71 14), *métro*: Opéra. Old favorite. Pub atmosphere stimulating enough for Gershwin to compose *American in Paris* here. Mature, tanked-up crowd.

Kitty O'Shea's, 10 rue des Capucines, 75002 (tel: 01 40 15 00 30), *métro*: Opéra. Warm, pub atmosphere frequented by sonorous Irish expatriates and business people revving up.

La Luna, 28 rue Keller, 75011 (tel: 01 40 21 90 91), *métro*: Bastille, Ledru-Rollin. Two lively high-tech floors for Bastille troopers.

Mayflower, 49 rue Descartes, 75005 (tel: 01 43 54 56 47), *métro*: Cardinal-Lemoine. Lively all-night pub. Stagger out at dawn for breakfast on the place de la Contrescarpe.

Moloko, 26 rue Fontaine, 75009 (tel: 01 48 74 50 26), *métro*: Blanche. Newly "in" late-night bar for Pigalle clubbers and party crowd.

Rosebud, 11 bis rue Delambre, 75014 (tel: 01 43 35 38 54), *métro*: Vavin. Shady Montparnasse bar, intimate atmosphere for discreet tête-à-têtes.

Night-clubs/discos

Les Bains, 7 rue du Bourg l'Abbé, 75003 (tel: 01 48 87 01 80), *métro*: Etienne-Marcel. Still top, still sniffish at the door, but a nocturnal landmark for fashion, showbiz, and media personalities. Go late. Restaurant.

Le Balajo, 9 rue de Lappe, 75011 (tel: 01 47 00 07 87), *métro*: Bastille. A survivor of the 1930s, incomparably ritzy décor for hip young things. Monday and Thursday nights are best.

Bobino, 20 rue de la Gaîté, 75014 (tel: 01 43 27 24 24). A top disco spread over two floors of a converted variety theater. Good DJs.

Castel's, 15 rue Princesse, 75006 (tel: 01 43 26 90 22), *métro*: Odéon. Members' club for monied, older generation. Bar upstairs and dance floor downstairs. Twinkle a diamond cufflink and you may get in.

La Chapelle des Lombards, 19 rue de Lappe, 75011 (tel: 01 43 57 24 24), métro: Bastille. Swinging rhythms from Latin America, Africa, and the Caribbean. Friendly atmosphere.

Le Cithéa, 114 rue Oberkampf, 75011 (tel: 01 40 21 70 95), *métro*: Parmentier. Crowded small bar open very late. Funk, soul, salsa, world, jazz; live music Thu–Sat.

Le Divan du Monde, 75 rue des Martyrs, 75018 (tel: 01 44 92 77 66), *métro*: Pigalle. Live indie rock, world, and French pop followed by DJs' selection of soul, funk, and hip hop.

La Locomotive, 90 boulevard de Clichy, 75018 (tel: 01 53 41 88 88), *métro*: Blanche. Ambitiously scaled, three-tiered basement club below Moulin Rouge. Latest hip sounds sprinkled with '60s nostalgia. Concerts are given too.

Nouvelle Eve, 25 rue Fontaine, 75009 (tel: 01 45 26 68 18), *métro*: Pigalle. Gilded theater changes from cabaret to nightclub on stroke of midnight. Good DJs.

Planet Rock, Sheherazade, 3 rue de Liège, 75009 (tel: 01 42 85 53 78), *métro*: Liège. 1,001 nights oriento-exotico décor in former Russian cabaret. Changing nightly style of rap, house, rock, etc.

Rex Club, 5 boulevard Poissonière, 75002 (tel: 01 42 36 10 96), *métro*: Bonne Nouvelle. Part of gigantic art deco concert hall and cinema. Different DJ every night from house to rap, rock, disco, salsa. Good concerts.

Le Tango, 11 rue au Maire, 75003 (tel: 01 42 72 17 18), *métro*: Arts-et-Métiers. Hot-blooded Afro-Latin rhythms, tango, salsa, reggae keep this low-key club boogeying.

RUBBING SHOULDERS WITH THE RICH AND FAMOUS

The Champs-Elysées area still attracts those with true glitter, so try Villa Barclay to meet B.C.B.G. Parisians. On the other hand, you might trip over the toes of French showbiz personalities or just plain rich folk at Les Bains in with-it Beaubourg. Everything is a question of generation so you are more likely to find youthful successes (media, photographers, designers, etc.) at Les Bains, whose reputation never wanes. Finally, the long-standing Castel, theoretically a members-only club, is where you're most likely to sit next to mature French movie stars accompanied by their latest girlfriend.

Eating out on the Champs-Elysées

WATCH WHERE YOU PARK YOUR CAR
The army of traffic wardens marching daily through the streets of Paris hand out some 8 million tickets a year.

BOOKING AGENCIES
Looking for accommodations? Two agencies, Paris-Séjour-Réservation at 90 Avenue des Champs-Elysées, 75008 (tel: 01 53 89 10 50) or Ely 12 12 at 9 rue d'Artois, 75008 (tel: 01 43 59 12 12) will reserve accommodations on your behalf.

FOLLOWING IN THE FOOTSTEPS OF THE FAMOUS
Paris is famous for its luxurious hotels, frequented by the rich and famous. The Hôtel Crillon, built during the reign of Louis XV, is one of the favorite haunts of the jet-set, from politicians to pop stars, and the Second-Empire Grand Hôtel Inter-Continental was patronized by many distinguished guests, including Winston Churchill. L'Hôtel was the last home of Oscar Wilde and the Lutetia was recently revamped by top designer Sybille de Margerie. The Ritz, former haunt of the Duke of Windsor and Ernest Hemingway, is now Madonna's favorite Paris hotel.

Accommodations

With 1,500 or so hotels and an annual average of 18 million tourists spread between them, Parisian accommodations cater to all tastes and budgets. This is one of the rare European capitals which offers quite acceptable and affordable accommodations in central areas, often family-run in idiosyncratic fashion.

At the top end of the spectrum are the luxury hotels, straight out of another epoch, which cater to countless well-heeled travelers or business people. Their prices, on a one-off basis, are very high, but some make discount arrangements with travel agents abroad, so it is often worth inquiring at home well in advance of your trip.

The season The Paris "season" is a strange one and is worth bearing in mind if you want good value. May, June, September, and October are the hardest months to find rooms and prices often go down in July and August, particularly in the 3-star establishments, which are sorely missing their business clientèle at that time. Remember that check-out time is midday. On arrival, make sure you check in before 6 PM as after this time the hotel has the right to give the room to someone else, even if they hold a deposit from you. Breakfasts are always continental-style (coffee or tea and rolls or croissants plus a fruit juice if you are lucky). Only 3-star hotels upward are obliged to offer service in the rooms, otherwise you will have to head for the dining room. Not all 1-star hotels offer breakfast. No hotel can charge you for breakfast unless you have ordered it, and you may prefer to join in the city bustle outside for better coffee at a lower price.

If you come to Paris by car remember that you will undoubtedly encounter parking problems. Hotels that have parking lots are generally the uninspiring modern blocks to be found outside the center: many are, however, located close to public parking lots.

Finding a base Choosing your base *quartier* is tricky. Every part of Paris has its advantages and disadvantages, its charms and its horrors. For the heart of luxury go straight to the 8th *arrondissement* (Champs-Elysées, avenue George V, avenue Montaigne, Faubourg St.-Honoré and surrounding streets). Here is the highest concentration of luxury, and 4-star establishments, and this is where to stay if you need to pop out for a fitting at Dior's, pick up some presents at Hermès or impress your business acquaintances. Even if your budget does not stretch to these palaces of refinement, at least drop in for a drink at the bar to soak up some of its features—call-girls included. Although everyone has heard of the Ritz, the Crillon, the Bristol, the Plaza-Athénée, or the George V, not everyone knows the less monumental establishments, such as the **Hôtel de la Trémoille**, the **Raphaël**, or the **San Régis**, favorites with the more discreet variety of wealthy travelers.

Following closely in the luxury stakes is the 1st *arrondissement* (Tuileries, Louvre, place Vendôme), convenient for high-class jewelry and culture, yet whose sidestreets have a good sprinkling of 2- and 3-star hotels. Preening themselves in old-world splendor here are the **Ritz** and the **Meurice**, both of which have remarkable interiors and are wonderful for an early evening drink. Closer to most people's budgets are places such as **Le Molière**, the **Hôtel des Tuileries,** or the **Hôtel Saint-Roch**. Immediately north is the 2nd arrondissement, which, despite its small size, has a large number of 2- and 3-star hotels, catering mainly to the business community centered around the banks and the Bourse. **Timhôtel Palais Royal** is one of a chain of fairly reasonable hotels, usually extremely well situated, and in this case is particularly convenient for doing raids on all the designer boutiques in and around the place des Victoires.

Budget choice The adjacent 9th *arrondissement* (Opéra, *grands boulevards*, Faubourg Montmartre) has the densest concentration of hotels of any Parisian *arrondissement*, and over half of them are budget 2-star establishments. The Faubourg Montmartre and its sidestreets claims the majority; many of these are used by tour operators, giving a rather un-Parisian feel to this otherwise interesting neighborhood. There are popular nightclubs near by, including the Rex Club along the *boulevards* and Planet Rock north toward Pigalle; the Folies-Bergère is just round the corner in an area full of ethnic restaurants (kosher, Turkish, North African). Try the **Corona Opéra**, a 1930s establishment in an interesting backstreet lined with hotels, or the quiet **Chopin**, tucked away in one of Paris' historic covered arcades, just off the bustling boulevard Montmartre.

If you do decide to give these places a wide berth, then head farther north toward Pigalle and Montmartre, where a number of characteristic family-run hotels can be tracked down. Near the delightful place St.-Georges, try the **Hôtel de la Tour d'Auvergne**, an atmospheric, renovated 3-star place, which boasts four-poster beds in every room.

Paris atmosphere The area most visitors head for with alacrity is the Rive Gauche, the 5th, 6th and even 7th *arrondissements*. Less business-oriented in atmosphere and more *vieux* Paris, the Quartier Latin and St.-Germain-des-Prés provide all the ingredients for a classic vacation in Paris. Throughout this district is a host of reasonably priced 1-, 2- and 3-star hotels whose prices are generally lower than their equivalents across the Seine. In the same area you can find fairly basic student hotels and restaurants, gathered around the rue Mouffetard, the place de la Contrescarpe, and the rue des Ecoles, and the slightly more upscale **Hôtel du Collège de France**. Here, in a quiet sidestreet, simple but pleasant rooms rise up to the seventh floor, from where you can glimpse the spires of Notre-Dame. Similarly quaint in spirit is the **Timhôtel Jardin des Plantes**, whose freshly decorated rooms all with a floral theme look out over the park of the same name. Reasonable prices can also be had at the tiny **Hôtel des Carmes**, situated in an atmospheric sidestreet off the boulevard St.-Germain. With its strong student population, due to the proximity of the university, this lively part

LINGUISTIC HELP
In the more upscale establishments receptionists are usually bilingual, and any hotel with two or more stars must by law have a receptionist speaking a second language.

CHEAP CHAIN HOTELS
More and more chain hotels are springing up on the outskirts of Paris, including Ibis (tel: 01 60 87 91 00), Mercure (tel: 01 60 77 22 33), Campanile and Formule I. Although they lack Parisian character and are often located on a busy road, they offer a cheap, clean, practical solution for budget travelers in Paris.

A TIGHT FIT
France has the smallest minimum legal size in Europe for hotel bedrooms and bathrooms, and in Paris, where real estate does not come cheap, many hoteliers exploit this to the full. Thus the so-called bathroom is more than likely to be chopped out of the corner of the bedroom. When booking a room make sure you distinguish between a *salle d'eau* (shower-room) and a *salle de bains* (bathroom).

of the Rive Gauche is particularly recommended for those with a limited budget. Within easy reach of numerous monuments and museums, it has an easy-going atmosphere and caters well to young travelers.

Higher prices St.-Germain harbors a wide selection of good 3-star hotels, but prices can rocket here. The **Hôtel de l'Abbaye St.-Germain** is justifiably pricey within its category, but service is impeccable and the rooms are perfectly appointed, if limited in size (this is medieval Paris, after all). The delightful **Hôtel des Marroniers** is tucked away in its pretty courtyard in the heart of the antiques district, and here the prices are more reasonable if you can get a room. The area of the rue Jacob, the rue de l'Université and the rue de Seine is thick with small family-run hotels, and it is a chic and pleasant part of town. If you must overlook the river try the **Hôtel du Quai Voltaire**, a rambling old place where Baudelaire once stayed. A sure favorite for its location and price is the **Hôtel Michelet-Odéon**, on the place de l'Odéon, just a few steps from the Luxembourg Gardens.

Montparnasse makes a good base: transportation is easy and the bars of the boulevard stay open late. Here you could try squeezing into the tiny **Hôtel Danemark**, renovated from a charming old establishment into a more chic and elegant place. Near by, in the arty rue de la Grande-Chaumière, is a small family-run hotel, excellent for low

The place de l'Opéra, set in the 9th arrondissement, *where hotels are plentiful, often inexpensive, and within easy reach of the many theaters, bars, and restaurants in the area*

budgets: the **Hôtel des Académies**. Farther east and across the boulevard is the **Hôtel Istria**, part of the Montparnasse cultural legend, and reasonable value. Still following the artists' trail, go as far south as you can in Paris—almost—to the **Hôtel du Parc Montsouris**, a simple establishment but with all the necessary comforts and straight across the road from the park. In this charming, peaceful neighborhood are many of the artists' custom-built studios from the 1920s.

Le Marais This is a *quartier* not to be forgotten if you want up-to-the-minute Parisian life. Numerous hotels, old and new, pepper this animated district and you are more likely to find peace and quiet here than anywhere else on the Rive Droite. Although these are mainly 2- and 3-star establishments the occasional budget hotel can still be found such as the fun **Hotel du 7e Art** or the **Grand Hôtel Malher**. In the middle category, try the **Hôtel de la place des Vosges** or the historic **Caron de Beaumarchais**, deservedly popular. Once for low budgets, now with an extra star rising is the characteristic **Hôtel Saint-Merry**, perfectly located for avid visitors to Beaubourg. And for those seeking discreet refinement, the **Pavillon de la Reine** is the *crème de la crème*, modestly set back from the place des Vosges behind a pretty little garden.

See also pages 274–277

ROOM DECORATION
Oscar Wilde managed to keep on wise-cracking to his dying day. Apocryphal or not, he is said to have rung in his last moments for his landlady in the run-down establishment that is now the much more elegant L'Hôtel, rue des Beaux Arts, and whispered to her: "I am sorry, Madame, you must choose between this dreadful wallpaper and me. One of us must go."

MAKING THE BEST OF IT
Even if you can't afford to stay in the 5-star palaces, as the French call them, you can at least get a feel for their atmosphere by having a drink in the bar or tea in the lounge. Best 5-star bars: Crillon, Ritz, and Bristol; best tea: Plaza Athénée, and Meurice.

It's hard to generalize about 2 million people, but as a rule the best way to communicate with Parisians is by using their language. The tourist who relentlessly speaks loud English is much less welcome than the visitor who squeaks out s'il vous plaît, *however poorly pronounced.*

Could it be that old devil flattery at work? Whatever, once you have initiated contact, you then run the risk of hearing in return a slew of what seems to be unintelligible noises, impossible to decipher. To this you simply reply *Parlez-vous anglais?*. If the answer is a brusque *non*, do not despair. An increasing proportion of the younger generation (officially 59 percent of all age groups and 89 percent of the 15- to 19-year-olds) speak a foreign language and willingly help foreign visitors. So keep your eyes open for some bright-eyed teenager.

Forms of address For those who speak some remnants of French, it is worth bearing in mind other practical rules. Addressing people with a *Madame* or *Monsieur* tacked on the end is a sign of politeness that is appropriate no matter what the person's social status. It can work wonders in persuasive tactics. With strangers always stick to *vous*, and with acquaintances only use *tu* once they do. The younger generation is less rigid about this now, but the best rule is to play it safe.

As in many Latin countries, you may be pigeon-holed according to the way you dress—though less so than once imagined. The criterion these days is a certain elegance, but casual rather than formal. What matters is some sense of style and taste. Many Anglo-Saxons may be tempted to overdo it when trying to match Parisian chic. A sloppy appearance will be condemned, but scarcely more than an excessive effort to overdress.

Talking as tourists Because of its incredible popularity among visitors (close to 20 million annually), Paris has its fair share of locals who believe that tourists equal money, and that is the end of it. Yet they love to hear foreigners praise their city, and waiters and waitresses are only too pleased to hear that the food and/or wine they are serving is good. Humor will also take you a long way—contrary to general belief, the Parisians are blessed with a subtle sense of irony and love to share it. Waiters will change from apparently surly monsters to cheerful fellow humans if your French is up to this kind of exchange. Otherwise, a friendly smile will always be appreciated.

Although there is no traditional drinking hour in French cafés to facilitate striking up conversations, curiously enough the restaurants can oblige. Bistros and brasseries—those bustling, old-fashioned dining-halls where tables are squeezed in and customers barely have enough room to raise their fork—are ideal meeting places. Mealtimes are the moment when the French at last drop their guard and relax, and many a conversation

A PARISIAN VINEYARD

The French are passionate about wine. Indeed it is a way of life and even in Paris, wine is produced. Wine-growing is one of the most ancient traditions of Montmartre: the slopes of the Butte Montmartre were formerly covered in vineyards. Nowadays the only remaining vineyards are at the corner of the rue St.-Vincent and rue des Saules, with an annual wine festival celebrated in October.

has been started over the label of a bottle of wine or the relative merits of an unusual dish.

Points of etiquette If you manage to break down the barriers and get to know a French person, a number of rules should be remembered. Two men always shake hands when greeting each other and on leaving, even when they know each other. Members of the opposite sex kiss each other once on each cheek, though suburbanites and people from the provinces actually go through this procedure two or three times. The "Continental Kiss" may seem strange, but it is truly commonplace for ordinary, non-professional encounters, even when you've only met the person an hour earlier.

When entering a room full of strangers, it is usual practice to do the rounds of each person, shaking hands and giving your name, as they do theirs. When you leave, you have to go through the same ritual as you say *au revoir*, shaking hands or giving the *bise* (kiss), depending how much communication has taken place.

Lastly, a universal piece of advice holds equally true for Parisians: if you are invited to someone's home for dinner, make an effort to take flowers, chocolates, or other small gift. It always works wonders.

PROTECTING THE FRENCH LANGUAGE
The French are so protective about their language that there is a special society within the Académie Française, whose job it is to prevent English words from becoming part of daily French vocabulary. Words like *le weekend* and *le foot* somehow slipped through the net and I.T. language has injected a whole new vocabulary.

Striking up a conversation over a drink or a meal is an ideal way of breaking the ice

The Paris métro

Steady amidst the chaotic swirl of Parisian traffic, the Arc de Triomphe gives superb views of the city

Travel Facts

Arriving

U.S. citizens need a valid passport to enter France for stays of up to 90 days. First-timers should apply in person at least five weeks before departure to one of the 13 U.S. Passport Agency offices. Also, local county courthouses, many state and probate courts, and some post offices accept applications. Necessary documents are: (1) a completed passport application (Form DSP-11); (2) proof of citizenship (certified birth certificate issued by the Hall of Records of your state of birth, or naturalization papers); (3) proof of identity (valid driver's license or state, military, or student I.D. card with your photograph and signature); (4) two recent, identical, two-square-inch photgraphs (black-and-white or color head shot with white or off-white background); and (5) $60 for a 10-year passport (those under 16 pay $40 for a five-year passport). Check, money order, or cash (exact change) is accepted. Passports are sent in 10 to 15 business days. You may renew in person or by mail. Send a complete Form DSP-82; two recent, identical passport photographs; your current passport (if it's less than 12 years old and issued after your 16th birthday); and a check or money order for $40.

Air Paris is served by two airports: Orly in the south and Roissy (Charles-de-Gaulle) in the north. Most American flights now arrive at the expanding Roissy Airport. Orly-Ouest terminal is monopolized by internal French flights. There are no airport taxes paid on arrival or departure.

Both Orly and Roissy have extensive international airline facilities including car rental, duty-free stores, restaurants, post offices, hotels in the proximity, and ground transportation into the city center. Air France and airport staff are, on the whole, helpful and can, generally, speak English.

Transportation to and from Roissy: Two possibilities exist apart from a rather costly taxi ride (250 francs) covering the 14 miles. The easiest is the Air France airport bus, which leaves every 15 minutes (5:40 AM–11 PM) and in 40 minutes whisks you straight into the central Arc de Triomphe (Etoile) or the nearby Porte Maillot. Taxis usually await the bus, and the *métro* station is a few yards away. On leaving, pick it up again at Etoile, avenue Carnot. An alternative is Roissy-Bus, an airport bus serving all terminals which heads for Opéra in central Paris. It runs every 15 minutes.

Eurostar trains from London Waterloo terminate at Gare du Nord

The budget transportation system is the RATP shuttle, which links with Roissy-Rail (*RER* line B). If you have a lot of baggage, it's not so easy heaving cases on and off the bus and then down escalators to the *RER* express train, but it will take you directly into the Gare du Nord, or Châtelet-Les Halles. Allow 30–40 minutes. Trains run from 5:30 AM–12 AM every 15 minutes.

Transportation to and from Orly: Only 9 miles from the center, Orly is more feasible by taxi, but it also has more transportation possibilities. The Air France bus (departures every 15 minutes) goes to Invalides but will drop you off, if requested, at Porte d'Orléans or Duroc *métro*. Allow 30 minutes. Much cheaper but less plush is the Orlybus, which arrives at the *RER* and *métro* station of Denfert-Rochereau in south Paris. You can also take the *RER* line C, called Orly-Rail, from St.-Michel, but the shuttle connection is not as well organized as at Roissy. Orly-Val connects a shuttle with the *RER* line B. Passenger information in English is available at both airports (Roissy tel: 01 48 62 22 80; Orly tel: 01 49 75 15 15).

Camping

There are altogether about 120 campgrounds scattered throughout the Ile-de-France, many of which are in or near the forests. Rating, as it is with hotels, ranges from 1-star to 4-star; those at the top end usually have a swimming pool or are close to a swimmable lake or river.

Useful guidebooks can be obtained from the **Fédération Française de Camping Caravaning** (a campers' association), 78 rue de Rivoli, 75004 (tel: 01 42 72 84 08) or the **Espace du Tourisme d'Ile de France**, Carrousel du Louvre, 99 rue de Rivoli, 75001 (tel: 01 44 50 19 98), which also has a free guide to the campgrounds in the Paris area.

Many Parisians park their camper vans year round on a site just outside Paris and use it as a weekend retreat. This is why, although the high season runs April through September, it is not too difficult to find a space in July or August when the Parisians have taken off. It also explains why the 3-star campground in the **Bois de Boulogne** (between Longchamp racecourse and the Seine) is strictly reserved for non-Parisians (tel: 01 45 24 30 00). Otherwise head for **Versailles** (tel: 01 39 51 23 61), **Rambouillet** (tel: 01 30 41 07 34) or **St.-Quentin-en-Yvelines** (tel: 01 30 58 56 20)—three countrified sites that have excellent transportation connections into Paris. Always beware of school holidays (Easter, Pentecost). For on-site rental, check the guidebook published by the Federation: each campground offers different facilities.

As a general rule, municipal campgrounds, though up to reasonable standards, are not particularly dynamic in their upkeep and equipment. However, if you aim for 4-star sites such as at **L'Isle-Adam**, situated beside the biggest river beach in France (tel: 01 34 69 08 80), or **Ormoy-la-Rivière** (tel: 01 64 94 21 39), you should be well installed. The best shop for camping equipment in Paris is **Au Vieux Campeur**, 48 rue des Ecoles, 75005 (tel: 01 53 10 48 48).

Children

Children can fit in well with visiting Paris. Restaurant staff do not generally turn up their noses at the sight of a stroller, and Parisians are generally tolerant of the presence of children. Hotels obviously vary in terms of the services they provide, but all will provide extra beds or sometimes cribs in a double room at little more than the usual room price. The Novotel chain even allows up to two children under 15 to stay free in their parents' room. Other chains offer good deals, particularly in July and August when there are no business customers. Squares and parks all have specific areas with slides, sandboxes, and more set aside for children. River trips, science museums, and certain parks (see pages 26–27) are always favorites.

English-speaking baby-sitters can be found through **Baby Sitting Express**, a private service that also arranges day-trips and tea parties (*Open* daily, tel: 01 45 50 32 32). Qualified baby-sitters or nannies can

Paris has plenty to offer young people and children

also be obtained through **Kid Services** (tel: 01 42 61 90 00). **Inter-Service Parents** (tel: 01 44 93 44 93) is a free advisory service giving details of baby-sitting agencies and children's activities all over Paris. When dining out with children, aim for family-style bistros where staff are more helpful. Elegant, upscale restaurants are less enthusiastic about strollers and juvenile voices.

Climate

Cool but gloriously sunny days often surprise the population in October

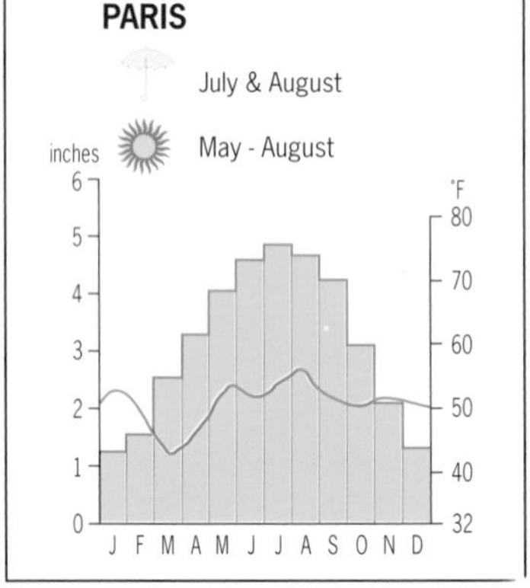

Weather chart conversion
1 inch = 25.4mm
°F = 1.8 x °C + 32

and late February, whereas the old cliché of "Paris in the spring" does not usually apply until well into May. Rarely stifling in midsummer, Paris tends to get very muggy after a few consecutive days of sun. This is when much of the population heads down to the *quais* beside the Seine for a fresher breeze and a chance to sunbathe. Blessed with a fairly low rainfall overall, Paris nevertheless commonly sees showers, above all during March and April as well as November (possibly the least inspiring month climatically, along with chilly January).

Crime

Street crime varies from *arrondissement* to *arrondissement*. Generally speaking, if you stick to the more touristy inner areas you are safe—except for pickpockets. Followers of this pursuit are particularly prevalent on public transportation. *Never* keep your wallet in a back pocket, and ladies should make sure their bags are firmly closed and held onto. Be careful, too, in crowded cafés, flea markets, restaurants, and movie theaters. If you lose something, the first step is to make a declaration at the local police station, which you will need in case you are claiming insurance. Ask for the nearest *commissariat*. Stolen credit cards should be reported immediately to any of the following 24-hour services: American Express (tel: 01 47 77 72 00); Diners Club (tel: 01 47 62 75 75); Visa/MasterCard (tel: 08 36 69 08 80, 2,23 francs/min). You will need to follow this up with written confirmation and a copy of your police declaration. If you are using travelers' checks, make sure you keep a separate note of their numbers, along with the relevant phone number to contact in case of theft.

If your car is stolen (unlikely) or broken into (more likely), you will need to follow the same procedure at the *commissariat* and should contact your insurance office as soon as possible.

The police lost-property office does not deal with phone inquiries but is open Mon, Tue, Thu, 8:30–5, Wed, Fri 8:30–4 at 36 rue des Morillons, 75015, *métro*: Convention. It is worth checking here several days after any theft, as most thieves are only interested in cash and credit cards and so dump the rest. In fact, there is a notable rise in "gentlemen thieves" who actually return the unwanted contents of wallets to owners' addresses.

Victims of more serious crimes should call S.O.S. Help, an English-language crisis hotline that offers advice and counseling (tel: 01 47 23 80 80. *Open* daily).

❑ Serious crime (armed robbery, muggings) in Paris dropped during the 1990s, as did car thefts, but burglaries are on the increase, as are fake identity papers, bounced checks and graffiti. ❑

Customs regulations

You may bring home up to $400 of foreign goods duty-free, provided you've been out of the country for at least 48 hours and you haven't made an international trip in the past 30 days. Each member of the family, regardless of age, is entitled to the same exemption; exemptions may be pooled. For the next $1,000 of goods, a flat 10 percent rate is assessed; above $1,400, duties vary with merchandise. Travelers 21 or older are allowed one liter of alcohol, 100 cigars (non-Cuban), and 200 cigarettes, and one bottle of perfume trademarked in the United States. Antiques and works of art over 100 years old are duty-free. Exceed these limits, and you'll be taxed at the port of entry and additionally in your home state. Gifts under $50 may be mailed duty-free to stateside friends or relatives, with a limit of one package per day per addressee; perfumes over $5, tobacco, and liquor are prohibited. For "Know Before You Go," a free brochure detailing what you may and may not bring back to America, contact the U.S. Customs Service (1301 Constitution Ave., Washington, DC 20029, tel: 202/927-6724).

Travelers with disabilities

The national organization for people with disabilities is **ACNRH**, 236 bis rue de Tolbiac, 75013 (tel: 01 53 80 66 66), which publishes *Paris Ile de France pour Tous*, available from abroad on request; they will also provide advice on all relevant matters. The **Centre d'Information et de Documentation Jeunesse**, 101 quai Branly, 75015 (tel: 01 44 49 12 00), also helps with information for young people with disabilities and publishes a booklet called *Vacances pour personnes handicapées*. Bus route 20 is suitable for wheelchair users and the express RER A and B have access in parts. A leaflet listing stations equipped with elevators, and showing which connections are feasible, is published by the Paris transportation system, the **RATP**, 53 ter, quai des Grands Augustins, 75006 (tel: 08 36 68 77 14). The *RER* express train, being more modern, is better equipped for wheelchairs, and certain SNCF trains are now specifically designed for them, but you should inquire with the information service

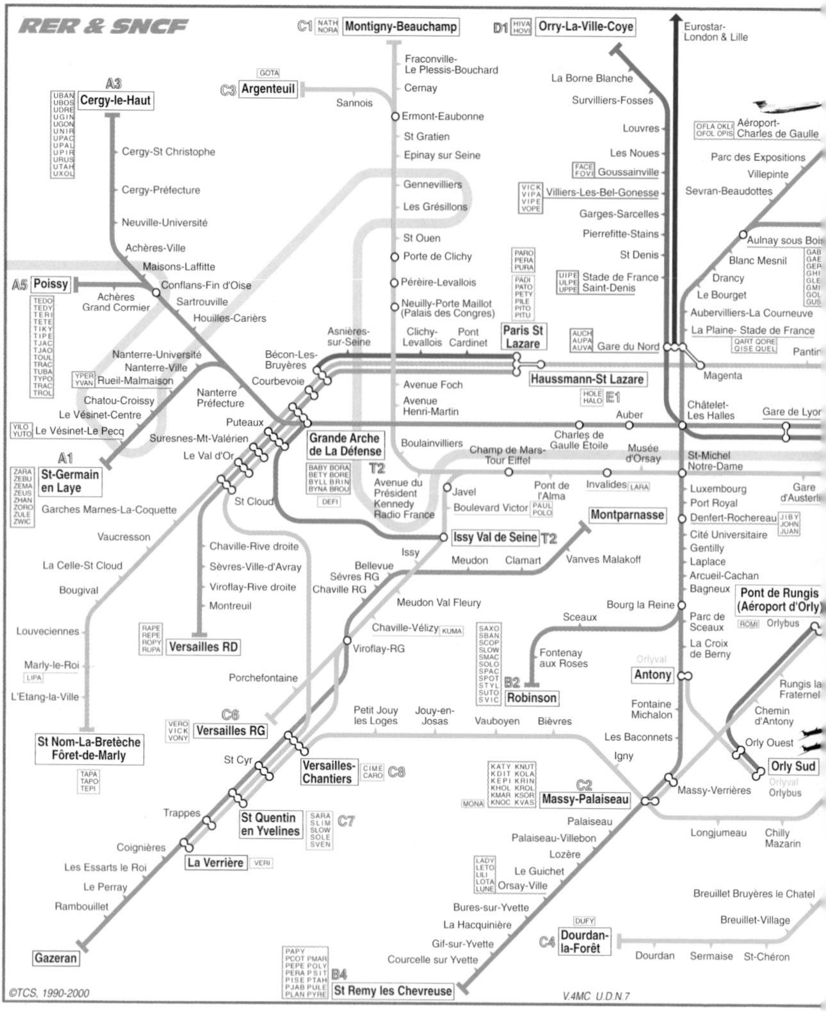

in advance (tel: 01 53 90 20 20). All Parisian train stations have wheelchair access, special restroom facilities, and phones; ask for assistance at the *accueil* in each station.

Both Orly and Roissy airports are well equipped for people with disabilities. For more specific information, contact the **Service Image et Communication**, Aéroports de Paris, 291 boulevard Raspail, 75014 (tel: 01 43 35 70 00). It publishes a brochure, *Guide des personnes handicapées*, describing facilities available.

A specially equipped shuttle transports passengers between the terminals at Roissy, but there is nothing between Orly and Roissy. For getting to Orly Sud or Ouest, contact **AIHROP** (tel: 01 40 24 34 76).

Parisian taxis must by law accept clients with disabilities. There is no longer a specific service for travelers with disabilities, but it is possible to rent minibuses through a number of nonprofit organizations. Try **Valem** (tel: 01 43 14 79 79). Most pharmacies have a service for renting wheelchairs. Try centrally located **Pharmacie Matignon**, 2 rue Jean-Mermoz, 75008 (tel: 01 43 59 86 55). Specially equipped cars can be rented from **Inter Touring Service**,

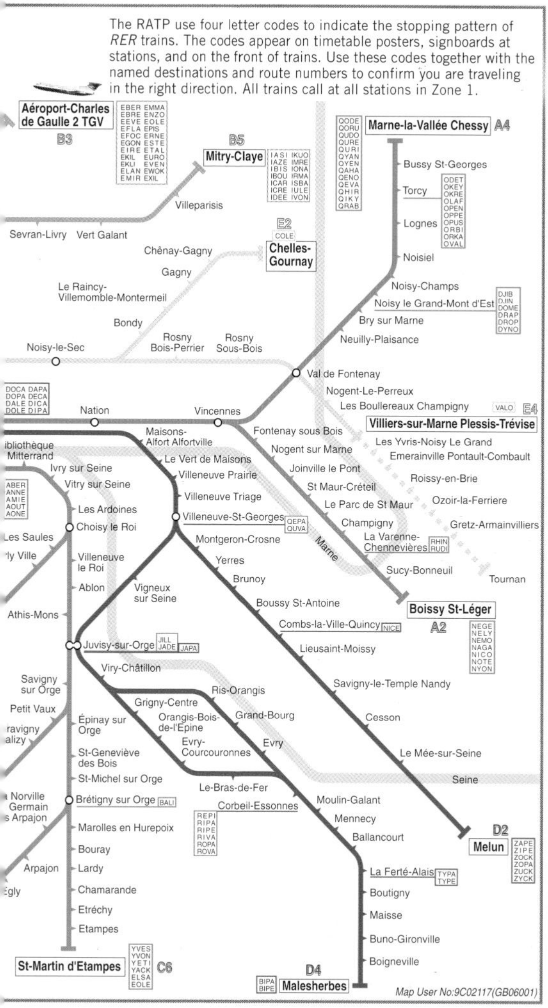

117 boulevard Auguste Blanqui, 75013 (tel: 01 45 88 52 37). Hotels (particularly in the budget category) are not always easily accessible, but the red Michelin hotel and restaurant guide shows which ones are, as does the list published by the Office de Tourisme de Paris. The Paris branch of the **Association des Paralysés de France**, 17 boulevard Auguste, Blanqui, 75013 (tel: 01 40 78 69 00) publishes *Où ferons-nous étape?*, a guide listing specially equipped hotels and motels in France.

Although Paris is not an easy city for people with disabilities (kerbs are high, ramps are few, and elevators

The Arc de Triomphe and the Champs-Elysées—the world's most famous street and scene of many great historical processions

sometimes too small), facilities are improving and awareness of needs is growing. All renovated and newly constructed buildings are now well equipped.

The **Information Center for Individuals with Disabilities**, 20 Park Plaza, Room 330, Boston, MA 02116 (tel: 617/727-5540, TDD tel: 617/727-5236) provides information and a referral service. The center also publishes two fact sheets, "Tips on Planning a vacation" and "Tour Operators and Travel Agencies." There is no charge for the fact sheets, but donations are always appreciated.

Moss Rehabilitation Hospital Travel Information Service, a telephone information resource center (tel: 215/456-9603, TDD tel: 215/456-9602), provides information on tourist sights, transportation, and accommodations in destinations around the world for a small fee. They also provide toll-free telephone numbers for airlines, with special lines for the hearing impaired.

The **Society for the Advancement of Travel for the Handicapped** (SATH, 347 5th Avenue, Suite 610, New York, NY 10016, tel: 212/447-7284, fax:212/725-8253) provides information on tour operators specializing in travel for those with disabilities. Annual membership is $45, $25 for students and senior citizens. Send $3 and a SASE for information on specific destinations.

Driving

Drivers in Paris should be 18 or over, have valid car registration papers, a driver's license, and car insurance.

France follows international road signs and regulations. All road signs are those of the international code except one: *Vous n'avez pas la priorité* (you do not have priority).

Paris streets are regularly resurfaced. August is the peak month for any kind of road works; it's also when driving is most

A bird's-eye view down the Champs-Elysées

pleasurable, as the capital is relatively empty. For the rest of the year, you will find a car more of a hindrance than a help, and Parisian traffic manners need getting used to. Nobody waits or watches out for anyone else, cars move fast when possible, pedestrians dive across streets risking life and limb. However dangerous all this may seem, drivers do have fast reactions and are used to getting out of unexpected situations. Several main north-south and east-west axes have now been declared *axes rouges*, which means parking or even stopping is absolutely forbidden. If you are traveling through France call 08 36 68 10 77 for highway information.

Accidents/breakdown 24-hour breakdown service can be obtained through the garages listed below. Others are listed in the yellow pages under *Dépannages et remorquages*:

AAA Dépannage, 19 rue Jean Maridor, 75015, (tel: 01 45 58 49 58).

Alfauto 19 rue de Dantzig, 75015 (tel: 01 45 31 61 18).

Auto Dépannage Ampère, 15 rue Rosenwald, 75015 (tel: 01 45 31 16 20).

S.O.S. Dépannage (official breakdown number) tel: 01 47 07 99 99.

Car/motorcycle/camper rental Most major car-rental companies are represented in France, and visitors are advised that it is usually best to make a reservation in advance. Usually, you must be over 21 (25 in some cases) to rent a car, and restrictions may apply to drivers over 60. Your current driver's license is usually acceptable, but some require an International Driver's Permit, available through an Automobile Club (AAA or CAA) office.

For reservations call:
Avis (tel: 800/331-1084);
Budget (tel: 800/527-0700);
Dollar (tel: 800/800-4000);
Hertz (tel: 800/654-3131);
National (tel: 800/328-4567).

Fuel Super, *sans plomb* (unleaded) and diesel are the three types of fuel available. Fuel pumps are located above ground as well as in parking

Motorcycles are available for rent at several outlets—and can be the object of admiration ...

garages. There are several 24-hour pumps:
corner Champs Elysées/avenue Georges V, 75008;
1 boulevard de la Chapelle, 75010;
avenue de la Porte de Chatillon, 75014;
6 avenue de la Porte de Clichy, 75017;
avenue de la Porte de Saint-Ouen, 75018.

Parking This is Paris' perennial problem. Most central streets are now metered, a system that costs residents considerably less than it does visitors. Meters are situated at intervals along streets: put in the coins corresponding to the length of time you want to park, press the button, collect the ticket, and put it inside your car so that it is visible on the dashboard. More and more underground parking garages are

❑ Of all major European cities Paris has one of the highest rates of lead and carbon-monoxide pollution. Cars are responsible for 75 percent of city pollution, and 59 percent of Parisians favor a limitation of traffic in the center. ❑

being constructed to meet the growing demand, and these can be spotted by their blue signs marked with a large P. If you decide to park your car for a few days and visit

Paris in a more leisurely fashion, the cheapest 24-hour parking facilities are situated on the perimeter (Porte de Saint-Ouen, Porte de Clignancourt, Porte d'Italie). Otherwise, central underground parking costs considerably more.

Boots (clamps) and car pounds (*fourrière*): Although clamps are uncommon, they do appear, so avoid parking illegally (pedestrian crossings, loading zones, bus lanes, *axes rouges*, etc). You may also be towed away to one of the six Paris car pounds that cover all *arrondissements*. Contact the local police station to find out where you have to go.

Speed limits 50 km/h (31 m.p.h.) in cities; 90 km/h (56 m.p.h.) outside cities; 80 km/h (50 m.p.h.) on the *périphérique* (ring road); 130km/h (80mph) on motorways 110 km/h (68 m.p.h.) on four-lane highways; 130 km/h (81 m.p.h.) on four to six-lane highways (called *Autoroutes*).

Electricity

Voltage is 220 V, and sockets take two round pins. Americans will need to purchase an adapter.

Embassies and consulates

Always check opening hours by phone in advance: many consulates are only open in the morning and close for both French public holidays and those of their own country.

In general the consulate deals with day-to-day problems facing their resident citizens or travelers to the country, whereas the embassy is for more official business. Other embassies are in the phone book under *Ambassades*.

U.S. Embassy: 2 avenue Gabriel, 75008 (tel: 01 43 12 22 22), *métro*: Champs-Elysée-Clémenceau. Consulate/visas: 2 rue St.-Florentin, 75001 (tel: 01 42 96 14 88), *métro*: Concorde.

> ❑ 1,300,000 vehicles circulate in Paris daily—four times as many as 20 years ago. About 85 percent of traffic jams in France occur in and around Paris. ❑

Emergency phone numbers

Ambulance (Samu) tel: 15 (or 01 45 67 50 50)

Fire tel: 18

Police tel: 17

Anti-poison tel: 01 40 05 48 48

Doctor (S.O.S. Médecins) tel: 01 47 07 77 77. Emergency house calls only. Ask for an English-speaking doctor or contact **The American Hospital**, 63 boulevard Victor Hugo, Neuilly (tel: 01 46 61 25 25), which has a 24-hour emergency service—at a price. **The Franco-British Hospital**, 3 rue Barbes, Levallois-Perret (tel: 01 46 39 22 22) provides a similar emergency service.

For burns go to the **Hôpital St.-Antoine**, 184 rue du Faubourg St.-Antoine, 75012 (tel: 01 49 28 20 00). Emergency treatment for children can be obtained at the **Hôpital Necker**, 149 rue de Sèvres, 75015 (tel: 01 44 49 40 00).

Dentist (S.O.S. Dentistes) 01 43 37 51 00. Emergency house calls only.

Motorway and road information (tel: 08 36 68 10 77; in French only).

S.O.S. Help (tel: 01 40 42 22 22) is a crisis line for English speakers.

The Panthéon

Etiquette
French etiquette is a bit more formal than the variety most Americans are familiar with, although that is disappearing with the younger generations. Handshaking is more prevalent when meeting someone, even when you have already been introduced. You can feel justifiably proud when the local bartender or restaurant owner proffers hisor her hand on your arrival. This is a sign of respect and acceptance. Do not use Christian names unless you yourself have been addressed in this way. Smoking is more widespread but is completely banned in movie theaters and inside Paris buses and *métros*. Taxis will display a no-smoking sign when drivers are averse to it; but if you find yourself with a smoking taxi driver, there is little you can do. Cafés and restaurants are now required by law to provide a no-smoking section.

Health
There are no inoculations necessary to enter France, but if you plan on staying more than three months, a medical check-up is required for non-E.U. nationals.

France offers no more health risks than any other European country (apart from the effects of overeating and drinking, so bring a stock of Alka-Seltzer with you). Paris tap water is perfectly drinkable, though you may prefer the taste of bottled mineral water.

If you need to buy prescription drugs, have your doctor write a prescription using the drug's generic name; brand names vary from country to country. The International Association for Medical Assistance to Travelers (in the U.S.: 417 Center St., Lewiston, NY 14092, tel: 716/754-4883) offers a free worldwide list of approved physicians and clinics whose training meets American and British standards.

Hospitals Public hospitals are found all over Paris (listed in phone book under *Hôpitaux*), the most central being the Hôtel Dieu, right outside Notre-Dame. All have a 24-hour emergency service (*urgences*), as well as specialty doctors in every field.

Payment is made on the spot for any kind of consultation, but if for any reason you are hospitalized ask to see the *assistante sociale* to arrange

Making contact in a restaurant on the Left Bank

reimbursement directly through your own insurance. By law, any emergency case must be treated and, once out of danger, foreign patients are flown home. Private hospitals are a lot more expensive, and treatment is not necessarily better, but for linguistic reasons you may prefer one of the following:

American Hospital 63 boulevard Victor Hugo, Neuilly (tel: 01 46 61 25 25).

Franco-British Hospital 3 rue Barbès, Levallois-Perret (tel: 01 46 39 22 22).

Local doctors can be found by asking at a nearby *pharmacie*. Appointments are usually made in advance, but very few will refuse to see an emergency case. House calls can be arranged by calling **S.O.S. Médecins** (tel: 01 47 07 77 77). A similar dental service exists (tel: 01 43 37 51 00).

Specific problems

AIDS advice (in English): **FAACTS** (Free Anglo American Counseling Treatment Support), Mon, Wed, Fri 6–10 PM (tel: 01 44 93 16 69).

Kiosque Info Sida, 36 rue Geoffrey l'Asnier, 75004 (tel: 01 44 78 00 00).

Poison center (tel: 01 40 05 48 48).

Burns center (tel: 01 42 34 17 58).

Centre de Soins MST (sexually transmitted diseases), **Institut A. Fournier**, 25 boulevard Saint Jacques, 75014 (tel: 01 40 78 26 00), *métro:* St.-Jacques.

S.O.S. Help English Hotline (tel: 01 40 42 22 22).

S.O.S. legal services (tel: 01 43 29 33 00).

Hitchhiking

Hitching in France is legal except on highways. As in any city, hitching inside Paris will get you nowhere unless there is a general transportation strike. However, if you are heading out of the capital to the rest of France, the best places are at the relevant *portes* leading to the main highways—but do not stand where traffic is already traveling at speed. Firstly, it is dangerous and, secondly, nobody will stop. At the Porte d'Orléans there is usually a line of hopeful hitchers on the slip road leading down to the southbound Autoroute du Soleil, and a similar crowd of optimists gathers at the Porte de la Chapelle for the Autoroute du Nord. For those heading west, go to the Porte d'Auteuil, while for eastern destinations go to the Porte de Bercy.

It is a good idea to have a sign declaring your destination, but do make sure you are standing where cars can pull in safely without stopping the traffic flow, otherwise the local *gendarmes* will pick you up instead. A much safer and surer method is to contact a hitchhiking service. This links up drivers with potential passengers, who contribute to fuel costs: **Allostop-Provoya**, 8 rue Rochambeau, 75009 (tel: 01 53 20 42 42. *Open* Mon–Fri 9–7:30, Sat 9–1 and 2–6), *métro:* Cadet-Poissonnière. This is a reliable agency.

Insurance
Travel insurance should be taken out before leaving home. Travel agents can usually provide information, and certain credit cards also provide cardholders' insurance if tickets are purchased with their card.

Language
Numbers

1	un/une
2	deux
3	trois
4	quatre
5	cinq
6	six
7	sept
8	huit
9	neuf
10	dix
11	onze
12	douze
13	treize
14	quatorze
15	quinze
16	seize
17	dix-sept
18	dix-huit
19	dix-neuf
20	vingt
30	trente
40	quarante
50	cinquante
60	soixante
70	soixante-dix
80	quatre-vingt
90	quatre-vingt-dix
100	cent
1000	mille

Days of the week

Monday	lundi
Tuesday	mardi
Wednesday	mercredi
Thursday	jeudi
Friday	vendredi
Saturday	samedi
Sunday	dimanche

Basic phrases

yes/no	oui/non
please	s'il vous plaît
thank you	merci
excuse me	excusez-moi
I'm sorry	Je suis désolé
hello	bonjour
goodbye	au revoir
How are you?	Comment allez-vous?
Very well, thanks	Très bien, merci
Do you speak English?	Parlez-vous anglais?
I don't understand	Je ne comprends pas
why?	pourquoi?
who?	qui?
what?	quel?
when?	quand?
how?	comment?
how much?	combien?
today	aujourd'hui
yesterday	hier
tomorrow	demain
this morning	ce matin
this afternoon	cet après midi
tonight	ce soir

Directions

Where is ...	Où est ...
the nearest métro	le métro le plus proche
the telephone	le téléphone
the bus stop	l'arrêt de bus
the bank	la banque
the bookshop	la librairie
Where are the rest rooms?	Où sont les toilettes?
in the basement	au sous-sol
on the ground (first) floor	au rez-de-chausée
on the second floor	au premier étage
turn right/left	tournez à droite/gauche
go straight on	allez tout droit

the first street before the intersection	la première rue avant le carrefour
after the rotary	après le rondpoint
at the traffic lights	aux feux rouges

Hotels

Do you have ...?	Avez-vous ...?
a double room	une chambre double
with bathroom	avec salle de bains
with shower room	avec salle d'eau
a single room	une chambre simple
We need an extra bed	Nous avons besoin d'un lit supplé - mentaire
What time is breakfast?	A quelle heure est le petit déjeuner?
Do you accept credit cards?	Prenez-vous les cartes de crédit?
We leave tomorrow	Nous partons demain
Please prepare our bill	Pouvez-vous préparer la note s'il vous plaît?

Restaurants

Waiter! Waitress!	Monsieur! Madame!
We want to book a table for 9 o'clock	Nous voulons réserver une table pour neuf heures.
Do you have a fixed price menu?	Avez-vous un menu?
I am a vegetarian	je suis végétarien
a bottle of ...	une bouteille de ...
a glass of ...	un verre de ...
Can I have the menu please?	Donnez-moi la carte, s'il vous plaît
the bill	l'addition
breakfast	le petit déjeuner
lunch	le déjeuner
dinner	le dîner

Lost property

The central lost property office (*Open* Mon, Tue, Thu 8.30–5, Wed, Fri 8.30–4) for anything handed to the police, is at 36 rue des Morillons, 75015, *métro:* Convention.
No information will be given over the phone.

Maps

The Office du Tourisme—at 127 avenue des Champs-Elysées, 75008 (tel: 01 49 52 53 54), *métro:* Charles-de-Gaulle-Etoile—is open daily 9–8 PM (Sun 11–6) and provides extensive free information. City maps can also be found free in most hotels, while *métro* stations and some buses have free transportation maps. If you are staying for a longer period, it is worth investing 40 francs or so in a *Paris par Arrondissement*, a small publication with road index and *arrondissement* maps.

Media

Parisian press Unlike readers in the United States, Parisians do not spend their Sundays perusing bulky supplements to catch up on the week's news. This role is filled by weekly magazines (similar to *Time* or *Newsweek*), all published on Thursdays. Covering the political spectrum, they range from *Le Nouvel Observateur* and *L'Evénement du Jeudi* (broadly left wing) to *L'Express* (center) and *Le Point* (center-right). *Paris-Match* still deals in society gossip or disaster-related scoops, while political scandals are dug up in the investigative satirical weekly newspaper, *Le Canard Enchainé*. The most lively weekly for young adults is *Les Inrockuptibles*, providing first-class cultural coverage with a social viewpoint.

There are seven main daily newspapers, none of which has an enormous circulation. Most respected intellectually, although sometimes tough to read, is *Le Monde*, which goes on sale at

2:30 PM except Sunday. Its entertainment supplement, published on Wednesday afternoon, gives a useful overview of the best current shows and exhibitions. It is now the only daily newspaper which comes out in the afternoon. Despite its name, *France-Soir* is now a morning paper, having switched from broadsheet to a tabloid format more in keeping with its breezy news treatment.

The Parisian daily *par excellence* is *Libération*, a young, witty daily carrying on much of the 1968 radical thought, although many of its readers are now affluent and middle-aged. Its coverage of the arts is excellent.

Le Figaro, historically the most established (since 1866), veers from being ultraconservative to providing a useful antigovernment voice, while its classified ads constitute the bible of property and job-seekers. The popular morning tabloid, *Le Parisien* has brightened up and modernized its coverage of local and national affairs. Canny politicians recognize its importance as it drains working-class readers from the venerable *L'Humanité*. This Communist newspaper struggles gamely to free itself of the old Party image.

Foreign press Central newspaper stands usually carry a fairly reasonable selection of European dailies, and you can always pick up the Paris editions of the *International Herald Tribune* and *Wall Street Journal*.

For a wide range of European and American press and magazines, go to one of the NMPP bookshops, (52 rue Jacques Hillairet, 75012, or 87 rue Charolais, 75012). This is the central distribution organization for all press in France and so carries the gamut of the extensive French regional press too.

Entertainment magazines All three come out on Wednesday, the day new movies are released. Take your pick from the old mainstay *Pariscope*, *L'Officiel des Spectacles* (less easy to follow the latter's classifications, but

CONVERSION CHARTS

FROM	TO	MULTIPLY BY
Inches	Centimeters	2.54
Centimeters	Inches	0.3937
Feet	Meters	0.3048
Meters	Feet	3.2810
Yards	Meters	0.9144
Meters	Yards	1.0940
Miles	Kilometers	1.6090
Kilometers	Miles	0.6214
Acres	Hectares	0.4047
Hectares	Acres	2.4710
Gallons	Liters	4.5460
Liters	Gallons	0.2200
Ounces	Grams	28.35
Grams	Ounces	0.0353
Pounds	Grams	453.6
Grams	Pounds	0.0022
Pounds	Kilograms	0.4536
Kilograms	Pounds	2.205
Tons	Tonnes	1.0160
Tonnes	Tons	0.9842

MEN'S SUITS

UK	36	38	40	42	44	46	48
Rest of Europe	46	48	50	52	54	56	58
US	36	38	40	42	44	46	48

DRESS SIZES

UK	8	10	12	14	16	18
France	36	38	40	42	44	46
Italy	38	40	42	44	46	48
Rest of Europe	34	36	38	40	42	44
US	6	8	10	12	14	16

MEN'S SHIRTS

UK	14	14.5	15	15.5	16	16.5	17
Rest of Europe	36	37	38	39/40	41	42	43
US	14	14.5	15	15.5	16	16.5	17

MEN'S SHOES

UK	7	7.5	8.5	9.5	10.5	11
Rest of Europe	41	42	43	44	45	46
US	8	8.5	9.5	10.5	11.5	12

WOMEN'S SHOES

UK	4.5	5	5.5	6	6.5	7
Rest of Europe	38	38	39	39	40	41
US	6	6.5	7	7.5	8	8.5

pocket-sized like *Pariscope*), *Le Figaro* also enters the fray on Wednesdays with a well-listed entertainments supplement, *Figaroscope*.

Radio If you tune in to F.M. in Paris, you will be amazed at what bounces off the crowded and varied airwaves. No longer the bonanza that it was in the early 1980s, when anybody and everybody jumped on the free-radio bandwagon, the number of stations is now—thankfully—controlled. Minority tastes are catered for, from **Judaïque FM** (94.8 MHz) to **Radio Notre-Dame** (100.7 MHz) for Christians, or **Beur FM** (106.7 MHz) for the North African community. **Tropic FM** (92.6 MHz) takes you even farther, specializing in African and Caribbean sounds. The quaint sounding **Cherie FM**. broadcasts on 91.3 MHz. News is broadcast around the clock on **France Infos** (105.5 MHz), while the latest update on traffic jams in the capital interjects a mixed music program on **FIP** (105.1 MHz).

Classical music fans should tune in to **France Musique** (91.7 and 92.1 MHz), though presenters tend to chat, whereas **Radio Classique** (101.1MHz) provides virtually nonstop music. Not as influential as they were, but still powerful, are current affairs and variety stations such as **France Inter** (87.8MHz), **RTL** (104.3MHz), **Radio Monte Carlo** (103.1MHz), and **Europe 1** (104.7MHz). For unadulterated rap/rock/House/ world music, your best bet is to tune in to **Radio Nova** (101.5 MHz) or **NRJ** (100.3 MHz).

The **BBC World Service** can be found on medium wave, 648 KHz.

Television The two main state channels, **France2** and **France3**, still have a long way to go in the quality of their programs, but the now privatized **TF1** is even worse. Addicted to trite panel discussions, variety shows, reruns of "family" movies, and dubbed American police shows, none of the channels has a clear identity. France2 occasionally rises out of mediocrity with a good documentary and, like France3, gives cultural events reasonable coverage.

Canal Plus, a private subscribers' channel launched in 1983, has been very successful in its rotation of recent movies, good documentaries, sports events, and children's programs. It starts the day at 7 AM with the CBS

evening news. When Berlusconi's **La Cinq** finally disappeared its slot was taken by the French/German cultural channel **Arte**. On the other hand, the sixth channel (M6), created in 1987, is increasingly popular. Mixing music videos with movies, it also schedules some excellent BBC documentaries and T.V. movies (dubbed). Arte, whose programs are all coproduced with Germany, provides an interesting alternative to mainstream channels, devoting much of its coverage to cultural and minority interest. Most big hotels are linked up to cable or satellite for **CNN** and **BBC** T.V.

Money matters

The unit of currency is the Euro; during the transitional period for full change-over (until December 2001), the franc will continue to be used as a "subunit" of the Euro and a dual pricing system will operate. In January 2002, Euro banknotes and coins will be introduced. Banknotes will be introduced in denominations of 5, 10, 20, 50, 100, 200 and 500; coins will come in denominations of 1, 2, 5, 10, 20 and 50 centimes, 1 and 2 Euros. The franc will cease to be legal tender in June 2002.

Higher denomination notes are hard to change in taxis and small stores, so try to avoid being given them when you change money. Foreigners can bring in currency, up to the generous limit of 50,000 francs, in any form: cash, travelers' checks, Eurocheques, etc.

Banks Most Parisian Banks are open 9–4:30 Monday to Friday, but shut at noon the day before any public holiday (see page 258). They usually have a foreign exchange counter, which charges a small commission on any operation. If you are confronted with a choice, BNP is likely to offer the best rates and lowest commission. Banks that display credit card symbols outside will also advance cash on the basis of your card. Remember to have your passport on you for any transaction. Exchange bureaus outside any bank take Visa, sometimes Diners Club and MasterCard, and give instructions in English. For emergency exchange on weekends, go to the Champs-Elysées, where the CCF (115 Champs-Elysées, *métro:* George V) remains open daily except Sunday till 8 PM. There is also a 24-hour exchange cash dispenser at this address and another at 2 Carrefour de l'Odéon, 75006. If you have large amounts of cash to change, it may be worthwhile going to the rue Vivienne near the Stock Exchange (*métro:* Bourse), where numerous private money-changers give good rates and charge no commission. Some are open till 7 PM.

If you're desperate, it's 8:30 PM, the exchange machine on the Champs-Elysées has run out of notes and you have no credit cards, you have no other choice than to go to a *bureau de change* at one of the main train stations (*Open* 6:30–10:30 PM daily at the Gare du Nord and the Gare de Lyon; Monday to Saturday at the Gare St.-Lazare and Austerlitz) or at St.-Michel (daily 8–11 PM). Exchange bureaux at Orly and Roissy airports are open 7 AM–11 PM daily.

Foreign banks

American Express is at 11 rue Scribe, 75009 (tel: 01 47 77 79 50), *métro:* Opéra. Here you can cash personal checks if you are a cardholder, as well as having funds rapidly transferred from the United States, but with a high commission.

Barclays (main branch), 21 rue Laffitte, 75009 (tel: 01 44 79 79 79), *métro:* Richelieu-Drouot. Many other branches throughout Paris.

Citibank 30 avenue des Champs-Elysées, 75008 (tel: 01 40 76 33 00), *métro*: Franklin-D.-Roosevelt.

Lloyds 15 avenue d'Iéna, 75016 (tel: 01 44 43 42 41), *métro:* Opéra.

National Westminster no longer has any branches open to the public.

Credit cards are now widely accepted anywhere from supermarkets to restaurants. Top of the popularity list is any card linked to the Visa network, including MasterCard, but always check before making assumptions. American Express is less popular due to the relatively high percentage the trader loses on any transaction.

Bring a combination of cash, travelers' checks (in French called simply *travellers'* with a heavy Chevalier

❑ Although central Paris represents only 0.022 percent of the total French territory with 4 percent of its population, it possesses 96 percent of bank head offices, 70 percent of insurance company head offices, 39 percent of all professional people and furnishes 45 percent of income tax revenue. ❑

accent), and credit cards, and you can't go wrong. Travelers' checks are not accepted in place of currency and need to be changed at banks. Avoid changing large amounts in hotels, as rates are considerably worse.

National holidays

The many public and religious holidays in France are known as *jours fériés*. Transportation timetables change, banks, most museums, and stores close, even newspapers do not come out. So bear this in mind when booking your holiday. Parisians make a habit of stretching a public holiday to bridge with a weekend, commonly known as *le pont*, which gives them a four- or five-day holiday. This is particularly visible in May, when there are no fewer than three public holidays. The following are the official one-day *jours fériés:*

January 1	New Year's Day
March/April	Easter Monday
May 1	Fête du Travail (Labor Day)
May 8	Armistice (WWII)
Late May	Ascension
Early June	Whit Monday
July 14	Bastille Day
August 15	Assumption
November 1	Toussaint (All Saints)
November 11	Armistice (WWI)
December 25	Christmas

The most steadfastly respected of the above are January 1, May 1, November 1, November 11 and December 25, when nearly everything is closed. Always check with museums and monuments to see if they remain open on public holidays. Some smaller ones even shut up shop for all of August.

Whatever the cultural potential, you will, however, never starve. Restaurants do a good trade on these days, as do certain local grocery stores, but public transportation slows down considerably, so do not try to venture far afield. Hotels are notoriously difficult to book in May, June, September, and October, when trade fairs and fashion shows abound, attracting thousands of business visitors. July and August are, surprisingly, not particularly booked up, as this is when most of the Parisian population heads for the coast and hills.

Opening hours

Banks respect to the letter every public holiday and close on the preceding afternoon, so beware! Otherwise their hours are generally 9–4:30, although smaller branches may close for lunch and remain open an hour longer.

Shops Most shops open at 9 AM and close at 7 PM, although many fashion boutiques wait till 10 AM or even later. Few large food stores in central Paris close for the lunch hour, although small specialty traders may take a one- or two-hour break. Department stores, supermarkets and central boutiques all remain open. Saturday is a major trading day. Sunday—apart from Le Marais boutiques, food markets and the odd local grocer (who often remains open daily till 10 PM)—is definitely closed, while Monday provides a balance between the two.

Museums These, too, vary. On the whole, the golden rule is the larger the museum the less likely it is to close for lunch, but watch out for the common closing days of Monday or Tuesday. National museums close on Tuesdays (except the Musée d'Orsay, the Musée d'Arts Décoratifs and the Musée de la Mode et du Textile which opt for Monday), while municipally financed museums close on Mondays. Most remain open on Sunday, when entrance fees are reduced or waived.

Opening hours vary. The more traditional museums stick to about 9:30–5 while certain avant-garde art museums (Centre Pompidou, Jeu de Paume, Arts Décoratifs, la Mode) don't open their doors till later. The important museums usually have a late-night opening (*nocturne*), and this is often a good opportunity to avoid queues (for example the Musée du Louvre remains open late on Wednesday and the Musée d'Orsay on Thursday). Check small museums in advance; their habits can be idiosyncratic, and the renovation craze has not helped matters.

Organized tours
Bicycle tours
Paris á Velo, c'est sympa, 37 boulevard Bourdon, 75004 (tel: 01 48 87 60 01) organizes tours of Paris by bike.

Boat trips
One of Paris' greatest pleasures is the Seine, so try to see some of the monuments from this perspective.

The enormous glass-roofed Bateaux-Mouches leave every half-hour from the Pont de l'Alma (Right Bank), take you east to beyond the Ile-Saint-Louis, then circle back. The entire trip takes over an hour and commentaries are given in six languages.

In summer, trips start at 10 AM and the last one at night leaves at 11:30 PM. In winter (mid-November to mid-March) departures are every half hour starting at 10 AM. Try the extra-long lunch trip or even longer dinner trip—a spectacular way to see the monuments (leaving at 1 PM and 9:15 PM respectively). Reductions for children under 14 (tel: 01 42 25 96 10).

Very similar, but more central and easier to get to, is the flotilla of **Vedettes du Pont-Neuf** (tel: 01 46 33 98 38), which leave from the tip of the Ile-de-la-Cité at Pont-Neuf. These boats

Galeries Lafayette, queen of department stores

accomplish a one-hour trip around the islands and down to the Eiffel Tower, but have the advantage of dropping you back in central Paris. In French and English, the slightly more expensive summer departures start at 10 AM, running almost every half-hour through to the last boat at 10:30 PM. The evening tours do not include dinner. The winter service is more limited. Reductions for children under 10.

The **Bateaux Parisiens** leave from the Left Bank side of the Pont d'Iéna and provide an almost identical service to the Bateaux-Mouches (tel: 01 44 11 33 44).

Canal St.-Martin

Paris Canal Croisières organizes three-hour boat trips that take you along the Seine from the Musée d'Orsay to the Canal St.-Martin and north to the Parc de la Villette. Commentaries are in French and English. This is a more unusual trip, perfect for a sunny afternoon, and will take you through parts of Paris you have probably never seen. Departures are at 9:30 AM and 2:35 PM from the Musée d'Orsay and 2:30 PM from La Villette (late Mar–early Nov). Booking by phone is essential (tel: 01 42 40 96 97).

Prices are reasonable for the length of the trip, children under 11 and young people under 25 get a reduction. Trips along the Canal St.-Martin, spanned by picturesque footbridges, with **Canauxrama** between the Bastille and La Villette leave at 9:30 AM and 2:45 PM from 13 quai de la Loire, 75019 (*métro:* Jaurès), or 9:45 AM and 2:30 PM from the Port de l'Arsenal opposite 50 boulevard de la Bastille (*métro:* Bastille).

The same company organizes a delightful one-day trip through canals or along the River Marne out into very pretty countryside. Commentaries are in French and English. Reductions for children under 12. Booking is essential (tel: 01 42 39 15 00).

Bus tours

For first-time visitors without much time, a bus tour is ideal to orient yourself if you don't mind the group-style travel. All these tours are in comfortable double-decker buses, with a live or recorded commentary (in whatever language you want) and last two to three and a half hours.

A detail from the Grand Palais—one of the museums with late-night opening on Wednesdays

One of the great riverside sights of Paris: the Louvre

Two companies, **Paris Vision** and **Cityrama**, monopolize the field; their services are virtually identical, although Cityrama is slightly cheaper. Both organize thematic tours (Paris by Night, Artistic Paris, Erotic Paris, Cabarets) as well as excursions to Versailles, Fontainebleau, Chartres, and the Loire Valley.

Brochures are available and bookings can be made through the Office du Tourisme, 127 Champs-Elysées (tel: 01 49 52 53 54), *métro:* Charles de Gaulle-Etoile.

Paris Vision (terminus), 214 rue de Rivoli, 75001 (tel: 01 42 60 30 01), *métro:* Tuileries (*Guided tours* at 9:30 AM and hourly till 2:30 PM. Arrive at least 15 minutes in advance).

Cityrama (terminus), 4 place des Pyramides, 75001 (tel: 01 44 55 60 00), *métro:* Pyramides, Palais-Royal. The same conditions apply as for Paris Vision.

A third company, **Parisbus** (tel: 01 43 66 55 50), entered the field a few years ago sporting red double-decker buses and a system leaving you free to get on and off their buses at any of the nine stops. Buses leave from the place du Trocadéro at 9:30 AM and the Eiffel Tower at 9:55 AM. There are now 12 departures a day with a bus arriving every 50 minutes at each stop (in theory), so waiting time is not long.

Your ticket is valid for two consecutive days and commentaries are in French and English on all the buses.

Walking tours

An excellent daily program of walking tours of Paris covering specific areas or themes (often with entrance to monuments closed to the general public) is organized by the **Caisse Nationale des Monuments Historiques**, Hôtel de Sully, 62 rue St.-Antoine, 75004 (tel: 01 44 61 20 00). Many walking tours are listed in the weekly entertainment magazines (under *Conférences*), and you can simply turn up at the appointed time and place. The only problem is that many of the guides speak only French but the accessibility of unusual sites may outweigh this.

Pharmacies

The hundreds of pharmacies in Paris are identified by large illuminated green crosses in front of their

Inside-out architecture at the Centre Georges Pompidou

entrances. Most are open Mon–Sat 9–7 or 9–8. Out of hours, a list of other local pharmacies that are open is provided on the door.

Authorized to supply medication under prescriptions, they also have a monopoly on the sale of certain beauty and health products.

Generally helpful, pharmacists also give immediate first aid (bad cuts, etc), and you will probably find that there is at least one who speaks English. They can also direct you to local doctors and specialists. For ordinary items (soap, toothbrushes, razors, etc) it is cheaper to go to a supermarket. All health needs are available in pharmacies, from aspirin to condoms to tampons or baby requisites.

Late-night pharmacies:

Pharmacie Opéra, 6 boulevard des Capucines, 75009 (tel: 01 42 65 88 29. *Open* Mon–Sat 8 AM–12 AM, Sun 8 AM–12:30 AM), *métro:* Opéra.

Drugstore Champs-Elysées, 133 avenue des Champs-Elysées, 75008 (tel: 01 47 20 39 25. *Open* daily 8:30 AM–2 AM), *métro:* Charles-de-Gaulle.

Dhéry, 84 avenue des Champs-Elysées, 75008 (tel: 01 45 62 02 41. *Open* 24 hours daily), *métro:* George V.

Pharmacie Européenne, 6 place de Clichy, 75009 (tel: 01 48 74 65 18. *Open* 24 hours daily), *métro:* Place de Clichy.

Places of worship

Worshipers of any religion should be able to find the appropriate church, temple, or synagogue in Paris, although Catholics obviously get the most choice.

Below is a selection.

Anglican Protestant

American Cathedral 23 avenue George V, 75008 (tel: 01 53 23 84 00), *métro:* Alma-Marceau.

American Church 65 quai d'Orsay, 75007 (tel: 01 40 62 05 00), *métro:* Invalides.

Church of Scotland 17 rue Bayard, 75008 (tel: 01 48 78 47 94), *métro:* Franklin-D.-Roosevelt.

St. George's English Church 7 rue Auguste Vacquerie, 75016 (tel: 01 47 20 22 51), *métro:* Etoile.

St. Michael's Church of England 5 rue d'Aguesseau, 75008 (tel: 01 47 42 70 88), *métro:* Madeleine.

Centre d'Information et de Documentation Religieuse, 8 rue de la Ville'Evêque, 75008 (tel: 01 49 24 11 44), *métro:* Madeleine. Helpful people at the end of the phone offer information on times of services, nearest churches, etc., for Catholic, Protestant and Orthodox churches. English spoken.

Roman Catholic

See listing on pages 140–141. Every *arrondissement* has at least four or five.

Jewish

Synagogue 21 bis rue des Tournelles, 75004 (tel: 01 42 74 32 65), *métro:* Bastille.

Synagogue Nazareth 15 rue Notre-Dame de Nazareth, 75003 (tel: 01 42 78 00 30), *métro:* République.

❑ Only about 50 of the 300 churches which stood in 18th-century Paris remain today. A further 150 have been built since World War II. ❑

Synagogue 44 rue de la Victoire, 75009 (tel: 01 45 26 95 36), *métro*: Notre-Dame-de-Lorette.

Orthodox

Eglise Grecque Orthodoxe 2 bis rue Laferrière, 75009 (tel: 01 42 81 42 67), *métro:* St.-Georges.

Saint Alexandre Nevsky (Russian Orthodox), 12 rue Daru, 75008 (tel: 01 42 27 37 34), *métro:* Courcelles.

Police

No longer those familiar figures sporting *képis*, Parisian police now look like any other national police force and wear flat caps.

There are over 16,000 uniformed police officers—a few young ones even patroling on in-line skates. The fire brigade is loosely related and will deal with immediate first aid, lost cats, victims of accidents, gas leaks, etc., apart from dealing with fires.

Each *arrondissement* has several police stations, including a main one open 24 hours a day which is often integrated into the *arrondissement* town hall. The *arrondissement* police will help with most problems (finding a plumber, vet, doctor, etc)

The Catholic Eglise St.-Germain-des-Prés was founded in the 10th century

as well as administrative matters, drug problems and, of course, crime.

1e place du Marché St.-Honoré (tel: 01 47 03 60 00)
2e 5 place des Petits Pères (tel: 01 44 58 97 50)
3e 5 rue Perrée (tel: 01 53 01 93 60)
4e 2 place Baudoyer (tel: 01 44 78 61 00)
5e 4 rue Basse des Carmes (tel: 01 44 41 51 00)
6e 78 rue Bonaparte (tel: 01 43 29 76 10)
7e 9 rue Fabert (tel: 01 44 18 69 07)
8e 1 avenue du Général Eisenhower (tel: 01 53 76 60 00)
9e 14 bis rue Chauchat (tel: 01 44 83 80 80)

The basilica of Sacré-Cœur on Montmartre has hourly services every morning, and also evening mass

10e 26 rue Louis-Blanc (tel: 01 53 71 60 00)
11e 107 boulevard Voltaire (tel: 01 44 93 27 30)
12e 80 avenue Daumesnil (tel: 01 44 87 50 12)
13e 144 boulevard de l'Hôpital (tel: 01 40 79 05 05)
14e 112-116 avenue du Maine (tel: 01 53 74 14 06)
15e 250 rue de Vaugirard (tel: 01 53 68 81 00)
16e 58 avenue Mozart (tel: 01 55 74 50 00)
17e 19 rue Truffaut (tel: 01 44 90 37 17)
18e 79 rue Clignancourt (tel: 01 53 73 63 00)
19e 2 rue André Dubois (tel: 01 48 03 82 00)
20e 6 place Gambetta (tel: 01 40 33 34 00)

The central Préfecture de Police on the Ile de la Cité deals with driver's licenses, residence and work permits, licenses for various activities, etc. (tel: 01 53 71 53 71).

Another section of the police force is the river police, which controls crime and administrative matters on the Seine.

Parking fines are usually dished out by a separate section, whose officers are generally female and dressed in navy-blue uniforms. The CRS is the military-looking, shield-bearing riot police, who hang around in vans near any demonstration, ready for action.

Emergency calls
Police: 17
Fire Department (*pompiers*): 18
SAMU (*24-hour ambulance*): 15

Post offices

French post offices are known as *la poste*, officially the PTT, and in Paris each is signposted in the street. Many post offices have outside A.T.M.s that accept bank cards.

Opening hours are: Monday to Friday, 8–7 PM, Saturday, 8–noon. Avoid lunch hours and late afternoon when office workers dealing with business mail create endless lines. Most post ofices have phone booths, photocopiers, fax (*télécopieur*), and free access to the Minitel directory

service. Express post facilities (called *Chronopost*) for within France and abroad are also available. Stamps can also be bought at *tabacs* (tobacco shops) and yellow mailboxes are situated immediately outside.

The central post and sorting office of the Louvre is open 24 hours, but at night this is only for sending mail and general delivery (*poste restante*). PTT, 52 rue du Louvre, 75001 (tel: 01 40 28 20 40), *métro:* Louvre.

General delivery Use the Louvre post office for convenience; it is central and you can pick up mail at any time. Otherwise, every post office provides this service as long as the full address is given. American Express (see Banks) also has a *poste restante* service.

Other central post offices

PTT Paris Archives, 67 rue des Archives, 75003.

PTT Hôtel de Ville, 9 place de l'Hôtel de Ville, 75004.

PTT Paris Bastille, 12 rue Castex, 75004.

PTT Paris Sorbonne, 13 rue Cujas, 75005.

PTT Paris St.-Germain-des-Prés, 53 rue de Rennes, 75006.

PTT Paris Pigalle, 47 boulevard de Clichy, 75009.

PTT Paris Champs-Elysées, 75008.

Public transportation

The capital's public transportation is one of the best systems in the world. *Métro/RER* and bus maps are available free from any *métro* station and from some hotels. Bus routes are clearly marked at every bus stop and again inside the bus, so don't be afraid to use this as an excellent and cheap sightseeing service. As in every big city, avoid the morning and evening rush hours, when travel can become unbearable (roughly 8:30–9:30 AM and 5–7 PM).

Buses Buses should be hailed from bus stops. Use one *métro* ticket within Paris (possibly more in the suburbs, depending on the length of journey), which you punch in a machine beside the driver. It is possible to buy a single ticket on the bus, but it costs more this way. Most routes operate from 6:30 AM–8:30 PM, with a few exceptions carrying on till midnight. Night buses (*noctambus*) radiate out hourly from Châtelet between 1:30 AM and 5 AM.

Métros Identified by a large 'M' in a circle, *métro* stations are easily spotted. The network of lines covers central Paris, and every station has clear indications, so you are unlikely to need help. Lines are identified by their end station; only two have branches, which means checking the destination on the front of the train.

Doors open easily—press the button or lift the handle—and they shut automatically. Connections are called *correspondances*, and an orange sign on the platform indicates directions to your connecting line. Blue signs marked *sortie* indicate the exits.

One ticket is valid for every uninterrupted journey. After braving the automatic barriers, keep the ticket on you until you end your journey in case of inspectors. There is no longer a first-class carriage service. First *métros* start at 5:30 AM, the last leave around 12:30 AM.

Radio taxis

Alpha-taxis:	01 45 85 85 85
Taxis Bleu:	01 49 36 10 10
Taxi Etoile:	01 42 70 41 41
G7	01 47 39 47 39

All the above take advance bookings for travel to airports.

RER This express train system runs underground in the city center and stretches far out into the suburbs. It can be a good time-saver if you are going from one side of Paris to the other, but access to platforms is often long and complicated, so it is not often worth it for a short trip. *Métro* tickets can be used for trips in central Paris; otherwise buy a ticket from a machine. Keep it with you, as you have to slot it into a ticket machine when you enter and exit the train.

Taxis These can be hailed in the street (when the roof light is switched on completely), picked up from taxi ranks or ordered by phone. Not the most open-minded of species, some taxi drivers may also be accompanied by a faithful, slavering hound. Few accept more than three passengers. Fares (displayed on a meter) are reasonable, and it is normal to add a 10 percent tip.

The métro: a convenient means of transportation and a work of art

Tickets/Travel passes Various formulas exist for travel passes, but even if you don't use one of them, make sure you buy a *carnet* (book) of 10 tickets (*métro/RER/bus*) rather than the more costly individual tickets. A special tourist pass called *Paris Visite* gives you unlimited travel for two, three, or five days. You can choose how many travel zones it covers (from two to five, including the suburbs and airports).

❑ Opened in 1900, the *métro's* 14 lines measure over 125 miles placed end to end and have 368 stations. The *RER* has added a further 63 miles. ❑

Mobilis is a one-day pass, also valid on *métro*, *RER* and bus, with a similar choice of zones.

Parisians themselves rely on *Carte Orange* travel passes for a week (*coupon hebdomadaire*) or a month (*coupon mensuel*) but for both of these you need a photo to have a special pass made on the spot. They are valid from the first day of the month or, for weekly passes, from Monday.

Rest rooms

Public rest rooms can be found all over the city. Large off-white plastic affairs, they function with 1F or 2F pieces, have automatic flushing and disinfecting systems, and are usually well-maintained. Every café has a toilet, ranging from old smelly squatters to pristine affairs reeking of chlorine. These are designed for customers only, so don't tempt fate by using one without first ordering a drink. They are nearly always in the basement. A small number are coin-operated. The old *pissoirs* have gone but some *métro* stations still house relics from the old days of public rest rooms, those at the Madeleine being particularly characterful.

Senior citizens

If you can prove that you are over 60, you will be given discounts for entry to museums and monuments and sometimes other attractions. It is always worth checking. There is, however, no reduction on Paris public transportation, although Air Inter and SNCF do have special deals.

The American Association of Retired Persons (AARP, 601 E Street, NW, Washington, DC 20049, tel: 202/434-2277) has two programs for independent travelers: the Purchase Privilege Program, which offers

The Gare de Lyon

discounts on hotels, car rentals, and sightseeing; and the AARP Motoring Plan, provided by Amoco, which furnishes emergency road-service aid and trip-routing information for an annual fee of $39.95 per person or couple. AARP members are age 50 or older; annual dues are $8 per person or couple. AARP advises that all members can now purchase tours and cruises and pay for them with a credit card.

When using an AARP or other type of senior-citizen identification card for reduced hotel rates, mention it when booking, not when checking out. At participating restaurants, show your card before you're seated; be aware that discounts may be limited to certain menus, days, or hours. When renting a car, ask about promotional rates that might be cheaper than the senior-citizen discount.

Elderhostel (75 Federal St., 3rd floor, Boston, MA 02110–1941, tel: 617/426-7788) is an innovative educational program for people 60 and older. Participants live in dorms on over 1,200 campuses worldwide. mornings are devoted to lectures and seminars; afternoons to sightseeing and field trips. Fees for two- to three-week trips—including room, board, tuition, and round-trip transportation—range from $1,800 to $4,500.

❑ Over 45 billion francs are spent annually on the national lottery, Loto, horse-racing, and casino-gambling. This represents 12 billion francs in revenue for the government. ❑

Sports

Unless you are staying for a lengthy period in Paris, this is probably not what brought you to the City of Light. However, if you are desperate, there are some possibilities, notably swimming pools, gyms, and bicycle paths in parks (see pages 228–229).

Check the weekly entertainment magazine *Pariscope* in the *Sports et Loisirs* section for a list of bowling alleys, skating rinks, squash and tennis clubs. For more specific information contact the Hôtel de Ville phoneline, which specializes in municipal sports facilities and sporting events in the Paris area: **Allô-Sports**, 25 boulevard de Bourdon, 75004 (tel: 01 42 76 54 54), *métro*: Bastille.

Golf enthusiasts who want to keep their wrists supple should contact: **Fédération Française de Golf**, 69 avenue Victor-Hugo, 75016 (tel: 01 44 17 63 00), *métro*: Victor-Hugo. The Federation provides a list of golf courses in France, but remember that most of them are out in the suburbs.

Spectator sports

Palais Omnisport Paris-Bercy 8 boulevard de Bercy, 75012 (tel: 01 40 02 60 60), *métro*: Bercy. A vast, modern structure holding up to 17,000 spectators for cycling races, horse jumping, motocross, and hockey championships.

Parc des Princes 24 rue du Commandant-Guilbaud, 75016 (tel: 01 42 88 02 76), *métro*: Porte de St.-Cloud. The stadium, which holds nearly 50,000 spectators, is home to the famous Paris-St.-Germain soccer team. Once the king of Paris stadiums, it is now in direct competition with the new Stade de France in St.-Denis (north of the center), now the main home of football and rugby internationals.

Roland-Garros 2 avenue Gordon-Bennett, 75016 (tel: 01 47 43 48 00), *métro*: Porte d'Auteuil. Home to the French Tennis Open held in late May; but beware: many of the tickets are in the hands of black marketeers charging exorbitant prices at the gates. Book seats in advance, asking for a reservation form (by February)—contact: **FFT Service Réservation** BP 333-16, 75767 Paris Cedex 16 (tel: 01 47 43 48 00).

Racecourses

Hippodrome d'Auteuil Bois de Boulogne, 75016 (tel: 01 40 71 47 47. *Closed* Jul and Aug), *métro*: Porte d'Auteuil. Mainly hurdle racing.

Hippodrome de Longchamp Bois de Boulogne, 75016 (tel: 01 44 30 75 00), *métro*: Porte d'Auteuil. (*Closed* for part of summer) then shuttle bus. One of the world's most famous flat races, the Prix de l'Arc de Triomphe, is held here.

Hippodrome de Vincennes Bois de Vincennes, 75012 (tel: 01 49 77 17 17), *métro*: RER Joinville le Port. Mainly sulky racing, a colorful treat to watch. The big race is the Prix d'Amérique.

Student and youth travel

If you have a valid International Student Identity Card, it will earn numerous reductions (museums, movies, air and rail travel). Being a student city, Paris has endless facilities aimed specifically at the student population. The following organizations will set you in the right direction.

Carte Jeune is worth its 120 franc price at FNAC bookstores (see page 215) for its discounts on travel, museums, theaters, movies, sports facilities, and some restaurants. The Carte Jeune of **SMEREP** (Sociéte Mutualiste des Étudiants de la Région Parisienne), 54 boulevard St.-Michel (tel: 01 56 54 36 34) includes discounts on the Métro and Louvre.

Another useful address for information on discounts available:

O.T.U. Voyages, 2 rue Malus, 75005 (tel: 01 43 36 80 27. *Closed* Sun and Mon), *métro*: place Monge.

CIJD (Centre d'Information et de Documentation Jeunesse), 101 quai Branly, 75015 (tel: 01 44 49 12 00. *Open* Mon–Sat 10–6), *métro*: Bir-Hakeim. Excellent information center for young people looking for jobs, courses, sports, etc.

CROUS 39 avenue Georges Bernanos, 75005 (tel: 01 40 51 36 00. *Open* Mon–Fri 9–5), *métro*: Port-Royal. Useful student organization which runs university restaurants, organizes sporting and cultural events, and can provide information on jobs and accommodations.

Youth hostels

Cité Universitaire 19 boulevard Jourdan, 75014 (tel: 01 44 16 64 00), *RER*: Cité Universitaire. During the summer months, rooms are available in the student residences for anyone with an International Student Card.

UCRIF 27 rue de Turbigo, 75002 (tel: 01 40 26 57 64. *Open* Mon–Fri 9–6), *métro*: Les Halles/Etienne Marcel. Operates several cheap hostels in Paris as well as social events and language courses for foreigners.

Student travel agencies

Council Travel 1 place de l'Odéon, 75006 (tel: 01 44 41 89 89) or 66 avenue des Champs-Elysées, 75008 (tel: 01 40 75 95 45), specialize in cheap air fares, tours, and charters to the U.S.

Jeunes Sans Frontières (Wasteels), 150 avenue de Wagram, 75017 (tel: 08 03 88 70 14). Cheap flights and train fares.

Club Français du Tourisme de Jeunes (Maison de France) 20 avenue de l'Opéra, 75001 (tel: 01 42 96 70 00) have information about traveling throughout France.

SNCF

SNCF's Carissimo card is available to people aged from 12 to 25 years and gives reductions of up to 50 percent. Students under 26 can buy BIGE tickets and cut the cost of traveling around France by up to 20 percent. For going farther afield use Eurodomino. Ask at your local French Tourist or French Railway office.

The Latin Quarter

Telephones
Repairs: 13
Directory enquiries (national): 12; (international): 00 33 12 + country prefix.
Telegrams (national): 36 55; (international): 08 00 33 44 11 (all languages).

New 10-digit numbers have replaced eight-digit numbers by adding two figures before exisiting numbers as follows:

01	Paris and Paris outskirts
02	Northwest France
03	Northeast France
04	Southeast France
05	Southwest France

To call a number anywhere in France, just dial the 10 digits.

International calling If you are phoning France from abroad, dial the international code, then 33, then the 10-digit number, minus the initial 0. To dial abroad from France dial 00 followed by the country dialling code:

U.S.	00 +1	+area code
Canada	00 +1	+town code
U.K.	00 +44	+town code

For a free direct operator service, dial:

U.S.	08 00 9919 00 11 (AT&T)
Canada	08 00 9919 00 16
U.K.	08 00 9919 00 44

Public phones Nearly all of Paris' public phones now function with phone cards (*télécartes*). These can be bought at post offices or *tabacs* for 50 or 120 units.

Public phones in cafés and restaurants use coins or have to be switched on by staff, in which case you pay after the call (ask which system it is beforehand). For coin phones lift the receiver, insert a 1, 2, 5, or 10 franc piece, await the dial tone, then dial. Avoid using hotel phones for long-distance calls, as they are usually far more expensive.

Reduced rates The cheap-rate times have been considerably simplified and extended in the last few years, and it is liable to change again as France Telecom has now lost its monopoly. For calls within France the cheapest times are at night, 7 PM–8 AM, after noon on Saturday and all day Sunday.

International off-peak rates depend on the destination, but are generally 30 percent or so less than normal rates.

U.S. and Canada: Cheapest is from 7 PM to 1 PM the next day and all day Sunday.

Any public holiday has the same rates as Sunday.

Time
As the world has not yet agreed on a mutual start and finish of winter time and summer time, there is often a period in spring and fall when the winter time differences given below are incorrect for a week or so. However, for most of the year these differences apply. France changes its clocks in late September (back one hour) and late March (forward one hour). Its winter time is the same as that of Western Europe (except Portugal, which goes along with the U.K).

Australia	
Perth	+ 7 hours
Sydney/Melbourne	+ 9 hours
Canada	
Montreal	– 6 hours
Vancouver	– 9 hours
Ireland	– 1 hour
New Zealand	+ 11 hours
U.K.	–1 hour
U.S.	
New York	– 6 hours
Los Angeles	– 9 hours

Tipping
Tipping in France is a complex affair, varying from service to service. In hotels, restaurants, and cafés, service is included (up to 15 percent), but it is usual to leave a small extra tip if you are satisfied, ranging from 50 centimes for a coffee to at least 10 or 20 francs at a restaurant.

Theater ushers look for tips (5 or 10 francs) and movie theater attendants depend on them for a living, so slip them 2 francs when they tear your ticket. Taxi drivers expect 10 percent, as do hairdressers.

Hotel porters and bellboys should be given 10 francs or so per bag (going up with class of hotel) and chambermaids a banknote at the end of your stay. Room service also appreciates at least 10 francs.

If the hotel concierge has achieved the impossible for you, he or she, too, will appreciate a solid tip. Any tour guide should be tipped roughly 10–15 percent.

Tour groups

Apart from fending for yourself and making your own trip around Paris, there is also the option of a package tour. Creative itineraries abound, offering access to places you may not get to on your own, as well as the more traditional spots. They aslso tend to save you money on airfare and hotels. If group outings are not your style, cheack into independent packages; somewhat more expensive than package tours, they are also more flexible.

When considering a tour, be sure to find out exactly what expenses are included (particularly tips, fares, side trips, additional meals, and entertainment); governmental ratings of all hotels on the itinerary and the facilities they offer; cancellation policies for both you and the tour operator; and, if you are traveling alone, the price of the single supplement. Most tour operators ask that bookings be made through a travel agent (there is no extra charge for doing so). Initially, you should contact your travel agent or the French Government Tourist Office.

Tourist offices

L'Office de Tourisme de Paris 127 avenue des Champs-Elysées, 75008 (tel: 01 49 52 53 54; www.paris-touistoffice.com *Open* daily 9 AM–8 PM), *métro*: Charles-de-Gaulle. Drop by here to pick up free maps and leaflets about museums, tours, and châteaus in and around Paris. They will find you accommodations and are extremely helpful.

Other smaller tourist offices are situated in the main train stations (Gare du Nord, de l'Est, Austerlitz, Montparnasse, de Lyon), and in the summer the Eiffel Tower claims its own branch. The station offices can be very useful in getting last-minute accommodations. Each French region has its own tourist office in Paris and can be a useful source of information if you are traveling around the rest of the country. The Maison de la France, 8 avenue de l'Opéra, 75001 (tel: 01 42 96 10 23) regroups information from all of them, but in less detail.

Below is a selection of regional tourist offices.

Maison Alpes Dauphiné
2 place André Malraux, 75001 (tel: 01 42 96 08 43).

Maison de l'Alsace
39 avenue des Champs-Elysées, 75008 (tel: 01 53 83 10 10).

Maison de la Bretagne
203 boulevard St.-Germain, 75007 (tel: 01 53 63 11 50).

Maison des Hautes Alpes
4 avenue de l'Opéra, 75001 (tel: 01 42 96 05 08).

Maison du Nord-Pas de Calais
5 rue Bleue, 75009 (tel: 01 48 00 59 62).

Périgord: contact regional office in Périgueux (tel: 05 53 35 50 50).

Maison de Poitou-Charentes
68 rue du Cherche-Midi, 75006 (tel: 01 42 22 83 74).

Maison des Pyrénées 15 rue St.-Augustin, 75002 (tel: 01 42 86 51 86).

Maison de Savoie 31 avenue de l'Opéra, 75001 (tel: 01 42 61 74 73).

Local French tourist offices

The French Government Tourist Office (FGTO) publishes a great deal of literature in English, available from the following addresses:

U.S.: 444 Madison Avenue, 16th Floor, New York, NY 10022 (tel: (212) 838 7800, fax: (212) 838 7855).

676 North Michigan Avenue, 3360 Chicago, IL 60611–2819 (tel: (312) 751 7800, fax: (312) 337 6339).

9454 Wilshire Boulevard, Beverly Hills, CA 90212–2967 (tel: (310) 271 6665, fax: (310) 276 2835).

Valeting/laundry

For general laundry go to a launderette (*laverie automatique*), although these are not as common as dry cleaners. Dry cleaners (*pressing*) can be found all around Paris are not cheap. Some have an economy service, but this is not recommended for your best silk jacket.

Accommodations & Restaurants

ACCOMMODATIONS

(per standard double room)

($$$)	—over 1,000 francs
($$)	—600–1,000 francs
($)	—under 600 francs

Hôtel de l'Abbaye ($$)
10 rue Cassette, 75006 tel: 01 45 44 38 11
A classy but affordable hotel in a former convent. with a cobbled courtyard. There are elegant salons, terraced duplex rooms, and smiling staff.

Hôtel des Académies ($)
15 rue de la Grande-Chaumière, 75006 tel: 01 43 26 66 44
Located in an historic street for artists in Montparnasse, this is a family-run hotel with basic 1950s-style garrets. It is good value.

Hôtel de l'Angleterre ($$)
44 rue Jacob, 75006 tel: 01 42 60 34 72
This historic building boasts staircase murals and a courtyard garden. Bedrooms are spacious and the bathrooms vary from charming to opulent.

Hôtel l'Astor ($$$)
11 rue d'Astorg, 75008 tel: 01 53 05 05 05
This superbly renovated hotel boasts a beautiful *trompe l'oeil* dining room. The cuisine is inspired by the famed Joël Robuchon.

Hôtel Banville ($$)
166 boulevard Berthier, 75017 tel: 01 42 67 70 16
An elegant, well-decorated, small hotel. It is not centrally located, but it is excellent value.

Hôtel Beau Manoir ($$)
6 rue de l'Arcade, 75008 tel: 01 42 66 03 07
Renovated in 1994, this hotel boasts 19th-century chic with a discreet charm. The rooms are comfortable and well equipped.

La Bourdonnais ($$)
111 avenue de la Bourdonnais, 75007 tel: 01 47 05 45 42
Located in a residential district, this hotel offers provincial warmth and simplicity. The 1-star Michelin restaurant is a welcome bonus.

Hôtel Bradford-Elysées ($$)
10 rue St.-Philippe-du-Roule, 75008 tel: 01 45 63 20 20
Here you will find old-fashioned chic, and period furnishings. Impeccable service and large rooms. Consequently it is pricey, but worth it.

Hôtel de la Bretonnerie ($$)
22 rue St.-Croix de la Bretonnerie, 75004 tel: 01 48 87 77 63
This hotel offers traditional comfort in an attractive Old World interior. It is located in the Marais.

Hôtel le Bristol ($$$)
112 rue de Faubourg St.-Honoré, 75008 tel: 01 53 43 43 00
The Bristol offers old world charm, tranquillity and luxurious amenities, with expansive gardens. The hotel features an indoor pool, fitness center, and the excellent restaurants d'Hiver and d'Eté.

Le Britannique ($$)
20 avenue Victoria, 75002 tel: 01 42 33 74 59
This small hotel has clubby public areas with leather chesterfields. Rooms are comfortable and well-decorated.

Buci Latin ($$)
34 rue de Buci, 75006 tel: 01 43 29 07 20
This post-modern hotel has small but attractively decorated rooms. Look out for interesting modern artwork and designer graffiti on the stairwell.

Hôtel Castex ($)
5 rue Castex, 75004 tel: 01 42 72 31 52
The rather basic bedrooms are neat, clean and pleasant but without T.V. Most are fully en-suite, but there is no lift. It gets booked well in advance.

Hôtel Chopin ($)
46 passage Jouffroy, off boulevard Montmartre, 75009 tel: 01 47 70 58 10
Interestingly set in a 19th-century shopping arcade, this modest 2-star hotel is excellent value.

Hôtel le Colbert ($$)
7 rue de l'Hôtel-Colbert, 75005 tel: 01 43 25 85 65
This 36-room 18th-century inn offers views of Notre-Dame and a quiet courtyard. Some of the rooms have original fixtures and antique furnishings.

Hôtel Costes ($$$)
239 rue St.-Honoré, 75001 tel: 01 42 44 50 50
There are charming nooks facing on to the courtyard and the rooms are equipped with marble-topped basins. The restaurant is chic.

Le Crillon ($$$)
10 place de la Concorde, 75008 tel: 01 44 71 15 00
Commissioned in 1758 by Louis XV, this hotel is a superb example of 18th-century French architecture. The rooms and suites are handsomely decorated. There is a deluxe fitness center.

Hôtel Danemark ($$)
21 rue Vavin, 75006 tel: 01 43 26 93 78
A small friendly family-run hotel near the high spots of Montparnasse. A spruce up has increased its comfort level.

Hôtel du Danube ($$)
58 rue Jacob, 75006 tel: 01 42 60 34 70
The individually styled rooms are grouped around the small courtyard of this wood-paneled and stone Napoleon III house. It is good value.

Hôtel les Degrés de Notre-Dame ($)
10 rue des Grands-Degrés, 75005 tel: 01 55 42 88 88
Choose between a view of Notre-Dame at the front or tranquillity at the back in a very pleasant, well-kept hotel.

Hôtel Des Deux Acacias ($)
28 rue de l'Arc-de-Triomphe, 75017 tel: 01 43 80 01 85
This simple, bright hotel is in a quiet spot yet conveniently close to the Champs Elysées. The bedrooms are pretty.

Hôtel des Deux Iles ($$)
59 rue St.-Louis-en-l'Ile, 75004 tel: 01 43 26 13 35
This comfortable hotel is at the hub of the island. A charming patio and vaulted breakfast room add to its attraction.

Hôtel Esmeralda ($)
4 rue St.-Julien-le-Pauvre, 75005 tel: 01 43 54 19 20
The Esmeralda is located across from Notre-Dame, so many rooms have great views. The charming interior has characteristic 19th-century furniture and *objets d'art*.

Four Seasons George V ($$$)
31 avenue George V, 75008
tel: 01 49 52 70 00
A landmark hotel, just off the Champs-Elysées, the George V is a byword for Parisian glamor with a sumptuous and sophisticated interior. Many suites have private terraces. Modern amenities include a fully serviced business center, pool, and health club. Chef Philippe Legendre runs the hotel's flagship Le Cinq restaurant.

Le Grand Hôtel Inter-Continental ($$$)
2 rue Scribe, 75009 tel: 01 40 07 32 32
Originally built for Napoleon in 1862, this hotel is a favorite among visiting luminaries. The bedrooms are well equipped with every comfort.

Hôtel des Grandes Ecoles ($$)
75 rue du Cardinal-Lemoine, 75005
tel: 01 43 26 79 23
Well-kept rooms overlook the garden of this picturesque country-house hotel in a verdant corner of the Latin Quarter. It is advisable to book ahead.

Hôtel Henri IV ($)
25 place Dauphine, 75001
tel: 01 43 54 44 53
Extremely basic to the tune of one communal bathroom per floor, this hotel has a rare old-world atmosphere. It is located on one of Paris' most delightful squares. Advance booking is essential.

L'Hôtel ($$$)
13 rue des Beaux Arts, 75006
tel: 01 43 25 27 22
This Parisian legend has antiques galore, elegance and memories of Oscar Wilde. The restaurant and piano bar are much frequented.

Hôtel Istria ($$)
29 rue Campagne Première, 75014
tel: 01 43 20 91 82
Follow Montparnasse legends such as Rilke, Duchamp, Man Ray, and Aragon to this friendly, comfortable hotel.

Hôtel des Jardins du Luxembourg ($$)
5 impasse Royer-Collard, 75005
tel: 01 40 46 08 88
This no-frills, well-maintained and comfortable, 25-room hotel is in a very quiet street. Some of the rooms have balconies with wonderful views.

Hôtel Jeanne d'Arc ($)
3 rue de Jarente. 75004 tel: 01 48 87 62 11
This charming, clean and quiet provincial-style hotel in the Marais is very popular, so book ahead.

Hôtel du Jeu de Paume ($$$)
54 rue St.-Louis en L'Ile, 75004
tel: 01 43 26 14 18
The mezzanines and galleries offer contemporary comfort in period surroundings in this 17th-century building. It was used for the practice of *le jeu de paume*, the ancestor of indoor tennis.

Hôtel Lancaster ($$$)
7 rue de Berri, 75008 tel: 01 40 76 40 76
This ultra-elegant hotel was once favored by Coward and Garbo. The oriental-style Salon Vert café/bar leads on to a courtyard garden.

Hôtel Lenox ($$)
9 rue de l'Université, 75007
tel: 01 42 96 10 95
A favorite with the design and fashion world. Chase T.S. Eliot's ghost and enjoy the restored, stylish 1930s bar. Book well ahead.

Hôtel Louis II ($$)
2 rue St.-Sulpice, 75006 tel: 01 46 33 13 80
This atmospheric small hotel has exposed beams, lace spreads, and gilt mirrors. The bedrooms are mostly small. The salon is elegant.

Hôtel de Lutèce ($$)
65 rue St.-Louis-en-Ile, 75004
tel: 01 46 26 23 52
The Lutèce offers a country-house atmosphere. The bedrooms are understated and decorated with antiques.

Hôtel Lutétia ($$$)
45 boulevard Raspail, 75006
tel: 01 49 54 46 46
Huge, historic, a masterpiece of art deco, this elegantly renovated hotel was restyled by Sonia Rykiel. It has a good brasserie.

Hôtel des Marronniers ($$)
21 rue Jacob, 75006 tel: 01 43 25 30 60
It is advisable to book well in advance to enjoy the gracious and now famous country-house atmosphere (see page 147).

Hôtel Meurice ($$$)
228 rue de Rivoli, 75001 tel: 01 44 58 10 10
The sumptous 18th-century design designates this the "hotel of kings." Many rooms overlook the Tuileries Gardens. Enjoy the antiques-filled restaurant, or tea in the Pompador Salon.

Hôtel Montalembert ($$$)
3 rue de Montalembert, 75007
tel: 01 45 49 68 68
Built in 1926 in the beaux-arts style, this hotel retains its hip, Left Bank feel, while maintaining a serene and understated air. Enjoy fine cuisine at the wonderful Le Montalembert restaurant.

Hôtel Montpensier ($)
12 rue de Richelieu, 75001
tel: 01 42 96 28 50
Once the residence of Louis XV's mistress, this hotel is remarkably cheap and different. It is next to the Palais Royal.

Hôtel de Nevers ($)
88 rue de Bac, 75007 tel: 01 45 44 61 30
This former 17th-century convent, on a historic street, has only 11 rooms. It is basic, with no lift, but rooms are comfortable and all have either a bathroom or shower room. No credit cards.

Hôtel Parc St.-Séverin ($$)
22 rue de la Parcheminerie, 75005
tel: 01 43 54 32 17
A peaceful hotel in a pedestrianised street at the heart of the Latin Quarter, with beautiful views of the oldest sights in Paris. Some of the top floor rooms have a terrace.

Hôtel Pergolèse ($$$)
3 rue Pergolèse, 75016 tel: 01 53 64 04 04
This smart designer hotel has chic, contemporary furnishings. There are minimalist but soothing bedrooms with high-tech bathrooms, and a Japanese-styled garden seen through a curved glass wall. Philippe Starck chairs grace the breakfast room.

Hôtel de la place des Vosges ($$)
12 rue de Birague, 75004
tel: 01 42 72 60 46
This charming 17th-century town house offers modernized rooms. It is quiet, well-maintained, and a few steps from the place des Vosges.

Hôtel Plaza Athénée ($$$)
25 avenue Montaigne, tel: 01 53 67 66 65
An elegant, sophisticated hotel, this has a beautifully appointed courtyard, classic décor, and excellent service. The restaurant, Le Régence, has long been celebrated for its fine cuisine.

Hôtel Prima Lepic ($)
29 rue Lepic, 75018 tel: 01 46 06 44 64
In bustling Montmartre, this is an airy, light hotel with well-decorated, if smallish, bedrooms and a courtyard style reception area.

Hôtel du quai Voltaire ($$)
19 quai Voltaire, 75007 tel: 01 42 61 50 91
Despite the dusty 18th-century setting, the location is unbeatable overlooking the Seine, opposite the Louvre. Baudelaire and Wagner stayed here.

Hôtel Régina ($$$)
2 place des Pyramides, 75001
tel: 01 42 60 31 10
Excellently located, right off the rue de Rivoli, this hotel is filled with fresh flowers that create an air of opulence. There is a traditional French restaurant called Le Pluvinel.

Hôtel Regyn's Montmartre ($)
18 place des Abbesses, 75018
tel: 01 42 54 45 21
Look no farther for inexpensive lodgings at the bottom of the Butte. The rooms are small, but well equipped, and those at the front are double-glazed and some have great views.

Relais Christine ($$$)
3 rue Christine, 75006 tel: 01 40 51 60 80
Formerly a 16th-century cloister, this antiques-filled hotel is opulent and comfortable. The bedrooms are stylish, many with marble bathrooms.

Relais St.-Germain ($$$)
9 Carrefour de l'Odéon, 75006
tel: 01 43 29 12 05
This small luxury hotel is in the elegant St.-Germain des Prés district. The spacious yet cozy bedrooms are furnished with antiques.

Relais-Hôtel du Vieux Paris ($$)
9 rue Gît-le-Coeur, 75006 tel: 01 43 54 41 66
Near the action of St.-Michel, this original "beat" hotel was frequented by Burroughs, Ginsberg, and the like. The rooms are tiny but pretty.

Hôtel Ribouttè-Lafayette ($)
5 rue Ribouttè, 75009 tel: 01 47 70 62 36
Close to Opéra and *grands boulevards,* this is a peaceful, small place, and very reasonably priced.

Hôtel Richelieu-Mazarin ($)
51 rue de Richelieu, 75001
tel: 01 42 97 46 20
Come here for rock-bottom prices at a popular address. The rooms in this tiny hotel are basic, but clean, and some are surprisingly spacious. Avoid No. 20, however, which has no window!

Hôtel Ritz ($$$)
15 place Vendôme, 75001
tel: 01 43 16 30 30
This quintessentially Parisian hotel, frequented by Hemingway, exudes style and opulence. Enjoy fine cuisine at l'Espadon, and a magnificent pool.

Hôtel St.-André-des-Arts ($)
66 rue St.-André-des Arts, 75006
tel: 01 43 26 96 16
A 17th-century Latin Quarter classic, this is usually packed. It is lively and fun but often noisy.

Hôtel le Ste.-Beuve ($$$)
9 rue Ste.-Beuve, 75006 tel: 01 45 48 20 07
High style is to be had in this pricey but exquisite bed and breakfast establishment. It hosts stylish theme weekends and art exhibitions.

Hôtel St.-Louis Marais ($$)
1 rue Charles V, 75004 tel: 01 48 87 87 04
Exposed beams, stone walls, and a terra-cotta floor add a country flavor to this restful small hotel in the heart of the Marais. The elegant bedrooms have antique furniture.

Hôtel San Régis ($$$)
12 rue Jean Goujon, 75008
tel: 01 44 95 16 16
Elaborately redecorated a few years ago, this is a favorite with American movie stars. Each room has a personalized style with 4-star facilities.

Hôtel du 7e Art ($)
20 rue St.-Paul, 75004 tel: 01 44 54 85 00
Nothing if not fun, this hotel has a good line in film posters and movie memorabilia; plus it's in the budget-hotel starved Marais.

Hôtel Square ($$$)
3 rue des Boulainvilliers, 75016
tel: 01 44 14 91 90
This highly original boutique hotel also houses the sleek and trendy Zebra Square bar. The style marries colorful extravagance with zen minimalism and luxurious detail—trés hip. Contemporary artists exhibit in the atrium cum gallery.

Hôtel le Tourville ($$)
16 avenue de Tourville, 75007
tel: 01 47 05 62 62
Vibrant color schemes greet you as you enter this smart hotel designed by interior decorator Christian Badin. The furnishings are a mix of antique and modern. Rooms vary considerably in size and price; the staff are particularly helpful.

Hôtel des Trois Collèges ($)
16 rue Cujas, 75005 tel: 01 43 54 67 30
Picturesque and cozy, this hotel is in the shadow of the mighty university colleges. There is a view of the Sorbonne and the Panthéon from the beamed attic rooms.

Hôtel des Tuileries ($$)
10 rue St-Hyacinthe, 75001
tel: 01 42 61 04 17
Renovated in 18th-century style, this hotel is comfortable and quiet. Rooms are small.

Hôtel de l'Université ($$)
22 rue de l'Université, 75007
tel: 01 42 61 09 39
Impeccably decorated with antiques, this 17th-century town house is a lovely choice. Many rooms have terraces or access to a central courtyard.

Hôtel le Vendôme ($$$)
1 place Vendôme, 75001 tel: 01 42 60 32 84
Its opulent Second Empire style rooms are the height of luxury. Hedonistic detail runs to waterproof telephones, Guerlain toiletries and automated bedside consoles. Superb service is given by an army of immaculately drilled staff.

Hôtel Vernet ($$$)
25 rue Vernet, 75008 tel: 01 44 31 98 00
Classic Parisian style and ambience. The rooms, though somewhat small, are well equipped and furnished with antiques. The restaurant, Les Elysées, is a beautiful skylit room.

RESTAURANTS

($$$) —over 350 francs
($$) —200–350 francs
($) —under 200 francs

A la Cloche des Halles ($)
28 rue Coquillière, 75001 tel: 01 42 36 93 89
This is a typical animated local wine bar. It is good for lunch, but closes at 9 PM and on weekends.

Alain Ducasse ($$$)
55 avenue Raymond Poincaré, 75016
tel: 01 47 27 12 27
The iconic Michelin-starred chef Alain Ducasse's Parisian outpost is one of the most sought-after dining experiences. The modern French food is understated, but the prices are certainly not.

Alcazar ($$)
62 rue Mazarine, 75006 tel: 01 53 10 19 99
Terence Conran's slick brasserie is on the site of the old Alcazar cabaret. There is a great atrium and mezzanine interior in this large, noisy, and popular restaurant.

Allard ($$)
41 rue St.-André-des-Arts, 75006
tel: 01 43 26 48 23
This is truly an archetypal Parisian bistro. Enjoy a warm welcome and a classic menu that includes their signature duck with olives.

Ambassade d'Auvergne ($$)
22 rue du Grenier St.-Lazare, 75003
tel: 01 42 72 31 22
Genuine Auvergne food is served in a rustic setting. Don't miss the *aligot*—a luscious mix of potatoes, cheese, and garlic. At one of the last *table d'hôtes* in Paris, diners share tables.

L'Amis Louis ($$$)
32 rue de Vertbois, 75003
tel: 01 48 87 77 48
Prices may be astronomical but this legendary restaurant serves the best roast Challans chicken and *foie gras* in town. The interior is elegantly quaint with a wood-burning stove.

Apicius ($$$)
122 avenue de Villiers, 75017
tel: 01 43 80 19 66
Chef Jean-Pierre Vigato's cuisine is inventive and sophisticated, and few can rival his ability to track down the finest ingredients. Try the fabulous sweet and sour panfried duck *foie gras* with *confit* of black radish, or his new take on *tête de veau*.

Aquarius ($)
40 rue de Gergovie, 75014
tel: 01 45 41 36 88
This bright vegetarian restaurant has good salads, nut roast, mushroom quiche, and tofu croquettes. There is organic wine and a smokers' corner.

Arpège ($$$)
84 rue de Varenne, 75007
tel: 01 44 31 98 00
The newest restaurant to receive 3 Michelin stars, expect the most from Alain Passard's innovative French menu. Try the interesting dessert selections.

L'As du Fallafel ($)
34 rue des Rosiers, 75004
tel: 01 48 87 63 60
A good kosher food shop that sells delicious fallafels to eat on the spot or take out.

L'Assiette ($$)
181 rue du Château, 75014
tel: 01 43 22 64 86
Montparnasse is the traditional haunt of writers and politicians. Lulu, the chef/patronne, is an expert with game such as partridge with cabbage and *foie gras* or pheasant with beans.

Astier ($$)
44 rue Jean-Pierre Timbaud, 75011
tel: 01 43 57 16 35
There are no hidden surprises in Astier's copious, reasonable menu. Try the fantastic cheeses at this friendly, unpretentious local spot.

Asuka ($)
8–10 rue Léopold-Bellan, 75002
tel: 01 40 13 07 00
Check out the daily display of imaginative precision-cut *sushi*. They are all at remarkably low prices.

Au Bascou ($$)
38 rue Réamur, 75003 tel: 01 42 72 69 25
Great food is served at this unpretentious and lively little Basque restaurant. Regional specialties included are piperade, Pyrenees lamb, scallops with peppers, and Irouléguy wines.

L'Auberge Nicolas Flamel ($$)
51 rue de Montmorency, 75003
tel: 01 42 71 77 78
A trendy showbiz crowd is attracted to contemporary cuisine in one of Paris's oldest houses.

Au Bistrot de la Sorbonne ($)
4 rue Toullier, 75005 tel: 01 43 54 41 49
This bistro is crowded with students, noisy, and friendly. Dishes and prices are very basic.

Au Bon Acceuil ($$)
14 rue de Monttesuy, 75007
tel: 01 47 05 46 11
Creative cuisine using top-class ingredients features in this popular bistro near the Eiffel Tower. Desserts such as *clafoutis* with rhubarb and saffron *coulis* are particularly recommended.

Au Bon St-Pourçain ($$)
10 bis, rue Servandoni, 75006
tel: 01 43 54 93 63
This neighborhood bistro sports no frills. Simple, traditional dishes, such as oxtail terrine and *entrecôte marchand de vin* are hearty and generous.

Au Cochon d'Or ($$)
192 avenue Jean-Jaurès, 75019
tel: 01 42 45 46 46
A worldly Parisian crowd pours in here for its famed grilled meat dishes and gigantic steaks.

Au Grain de Folie ($)
24 rue de Lavieuville, 75018
tel: 01 42 58 15 57
Generous portions of vegetarian food are served here and organic wine is available. This is very good value. Credit cards are not accepted.

Au Petit Riche ($$)
25 rue Le Peletier, 75009
tel: 01 47 70 68 68
The superb 1880s interior is complimented by delicious bourgeois cuisine and impeccable service. A favorite for business lunches.

Au Pied du Cochon ($$)
6 rue Coquillière, 75001 tel: 01 40 13 77 00
This old classic from the market days of Les Halles is open nonstop. A good place for pig's trotters at 5 AM.

Au Sauvignon ($)
80 rue des Saints-Pères, 75007
tel: 01 45 48 49 02
Good for a quick snack after shopping in St.-Germain, this small, popular wine bar has a much frequented terrace in summer.

Aux Bons Crus ($)
7 rue des Petits Champs, 75001
tel: 01 42 60 06 45
This popular wine bar serves hot lunches. Barrels tower over tiny tables packed with locals.

Aux Charpentiers ($$)
10 rue Mabillon, 75006 tel: 01 43 26 30 05
Search out this evergreen bistro. It offers a consistently good rendition of old favorites such as *blanquette de veau* with rice.

La Baracane ($)
38 rue des Tournelles, 75004
tel: 01 42 71 43 33
Go for the traditional Gascon specialties, such as wonderful duck dishes, in a quaint bistro setting.

Le Bar au Sel ($$)
49 quai d'Orsay, 75007 tel: 01 45 51 58 58
This modish seafood restaurant is near Les Invalides with marine-style décor. House specialty is sea bass cooked in a salt crust.

Bar des Théâtres ($$)
6 avenue Montaigne, 75008
tel: 01 47 23 34 63
this sophisticated, animated bar/restaurant is opposite the theater. Actors and a chic audience mix here for reliable dishes.

Le Baron Rouge ($)
1 rue Théophile-Roussel, 75012
tel: 01 43 42 54 65
This classic bistro sells wine from its barrels and serves delicious little platters. It closes at 9:30 PM.

La Bastide Odéon ($$)
7 rue Corneille, 75006 tel: 01 43 26 03 65
Provençal chef Gilles Ajuelos is a rising star. His Southern classics in the Mediterranean-looking bistro include "*pieds et paquets*," more modern dishes include rabbit stuffed with aubergine.

Benoît ($$$)
20 rue St.-Martin, 75004 tel: 01 42 72 25 76
This much loved, deluxe bistro has a peerless belle époque interior. The menu is a monument to classic French cooking—blanquette, ballotine of boned duck with *foie gras, boeuf mode.*

Bhai Bhai Sweets ($)
77 passage Brady, 75010 tel: 01 42 46 77 29
This is one of many Indian and Pakistani restaurants in an atmospheric old passage. Excellent tandooris, lassis, and more are served.

Bistrot du Dôme ($$)
2 rue de la Bastille, 75004 tel: 01 48 04 88 44
Superb quality fish is offered here. There is another Bistrot in Montparnasse.

Blue Elephant ($$)
43 rue de la Roquette, 75011
tel: 01 47 00 42 00
This trendy Thai restaurant has over-the-top décor and spicy specialties.

Le Boeuf sur le Toit ($$)
34 rue du Colisée, 75008 tel: 01 53 93 65 55
This is part of Paris's famous chain of brasseries. A spectacular 1920s setting for fabulous seafood and *foie gras.*

Bofinger ($$)
5 rue de la Bastille, 75004 tel: 01 42 72 87 82
This is one of the most beautiful belle époque brasseries in the city, serving excellent food.

Les Bouchons de François Clerc ($$)
12 rue de l'Hôtel Colbert, 75005
tel: 01 43 54 15 34
This is one of a mini-chain of excellent, good value wine bars, where fine label bottles are served at wholesale prices. There are also good cheeses and a reliable four-course menu.

Brasserie dè l'Ile Saint-Louis ($$)
55 quai de Bourbon, 75004
tel: 01 43 54 02 59
This noisy, crowded, fun brasserie is on the tip of the island. Enjoy the sunny terrace and the reasonable prices.

Brasserie Flo ($)
Cour des Petites-Ecuries, 75010
tel: 01 47 70 13 59
This landmark early 20th-century brasserie has glorious stained-glass windows and is busy and bustling. Best bets are the *choucroute* and oysters; it is an after-theater favorite.

Brasserie Stella ($$)
133 avenue Victor-Hugo, 75016
tel: 01 47 27 60 54
At this large, animated, chic brasserie, classic seafood is complemented by original 1950s décor.

Café d'Angel ($$)
16 rue Brey, 75017 tel: 01 47 54 03 33
This trendy, small bistro has a bright stagey interior. Choose light and inventive dishes such as *carpaccio* of tuna and rabbit with wheatberries from the blackboard menu.

Café de la Poste ($)
13 rue Castex, 75004 tel: 01 42 72 95 35
Mosaic walls, banquette seating, and a beautiful wooden bar add character to this tiny relaxed Marais bistro. Go for its honest, fresh cooking.

Café des Lettres ($)
53 rue de Verneuil, 75007
tel: 01 42 22 52 17
Inexpensive Swedish family cooking is offered, such as gravlax and beef meatballs with cranberry preserve. The restaurant also doubles as an art gallery. There is a summer patio and Sunday brunch.

Café du Commerce ($)
51 rue du Commerce, 75015
tel: 01 45 75 03 27
A 1920s brasserie that has been made over to fill three floors around a plant-filled atrium. Expect a lively atmosphere, inexpensive set meals, and lines every lunchtime.

La Cagouille ($$)
10 place Constantin Brancusi, 74014
tel: 01 43 22 09 01
Fresh fish flawlessly cooked in minimal style and some of the best cognacs in Paris are served here. There is a terrace for summer dining.

Le Camelot ($)
50 rue Amelot, 75011 tel: 01 43 55 54 04
This gourmet budget bistro is run by a chef who worked with Christian Constant. Excellent soups, such as cream of crab with vermicelli always kick off the daily changing *prix fixe* menu.

Carré des Feuillants ($$$)
14 rue de Castiglione, 75001
tel: 01 42 86 82 82
A star attraction is Alain Dutournier's ultra-refined interpretation of the cooking of his native southwest. His autumn truffle menu is unmissable.
Cartet ($$)
62 rue de Maite, 75011 tel: 01 48 05 17 65
This modest Lyonnaise restaurant was established in 1936. It compensates for lack of size with oversized portions of terrines and sausages and a friendly, family atmosphere.
Casa Miguel ($)
48 rue St-Georges, 75009 tel: 01 42 81 09 61
This world-famous soup kitchen has rock-bottom prices and endless queues. *Open* noon–1 and 7 PM–8PM only.
Chartier ($)
7 rue du Faubourg-Montmartre, 75009
tel: 01 47 70 86 29
A famous food institution that is popular with tourists but still a must. You will have to share tables but the service is fast and the atmosphere charged.
Chen ($$)
15 rue du Théâtre, 75015
tel: 01 45 79 34 34
Devotees claim this is the best Chinese restaurant in Paris. Peking duck is served in three stages for an imperial feast.
Chez Aïda ($)
48 rue Polonceau, 75018
tel: 01 42 58 26 20
Robust Senegalese cooking and powerful rum aperitifs are offered in a warm and friendly atmosphere. It's closed on Wednesdays.
Chez Denise ($$)
5 rue des Prouvaires, 75001
tel: 01 42 36 21 82
This famous eating place near Les Halles packs them in all night long for filling helpings of *pot-au-feu* and home-made crème caramel. Note that it's closed on weekends.
Chez Germaine ($)
30 rue Pierre-Leroux, 75007
tel: 01 42 73 28 34
This simple, local bistro is popular with all ages. Egg mayonnaise, brandade, and roast pork with prunes are frequently on the unpretentious, good value menu.
Chez Gladines ($)
30 rue des Cinq-Diamants, 75013
tel: 01 45 80 70 10
Simple food from southwest France is served in this lively neighborhood bar up to midnight. Specially recommended are their pipérade and basque chicken.
Chez Gramond ($$$)
5 rue de Fleurus, 75006
tel: 01 42 22 28 89
A tiny, traditional bastion of classic French cuisine that is much patronized by members of the nearby Senate. In season, try the young partridge from the Beuce and the vintage wines.
Chez la Vieille ($$)
1 rue Bailleul, 75001 tel: 01 42 60 15 78
Reliable bistro cooking is served in generous portions. Indulge in their chocolate mousse served in a huge fruit bowl.
Chez Maître Paul ($$)
12 rue Monsieur-le-Prince, 75006
tel: 01 43 54 74 59
In this friendly little bistro, delicious specialties from eastern France are served.
Chez Michel ($$)
10 rue de Belzunce, 75010
tel: 01 44 53 06 20
Inventive Breton cooking is served in a popular, rustic looking bistro tucked away near the Gare du Nord. Try their regional classics such as eel terrine and slow-cooked pig's cheek.
Chez Paul ($$)
13 rue de Charonne, 75011
tel: 01 47 00 34 57
This favorite with local gallery owners, artists and clients is a revamped old bistro with traditional dishes. Booking is essential.
Chez René ($$)
14 boulevard St-Germain, 75005
tel: 01 43 54 30 23
This venerable Lyonnaise bistro has a loyal following. Go for *coq au vin* and *boeuf bourguignon* as they should be made.
Chez Toutoune ($$)
5 rue de Pontoise, 75005 tel: 01 43 26 56 81
At this fashionable, busy restaurant serving fresh, hearty cooking, service is slow. It can be quite expensive.
La Closerie des Lilas ($$)
171 boulevard du Montparnasse, 75006
tel: 01 40 51 34 50
A piano tinkles in the background as you eat at this famous old Montparnasse bar/brasserie/restaurant. The atmosphere is sophisticated and bustling.
Le Cochon à l'Oreille ($)
15 rue Montmartre, 75001
tel: 01 42 36 07 56
Always crowded, this old-time Les Halles classic bar is good for early risers and late-nighters. Delicious hot dishes are served. *Open* 4 AM–3 PM.
La Coupole ($$)
102 boulevard du Montparnasse, 75014
tel: 01 43 20 14 20
The restored art deco interior is still magnificent at this Montparnasse institution. The vast, noisy spot attracts tourists and regulars for classic seafood and brasserie fare.
Crêperie de Josselin ($)
67 rue de Montparnesse 75014
tel: 01 43 20 93 50
Crowd into this cheap, delicious crêperie for classic Parisian fare. A cut above the many similar spots.
Dame Jeanne ($$)
60 rue de Charonne, 75011
tel: 01 47 00 37 40
Explore taste on a trendy Bastille street. Big, bold flavors are crafted by the Apicius-trained chef.
Dîlan ($)
13 rue Mandar, 75002 tel: 01 42 21 14 88
Sit at large tables in this friendly, basic setting, and sample Kurdish and Turkish specialties.
Le Dôme ($$$)
108 boulevard du Montparnasse, 75014
tel: 01 43 35 25 81
This classic seafood brasserie was once frequented by Sartre. It still serves some of the best oysters and *bouillabaisse* in Paris.

Drouant ($$$)
place Gaillon, 75002 tel: 01 42 65 15 16
This illustrious old literary sanctuary has superb décor. Specialties are expensive, but the evening menu reasonably priced.

Au Duc des Lombards ($)
42 rue des Lombards, 75001
tel: 01 42 33 22 88
Choose from the reasonably priced menu in a young, friendly setting. There is a late-night first floor jazz bar.

L'Ebauchoir ($)
43–45 rue de Cîteaux, 75012
tel: 01 43 42 49 31
This is one of the Bastille's busiest spots. The blackboard menu offers great value meals that feature simple, well-prepared dishes such as leeks vinaigrette and fricassée of chicken with lemon.

Ecaille et Plume ($$)
25 rue Duvivier, 75007 tel: 01 45 55 06 72
Superb fresh fish and game (there's no freezer on the premises) are the specialties at this rather cramped little restaurant near the Ecole Militaire. At its best, the cooking can be inspired.

L'Ecluse ($$)
15 place de la Madeleine, 75008
tel: 01 42 65 34 69
One of a small chain of wine bars where you can sip Bordeaux by the glass while nibbling cold snacks. Watch the fashionable clientèle.

L'Epi du Pin ($$)
11 rue Dupin, 75006 tel: 01 42 22 64 56
Book well in advance for this intimate and pretty bistro where François Pasteau serves some of the most delicious, contemporary food in Paris. The *prix fixe* menu is unbeatable value.

Fakhr el Dine ($$)
3 rue Quentin Bauchart, 75008
tel: 01 47 23 44 42
Sample the striking *mezze* at this flower-filled Lebanese restaurant. There are good lamb main courses and a choice of local *crus* such as Château-Kefraya.

La Fermette Marbeuf ($$)
5 rue Marbeuf, 75008 tel: 01 53 23 08 00
The stunning setting compliments the imaginative cuisine, featuring seasonal dishes. The clientèle is elegant, stylish.

Le Flamboyant ($$)
11 rue Boyer-Barret, 75014
tel: 01 45 41 00 22
This is reasonable value for one of Paris' best antillais restaurants. Specialties include spicy accras, stuffed crab, and turtle kebob.

Les Fontaines ($)
9 rue Soufflot, 75005 tel: 01 43 26 42 80
There is an extensive menu. Most people come for top-notch beef dishes at wallet-friendly prices.

La Frégate ($)
1 rue du Bac, 75007 tel: 01 42 61 23 77
This is great value for a chic *quartier* beside Musée d'Orsay. There is an old-fashioned, stilted brasserie and a slightly pricier restaurant.

La Galoche ($$)
41 rue de Lappe, 75011 tel: 01 47 00 77 15
This is a rare survivor in a hub of trendiness. Experience robust, central France in an old-fashioned clog-lined setting.

Gérard Besson ($$$)
5 rue Coq Héron, 75001 tel: 01 42 33 14 74
Impeccable technique and seemingly effortless style are the hallmarks of Besson's small restaurant. Honors go to his exceptional game dishes.

Goumard-Prunier ($$$)
9 rue Duphot, 75001 tel: 01 42 60 36 07
There is extravagant luxury with prices to match at this splendid seafood restaurant. It has become an institution.

Le Grizzli ($$)
7 rue Saint-Martin, 75004 tel: 01 48 87 77 56
Traditional Auvergne cooking is served in a pretty dining room. Specialties include grilled meat and fish.

Guy Savoy ($$$)
18 rue Troyon, 75017 tel: 01 43 80 40 61
Ground-breaking, innovative techniques and an exploration of flavors are presented here with insight and intelligence in an understated setting hung with modern art. Uncooked duck *foie gras* with sea salt is one of the star turns. The seasonal truffle menu is sensational.

Haynes ($$)
3 rue Clauzel, 75009 tel: 01 48 78 40 63
A soul food restaurant in Paris? Since 1949 Haynes has been delighting Parisians, and soothing homesick, ex-pat Americans, with authentic, down-home fare such as okra and barbecues. Open for dinner only; closed Sunday and Monday.

Higuma ($)
32 bis, rue Ste-Anne, 75001
tel: 01 47 03 38 59
A fast and filling noodle bar situated near the Opéra. It's very popular with Japanese office workers.

Isse ($$$)
56 rue Ste-Anne, 75002 tel: 01 42 96 67 76
This Japanese restaurant near the Opéra numbers the fashion designer Kenzo amongst its regulars. The *sushi* and *sashimi* are consistently excellent.

Jacques Mélac ($$)
42 rue Léon-Frot, 75011 tel: 01 43 70 59 27
An exuberant patron keeps the bistro overflowing with clients and wine. Good for daytime sustenance and also open until midnight Tuesday to Saturday.

Jo Goldenberg ($)
7 rue des Rosiers, 75004 tel: 01 48 87 20 16
Here is a legendary Jewish deli-diner. Go for the plates piled-high with Eastern European specialties such as stuffed carp, chopped liver, and pastrami.

Juveniles ($)
47 rue de Richelieu, 75001
tel: 01 42 97 46 49
Tapas-style snacks and salads are served with wine by glass here. Go early because it's small, crowded, and hard to squeeze in.

Krung Thep ($)
93 rue Julien-Lacroix, 75020
tel: 01 43 66 83 74
Enjoy a truly authentic Thai experience, even to the extent of eating off low tables. Choose from an extensive catalog of fragrant dishes—but evenings only.

Lao Siam ($)
49 rue de Belleville, 75019
tel: 01 40 40 09 68
This is recommended as a reliable Thai-Laotian restaurant. On offer are some intriguing dishes such as shrimps with banana flowers.

Ledoyen ($$$)
1 avenue Dutuit, 75008 tel: 01 53 05 10 01
Chef Christian le Squer is already gaining plaudits for his cooking at this fine old Napoleon III dining-room in the gardens of the Champs-Elysées. Elegant presentation and precise execution.

Lucas-Carton ($$$)
9 place de la Madeleine, 75008
tel: 01 42 65 22 90
This is extremely pricey and smart. Beautiful *belle époque* architecture compliments inventive cuisine.

Ma Bourgogne ($$)
19 place des Vosges, 75004 tel: 01 42 78 44 64
Tables spill out onto the sidewalk in one of Paris' loveliest squares. Unpretentious food such as steaks and salads is served.

Maison Prunier ($$$)
16 avenue Victor Hugo, 75016
tel: 01 44 17 35 85
The magnificent art deco fish restaurant has refined cooking, excellent wines and a highly civilized atmosphere. Enjoy oysters on seaweed at the mosaic bar or retire to the plush comfort of the second-floor restaurant for a seafood feast.

Le Mansouria ($$)
11 rue Faidherbe, 75011 tel: 01 43 71 00 16
This fashionable Moroccan restaurant has elegant décor. It serves delicate *tajines*.

La Marée ($$$)
1 rue Daru, 75008 tel: 01 43 80 20 00
Try this polished seafood restaurant for superb *bouillabaisse* and modern fish dishes. The setting is stylish and "clubby."

Marie et Fils ($$)
34 rue Mazarine, 75006 tel: 01 43 26 49 49
Experience the warmth and hospitality of the mother-and-son team that run this friendly restaurant. The food is excellent, as is the mood.

Michel Rostang ($$$)
20 rue Rennequin, 75017 tel: 01 47 63 40 77
Rostang's most elegant of restaurants serves a first-rate menu from warm bitter chocolate tart to his gourmet family recipe for creamy *gratin dauphinois*. Try the seasonal asparagus menu.

Moissonnier ($$)
28 rue des Fossés-St-Bernard, 75005
tel: 01 43 29 87 65
This solid, bourgeois Lyonnaise bistro has barely changed in 30 years. Tripe and andouillette sausage are the real thing.

New Hoa Khoan ($)
15 avenue de Choisy, 75013
tel: 01 45 85 81 31
This is a busy, Hong Kong style canteen in Chinatown. *Open* 9 AM–11 PM.

Nioullaville ($$)
32/34 rue de l'Orillon, 75011
tel: 01 40 21 96 18
Hong Kong comes to Paris, or Belleville in this vast kitsch Chinese restaurant with endless menus and passing trolleys for sampling.

L'O à la Bouche ($$)
124 boulevard du Montparnasse, 75014
tel: 01 56 54 01 55
Franck Paquier comes with a good pedigree after training with Guy Savoy and Troisgros. Stylish, upbeat cooking incudes fresh ideas as well as Savoy signatures such as *dorade en écailles*.

Les Olivades ($$)
41 avenue de Ségur, 750057
tel: 01 47 83 70 09
Flora Mikula is one of the best female chefs in Paris. She brings a Provençal taste of the sun to veal sweetbreads with rosemary, honey, and lemon, and lavender-accented crème brûlée.

Osteria del Passepartout ($)
20 rue de l'Hirondelle, 75006
tel: 01 46 34 14 54
This simple Italian restaurant is located down a minuscule alley. Come here for inventive pasta dishes at reasonable prices.

Le Pain Quotidien ($)
18 place du Marché-St.-Honoré, 75001
tel: 01 42 96 31 70
A convivial bakery is combined with a restaurant. Try the delicious cramique cakes for breakfast, lunchtime salads, and excellent wheatbreads.

Paul Minchelli ($$$)
54 boulevard de la Tour-Maubourg, 75007 tel: 01 47 05 89 86
This superchic, megabucks restaurant has an interior designed by Slavik. Skate fin with tarragon vinegar and bass tartar are examples of a minimalist approach to fish cooking.

Pavillon Montsouris ($$$)
20 rue Gazan, 75014 tel: 01 45 88 38 52
This 1900 pavilion affords Paris's most bucolic setting in the Parc Montsouris. Go for a discreet summer lunch to enjoy adventurous dishes.

Le Pavillon Puebla ($$$)
Parc des Buttes-Chaumont, 75019
tel: 01 42 08 92 62
In the incomparable setting of the landscaped park, this elegant restaurant serves imaginative cuisine influenced by its Catalan owner.

Le Petit Marguery ($$)
9 boulevard de Port-Royal, 75013
tel: 01 43 31 58 59
Taste excellent, rather grand cooking by the Cousin brothers in the Gobelins district. Game is a specialty—hare à la royale, terrine of pheasant *foie gras*, and purée of partridge with juniper are all superb.

Le Petit Saint-Benoît ($)
4 rue Saint-Benoît, 75006
tel: 01 42 60 27 92
This is a favorite cheap restaurant. Its décor and waitresses seem unchanged since the 1930s.

La Petite Chaise ($)
36 rue de Grenelle, 75007
tel: 01 42 22 13 35
This establishment was founded in 1680. The copious all-in menu has something for everyone. It is a smart, popular, fun place.

Les Philosophes ($)
28 rue Vieille du Temple, 75004
tel: 01 48 87 49 64
Join the crowd at this Marais bistro. There is good food, inexpensive wine by the glass and a fine selection of beers. *Open* 9 AM–2 AM daily.

Piccolo Teatro ($)
6 rue des Écouffes, 75004
tel: 01 42 72 17 79
This easy-going vegetarian bistro/café is open until 11 PM. It is impossible to go wrong with a choice of salads, gratins, organic beer, and freshly squeezed fruit juices.

Pierre au Palais Royal ($$)
10 rue Richelieu, 75001 tel: 01 42 96 09 17
A classic spot, marked with a florist at the entrance. The updated menu still retains favorites such as *boeuf à la ficelle*, peach Melba, and *tarte tatin.*

La Poule au Pot ($$)
9 rue Vauvilliers, 75001 tel: 01 42 36 32 96
Open till 6 AM. Spend all night here sampling traditional dishes in a very animated atmosphere.

Le Pré Catalan ($$$)
route de Suresnes, Bois de Boulogne, 75016
tel: 01 44 14 41 14
Very expensive, but if you must dine in a Parisian rose-garden, this is it. Don't skip the desserts.

Les Quatre et une Saveurs ($)
77 rue du Cardinal-Lemoine, 75005
tel: 01 43 26 88 80
Macrobiotic fans should trek to this minimalist, Japanese restaurant. Good vegetable soups to sample include tofu bouillon.

404 ($$)
69 rue des Gravilliers, 75003
tel: 01 42 74 57 81
Low seats, low lighting, high ceilings make this excellent Moroccan restaurant popular with a lively young crowd.

La Régalade ($$)
49 avenue J. Moulin, 75014
tel: 01 45 45 68 58
This contemporary bistro is filled with a stylish and exuberant crowd. Prices are reasonable and the menu selections are updated versions of classics.

Rendez-Vous Des Chauffeurs ($)
11 Rue des Portes-Blanches, 75018
tel: 01 42 64 04 17
This atmospheric old trooper soon gets crowded out by those in the know. Go for the good home cooking at unbelievably low prices.

Restaurant des Beaux Arts ($)
11 rue Bonaparte, 75006
tel: 01 43 26 92 64
This is a popular meeting place for art students and impoverished philosophers. You'll find inspiring décor and classic family cuisine.

Sousceyrac ($$)
35 rue Faidherbe, 75011 tel: 01 43 71 65 30
Cassoulet to dream about, but leave room for the rum baba. This old-time restaurant has been serving southwestern French food for more than 70 years.

Spoon, Food & Wine ($$$)
14 rue de Marignan, 75008
tel: 01 40 76 36 66
Love it or loathe it, but Alain Ducasse's foray into global cuisine is one of the hottest spots in town. The menu ranges from BLTs to Asian noodle dishes—exceptionally for Paris, French wines are almost nowhere to be seen.

Le Square Trousseau ($)
1 rue Antoine-Vollon, 75012
tel: 01 43 43 06 00
Superb old zinc bar, mosaics, and red moleskin banquettes transport you back to the 1900s. The menu changes monthly and is written up on large blackboards. Refined cooking attracts an urbane clientèle.

La Table d'Aude ($)
8 rue de Vaugirard, 75006
tel: 01 43 26 36 36
A regional inn that seems to have been transported lock, stock and barrel from the Aude region. The fixed price menu—look out for their abundant *cassoulet à la Castelnaudary* – includes wine.

Tan Dinh ($$$)
60 rue de Verneuil, 75007
tel: 01 45 44 04 84
Exquisite creative Vietnamese cuisine is served with equal delicacy. The wine list is renowned, and the décor is chic Oriental.

La Taverna Henri IV ($)
13 place du Pont-Neuf, 75001,
tel: 01 43 54 27 90
This place is ideal for a quick snack. A specialty is the open sandwiches on Poîlane bread.

Thanksgiving ($)
20 rue St.-Paul, 75004 tel: 01 42 77 68 28
This down-home American restaurant serves regional dishes. Try their Cajun jambalaya and Maryland crab cakes, as well as meatloaf and hamburgers and a great Sunday brunch.

Thoumieux ($$)
79 rue Saint-Dominique, 75007
tel: 01 47 05 49 75
Part bistro, part brasserie, this fashionable, friendly, animated place serves southwestern specialities.

La Tourelle ($)
5 rue Hautefeuille, 75006
tel: 01 46 33 12 47
An unpretentious restaurant resides in an historic building. It is a local favorite, with fast service and reliable simple dishes.

Train Bleu ($$$)
Gare de Lyon, 75012 tel: 01 43 43 09 06
A stunning belle époque décor overpowers the Lyonnais cuisine. Choose simple dishes and revel in the setting.

Le Trumilou ($)
84 Quai de l'Hôtel-de-Ville, 75004
tel: 01 42 77 63 98
A range of very reasonably priced menus are on offer here. Expect generous helpings and a provincial atmosphere.

Le Violon d'Ingres ($$$)
135 rue St-Dominique, 75007
tel: 01 45 55 15 05
The paneled setting is as elegant and refined as the cooking of Christian Constant, also a distinguished chocolatier. Try his well-flavored dishes such as guinea fowl with turnip *choucroute* and braised peaches with verbena.

Yugaraj ($$$)
14 rue Dauphoine, 75006
tel: 01 43 26 44 91
One of the city's best Indian restaurants, this has charming and friendly Sri Lankan service. The atmosphere is very discreet.

La Zygotissoire ($)
101 rue de Charonne, 75011
tel: 01 40 09 93 05
This small rôtisserie restaurant offers cooking that is a cut above the norm. The set menu is unbeatable value for money.

A

B

C

D

E

F

N

O

P

Q

R

S

Picture Credits

The Automobile Association would like to thank the following photographers and libraries for their assistance in the preparation of this book:
CORBIS 19, 22–23 (bottom); **ALL SPORT (UK) LTD** 95a (Gerard Vandy Stadt); **ART DIRECTORS & TRIP PHOTO LIBRARY** 256; **CORBIS** 19 (O. Franken), 22a, 23a, 23b (Reuters New Media Inc), 22b, 22c, 22d (AFP); **DIAF** 158 (Thierry); **FULTON PICTURE LIBRARY** 14, 46/7; **MARY EVANS PICTURE LIBRARY** 30b, 31a, 33, 36a, 37a, 37b, 38a, 38b, 39a, 40, 42b, 43a, 48b, 49, 112; **MUSÉE BACCARAL** 79; **MUSÉE DE CLUNY** 105a, 140a; **PHILIPPE COVETTE** 84; **PICTOR INTERNATIONAL** 241; **POPPOFOTO** 115; **REX FEATURES LTD** 82, 83; **WORLD PICTURES** 242; **ZEFA PICTURE LIBRARY** 82, 83.

The following photographs were taken by Bertrand Rieger and from the Automobile Association's picture library (© AA Photo Library).
P. ENTICNAP 9, 56b, 97, 114, 134/5, 137a, 137b, 171; E. MEACHER 24c, 181b; D. NOBLE 29a, 35, 61a, 191, 192a, 193, 194, 198, 199, 202/3, 204, 205, 209a, 209b, 210, 211, 212a, 212b; K. PATERSON 5, 6, 13, 16, 20a, 21, 26/7, 41, 46a, 52, 55a, 56, 69b, 71b, 76a, 87a, 88a, 89b, 91a, 93a, 94a, 98a, 101a, 101b, 106, 110a, 116a, 120b, 122a, 139, 140b, 166, 172, 177a, 177b, 184, 185, 186a, 186b, 187, 216, 226, 227, 232, 238, 244, 248, 249, 250/1, 262, 263, 268/9, 270, 273, 277; B. RIEGER 6/7, 14, 20b, 26, 29, 30, 32, 34, 44a, 48a, 54, 58a, 59a, 59b, 60a, 63, 66, 66/7, 68, 69a, 70, 71a, 73b, 75a, 75b, 76b, 77, 87b, 88b, 89a, 92a, 92b, 93b, 95b, 96a, 97b, 98b, 99a, 102, 107a, 107b, 109a, 109b, 111a, 113a, 113b, 117a, 118, 119a, 119b, 120a, 123a, 124, 125, 126, 127, 128a, 128b, 130a, 130b, 134, 136, 143, 144a, 144b, 146, 148, 149a, 149b, 150, 151a, 163, 165b, 170, 173, 178a, 180a, 181a, 182a, 188, 189, 192b, 203, 207, 217, 218, 219, 220, 222, 223, 225, 228, 236/7, 239b, 247, 260a, 261, 264, 267, 274, 275, 278, 281; C. SAWYER 73a, 200, 201; B. SMITH 237; A. SOUTER 3, 6 b, 8a, 17, 18, 24a, 36b, 42a, 45a, 61b, 64, 81, 82a, 85b, 100a, 121a, 132a, 138a, 145, 156, 159, 161, 164, 165a, 168, 169, 174, 175, 179a, 179b, 224, 229, 230, 231, 233, 239, 252, 259, 265, 266; J. A. TIMS 4, 5b, 80, 107; W. VOYSEY 5a.

Acknowledgments

The writers and editors would like to thank the following for their help in the production of this book: Musée National du Moyen-Age Thermes de Cluny; Musée du Louvre; Centre National d'Art et de Culture Georges Pompidou; Union Centrale des Arts Décoratifs.

Contributors

Original copy editor: Nia Williams
Revision editor: Lodestone Publishing Limited Revision verifier: Jack Altman, Clarissa Hyman